EUROPEAN SUCCESSION LAWS

EUROPEAN SUCCESSION LAWS

Edited by
Professor David Hayton LLD
School of Law, King's College, London University
Barrister and Recorder, 5 Stone Buildings, Lincoln's Inn

JORDANS
1998

Published by Jordan Publishing Ltd
21 St Thomas Street
Bristol BS1 6JS
United Kingdom

British Library Cataloguing-in-Publication Data
A catalogue record for this book is available from the British Library.

ISBN 0 85308 444 0

Typeset by Mendip Communications Ltd, Frome, Somerset
Printed in Great Britain by MPG Books Ltd, Bodmin, Cornwall

CONTRIBUTORS

Professor David Hayton, LLD (General Editor)
Barrister, 5 Stone Buildings, Lincoln's Inn and
School of Law, King's College, University of London

AUSTRIA

Dr Andreas Lintl
Rechtsanwalt, Vienna

BELGIUM

Professor Dr Alain Verbeke LLM
Professor of Private and Comparative Law
at the Universities of Leuven (KUL) and Antwerp (UIA);
Partner, Casman and Verbeke, Antwerp

BRITISH ISLES
ENGLAND

James Denker
Solicitor and Partner, Rowe and Maw, London

ISLE OF MAN

Neil Morris
Solicitor, Eversheds, London,
with the assistance of John Wright
Simcocks, Douglas

JERSEY

Steven Meiklejohn
Partner, Ogier and Le Masurier
(Jersey Advocates & Solicitors) St Helier

SCOTLAND

Ross Macdonald
Department of Law, University of Dundee

DENMARK

J Qviste
Ronne & Lundgren, Copenhagen

FINLAND

G O Z Sundström

Associate Professor, University of Helsinki
and Senior Partner, Nordic Law, Helsinki

FRANCE

Marie L Revillard

Docteur en droit, Juriste Consulte au Cridon de Lyon

GERMANY

Dr Karsten Kühne

Rechtsanwalt and German Notary Public, Berlin and London

GREECE

K D Magliveras

11 Hatzikosta, GR 11521, Athens

ITALY

D B Macfarlane

Solicitor, via Visconti Pi Modrone, Milan

THE NETHERLANDS

F A A Duynstee
and
K M F J Houben

De Brauw Blackstone Westbroek of The Hague and Rotterdam

PORTUGAL

Grupo Legal Português

(F Castelo Branco, Nobre Guedes & P Rebelo de Sousa,
in association with Simmons & Simmons, Pinheiro Neto & Co
and J & A Garrigues) Lisbon

SPAIN

Professor Julio D González Campos

Autonomous University of Madrid
and Judge at the Constitutional Court

Professor Alegría Borrás

University of Barcelona

SWITZERLAND

Duri Berther

Attorney-at-Law, Chur

PREFACE

This work first appeared in encyclopaedic loose-leaf form in 1991 and was annually updated. With the encouragement of Jordans, however, we have converted to the bound volume format. After all, succession laws do not change at a rapid rate, and a bound volume is cheaper and more manageable than a loose-leaf. A new edition every five years or so seems the best way forward.

The book covers domestic law and private international law rules of relevant jurisdictions in matters involving administration of deceased persons' estates and succession to such estates. Taxation matters are deliberately only touched upon, the idea being to provide a lawyer, or other person concerned with a client or a deceased's estate, with enough basic knowledge to liaise effectively with a foreign lawyer or other person. A tax specialist should be consulted on tax law which is complex and ever-changing.

As will become increasingly apparent as use is made of this book, succession matters can be very complex when international elements are present; international elements will inevitably arise in an increasing number of estates due to the increasing mobility of the labour force and of retired people, and as a result of increasing wealth.

To provide full advice, it becomes necessary to ascertain a client's domicile, nationality and habitual residence and the physical location of immovables and of valuable movables. Warnings may then have to be given about the dangers of changing any of the above factors so as to invoke the application of a law that will frustrate the client's intentions, for example by furthering forced heirship claims against his estate.

In providing good advice or chasing up matters involving a foreign estate, it will become necessary to consult and liaise with foreign lawyers. This book is intended to provide a good knowledge of a foreign *lex successionis* and of foreign terminology, especially where it appears misleadingly similar to local terminology. This should help to expedite matters and prevent persons being at cross-purposes with each other.

Naturally, I desire to record my sincere thanks for those who have collaborated with me in providing chapters relating to their own countries, especially those remarkable souls who provided their chapters on time. Our helpful publishers benignly condoned a significant slippage in the production schedule, hoping for forgiveness from punctual contributors, so that a wider range of countries could be dealt with. However, delayed contributions must await a new edition. Anyone experienced enough to provide a chapter on an unrepresented jurisdiction is encouraged to contact me so that the next edition may be enlarged.

Finally, particular thanks are due to Richard Hudson and Melanie Andrews of Jordans for their support and patience.

It is hoped that the law is accurately stated at 1 October 1997, but on foreign matters, recourse should always be had to foreign practitioners.

David Hayton
January 1998

CONTENTS

TABLE OF CASES

References are to paragraph numbers; n indicates that the reference is to a footnote to the paragraph indicated. Bold indicates that the text of the provision can be found at the reference.

AUSTRALIA

AUSTRIA

BELGIUM

FRANCE

GREECE

ITALY

NEW ZEALAND

SPAIN

UNITED KINGDOM

USA

TABLE OF INTERNATIONAL CONVENTIONS

References are to paragraph numbers; n indicates that the reference is to a footnote to the paragraph indicated. Bold indicates that the text of the provision can be found at the reference.

NATIONAL LEGISLATION

UK STATUTES

AUSTRIA

BELGIUM

DENMARK

FINLAND

FRANCE

GERMANY

GREECE

ISLE OF MAN

ITALY

JERSEY

NETHERLANDS

PORTUGAL

SPAIN

USA

INTRODUCTION[†]

THE RELEVANCE OF FOREIGN SUCCESSION LAW FOR A LOCAL PRACTITIONER

A client's needs may require a local practitioner to have, or to acquire, knowledge of some foreign succession law in more cases than one might imagine. Indeed, the practitioner may require, even for one client, a knowledge of the foreign succession law of more than one country. He cannot assume that there will only be one relevant *lex successionis* or, if it is common law, that the deceased's property will vest in personal representatives or, if it is civil law, will vest directly in the heirs.

If a client, T, dies domiciled (in the technical common law sense) in State A (eg England, Ireland), habitually resident in State B (eg France or Belgium or Denmark) but a national of State C (eg Spain, Portugal, Germany, Austria, Netherlands, Italy), it is possible for State A to apply its *lex successionis* to assets situated in State A; for State B to apply its *lex successionis* to assets situated in State B; for State C to apply its *lex successionis* to assets situated in State C; and for State D to apply its *lex successionis* to immovables situated in State D, where State D is a State which applies the *lex situs* to immovables, although having succession to movables governed by the law of the deceased's last domicile or habitual residence or nationality.

A yet further complication is to relate to the relevant *lex successionis* any relevant matrimonial property regime so as to ascertain what property is available to pass under the relevant *lex successionis* as opposed to the relevant matrimonial property regime.

To properly assist a client with his estate planning thus requires ascertaining the client's likely last domicile or habitual residence or nationality, discovering which States apply domicile or habitual residence or nationality, and ascertaining the *situs* of the client's assets. It is then important to discover which States are 'schismatic' (like England, France and Belgium) in having one law governing succession to movables and another law governing succession to immovables, and which States are 'unitarians' in having one *lex successionis* for movables and immovables. In some cases, it may be necessary to know how a relevant State characterises what is a movable and what is an immovable where this distinction is significant.

---

† Written by Professor David Hayton.

If a client's domicile, habitual residence and nationality are all that of the local jurisdiction, there can still be problems if he owns foreign immovables and the local State is a schismatic one letting immovables be governed by the *lex situs* or if the immovable is situate in a schismatic jurisdiction applying its *lex situs*. Thus, if an English citizen, habitually resident and domiciled in England, dies owning an immovable in Suntopia, does Suntopia accept the reference from English law to its law as the *lex successionis* for such immovable or is it one of the rare jurisdictions like Spain or Denmark which rejects such 'renvoi' in favour of English law governing the whole estate of the deceased? If 'renvoi' is not rejected then if Suntopia has forced heirship rules requiring a sizeable fraction (eg half or three quarters) of the immovable to pass to the deceased's children and the client does not wish this, then avoidance measures have to be investigated (eg selling the house and buying a new one in a favourable jurisdiction or owning the immovable through a company, the shares in which will be movables passing under the *lex successionis* for movables).

There may be further 'renvoi' complexities if the client, although habitually resident and domiciled in the local jurisdiction, has a foreign nationality and owns foreign immovables. Thus, if a Portuguese national habitually resident and domiciled in England has succession in respect of his Suntopia villa referred by English law to Suntopian law, which regards nationality as the connecting factor for the *lex successionis*, then succession to the villa (and forced heirship share therein) will be governed by Portuguese law due to the reference on by Suntopian law.

If the client is domiciled abroad and the local jurisdiction accepts that the law of the domicile at death is the *lex successionis* then no will should be drawn up nor any *inter vivos* estate planning measures undertaken without a full appreciation of the impact of the foreign *lex successionis*. It will be sensible to liaise with a law firm in the foreign locality and to ensure that misunderstanding of familiar-sounding terminology does not lead to discussions at cross-purposes. By use of *inter vivos* joint tenancies or trusts in the local jurisdiction there may well be opportunities to avoid any unsatisfactory forced heirship rules of the foreign *lex successionis*.

If the client is domiciled and habitually resident in the local jurisdiction, but is a national of a foreign jurisdiction which has nationality law as the *lex successionis*, while the local jurisdiction has as the *lex successionis* the law of domicile or habitual residence, it will be necessary to appreciate the potential impact of the foreign *lex successionis* in respect of assets or beneficiaries within its jurisdiction or another foreign jurisdiction which recognises nationality law as the *lex successionis*. The use of *inter vivos* joint tenancies or trusts in the local jurisdiction may obviate some of the foreign problems, so long as none of the relevant assets find their way into the foreign jurisdiction until after forced heirship claims in such jurisdiction have become time-barred and so long as a relevant beneficiary is not within the foreign jurisdiction where he can be compelled to bring his share of trust assets within the jurisdiction for the benefit of the settlor's forced heirs or to pay an equivalent amount to such heirs.

Finally, a local client may believe that he has inherited assets passing under a foreign *lex successionis* and wants to ensure that he receives whatever is his full entitlement as soon as possible. This will involve liaising with or chasing up lawyers or heirs or executors in the foreign jurisdiction: some knowledge of the foreign *lex successionis* and of foreign terminology will prevent persons being at cross-purposes and will expedite matters.

CHAPTER 1

THE PROBLEMS OF DIVERSITY†

1. INTRODUCTION

The differences between common law systems and civil law systems afford much scope for misunderstanding, especially where similar terminology obscures fundamental differences. 'Succession' and 'domicile' have different meanings in a civil law context from those in a common law context. Civil law systems may be seen to be excessively rigid as to matrimonial property regimes and heirs' indefeasible inheritance shares and their inter-relationship, while common law systems may be seen to be excessively flexible in relying on discretionary provision by the courts in such circumstances. 1.1

When international elements are present not only do matters become expensively complex but injustices may result. A wife, whose deceased husband's estate is governed by Utopian law and whose matrimonial property regime is governed by Erewhon law, may find that she obtains a double benefit (each law assuming that she would otherwise receive nothing under its related domestic law) or no benefit (each law assuming that she would otherwise benefit under its related domestic law): see paras **1.24–1.29**. In private international law matters, much may depend on the forum for resolving a particular dispute, such as whether an asset is a movable or an immovable. Moreover, the Utopian forum, (eg France) might characterise S's *inter vivos* transfer of property to T as encroaching upon S's heirs' indefeasible inheritance shares so as ultimately to be subject to the *lex successionis* governing S's estate. The Erewhon forum (eg England) might characterise the gift simply as a transfer of property and so subject to the *lex situs*, so that the gifted property is no longer part of S's estate and thus is not available to be subject ultimately to the *lex successionis* governing S's estate. 1.2

When it comes to ascertaining the *lex successionis* for S's estate, one forum may apply as the connecting factor the law of S's nationality, another the law of S's domicile in the strict common law sense, another the law of S's domicile in the common law sense but as liberalised by statute (eg so that on giving up an acquired domicile of choice such domicile, rather than the domicile of origin, continues as the connecting factor until a new domicile of choice is acquired), another the law of S's habitual residence, and another, in respect of immovables, the *lex situs*. By making a will, S can make matters worse if he chooses concepts known to one system of law, such as trusts and joint tenancies, where another system of law not having such concepts in its own law turns out to be the *lex successionis*. Legal systems 1.3

† This chapter was written by David Hayton, LLD, Barrister of 5 Stone Buildings, Lincoln's Inn, and Professor of Law, King's College, University of London, tel 0171 873 2452, fax 0171 873 2465.

can also make matters complex as where system A refers succession to the law of system B which refers it back to the law of system A or on to the law of system C.

1.4 Hague Conventions on Administration of Estates, on Matrimonial Property Regimes, on Recognition of Trusts and on Succession to Deceased Persons' Estates have grappled with the above problems and come up with some solutions. However, so far, few States have ratified these conventions and there remains a further need for a convention on jurisdiction and recognition of judgments in this area.

2. SUCCESSION AND ADMINISTRATION OF ESTATES

1.5 Common law systems make a distinction between matters of succession and matters of administration of estates whilst civil law systems have no such distinction, regarding both under the rubric of 'succession'. Classically, in civil law systems the assets and liabilities of the deceased are automatically transmitted on death directly to his heirs, although they have the option to reject their inheritance or to accept it with benefit of inventory so as to protect themselves in case unexpected liabilities are discovered. In common law systems, in contrast, the deceased's estate vests in his personal representatives who collect in the assets and discharge the liabilities (the process of 'administration of the estate' governed by the law of the forum) and who then distribute the net assets remaining to the beneficiaries under the deceased's will or intestacy who succeed to such assets (the 'succession' process governed by the *lex successionis*, being the *lex situs* for immovables and the law of the deceased's last domicile for movables).

1.6 The personal representatives will be the persons named as 'executors' in the deceased's will or, otherwise, will be the 'administrators' appointed by the court (normally by a mechanical bureaucratic process as opposed to a court hearing). They become full legal and beneficial owners of the deceased's property so that they can transmit full legal and beneficial title whether to purchasers, when selling assets to enable liabilities to be discharged, or to beneficiaries who, until transfer of assets to them, have merely a *chose in action* to have the estate duly administered by the personal representatives.

DOMICILE AND HABITUAL RESIDENCE

Domicile

1.7 In common law systems, domicile has a technical meaning which distinguishes it from the concept of habitual residence. It is crucial that no person may be without a domicile and that no person may have more than one domicile. A person's domicile is determined by the law of the forum.

On 19 October 1991 (HC Deb, vol 196, col 177) the government stated that it would be implementing the Law of Domicile Report by The Law Commission and the Scottish Law Commission ((1987) Cm 200, HMSO). In line with liberal legislation in other common law States, the Report recommends the abolition of the domicile of origin so that it will no longer apply where a domicile of choice has been abandoned without the acquisition of a new domicile of choice. 1.8

A draft Bill appended to the Report sets out new rules to determine domicile as follows:

'1 **Domicile of Children**

(1) A child is domiciled in the country with which he is for the time being most closely connected.

(2) Where the child's parents are domiciled in the same country and he has his home with either or both of them, it is to be presumed, unless the contrary is shown, that the child is most closely connected with that country.

(3) Where the child's parents are not domiciled in the same country and he has his home with one of them, but not with the other, it is to be presumed, unless the contrary is shown, that the child is most closely connected with the country in which the parent with whom he has his home is domiciled.

2 **Domicile of adults**

(1) On becoming an adult, a person retains (subject to paragraph (2) below) the domicile he has immediately before that time.

(2) An adult acquires a domicile in another country if –

(a) he is present there, and

(b) he intends to settle there for an indefinite period.

3 **Domicile in federal or composite State**

In any case where –

(a) an adult is present in a State comprising two or more countries and intends to settle in that State for an indefinite period, but

(b) the application to him of the other rules in this Schedule does not show that he is domiciled in any particular country within the State,

then notwithstanding the other rules in this Schedule he is to be treated until he next obtains a domicile in accordance with these rules as domiciled in the country within that State with which he is for the time being most closely connected.

4 **Domicile of adults under disability**

(1) An adult lacking the capacity to form the intention necessary for acquiring a domicile is domiciled in the country with which he is for the time being most closely connected.

(2) When that capacity is restored to an adult, he retains the domicile that he had immediately before it was restored.

Domicile

5 **Continuity of adult domicile**

An adult's domicile under rule 2 or 4(2) continues until he obtains another domicile.

6 **Standard of proof**

A person is to be taken for the purposes of these rules to have intended to settle in a country for an indefinite period if it is shown on a balance of probabilities that he had that intention.

7 Interpretation
In these rules –
"child" means a person who has not attained the age of sixteen, and "adult" is to be interpreted accordingly, and
"country" includes territory and means, in relation to a person whose domicile at a particular time is in question, a country which has its own system of law at that time.'

1.9 However, on 16 January 1996 (HC Deb, vol 269, col 489), Jonathan Evans MP on behalf of the Government stated:

> 'The Government has decided not to take forward these reforms on the basis that, although desirable in themselves, they do not contain sufficient practical benefits to outweigh the risks of proceeding with them and to justify disturbing the present long-established body of case-law on this subject.'

It is possible that the new Labour government may see advantages in proceeding with the domicile proposals, so it is as well to be aware of them as well as the inheritance tax deemed domicile provisions in s 267 of the Inheritance Tax Act 1984 (residence for not less than 17 years out of the 20 preceding years).

1.10 In English law, until any reforms are enacted, a person commences life with a domicile of origin which may, until the age of 16 years, be changed as a domicile of dependency by the relevant parent's change of domicile. Upon attaining the age of 16, a person remains domiciled as then domiciled unless and until he abandons that domicile and either acquires a domicile of choice or his domicile of origin revives (because he abandons his domicile of choice without acquiring another domicile of choice).

1.11 The domicile of origin of a legitimate child born during his father's life is the country of his father's domicile at the time of his birth while, for a posthumous legitimate child or for an illegitimate child, it is the country of his mother's domicile at the time of his birth. A foundling's domicile of origin is the country where he is found.

1.12 A child's domicile until attaining the age of 16 can be changed only if the parent on whom the child's domicile depends changes his or her domicile. Special rules apply where a legitimate child's parents are living apart: see s 4 of the Domicile and Matrimonial Proceedings Act 1973.

A person over 16 can acquire a domicile of choice if:

(1) he takes up residence in a country; and
(2) has an intention to make his home in that country permanently or (probably) indefinitely.

1.13 A lengthy period of residence is on its own not sufficient, while a very short physical presence can be sufficient if coupled with an intent to make a home in that country from that time on. An illegal entrant to England cannot, as a matter of English public policy, acquire domicile in England. As for the requisite intention, it must be an intention unlimited in period but it need not be irrevocable in character. The vague possibility that if one won the football pools or a national lottery one might return to the land of one's birth will not prevent the acquisition of a domicile of choice but an intention to return upon a clear realistic contingency, such as upon one's retirement or the death of one's spouse, will prevent the acquisition of such a domicile.

A person's domicile of origin automatically revives (irrespective of where he is resident or what he may intend for the future) if he abandons his domicile of choice by ceasing to reside in a country and losing the intention to make his home there permanently or indefinitely, and does not acquire another domicile of choice. 1.14

Habitual residence

In contrast to domicile with its technicalities and its heavy subjective emphasis on intention (for a domicile of choice), the concept of habitual residence is much more of an objective question of fact without any legal artificialities, although there is some uncertainty as to the degree of importance to be given to intention in deciding whether residence is habitual and as to the distinction, if any, between habitual residence and ordinary residence. 1.15

Under English law, 'habitual' residence in England is used as an alternative to domicile in respect of the English courts' jurisdiction to grant decrees of divorce, judicial separation and nullity of marriage, and in respect of the law governing formal validity of wills. It is also used as an alternative to nationality as a basis for recognising the jurisdiction of a foreign court when recognition of a divorce decreed by it is in issue. The habitual residence of a child is critical to the application of the Hague Convention on International Child Abduction as implemented in the UK by the Child Abduction and Custody Act 1985: see, for example, *Re S* (1997) *The Times*, 30 July. 1.16

'Ordinary' residence in England is used as a basis for charging tax and was originally used to give a wife the right to petition for divorce notwithstanding the foreign domicile of her husband and her corresponding foreign domicile of dependency in the days when she could not acquire an independent domicile. In these cases there can, or could, be a duality of ordinary residence and in *obiter dicta* Lord Scarman (with whom the other four Lords concurred) has treated habitual and ordinary residence as if they had the same meaning for supplanting domicile as the test of jurisdiction in family law: *Barnet London Borough Council v Shah* [1983] 2 AC 309 at 344. 1.17

This case concerned whether the respondent had been ordinarily resident in the UK for three years so that Barnet LBC had to make him a grant to study at university. It was held that a person is ordinarily resident if he has his: 1.18

> 'abode in a particular place which he has adopted voluntarily and for settled purposes as part of the regular order of his life for the time being, whether of short or long duration. ... The law requires that there is a settled purpose. This is not to say that the propositus intends to stay where he is indefinitely; indeed his purpose, while settled, may be for a limited period. Education, business, employment, health, family or merely love of the place spring to mind as common reasons for a choice of regular abode. ... All that is necessary is that the purpose of living where one does has a sufficient degree of continuity to be properly described as settled. ... If there be proved a regular, habitual mode of life in a particular place, the continuity of which 1.19

> has persisted despite temporary absences, ordinary residence is established provided only it is adopted voluntarily and for a settled purpose.'

The House of Lords rejected the suggestion that a person's ordinary residence is his one 'real home' and implicitly accepted that a person can be ordinarily resident in two different countries.[1]

1.20 One can accept such possible duality of ordinary or habitual residence to enable divorces and university grants to be given to foreigners but in the context of succession there can only be one law that is the *lex successionis*. Thus, if habitual residence is to be the connecting factor for the *lex successionis* it is necessary for each person to have only one habitual residence or, if it is lawfully possible to have more than one habitual residence, then it is necessary for the dominant or primary habitual residence to be used as the *lex successionis* (as in the case where nationality is used as the connecting factor and a person has two nationalities so that succession to his estate is governed by the law of his dominant nationality).

1.21 Essentially, for habitual residence to be a connecting factor for succession purposes it must represent the current centre of a person's business, social and family life (his current headquarters), irrespective of his intentions as to where he may subsequently settle permanently or for an unlimited period. Significantly, para 51 of the Waters Report on the Hague Succession Convention, which makes habitual residence the connecting factor for many succession purposes, states:

1.22
> 'A person can have only one habitual residence because it is the centre of his living, the place with which he is most closely associated in his pattern of life.... It is a regular physical presence, enduring for some time, and a clearly stronger association that "ordinary" or "simple" residence of which the de cuius may have two or more.'

Clarifying reform

1.23 If habitual residence is to be introduced into England to govern succession matters, as envisaged by the Hague Convention, then legislation may be needed to clarify some matters left unclear by the courts, eg what degree of importance is to be given to intention in determining whether residence is habitual? how long must residence persist to become habitual? can an individual have more than one habitual residence, in which case how does one determine the dominant habitual residence? It may be best for statute to provide that for succession purposes an individual can have only one habitual residence, being the centre of his personal, social and economic interests. In determining an individual's habitual residence, account should be taken of the duration of those three interests and of the intentions of the person relating thereto, but the weight to be given to each of those factors has to be left to the discretion of the judge, notary or lawyer involved in locating the centre of the individual's personal, social and economic interests.

---

1 Further see Dicey and Morris, *The Conflict of Laws* (12th edn) vol 2, pp 161–3, *Re M (Minors) (Residence Order: Jurisdiction)* [1993] 1 FLR 495 at 499 and, in the context of the Hague Child Abduction Convention, *Re J (A Minor) (Abduction)* [1990] 2 AC 562.

MATRIMONIAL PROPERTY REGIMES

Succession law cannot be considered in isolation from matrimonial property regimes for two reasons. First, if the applicable matrimonial property regime is some form of community of property, conferring *inter vivos* property rights on both spouses irrespective of which one has title to the property, then this limits the estate of which a spouse can dispose by will. It also limits or even excludes any need for a spouse to be protected from the other spouse's power of testamentary disposition by a restriction on the other's power of testation. Thus, such a restriction reserving part of the testator's estate may well be in favour of descendants (or ascendants) and not in favour of the surviving spouse. 1.24

Secondly, if marriage as such confers no matrimonial property rights on the spouses, a surviving spouse will have a greater need to be protected by a restriction on the testamentary power of the other spouse with title to property. Thus, the treatment of a surviving spouse (and other family members) by State A's succession law will be determined by State A's matrimonial property regime, if any. 1.25

However, the harmonious balance within State A can be upset if State B's law becomes applicable on a spouse's death, the *lex successionis* being determined at the date of death while the law applicable to matrimonial property will have been determined much earlier. Problems arise where the deceased moved from a jurisdiction having a community property regime to die in a jurisdiction having a separate property system or vice versa. 1.26

In the former situation the surviving spouse may obtain double protection, having vested property rights under State A's matrimonial property regime and a fixed indefeasible inheritance share under the *lex successionis* of State B. If State B, like England, has no fixed indefeasible share but, instead, discretionary family provision ordered by the court, then the court in its discretion will take into account existing matrimonial property rights, so preserving a proper equilibrium. If State B has fixed indefeasible shares then a proper equilibrium can only be achieved if it enacts internal legislation on the lines of the Uniform Disposition of Community Property at Death Act adopted by several American States. This Act recognises and preserves the community property rights under State A but deprives the surviving spouse of succession rights in the deceased's share of community property acquired by him so as to prevent double protection. 1.27

In the situation where the deceased moved from a separate property system to a community property State whose law is the *lex successionis*, the surviving spouse may have little or no protection, having no vested matrimonial property under the former system and little or no fixed indefeasible succession rights under the latter system. A proper equilibrium can only be achieved if the latter system enacts internal legislation to redress the balance by a process of adaptation as in the California Probate Code. This reclassifies the deceased's separate property at his death, so that one half of his movable property wherever situated and all Californian immovable property acquired by the deceased while domiciled outside California, which would have been community property of the deceased 1.28

and the surviving spouse had the deceased been domiciled in California at the time of its acquisition, are to belong to the surviving spouse.

1.29 Finally, it is worth noting that the distinction between community property regimes and systems without community of property may not be so great in practice as in theory. In England and other common law States, savings and immovables are increasingly being held by spouses in joint tenancy with right of survivorship: this can be regarded as a form of quasi-community property because it is a system of community property voluntarily undertaken with respect to each particular asset as opposed to a common fund designated by operation of law.

MANDATORY FAMILY PROTECTION PROVISIONS

1.30 All civilised systems of law (except for South Dakota) provide some protection against a testator leaving his family too little by giving or bequeathing his estate to others. Civil law systems tend to have rigid, compulsory shares for the deceased's close relatives while common law systems tend to have discretionary judicial provision available. The lack of the concept of the trust in civil law systems and its presence in common law systems may partly justify the distinction between the rigid and the flexible approach. After all, in common law systems it makes dynastic and financial sense in one's lifetime to transfer majority shareholdings in companies to trustees to manage for the benefit of one's spouse and descendants rather than allow small minority shareholdings to pass absolutely to each of one's heirs. Such lifetime provision will be taken into account in any claim for discretionary relief upon the settlor's death.

1.31 Where the forum is applying a foreign *lex successionis* with rigid compulsory shares for close heirs few problems arise in giving effect to such mandatory family protection. However, if the foreign *lex successionis* simply provides for discretionary judicial protection of close relatives and dependants, what is the court of the forum to do?

1.32 The answer is that it must ascertain the scope of the discretionary judicial provision of the *lex successionis*. If England or Northern Ireland be the *lex successionis* then discretionary relief is only available if the deceased died domiciled in England or Northern Ireland respectively: if he died domiciled elsewhere then *cadit quaestio*. If discretionary relief is available under the *lex successionis*, irrespective of the deceased's domicile, so long as property is situated in the state of the *lex successionis* the court of the forum is likely to refuse to exercise the discretionary powers, regarding them as vested only in the courts of the State creating those powers: *Re Paulin* [1950] VLR 462 at 467, *Re Bailey* [1985] 2 NZLR 656 at 660.

1.33 Where the deceased dies owning immovables located in a Sate, such as the Republic of Ireland, which applies the *lex situs* to succession to immovables and has discretionary judicial relief available for close heirs and dependants, then a claim to such relief will have to be brought in that State (although, if that State be England or Northern Ireland the claim can only be made if the deceased died domiciled in England or Northern Ireland respectively). If the *lex successionis* for other property of the deceased has discretionary judicial relief available then an application will need to be made in the State whose law is the *lex successionis*. Application to courts in two or more countries is inconvenient but the second (or third) court to deal with an application will take into account what the first (or second) court has already decided in exercising its discretion. Indeed, if a court in one jurisdiction found itself in a difficulty in the exercise of its discretionary power in view of an application in another jurisdiction it could adjourn the application before it until the determination of the other application.

UNITY OR SCISSION OF SUCCESSION

The principle of scission which is applied in most common law jurisdictions and some civil law jurisdictions requires one law to govern succession to movables (whether the law of nationality or of domicile or of habitual residence) and the *lex situs* to govern succession to immovables. The principle of unity requires only one law to govern succession to all the deceased's property but has to face up to the harsh jurisdictional reality that it has to allow immovables in a foreign State to be governed by the law of that State if that State applies the principle of scission (a 'schismatic' state). 1.34

Nevertheless, in calculating the rigid compulsory shares of close heirs, a 'unitarian' State may take into account the value of the deceased's whole estate (including foreign immovables in a schismatic State) although only being able to satisfy the heirs' claims out of assets in the unitarian State. In such a case, any application by such an heir for discretionary judicial relief out of the immovables in the *lex situs* will be likely to be rejected by the court of such *situs*. 1.35

Correspondingly, in a schismatic State any rigid compulsory share will be presumed to exist only in that part of the deceased's estate not governed by a foreign *lex situs*. In any application for discretionary provision in a court of the *lex situs*, it will be open for the court to take the view, if the value of the immovables is high enough, that reasonable financial provision has not been made for the applicant and so order provision to be made. 1.36

The principle of scission is particularly unsatisfactory and anomalous when one considers the statutory legacy to which a surviving spouse is entitled in most common law States on her spouse's death intestate. It is possible that she may obtain the statutory legacy considered proper for her not just once but twice, eg under Trinidadian or Northern Irish law as the *lex domicilii* and under English law as the *lex situs*: *Re Collens* [1986] Ch 505. However, if the immovables are situated in a unitarian State which rejects the doctrine of *renvoi*, a domiciled Englishman's whole estate may be governed by his English *lex domicilii* or nationality so that intestacy rights arise only under one system of law, or, in the case of a deceased leaving a will, so that only the mandatory family protection rules of one system can apply. 1.37

THE DOCTRINE OF RENVOI

1.38 A judge's task is not over when he has decided:

(1) that his court has jurisdiction;
(2) how the issue before him is to be characterised in private international law terms; and
(3) that the choice of law rules applicable to the characterised issue make the law of State X applicable, unless State X be the local forum so that it is obviously the internal, ie domestic, law of State X which is applicable.

1.39 However, if State X law is foreign law the judge has three options. He can decide that State X law means the internal law of State X. Alternatively, he can apply the *renvoi* doctrine in the form of 'single' *renvoi* so that State X law means all State X law *including* its private international law. Thus, if a judge in State W is referred by his own choice of law rule to the law of State X, but the choice of law rule under State X's private international law principles refers the issue back to the law of State W, then the judge accepts the 'remission' (or *renvoi* to the first degree) as requiring him to apply the internal law of State W. If State X's choice of law rule referred the issue on to the law of State Y then the State W judge could accept this 'transmission' (or *renvoi* to the second degree) as requiring him to apply the internal law of State Y. While some countries, like Spain and Belgium, have accepted single *renvoi* or, like France, even *renvoi* to the second degree, English law has rejected it and in some circumstances has adopted the third option, which may be termed the doctrine of 'double' *renvoi* or 'total' *renvoi* or the foreign court theory.

1.40 This theory requires the English judge when referred by English choice of law rules to the law of State X to pretend that he is a State X judge and to apply whatever law such a judge would apply if he were hearing the case. Take the case where an English-domiciled, deceased, British national owned immovables in State X, so the English judge holds that the *lex situs* of State X governs succession to those immovables whether the issue is one of intestacy or of mandatory family protection rules. Expert evidence could then lead the English judge to hold that a State X judge would be referred by his choice of law rules to English law (whether as the law of the deceased's nationality or of his habitual residence) and so find that the case was remitted to him by English law. It then becomes crucial whether State X law accepts the doctrine of single *renvoi*. If, like France, it does then the State X judge will apply the internal law of State X: *Re Annesley* [1926] Ch 692. If, as used to be the case for Italy before Law 218 of 31 May 1995 and still is the case for Spain, Denmark and Greece, it does not, then the State X judge will apply the internal law of England: *Re Ross* [1930] 1 Ch 377, *Re Duke of Wellington* [1947] Ch 506.

1.41 Where the acceptance or rejection of single *renvoi* is unclear, the English judge faces an invidious task as used to be the position in the case of Spain. Prima facie, Article 12 of the Spanish Civil Code as amended in 1974 introduced single *renvoi* into Spanish law so that Spanish internal law on intestacy and on mandatory family protection rules would apply to Spanish immovables of British nationals. However, it was arguable that the strength of the Spanish concept of the unity and universality of a deceased's estate as embodied in Article 9 was such as to prevail over Article 12 in matters of succession so that the deceased's national law must govern all his estate as held by Browne-Wilkinson V-C in *Re Adams Deceased* (unreported, English High Court, Chancery Division, 31 July 1985), rejecting a son's claim to a compulsory share in respect of a Spanish immovable. Under English law, the resolution of expert evidence on foreign law is a question of fact binding only the parties to the case. However, under s 4(2) of the Civil Evidence Act 1972, any finding in an English Court on a question of foreign law shall, if reported in citable form, be admissible as presumptive evidence of the foreign law unless the contrary is proved. While subsequent Spanish case-law rejected the view of Browne-Wilkinson V-C, the Supreme Court has recently taken the same view (see para **14.113**).

Ascertaining the deceased's national law can, of course, be difficult where the country of nationality, like the UK, comprises several different systems of territorial law, eg England, Scotland, Jersey, Isle of Man, Northern Ireland. Normally, one will be concerned with the territorial unit where the deceased was domiciled at death, but real difficulties arise if the deceased British national dies domiciled in State X which provides for succession to be governed by the deceased's nationality law and which rejects any remission to it by the national law, having rejected the single *renvoi* doctrine: *Re O'Keefe* [1945] Ch 124. 1.42

The position is also unclear where an Englishman dies domiciled in Switzerland or the Netherlands, having chosen English law to govern succession to his estate as allowed by Swiss or Dutch law (see paras **15.16–15.17**). Under English law the Swiss or Dutch law of the deceased's last domicile is the *lex successionis*, but by Swiss or Dutch law the *lex successionis* is English law. It would seem that an English judge putting himself in the shoes of a Swiss or Dutch judge would be likely to apply English law as the *lex successionis*, the Maine Supreme Court decision in *Estate of Wright* (1994) 637 A 2d 106 providing support for this approach. 1.43

CHANGE OF CONNECTING FACTOR

For succession purposes, it is the law of the connecting factor (whether nationality, domicile or habitual residence) at the date of death which is crucial. It follows that the operation of a will made by reference to the connecting factor applicable at the date of making the will may be affected by a subsequent change of nationality, domicile or habitual residence, as the case may be, or by selling an immovable in one country and using the proceeds to buy an immovable in a schismatic country. The change may result in the removal of a restriction on the testator's power to dispose of his estate as he wishes (eg by becoming domiciled in England or if a wealthy Englishman escapes the Inheritance (Provision for Family and Dependants) Act 1975 by acquiring a foreign domicile in a country which applies his 'English' nationality law to succession and not its own mandatory rules) or the imposition of such a restriction (eg by taking up habitual residence in France). In the latter case, this may well upset the estate planning in the balanced 1.44

interests of the family members undertaken by a combination of the testator's will and his lifetime trusts or *pactes successoraux.*

1.45 Testators thus need to be warned of the need to review the position if they change their nationality, domicile or habitual residence, or if they sell an immovable in one country and purchase an immovable in another country, though this will be unnecessary if the country in which they die has fully implemented the Hague Succession Convention.

3. THE HAGUE SUCCESSION CONVENTION

1.46 Under Article 5 of the Hague Convention (1989) on the Law Applicable to Succession to Estates of Deceased Persons (see Appendix B) (ratified by The Netherlands and signed so far only by Switzerland and Argentina) a testator can choose either the law of his nationality or the law of his habitual residence *at the time of making his will* to govern succession to his estate, so that his plans stand even if he subsequently changes his nationality or habitual residence. Exceptionally, his choice and his plans will not stand if he has the misfortune to die a national of, and habitually resident in, a country which has made a reservation under Article 24(1)(c) of the Convention. This enables it not to recognise the choice of a person who at his death was not a national of, or habitually resident, in the country whose law he had chosen but was a national of, and habitually resident in, the reserving country. Only a very few chauvinist countries seem likely to make this reservation which greatly undermines the good sense of the Convention.

1.47 In the absence of an effective express choice of law, the law applicable to succession to the estate of a deceased, 'D', is by Article 3:

(1) the law of the State of D's habitual residence and nationality at his death or, if they do not coincide;
(2) the law of the State where at his death D had been habitually resident for no less than five years immediately preceding his death unless, exceptionally, at his death D was manifestly more closely connected with the State of his nationality, when the law of that State will apply or, failing which (ie less than five years' habitual residence);
(3) the law of the State of D's nationality at death, unless he was then more closely connected with another State, when the law of that State will apply.

1.48 Habitual residence thus becomes the major connecting factor with the possibility of a fall-back to nationality: domicile in the common law sense ceases to be a factor and so the Inheritance (Provision for Family and Dependants) Act 1975 will need to be amended so as to be available whenever English law is the *lex successionis.* Moreover, the principle of unity prevails over the principle of scission. By Article 5, one law alone governs succession to D's movables and immovables including the mandatory family protection rules. However, to facilitate the administration and distribution of D's assets in a foreign State X, D can make a will in that State choosing its law, eg in respect of a State X villa and its contents (see Article 6). The application of State X law is then incorporated or subsumed within the one subjectively chosen or objectively applicable law: *cf* the German concept *materiell-rechtliche Verweisung* (substantive law reference).

Special provisions deal with multi-composite States like the UK and Spain having territorial units therein with different systems of law. A national or habitual resident of such a State can expressly choose the law of a territorial unit therein where he had earlier resided. Article 19 also contains provisions allocating, where necessary, nationals or habitual residents of such States to particular territorial units therein. 1.49

The Convention covers matters treated as matters of succession in the common law sense but a Contracting State can extend it to such matters of administration as it may specify under Article 7, para 3. 1.50

The Convention excludes issues pertaining to matrimonial property, but it may well enable an express choice of law to be made that coincides with the law applicable to matrimonial property so as to preserve a proper balance between succession rights and matrimonial property rights. 1.51

Article 1(2)(d) specifically excludes 'property rights, interests or assets created or transferred otherwise than by succession' such as in joint ownership with right of survival or, as mentioned in the last part of para 46 of the Waters Official Report on the Succession Convention, 'the *inter vivos* trust'. It was intended that 'claw-back' rules (entitling relatives of a deceased subject to a civil law *lex successionis* to claim their forced heirship rights not only against the deceased's actual estate on death but also against assets given away by him in his lifetime) would not therefore be available in common law jurisdictions where the deceased had earlier created a joint tenancy of his assets with another or a trust of assets. However, because of the clause in Article 1(2)(d) 'otherwise than by succession' and because the meaning of 'succession' was distorted in the Convention (common law lawyers regarding succession as concerned only with dispositions on death but having to permit civil law lawyers a wider range of matters covered by Article 7), Article 7 could be regarded as giving a wider functional meaning of succession so as to include 'claw-back' rules under Article 7(2)(a) and (d) and drastically limiting the ambit of Article 1(2)(d). 1.52

It seems almost certain that common law countries implementing the Convention will clarify the ambiguous relationship between Article 1(2)(d) and Article 7 in favour of ousting 'claw-back' rules which would otherwise introduce a novel retrospective impeachability of title into such jurisdictions.[1] This could be done because it is up to the forum to determine the meaning of the terminology in Articles 1(2) and 7(2) as recognised by para 74 of the Waters Official Report or, unsatisfactorily, by virtue of the public policy Article 18, requiring trustees to have 1.53

1 Further see D J Hayton, 'Trusts and Forced Heirship Problems' [1993] 1 J Int T & C Pl 3 at 9, and D J Hayton, 'The Hague Conventions on Trusts and on Succession: A Common Law Perspective' in Borras (ed) (1996) *E Pluribus Unum: Liber Amicorum Georges Droz* Martinus Nijhoff Publishers.

protection against 'claw-back' rules by provisions similar to those in s 13 of the Inheritance (Provision for Family and Dependants) Act 1975.

4. THE HAGUE MATRIMONIAL PROPERTY CONVENTION

1.54 The 1978 Convention on the Law Applicable to Matrimonial Property Regimes has been signed by France, Luxembourg, Austria, The Netherlands and Portugal, while France, The Netherlands and Luxembourg have gone on to ratify it. It excludes succession rights of a surviving spouse.

1.55 By Article 3, before their marriage, the spouses can expressly choose the law of any State of which either spouse is then a national or the law of the State in which either spouse then has his habitual residence or the law of the first State where one of the spouses establishes a new habitual residence after marriage. A separate choice of the *lex situs* of immovables can also be made.

1.56 Subsequently, by Article 6, the spouses can jointly change the law applicable to their matrimonial property regime to a new law. They can change either to the law of the State of which either spouse is a national at the time of choice or to the law of the State in which either spouse has his habitual residence at the time of choice. Thus, by an appropriate choice, the spouses may be able to submit their matrimonial property regime to the interrelated law which will govern succession to their estates.

5. THE HAGUE ADMINISTRATION OF ESTATES CONVENTION

1.57 The 1973 Convention concerning the International Administration of the Estates of Deceased Persons has been signed by Italy, Luxembourg, The Netherlands, Turkey and the UK, while Portugal and Czechoslovakia have gone on to ratify it. The UK Law Commission, which was asked to consider it with a view to the UK implementing it, is believed to have concluded that its complexities make it impractical and unworthwhile to implement it: hence, the UK has produced no implementing legislation and has not ratified the Convention. Presumably, Italy, Luxembourg, The Netherlands and Turkey have by now come to the same conclusion.

1.58 If the Succession Convention proves successful so as to simplify matters, then it should prove possible to look again at the Administration of Estates Convention and produce a simpler procedure for establishing an internationally recognised certificate designating the person or persons entitled to administer the deceased's estate and indicating his or their powers, without being subject to too many restrictions and qualifications.

6. THE HAGUE TRUSTS CONVENTION[1]

The 1985 Convention on the Law Applicable to Trusts and on their Recognition (see Appendix A) looks like being a successful Convention. It has been signed by Luxembourg and the United States while Australia, Canada (excepting Ontario and Quebec), Italy, The Netherlands and the UK (as well as many of its dependent or associated territories like Hong Kong, Bermuda, Gibraltar, Guernsey, the Isle of Man and Jersey) have also gone on to ratify it. France produced a Bill to insert a concept to be known as *la fiducie* into its internal law, introducing the concept (novel to French law) of a person having a fiduciary patrimony separate from one's private patrimony, just like a trustee's private property is separate from the property he holds as trustee. However, difficulties over taxation of *la fiducie* and any recognised trusts have, however, caused the French not to proceed with the Bill: nor will they implement the Convention to favour foreign trusts until they have a satisfactory domestic quasi-trust. Nevertheless, even before the Convention is in force, foreign courts are likely to take it into account as reflecting common law States' private international law rules and as a model to help resolve particular issues concerning trusts, as has been done by the Paris Court of Appeal and the Hague District Court for issues covered by other Conventions not yet in force. 1.59

The Convention does not introduce the trust concept into the internal law of non-trust States. There is no question of such States having to introduce into their internal law new property concepts, such as equitable interests and having to recognise the owner of an equitable interest in property as having a right to trace such property or the product of such property against all but a bona fide purchaser of the property: (see Article 15(1)(d) and (f) and the last sentence of Article 11). 1.60

The Convention does make non-trust States recognise trusts as such as a matter of private international law (subject to significant safeguards) and it establishes common private international law rules on the law applicable to trusts. It then goes on pragmatically to emphasise the consequences of recognising a trust created under the applicable law of some trust State. This will assist lawyers in non-trust States to cope expeditiously and effectively with trust issues raised within their jurisdictions. Such issues increasingly arise as more and more trust assets, beneficiaries and trustees are to be found in non-trust States. 1.61

Common law testators increasingly die owning property in non-trust States and may make a fairly standard common law will leaving all their estate on particular fixed or discretionary trusts. If they see a lawyer in the non-trust State where certain assets are situated, so as to make a foreign will disposing of such assets, then 1.62

1 Further see (1987) 36 ICLQ 260 (D J Hayton) and chapter 12 of Hayton & Marshall *Cases & Commentary on the Law of Trusts* (10th edn); Underhill & Hayton *Law of Trusts and Trustees* (15th edn) pp 826–838 and 'International Recognition of Trusts' in Glasson *International Trust Laws*; Albisinni and Gambino, 'Italian Civil Law and The Hague Convention on Trusts' [1993] 2 J Int T & C PL 73; O'Sullivan, 'The Hague Convention on Trusts – Further considerations' [1993] 2 J Int T & C PL 65; Schoenblum, 'The Hague Convention on Trusts: Much Ado About Very Little' [1994] 1 J Int T & C PL 5; Hayton, 'The Hague Convention on Trusts: A Little is Better than Nothing But Why So Little?' [1994] 1 J Int T & C PL 23.

they may be encouraged to utilise foreign concepts to implement their wishes, eg a Dutch *bewind*, a German *Treuhand*, or foreign concepts similar to life interests and interests in remainder but the life tenant or remainderman may have more or less extensive powers than would be the case under a common law system. If the Trusts Convention is implemented, then a national or habitual resident of a common law trust State will be able to create a trust as such in a foreign will covering foreign property rather than rely on local foreign concepts which he may misunderstand. He should expressly designate the law to govern his trust as recognised in Article 6 rather than rely on the law that is judged to be most closely connected with the trust under Article 7.

1.63 However, the Convention applies only to a trust once it has been effectively created by a will or other instrument: it applies to the 'rocket' and not to the 'rocket launcher'. Antecedent preliminary issues that may affect the validity of wills or other instruments by which property is allegedly subjected to a trust fall outside the Convention by Article 4. Thus, the Convention cannot apply if the applicable *lex successionis*, with its mandatory family protection rules reserving fixed shares for close heirs, prevents the relevant property from being available to be subjected to a testamentary trust.

1.64 Even where a trust survives Article 4, Article 15 makes provision for the applicable law of a trust to be overridden by the mandatory rules of a State whose substantive law is applicable according to the private international law rules of the forum. This can significantly undermine the effect of Article 11, especially if the Convention is restrictively interpreted so that all property (whether trust or private property) owned by a trustee is available to his creditors, although para 108 of the official von Overbeck Report on the Convention favours a broad interpretation because the separateness of the trust assets from the private assets of the trustee 'is an essential element of the trust, without which its recognition would have no meaning'. To avoid any doubt, the Dutch, in implementing the Convention, expressly ousted the application of Article 15(1)(d) and (e) so that the trust assets on the bankruptcy of the trustee are not available to his creditors[1]. Mandatory rules within Article 15 concern matters such as transfer of title to property to third parties, bankruptcy, matrimonial property and succession: they may lead to the *lex fori* or a foreign *lex successionis* or *lex situs* being applied so as wholly or partly to undo the effects of a trust. Mandatory succession rules concerned with bringing into account lifetime gifts by the deceased in order to ascertain the amount of heirs' reserved shares have special significance, particularly if the deceased settlor's trust assets are found situated in the civil law forum of such heirs. *Holzberg v Sasson* (Cass Civ, 4 February 1980, (1986) Rev crit de dr int pr 685) reveals that such forum will enable the heirs to claim their reserved shares out of such assets.

Heir's claims to reserved shares

1.65 However, if a settlor domiciled, habitually resident and a national of a non-trust State, 'Nontrusto', transfers assets situated in England to English trustees of an English trust for Nontrusto beneficiaries then, so long as assets which can be

1 Further see D J Hayton [1996] J Int T & C PL 128.

traced to the trust are not found in Nontrusto (or a similar civil law country also characterising lifetime gifts of the inheritance reserved for forced heirs as governed by the *lex successionis*), the settlor's heirs will not be able to claim anything against the trustees, assuming the trustees do not by a stay in Nontrusto make themselves personally subject to the jurisdiction of the Nontrusto courts. Any claim in the English courts against the English resident trustees of English assets (or foreign assets purchased with the proceeds of sale of English assets) should fail on the basis that by the English *lex situs* applicable to *inter vivos* transfers of English property and by the English trust law there is a valid trust, so that the trust assets are not part of the settlor's estate on his death to be governed by the Nontrusto *lex successionis* (applicable to assets other than English immovables, succession to which is, anyhow, governed by the English *lex situs*). Indeed, the trustees may well be able to invoke Article 15(1)(d) (in the Schedule to the Recognition of Trusts Act 1987) as preserving the supremacy of the rules of the English *lex situs* on the transfer of title to property, which is how English private international law rules should characterise the issue: see New York law in *Hutchinson v Ross*, 211 NE 2d 637 (1965) and *Wyatt v Fulrath*, 187 NE 65 (1933), and Florida Law in *Sanchez v Sanchez* (1989) 547 So 2d 945.[1] The position is analogous to the case where there would be outright rejection of any claims by the foreign heirs of a deceased joint tenant of English property against the surviving joint tenant.

If the heirs' claims were in the Nontrusto court (eg because proceeds of sale had been invested by the trustees in Nontrusto assets or trust assets had been transferred in specie to Nontrusto resident beneficiaries) then it would characterise the gift to trustees of the inheritance reserved for the heirs as governed by the Nontrusto *lex successionis*, the supremacy of which is preserved by Article 15(1)(c) if the Convention is in force in Nontrusto. Thus, the heirs' reserved shares should be satisfied so far as possible. **1.66**

If in a claim brought in an English court it was argued that the Nontrusto *lex successionis* would so operate in favour of the heirs, so that the English court should apply the Nontrusto *lex successionis* under Article 15(1)(c) and so find in favour of the heirs, there are two good grounds for rejecting this. First, English private international law rules do not characterise the issue as one of succession so that the *lex successionis* is not relevant: they prevail over the Nontrusto rules which so characterise the issue and thereby make the *lex successionis* relevant. Secondly, if the argument succeeded then such possible application of the prospective *lex successionis* (which might at the settlor's death not be the actual *lex successionis*) enabling the trust to be set aside *pro tanto* (whether in law or in substance) would so inhibit the trustees in discharging their fundamental functions or, even, deter persons from acting as trustees (for fear of having to repay their remuneration or otherwise becoming personally liable to the heirs) as to be manifestly incompatible with English public policy. Thus, Article 18 enables the argument to be **1.67**

1 However, if say A and B had litigated the matter in Civilopia where judgment was in A's favour then B should not be able to litigate the matter again in Trustopia because of *res judicata* principles: *Watts v Savings Bank Corpn* (1970) 27 New York 2d 270. Further see Underhill and Hayton, *Law of Trusts and Trustees* (15th edn) pp 203–204.

rejected, especially when, if the argument succeeded it could mean the introduction into internal English substantive law of a special instance of retrospective voidability of title if under Nontrusto law the heirs' claim amounted to a proprietary, rather than a personal, claim.

1.68 The practical lesson is that trustees must not allow assets which can be traced to the trust to be found in Nontrusto (or a similar State) nor must they themselves become subject to the jurisdiction of Nontrusto (or a similar State) if such jurisdiction could make orders compelling them to bring trust assets within the jurisdiction. If a Nontrusto resident beneficiary becomes entitled to trust capital or income, he should leave it outside Nontrusto (or a similar State), although it is possible that Nontrusto law may enable legal pressure to be brought to bear on him within the jurisdiction, so that he is compelled to bring the foreign property within the jurisdiction for the forced heir or to pay such heir compensation. Indeed, if the Nontrusto beneficiary under the English trust is also a beneficiary under the settlor's will or intestacy, it may well be that Nontrusto succession law enables the forced heir to make up his reserved share out of the beneficiary's interest in the deceased settlor's estate. This compensation arrangement may even apply in respect of English immovables, succession to which is governed by the English *lex situs*, where the forced heir's reserved share extends to such immovable under the unitarian Nontrusto *lex successionis* and the person acquiring the immovable (directly or under a trust) is a beneficiary under the will or intestacy of the deceased donor/settlor.

7. MEANS OF MINIMISING PROBLEMS

1.69 One can outline the techniques for minimising problems which are discussed in context in each of the chapters on particular countries. To facilitate the administration and distribution of assets in a foreign State, it is very useful to have a local foreign lawyer draw up the will in the foreign language so as to dispose of those assets. One must be careful that the will deals only with those assets and does not revoke any wills other than any earlier will dealing with such assets.

1.70 A person who is domiciled or habitually resident in a schismatic state which applies the *lex situs* to immovables and the *lex domicilii* (like England) or the law of habitual residence (like France) to movables will need to be careful where foreign immovables are concerned. He must check whether the foreign system of law accepts *renvoi* to itself as the *lex situs*, as in Germany, Austria or Italy, so that its intestacy rules will apply or, if there is a will, its mandatory family protection rules (providing fixed reserved shares for close heirs) will apply. If this is the case, then he should consider owning shares in a company (movables) that owns the foreign immovable. If he is to be co-owner of a foreign immovable, he should consider whether the foreign law allows a tontine arrangement whereby the survivor takes all the property free from any claims of forced heirs of his predeceased co-owner.

1.71 If the foreign system (like Spain, Denmark or Greece) rejects *renvoi* in favour of the application of only one *lex successionis* which it regards as English law by virtue of the deceased's English domicile, habitual residence or nationality, then all is fine because there is then no application of foreign forced heirship or intestacy rules. If, however, it applies the law of the deceased's nationality as the appropriate connecting factor rather than his English domicile, the testator, if he is a foreign national, will need to check whether his national law creates problems similar to those under the internal *lex situs*, in which case steps need to be taken as suggested in the preceding paragraph.

Mandatory family protection rules can be avoided altogether by a British national, considered linked to the English system, who is not domiciled in England, and so falls outside the Inheritance (Provision for Family and Dependants) Act 1975, if the foreign State where he is domiciled applies as the *lex successionis* his nationality law, namely English law. **1.72**

If a foreign-domiciled person owns English immovables then English law governs succession to such immovables but no discretionary provision is available under the 1975 Act. If the applicable *lex successionis* is otherwise that of a foreign schismatic State then normally forced heirship shares and intestacy shares will be calculated excluding the value of the English immovables. However, if the State is unitarian then it may well be that the value of English immovables is taken into account in calculating the forced heirship amounts. **1.73**

A foreigner (or an Englishman) may well find for estate planning purposes that an Isle of Man or Jersey or Cayman or English trust will be useful, although, as seen in paras **1.65** *et seq* the foreigner's State can still intervene in respect of assets or people in its jurisdiction. **1.74**

Finally, for proper estate planning it normally makes sense to try to have the same law governing matrimonial property as will govern succession matters or, at least, have the law governing matrimonial property have a similar approach to that of the State whose law appears to be the law that will govern succession matters. If the spouses are estranged then countervailing considerations may apply. **1.75**

The impact of any change of nationality or domicile or habitual residence on a testator's will and associated inter vivos dispositions must always be considered. A brief summary of tax considerations is given in each of the chapters on particular countries. However, practitioners are strongly advised to check the situation when drawing up a will, because tax law and practice are ever-changing and always complex where international elements are concerned. **1.76**

To avoid forced heirship complications a settlor should not reserve in his settlement a general power to appoint capital to himself or to revoke his trust because trust assets subject to such powers are treated as part of his 'net estate' for the purposes of claims under the Inheritance (Provision for Family and Dependants) Act 1975 if he died domiciled in England, and this can create problems even if he died domiciled in Nontrusto. If English law regards such assets as governed by the English *lex successionis* for English domiciliaries, it may **1.77** very well accept that such assets can be regarded as available for claims governed by the Nontrusto *lex successionis* for Nontrusto domiciliaries.[1]

1.78 It has thus been seen that when confronted with an international estate one must consider which law will govern the various parts of the estate and whether the inheritance rights in the various jurisdictions will correspond with the provisions of the testator's will. The forum for resolution of any disputes will often be crucial, the general rule being that if the relevant assets are situated in State X, then the court of State X will have jurisdiction and so will determine what is the relevant connecting factor for ascertaining the *lex successionis*.

1.79 One also needs to consider whether the bases for taxation in the various jurisdictions match, eg the USA taxes the world-wide estate of a citizen or resident of the USA, the UK taxes only UK domiciliaries or those who own assets situated in the UK, while the French use residence as the connecting tax factor. However, ss 158 and 159 of the Inheritance Tax Act 1984 provide bilateral relief (where there are double tax treaties) and unilateral relief from tax.

1 Further see D J Hayton, 'Trusts and Forced Heirship Problems' [1993] 1 J Int T & C PL 3 at 5–6.

CHAPTER 2

AUSTRIA†

1. INTRODUCTION

AUSTRIAN CIVIL LAW SYSTEM

Austria has a system of complete codified law (civil law system). It is, in fact, one of the oldest systems of codified law on the European continent, dating back from the days of the Austrian empire. The main code, the 'ABGB' (*Allgemeines Bürgerliches Gesetzbuch*, or Austrian General Civil Code), was introduced throughout the empire in 1811, nearly a century before the German Bürgerliches Gesetzbuch came into being. The statutory provisions concerning national Austrian law of inheritance are contained in ss 531 to 824 ABGB. 2.1

The national Austrian law of inheritance tax is likewise codified and is found in 'ErbStG' (*Erbschafts- und Schenkungssteuergesetz 1955*, or the Inheritance and Gift Tax Act 1955). 2.2

Austrian conflict of laws rules relating to inheritance issues including non-Austrian elements are governed by 'IPRG 1978' (*Internationales Privatrechtsgesetz*, or the International Private Law Act 1978). Particular regulations with regard to the law of inheritance are contained in ss 28 to 30 thereof. In addition, the *Haager Testamentsübereinkommen*, or Hague Convention concerning the form of wills was ratified by Austria and came into force there in 1963 when it was promulgated in the BGBI (*Bundesgesetzblatt* or Austrian Federal Law Gazette) number 295/1965. 2.3

Probate procedures, which play an important role in Austria, are governed by 'AußStrG 1984' (*Außerstreitgesetz*, or the Non-Contentious Proceedings Act). 2.4

Contentious proceedings are instituted in cases of inheritance disputes, and such proceedings are governed by the 'JN' (*Jurisdiktionsnorm* or Jurisdiction Act) and 'ZPO' (*Zivilprozeßordnung* or Civil Proceedings Act), both of which date from 1895. 2.5

In respect of international inheritance tax law, there are several double taxation treaties in existence between Austria and other countries (France, Germany, Lichtenstein, Sweden, Switzerland, Hungary, United States). At the moment, however, no such treaty is available between Austria and the UK. 2.6

---

† This chapter was written by Dr Andreas Lintl, Rechtsanwalt, Lugeck 7, A-1010 Vienna, Austria, tel (0043 1) 512 60 50, fax (0043 1) 512 8605 and London, tel 0171-972 9720, fax 0171-972 9723.

2. PROCEDURAL ISSUES

2.7 Heirs, no matter whether they have an entitlement under a will or as a consequence of the statutory intestacy rules, are not allowed simply to take possession of the estate or parts thereof. A formal procedure, called '*Verlassenschaftsabhandlung*' (deceased's estate proceedings), must be completed prior to the heir gaining legal title. The rules for such procedure are set out in ss 20 to 180 AußStrG.

2.8 The local district court in the jurisdiction of which the deceased was last resident is notified of the death by the registrar's office when a death certificate is issued. The district court, in its capacity as a probate court, opens a '*Verlassenschaftsakt*' (deceased's estate court file). This file is passed on to the competent notary public's office. Austrian notaries act as '*Gerichtskommissäre*' (officers of the court) in probate proceedings.

2.9 The preliminary proceedings are opened by the notary summoning the deceased's next of kin in order to draw up a list of all potential heirs and beneficiaries and to enquire if there is a will or other disposition made by the deceased and also to provide a preliminary list of all assets and liabilities of the deceased known to the next of kin. This meeting at the notary's office is called '*Todesfallsaufnahme*', and a document by the same name is issued (s 36 AußStrG). If a person dies outside Austria and proceedings are nevertheless commenced in Austria, this document is normally issued by the consular section of the relevant Austrian embassy.

2.10 It is compulsory under Austrian law that the *Todesfallsaufnahme* document is issued by a notary public (or an Austrian embassy in cases of death abroad). Once this document is issued, it is, however, possible for the potential heirs to apply for the deceased's estate proceedings to be carried out through a representative of the heirs (*Erbenmachthaber*) on the basis of written submissions to the probate court (*schriftliche Nachlaßpflege*). Austrian notaries as well as Austrian solicitors (*Rechstanwälte*) are entitled to act as representatives of the heirs in such proceedings. If no application for *schriftliche Nachlaßpflege* is made, the notary carries on his activity as officer of the court.

2.11 Wills and other last dispositions are opened and made known by the probate court '*Kundmachung des Testaments*' (ss 61 to 70 AußStrG). According to s 799 ABGB, the putative heir has to declare his intention to accept the inheritance (*Erbserklärung*) and prove his entitlement (*Erbrechtsausweis*). In the case of a conflicting declaration of another person claiming to be the heir, the probate court has to hear both parties and then instruct the party with the weaker evidence to institute contentious proceedings against the other party within a certain period of time. If such proceedings are not instituted within the given time, the probate proceedings are continued with the other party having the stronger title.

2.12 Finally, the non-contentious proceedings are closed by the issuing of the *Einantwortungsurkunde* (grant of probate) by the probate court. This document entitles the heir to take possession and dispose of all assets belonging to the estate. Due to the lengthy procedures prior to the *Einantwortungsurkunde* being issued, s 810 ABGB and s 145 AußStrG enable the putative heir to be granted leave to administer the estate (*Besorgung und Verwaltung des Nachlasses*). This, however, does not entitle the putative heir to sell or otherwise dispose of any of the assets of the estate without having obtained prior to approval by the probate court.

Full probate proceedings take place as described above only if a person was resident or left real estate in Austria. Otherwise, in the case of movable assets (eg investments or savings with Austrian banks) situated in Austria, a shorter and simpler procedure called '*Ausfolgungsverfahren*' applies. Such proceedings lead to the issuing of a court order entitling the heir to obtain the Austrian assets of the non-Austrian estate. As indicated, the most frequent occurrence of these proceedings is in the case of a foreign national having bank accounts in Austria. 2.13

3. INTESTATE SUCCESSION

GENERAL RULES

The ABGB provides for detailed rules if there is no valid last disposition (whether by will, codicil or inheritance contract). The estate will devolve upon the deceased's relatives and his surviving spouse in this situation (s 727 ABGB). Succession law follows the principle of family succession, according to which only relatives can qualify as statutory heirs. A son-in-law cannot be the statutory heir of his mother-in-law since he is related through marriage only. 2.14

Common law husbands and wives

'*Lebensgefaehrten*' (live-in partners, common law husbands or wives) are not statutory heirs. They can become entitled to the estate or parts thereof only under a valid last disposition. With regard to Austrian landlord and tenant law (*Mietrecht*), *Lebensgefaehrten* are treated like married spouses, ie they are entitled to take over the tenancy rights of the deceased person upon his death (s 14, para 3 'MRG' *Mietrechtsgesetz*, or Tenancy Law Act). 2.15

Illegitimate children

For the purposes of succession law, illegitimate children are treated like legitimate children (s 730, para 1 ABGB). Such equal treatment of illegitimate and legitimate children was introduced by *Erbrechtsnovelle 1989* (Inheritance Law Amendment Act 1989). 2.16

Adopted children

The adoption of a child creates between the adopting parent and his descendants on the one hand, and the adopted child and his children who are of minor age at the time of adoption on the other hand, the same mutual rights and obligations as in the case of natural children and their parents (s 182 ABGB). In addition, the right to inherit (*Erbrecht*) between the adopted child and his natural parents and 2.17

their relatives remains unaffected (s 182b ABGB). If the adopted child dies before his parents, the inheritance entitlement of the adopting parents prevails over that of the natural parents.

Order of inheritance in the case of intestacy

2.18 The heirs are divided into particular degrees (*Parentelen*) which determine the order of inheritance. The existence of relatives of an earlier degree prevents relatives of a later degree from becoming entitled to the estate (ss 70 *et seq* ABGB). The degrees can be illustrated through a family tree. Statutory heirs of the first degree, '*Erste Parentele*', are the descendants of the deceased himself (s 731, para 1 ABGB). The statutory heirs of the second degree, '*Zweite Parentele*' are the parents of the deceased and their descendants (s 731, para 2 ABGB). Statutory heirs of the third degree, '*Dritte Parentele*', are the grandparents of the deceased and their descendants (s 731, para 3). Statutory heirs of the fourth degree, '*Vierte Parentele*', are the great-grandparents of the deceased. Their descendants are not statutory heirs: their relationship to the deceased person is considered to be too remote ('*Erbrechtsgrenze*', inheritance entitlement limit).

2.19 As far as the degrees (*Parentelen*) are concerned, living relatives effectively exclude their descendants within the degree. For example, descendants living at the time of the deceased's death exclude their descendants who are related to the deceased through them, ie grandchildren cannot be the legal heirs of their grandfather as long as their father – the son of the deceased – is still alive (s 732 ABGB).

Republic of Austria as legal heir

2.20 If at the time of the inheritance there is neither an eligible relative nor a surviving spouse of the deceased, the State, ie the Republic of Austria, is the legal heir (s 760 ABGB).

Inheritance entitlement of spouse on intestacy

2.21 The inheritance entitlement of the spouse is specifically regulated in ss 757 to 759 of ABGB. If there are relatives of the first degree of the deceased (in particular children or grandchildren), the surviving spouse inherits one-third of the estate. If the nearest relatives are relatives of second degree or if grandparents are the closest relatives of the deceased, the spouse obtains two-thirds of the estate. If there are no relatives of the first or second degree or grandparents of the deceased alive, the spouse obtains the entire estate (s 757, para 1 ABGB). This statutory inheritance entitlement is available to a spouse who lives in valid marriage with the deceased person at the time of his death (s 757 ABGB). Hence, divorced spouses have no inheritance entitlements.

Statutory legacy of spouse (*Gesetzliches Vorausvermächtnis*)

2.22 This is a peculiarity under Austrian succession law. No matter whether the spouse's inheritance entitlement is based on an inheritance contract, a last will, or simply the statutory intestacy rules, or even where the spouse is not an heir of the predeceased spouse, the surviving spouse is entitled to the statutory preferential legacy (*gesetzliches Vorausvermächtnis*) (s 758 ABGB). This entitles the surviving spouse to the chattels which belong to the matrimonial household and also includes the right to carry on living in the matrimonial home. Such entitlements can be avoided only by a valid disinheriting disposition by the other spouse, based on most serious grounds (see section 5 below).

Inheritance entitlement of children on intestacy

In the case of all children of the deceased surviving him, the estate is divided between them per capita, ie all children obtain equal shares from the estate (s 732 ABGB). In the case of a predeceased child, its share devolves *per stirpes* to the descendants of such predeceased child (s 732 ABGB). For example, take the case where the deceased had three children and no surviving spouse. Two children survive him. The third, predeceased child, had two children herself. The two surviving children of the deceased obtain a one-third share of the estate each. The two grandchildren obtain jointly their mother's share, ie they obtain one-sixth of the estate each. 2.23

4. DISPOSITIONS ON DEATH

WILL (*TESTAMENT*), CODICIL (*KODIZILL*), INHERITANCE CONTRACT (*ERBVERTRAG*)

Non-delegable personal capacity to make will (*Testierfähigkeit*)

A person has full capacity to make a will after attaining his eighteenth birthday, provided he has the mental capacity to be aware both of the fact that he is making a will and of the contents of such will (s 569 ABGB). Last dispositions can only be made personally, and it is not possible for these to be done through a third party (s 564 ABGB). 2.24

Limited capacity to make a will

Minors in the age group between 14 to 18 years and persons of limited mental capacity can also make a will but only orally before a court or orally before a notary public. 2.25

Formalities and various kinds of wills

The following kinds of wills (*Testamentsformen*) are available:

Personally written will (Eigenhändiges Testament)

The entire will must be written by the testator in his own handwriting, and he has to sign it with his name. Putting the date and place as to when and where the will is drawn up is not required, but 'recommended' by the Act (s 578 ABGB). 2.26

According to precedents available, the will is properly signed by using the first name only or by signing 'your father'. The signature must be at the end. Amendments are only valid if they are signed as well. Use of the German language is not a prerequisite for the validity of a will. It is also important to note that a personally written will does not have to be witnessed.

Non-personally written will (Fremdhändiges Testament)

2.27 Such will is governed by ss 579 to 581 ABGB. In the case of this kind of will, it can be written by hand by a third party, or it can be typed. It is important to note that even if the testator types his own will and signs it, such will is considered a *Fremdhaendiges Testament.* In order for it to be valid, it has to be witnessed by three witnesses. At least two of the witnesses must be present at the same time. Their signature on the will must state that they signed as witnesses. Witnesses must be at least 18 years of age, they must have the necessary mental capacity, and must be capable of understanding the language of the testator (s 591 ABGB). Beneficiaries under the will and their next of kin cannot be witnesses (s 594 ABGB). The *Fremdhaendiges Testament* is the kind of will used if the testator wishes to make a will employing an Austrian solicitor.

Oral will (Muendliches Testament)

2.28 Sections 584 to 586 ABGB provide for the possibility of a testator making an oral will. This kind of will is a peculiarity of Austrian law and is considered to be quite problematic in this day and age. It is, however, applicable law that a will can be made orally in the presence of three persons having the capacity to witness the will (see above). It is a legal requirement, however, that the testator makes it known that he wishes to make a will and that he himself declares his last disposition. Hence, it is not sufficient for an oral will if another person proposes a will and the testator-to-be agrees to such proposal. If, in the probate proceedings one of the parties requests this, the three witnesses have to confirm the will by swearing an oath. If their statements given under oath do not match, the will is invalid.

2.29 All the above kinds of wills are considered private wills (*Private Testamente*). In addition, ss 587 to 590 ABGB and s 70 *et seq* (*Noatriatsordnung*/Notary Publics Act) provide for so-called public wills (*Oeffentliche Testamente*). These can be made orally or in writing before a court or a notary public.

2.30 Finally, ss 597 to 599 ABGB provide for the possibility of making a will in circumstances of threatening disasters. Due to the period in which the ABGB was drawn up, the potential disasters within its scope are: disasters at sea, or epidemics. In such cases the formality requirements are reduced, ie two witnesses of at least 14 years of age fulfil the legal requirements, Such wills, however, lose their validity upon expiry of a period of six months commencing from the end of the disaster threat.

Official registration of wills

2.31 It is not a requirement for the validity of a will to be registered. However, wills which are made before a notary public are registered with the central register of wills (*Zentrales Testament Register*) which is kept by the Austrian Chamber of Notaries (*Oesterreichische Notariatskammer*). Wills other than those made before notaries can also be registered with the central register of wills; however, this is optional. If a testator wishes to register his will, a registration form is filled in and sent to the Register. Such registration ensures that a will is, indeed, taken into account when it comes to the probate proceedings.

Codicil (*Kodizill*)

Whilst the will (Testament) is a last disposition in which the testator names one or more persons as his heir(s), a codicil is a last disposition which does not appoint heirs who would be universal legal successors (*Gesamtrechtsnachfolger*) of the deceased. It merely distributes the estate or parts thereof to various beneficiaries without appointing an heir in the technical legal sense. To find out who the heirs are in the case of a codicil alone, the statutory intestacy rules apply. As far as formality requirements for codicils are concerned, the statutory requirements for wills apply. 2.32

Possibilities with regard to dispositions

Wills can contain many different types of contents, in particular the appointment of heirs (s 553 ABGB), the declaration of persons with interests in possession and reversionary beneficiaries (s 608 *et seq* ABGB), legacies (ss 647 to 693 ABGB), conditions (ss 696 to 703 ABGB), obligations (ss 709 to 712 ABGB), direction of a disinheritance (ss 767 to 773 ABGB), the appointment of an executor of the will (s 816 ABGB), or the revocation of an earlier will (s 552 ABGB). 2.33

Substitutional heir (Ersatzerbe)

A testator can name one or more substitutional heir(s) in his will who will become heirs if the original heir, mentioned in the last disposition, cannot or does not want to accept the inheritance, eg if the original heir dies before the testator or does not want to accept the inheritance because of certain obligations attached to it (s 604 ABGB). 2.34

Beneficiary with interest in possession and reversionary beneficiary

In the case of an estate where there is an interest in possession and a reversionary interest, the testator can declare a person to be an heir on the basis that this person only becomes the heir (reversionary beneficiary/*Nacherbe*) after another person has earlier become the heir (person with an interest in possession/*Vorerbe*) in respect of the same estate (s 608 ABGB). This legal instrument can be used in particular in connection with safeguarding the continued existence of family assets. The testator can, for example, leave his wife or children an interest in possession, whilst making the children or grandchildren reversionary heirs. However, in order to prevent the testator from controlling the devolution of his family assets for an unduly long period of time after his death, he can only appoint reversionary heirs in unlimited number from persons who are already born (or at least conceived) at the time the will is made. If the testator chooses to appoint heirs who are not yet born (or conceived), he is limited to a total of two heirs in relation to movable property and to one heir in relation to immovable property. The *Vorerbe* (person with an interest in possession) is limited in his legal powers. In 2.35

particular, he is not allowed to sell any of the assets he owns in his capacity as *Vorerbe.* He is, however, entitled to take the income, eg rent or interest.

2.36 The reversionary beneficiary (*Nacherbe*) and the person with an interest in possession (*Vorerbe*) together, however, can dispose of the estate without limitation.[1]

Legacy

2.37 By means of the legacy (*Vermächtnis*) certain items of value can be bequeathed to persons who do not become heirs by virtue of such bequest (s 535 ABGB). The detailed statutory rules on legacies are contained in ss 647 to 693 ABGB. The legacy gives the legatee a legal claim against the heir or other beneficiary under the will. It is possible that in the will the heir is instructed to acquire a certain item which then should be passed on to the legatee. For example, take the case where the deceased leaves two brothers. The only asset in the estate is a house. In the will the testator leaves his house to one of his brothers and instructs this brother to buy a car which should then be given to the other brother as a legacy. The more common cases of legacies, however, are pecuniary legacies or specified items of commercial value.

Directions and conditions

2.38 The testator can set out directions (*Auflagen*) to be observed by heirs or legatees (ss 709 to 712 ABGB). The subject of directions can be anything which could be the subject of a legal duty. Often the obligation involves the funeral arrangements, care of the grave of the testator, looking after relatives or the testator's pets. A person who benefits under a direction set out by the testator has no legal claim to enforce the direction: otherwise, it would not be a direction but a legacy.

2.39 However, if there is an executor of the will appointed by the testator, the executor can take legal action to enforce the testator's directions (s 816 ABGB). This is one of the most important reasons why it does make sense to appoint an executor of the will under Austrian law.

2.40 The testator can in his last disposition make the heirs and legatees obtaining the estate or parts thereof subject to certain conditions (*Bedingung*). Such conditions are governed by ss 696 to 703 ABGB. Conditions can be conditions precedent (*aufschiebende Bedingung*) or forfeiting conditions subsequent (*auflösende Bedingung*). In the first case the heir obtains his inheritance if and when the condition is fulfilled, whilst in the second case the heir loses his inheritance if and at the time the condition is fulfilled.

Executor of the will

2.41 The testator can appoint an executor of the will (*Testamentsvollstrecker*). If the executor accepts this appointment, he has the duty to ensure that the last will of the testator is properly observed. In particular, the executor of the will participates in the probate proceedings when the inventory (itemisation of assets and

1 Koziol-Welser, *Grundriss des Bürgerlichen Rechts* II, 9. Auflage, Wien 1991 and Austrian Supreme Court in precedent published in *Juristische Blätter* 1974, 523.

liabilities of the estate) is drawn up, and he has the legal power to enforce directions given by the testator (s 816 ABGB).

Inheritance contract

2.42 Inheritance contracts are only valid if they are concluded between married spouses (s 602 ABGB). According to s 1 NotZwG (*Notariatszwangsgesetz*/Compulsory Notarial Deeds Act) they have to be executed by way of notarial deed (*Notariatsakt*). Being contracts, such last dispositions cannot be revoked unilaterally but by subsequent agreement only. Inheritance contracts, however, do not prevent either spouse from disposing of his/her assets without restrictions during their lifetime (s 1252 ABGB).

2.43 A statutory restriction in relation to inheritance contracts is that one-quarter of the entire estate of each spouse must remain unaffected by the inheritance contract (s 1253 ABGB).

2.44 Inheritance contracts, generally, are invalidated if spouses are divorced. The spouse, however, who is not responsible for the breakdown of the marriage keeps his entitlement under the inheritance contract in relation to the other spouse. (s 1266 ABGB).

Joint will

2.45 Married spouses are allowed to appoint not just each other but also third parties as heirs in one will. However, even such a will can be revoked (s 1248 ABGB). According to precedents given by the Austrian Supreme Court, joint wills are also available to couples engaged to be married so long as they enter into marriage subsequently.

2.46 A joint will is not considered a marriage contract and therefore does not require a notarial deed. Hence, all kinds of will (private and public) are available for making a joint will. Austrian legal commentaries, however, doubt the possibility of an oral will.[1] As far as the handwritten form of will is concerned, the Austrian Supreme Court requires both spouses to write the entire wording and sign it.[2]

5. THE STATUTORY INHERITANCE SHARE

2.47 Close relatives and the spouse of the testator are, in accordance with compulsory legal regulation, entitled to their so-called statutory share (*gesetzlicher Pflichtteil*) as participants in the value of the estate.

2.48 The claim for the statutory inheritance share can only be avoided by the testator on most serious grounds for disinheritance (*Enterbungsgründe*). Such grounds are: if the spouse or close relative was convicted for a crime and sentenced to lifetime imprisonment or imprisonment for 20 years, or if he grossly neglected his duties of care and support in relation to the testator when he was in a position of need.

1 See Kralik, *Das Erbrecht*, Vienna 1983, 141.
2 See Austrian Supreme Court in SZ10/327.

Precedents available accept as disinheritance grounds abandoning a sick old father, the non-fulfilment of maintenance duties towards children done with intent or gross negligence, and also failing to assist the testator in a position of financial need. The testator can also explicitly disinherit relatives and his spouse if they have committed an offence against the testator which can only be committed with intent and is punishable with imprisonment in excess of one year, eg causing grievous bodily harm with intent.

POSSIBILITY TO REDUCE STATUTORY INHERITANCE SHARE

2.49 With the introduction of equal inheritance entitlements for illegitimate children, Austrian legislation provides for the possibility of reducing the statutory portion to one half of its original amount if a parent and his child were never in a normal parent-child family relationship with each other (s 773a ABGB).

PERSONS WHO ARE ENTITLED TO STATUTORY INHERITANCE SHARE

2.50 Such persons are the spouse and descendants of the testator. If there are no descendants then the ascendants and the spouse are entitled to the statutory inheritance share (s 762 ABGB). The entitlement to the statutory inheritance share applies between illegitimate children and their parents and adopting parents and the adopted children. There is no statutory inheritance entitlement for descendants of ascendants of the testator. Hence, brothers and sisters or nephews and nieces of the testator have no statutory inheritance share claim.

AMOUNT OF THE STATUTORY INHERITANCE SHARE

2.51 The amount of the entitlement of descendants and the spouse of the testator is one half of the amount they would have inherited under the intestacy rules (s 765 ABGB). Ascendants of the testator are entitled to one-third of what they would have inherited under the intestacy rules (s 766 ABGB).

6. WAIVER AND DISCLAIMER OF INHERITANCE

2.52 Potential heirs, such as the spouse and children of the testator, can, by means of contract with the testator, waive their entitlement in the estate (*Erbverzicht*). To be valid, the contract must be executed by way of a notarial deed (*Notariatsakt*), or it has to be documented by a court protocol (*gerichtliches Protokoll*). The waiver cannot be withdrawn unilaterally but only with the agreement of the testator. On the other hand, a waiver does not prevent the testator from appointing the person who has previously waived his entitlement in the estate as an heir. If the waiver does not provide to the contrary, such waiver also affects the entitlement of the descendants of the person waiving his claim. A reason a potential heir might waive his claim could be that he had already received substantial payments or other benefits from the testator during the testator's lifetime, as where the testator had paid off his debts.

If the heir has not made any contract with the testator waiving his entitlement, and he decides after the death of the testator that he does not want to accept the inheritance, for whatever reason, then he disclaims his entitlement in the estate (*Erbschaftsausschlagung*). Disclaiming the inheritance means that the share of the estate does not pass to the person disclaiming, and the estate is treated as if the person disclaiming had not been alive at the date of the death. The disclaimer is made in the course of the probate proceedings which are compulsory for every estate. 2.53

7. LIABILITY OF THE HEIR

In the course of the probate proceedings, the heir is required to accept or disclaim the inheritance. If the heir is prepared to accept the inheritance, he has the possibility of a so-called conditional acceptance (*bedingte Erbserklärung*) and an unconditional acceptance (*unbedingte Erbserklärung*). The difference between the two for the heir is of the utmost importance because it is decisive as to the extent of the heir's liability for the deceased's debts. In the case of an unconditional acceptance (*unbedingte Erbserklärung*), the heir is personally liable with his entire assets for all debts of the deceased without limitation. It is irrelevant whether or not the heir was aware of particular debts at the time when he accepted the inheritance (s 801 ABGB). 2.54

If the heir accepts conditionally, he is also liable for debts of the deceased, but only up to the amount which equals the value of the estate (s 802 ABGB). By accepting the inheritance conditionally only, the heir cannot be liable for more than he himself receives from the estate. It should be noted, however, that the heir's liability is not limited to the actual items which he receives from the estate: all his personal assets are liable, though only up to the amount which equals the value received from the estate. 2.55

The personal liability of the heir commences at the time when the grant of probate (*Einantwortungsurkunde*) is issued. Before this, creditors have to enforce their claims against the estate itself, which, until the grant of probate is issued, is deemed to be a legal entity. 2.56

8. PRIVATE INTERNATIONAL LAW

2.57 According to Austrian private international law (s 28 IPRG), the devolution of the estate of a deceased person is dependent upon the law of the country of which the deceased was a national at the time of his death.

2.58 If probate proceedings are carried out in Austria, Austrian law applies in any event in relation to the acceptance or disclaimer of the inheritance and to the liability of the heir for debts of the deceased (s 28, para 2 IPRG). If the law of the country of the deceased's nationality refers the matter back to Austrian law, this referral back is accepted under Austrian law (s 5, para 1 IPRG).

2.59 Under English private international law, the law of the deceased's last domicile governs succession to movables and the *lex situs* governs immovables. Austria accepts a referral back. As a result, succession to immovables in England or in Austria is governed by the domestic *lex situs*, irrespective of the deceased's nationality or domicile. However, Austrian movables of a British national with English domicile will be governed by English law, while English movables of a person (whether British or Austrian) domiciled in Austria will be governed by Austrian law.

9. INHERITANCE TAX

2.60 Austrian inheritance tax legislation provides for five tax categories (*Steuerklassen*). Category 1 refers to spouse and children. The other categories refer to less close relatives and finally to beneficiaries who are not related to the deceased at all. Within the various categories there are bands, eg up to ATS 100,000; ATS 100,000 to ATS 200,000, etc. The lowest tax rate in category 1 is 2%, whilst the highest tax rate in category 5 is 60%! It is therefore of the utmost importance to take inheritance tax issues into account. In this connection, marriage and adoption also play a role, eg the inheritance tax burden on a common law wife can be seven times higher than it would be on a married spouse.

10. MEANS OF MINIMISING PROBLEMS WHERE INTERNATIONAL ELEMENTS ARE CONCERNED

2.61 Separate wills for property in different countries should be established, ensuring that proper formalities are observed, taking into account the 1961 Hague Convention concerning the form of wills which Austria has implemented, so that it suffices if a will complies with the national law of the testator or the law of the place where the will is executed.

Never rely on the fact that the intestacy rules would coincidentally provide for the beneficiaries the testator has in mind. Due to the fact that oral wills can be made under Austrian law, there is always the danger of somebody claiming that the deceased had made an oral will in that person's favour. Real estate in Austria leads to compulsory probate proceedings there with all its legal consequences. Moreover, '*Pflichtteil*' or forced heirship rules can apply due to the *lex situs* rules contained in private international law. It is therefore worth considering having real estate owned by a company in which the testator holds the majority of or the entire share capital. Shareholdings in such a company would not be considered immovable property. **2.62**

Finally, it should be mentioned that currently a new law on private foundations (*Privatrechtsstiftungen*) is being introduced in Austria. For family assets of considerable amount it might well be worth considering the use of opportunities under this new legislation. Section 1 PSG (*Privatstiftungsgesetz* or Private Foundations Act) defines a private foundation as a legal entity owning assets which were dedicated by the founder in order to achieve a purpose decided by the founder. **2.63**

By setting up a *Privatrechtsstiftung*, the *Stifter* (founder) can ensure that his assets are not divided unfavourably after his death but are kept as a unit, whilst beneficiaries receive payments of the income of the *Stiftung*. *Stiftungen* will be treated very advantageously taxwise since payments into the fund are to be subject to an inheritance and gift tax rate of only 2.5%. **2.64**

CHAPTER 3

BELGIUM†

1. GENERAL PRINCIPLES[1]

OPENING OF THE SUCCESSION

The succession process can only be opened on the death of an individual (article 718 BCC). The place where a succession 'falls open' is the place of the last domicile of the deceased. 3.1

It is possible to take protective steps to guard against dissipation of the estate as soon as the succession process commences. The attaching of seals by the Justice of the Peace (*juge de paix*) may be sought by the presumed heirs, their creditors, creditors of the estate and the testamentary executor (articles 1148 to 1174 of the Judicial Code). 3.2

An inventory can also be drawn up by notarial act (articles 1175 to 1184 of the Judicial Code). 3.3

TRANSMISSION OF THE SUCCESSION

Transmission of ownership: three options

General principles

A person who has the right to inherit is under no obligation to accept the inheritance (article 775 BCC). The law permits him either to accept the inheritance 'pure and simple', or to renounce it, or to accept the inheritance without liability for debts beyond the assets inherited. 3.4

---

† This chapter is written by Professor Dr Alain Verbeke. The 1992 version of this chapter was written by Mrs K Grumez-Vermeiren and Mr MA Hayes. For the purposes of this chapter, the Belgian Civil Code is abbreviated as BCC.

1 Selected general bibliography regarding sections 1–3: Dekkers, R, *Handboek Burgerlijk Recht, III. Howelijksstelsels, Erfrecht, Giften*, 2nd edn, Brussels, 1971; De Page, H, *Traité Élémentaire de Droit Civil Belge, IX. Les Successions*, 2nd edn, Brussels, 1974; Dillemans, R, *Erfrecht*, Brussels, 1984 and *Testamenten*, Brussels, 1977; Puelinckx-Coene, M, *Erfrecht*, 2nd edn, Antwerp, 1996; Raucent, L, *Les Successions*, 2nd edn, Brussels/Louvain-la-Neuve, 1988 and *Les Libéralités*, 2nd edn, Brussels/Louvain-la-Neuve, 1991; Verbeke, A and Leleu, Y-H, 'Harmonization of the Law of Succession in Europe' in *Towards a European Civil Code II*, 1998; *Commentaar Erfenissen, Schenkingen en Testamenten*, Antwerp: Kluwer, loose-leaf; *Repertoire Notarial*, Brussels: Larcier, loose-leaf. See also the regularly updated and very substantial case-law chronicles in such law journals as *Tijdschrift voor Privaatrecht*, *Revue Critique de Jurisprudence Belge* and *Journal des Tribunaux*.

3.5 This choice, known as an option, cannot be imposed by the deceased. The option is indivisible and therefore can only be exercised in respect of the whole of the inheritable estate. The option is an independent personal right and is not affected by the choices of other persons entitled to inherit. The effects of the option are determined by law and cannot be modified by a term or condition. In principle, the option once taken is irrevocable. On the opening of the succession process every person with inheritance rights may exercise the option. Special provisions exist for the various categories of persons lacking capacity. The option may be exercised during a period of 30 years after the opening of the succession process (article 789 BCC).

Acceptance 'pure and simple'

3.6 On acceptance 'pure and simple' the person entitled to inherit the estate receives the benefit of all the assets of the deceased and the burden of all his debts. Acceptance can be express or tacit. Express acceptance occurs if one holds oneself out as an heir in an authenticated or private document (article 778 BCC).

3.7 Tacit acceptance may be adduced from the heir's behaviour. If the heir carries out acts which necessarily imply his intention to accept and which he would have no right to do except in his capacity as heir, tacit acceptance is presumed (article 778 *in fine* BCC).

Renunciation

3.8 Renunciation of inheritance rights and liabilities will not be presumed. The formalities to be satisfied are prescribed by article 784 of the Civil Code. A declaration must be made to the registry of the court (*tribunal de première instance*) in the district where the succession process was opened. It is recorded in a register kept for that purpose.

Acceptance without liability for debts (acceptation sous bénéfice d'inventaire)

3.9 An heir who accepts *sous bénéfice d'inventaire* is only held liable for the debts of the deceased to the extent of the assets that he receives out of the deceased's estate. His own property is immune from claims of creditors of the deceased.

3.10 A declaration must be made to the registry of the court in the jurisdiction where the succession process commenced, and the declaration is also published in the *Moniteur Belge* (article 793 BCC). A notarial inventory which is faithful and exact as to the assets in the estate is drawn up (article 794 BCC).

Forced acceptance

3.11 An heir who has diverted or concealed the deceased's assets is deprived of his right to renounce the inheritance and remains an heir 'pure and simple' without having any right in the diverted or concealed assets (article 792 BCC).

Transmission of possession and administration

Saisine

3.12 Belgian law deals with the transmission of assets in the estate by adopting the system of direct factual possession (*saisine*). From the moment of death the heirs seised have the right to take possession of all assets, rights and actions of the deceased (article 724 BCC). Transmission of the inheritance operates directly and is not administered by a separate body (such as executors or administrators) as in common law countries. Under *saisine* an heir may take possession of the assets in the deceased's estate, administer them, derive any benefits from them and represent the estate in any litigation. He may exercise these rights even where he has not yet accepted the inheritance. However, he should be careful, because several actions might lead to the conclusion that he tacitly accepted.

Certain categories of heir do not derive their rights as from death, but must seek an order for possession (*envoi en possession*) from the court. That order confers *saisine* on them. This applies where the deceased's estate passes to the State. It also applies to the universal legatee, not faced with reserved heirs whose title derives from either a holograph will, or a will in international form. On the death of the testator, such wills must be presented to a notary who executes the formalities laid down in article 976 BCC. If such a legatee was appointed in a public will (see para **3.117** *et seq*) he has the *saisine*. 3.13

In all other cases, be it that of a universal legatee faced with reserved heirs claiming their rights or of a legatee under general title concerning a share of the estate or a specific legatee, delivery of the legacy is required. Delivery is not subject to any particular formality. 3.14

Testamentary executor

The law permits the testator to appoint one or more persons to supervise the implementation of his wishes; such persons are known as testamentary executors (*executeurs testamentaires*) (article 1025 BCC). They can only be appointed by will. In principle, the duties of a testamentary executor involve keeping a watchful eye over the heirs in the interests of the legatees. 3.15

However, the will may confer *saisine* on the testamentary executor, which permits him to take possession of movables in the estate for the period of one year and one day. The heirs are therefore deprived of the administration of the movables. The testamentary executor has power to sell the assets where there are insufficient funds to discharge all the legacies for which he is responsible. Once completed, he must render an account of his management of the estate (article 1031 BCC). 3.16

Other situations of administration

An heir who accepts the inheritance under the benefit of an inventory is obliged to administer the succession. He must render an account of his management to the creditors and the legatees (article 803 BCC). 3.17

In certain situations administration of the estate is conferred: 3.18

- on a curator for a 'vacant' succession, where no heir presents himself (article 813 BCC);
- on a provisional administrator appointed in cases of urgency by the court.

2. INTESTATE SUCCESSION

GENERAL PRINCIPLES

Unity of succession

3.19 The principle of unity of succession implies that all assets included in a deceased's estate devolve without a distinction being made as to the nature of the assets or as to their origin (article 732 BCC).

3.20 However, in Belgian private international law the *lex successionis* to be applied to movable and immovable property is governed by different rules (see para **3.157** below). Moreover, the principal residence of the family, and the furniture in it, are attributed preferentially to a surviving spouse (see article 1446 BCC).

3.21 In addition, in two situations where the deceased dies without issue assets given by ascendants or adopters return to those ascendants or adopters (or their heirs in direct line) (article 747 and 366, §§ 1 and 2 BCC).

Conditions to inherit

General principles

3.22 In order to inherit, a potential heir must be living at the date of the deceased's death (article 720 BCC). Neither a child who is not yet conceived nor an embryo who is not born capable of life can inherit (article 725). Where two or more individuals die in circumstances where it cannot be determined who died first, the deaths are held to have occurred simultaneously (article 721 BCC, introduced by the Law of 9 December 1977 enacting the Benelux Treaty on commorientes of 29 December 1972).

3.23 If one of the heirs is an individual whose existence is not confirmed (called 'absent'), the estate devolves exclusively on those co-heirs with whom he would have had a claim on the estate, or to those who would have inherited in his place (article 136 BCC).

3.24 The nationality of a heir is not relevant. Foreigners have the same rights as Belgian citizens to inherit in Belgium.

Bars on inheritance

3.25 (a) An heir may be deprived of the right to inherit on intestacy if he is held to be unworthy. Article 727 BCC sets out three situations in which an heir will be held unworthy:

- if he is convicted of the murder or the attempted murder of the deceased;
- if he has made an accusation of a capital nature against the deceased which is judged slanderous;
- if, having reached the age of majority, he has neglected to denounce the murder of the deceased.

(b) Parents are deprived of the right to inherit all or part of the estate of their children if they have been deprived of parental authority (articles 33 and 50, Law of 8 April 1965 on the protection of children). 3.26

(c) The surviving spouse may be excluded from his successoral rights, in whole or in part, if he has forfeited, in whole or in part, parental authority regarding children issued from the marriage with the deceased or if he has been excluded or dismissed from the guardianship of these children because of notorious misconduct (article 745 *septies* § 1 BCC). This action should be brought by descendants within one year after the opening of the estate, the forfeiting of the parental authority or the exclusion or dismissal from guardianship (article 745 *septies* § 2 BCC). It is in the discretionary power of the judge to pronounce the exclusion, or to do so in part only. 3.27

(d) The testator may always revoke his will. However, after his death a request for revocation of testamentary dispositions (article 1046 BCC) is possible in the same circumstances as the exceptional possibility of revocation of gifts *inter vivos*, laid down in articles 954 to 955 BCC. Thus, after the testator has passed away, it is possible to have a legacy revoked: 3.28

- because the conditions set by the testator are not fulfilled;
- because of ingratitude, as determined in article 955, §§ 1 and 2 BCC, ie if the legatee has made an attempt on the life of the testator or if the legatee is found guilty of cruelty, harm or serious injury towards the testator.

Some fundamental concepts

Heirship based on blood relationship or marriage

Only persons who are blood relatives of the deceased, living at the time of death, may inherit, if there is no will. The only exception is the surviving spouse, who is a legitimate heir even although not blood related. If there are no blood relatives, the surviving spouse will inherit everything. If there is no spouse then the succession is without a heir, and the State may inherit (article 768 BCC). If no one claims the estate (including the State) and any heirs that are known have renounced the succession will be declared vacant (article 811 BCC). 3.29

The blood relatives may be divided into three lines: 3.30

(1) the descending line (the children and their issue);
(2) the ascending line:
   - the privileged ascendants (the parents);
   - the ordinary ascendants (the greatparents and their ancestors);
(3) the collateral line:
   - the privileged collaterals (the brothers and sisters of the deceased and their issue);
   - the ordinary collaterals (the brothers and sisters of the deceased's parents and their issue).

To determine who of these blood relatives may inherit, it is necessary to establish first the category and, secondly, the degree within the category.

Category

3.31 A category is a group of blood relatives. Four categories exist:

3.32 (1) The first category of descendants (all the children or descendants of the deceased, whether legitimate, natural or adopted, have the same rights to inherit). Since the Law of 31 March 1987, no matter how filiation has been determined, children and their descendants have the same rights and obligations towards their parents and relatives, and vice versa (article 334 BCC). However, filiation has to be legally and definitively determined. This is not possible if the determination of filiation would reveal an incestuous relationship between the child's mother and father, both horizontally (brother and sister) and vertically (father and daughter, or mother and son) (articles 313 § 2, 314, second alinea and 321 BCC). Children born in and out of wedlock enjoy the same rights and, as such, the same inheritance rights. Children born out of wedlock are full and regular heirs, enjoying the *saisine* and a reserved portion (see further) in the same way as other descendants.

3.33 However, some discrimination still exists in relation to succession rights of children born out of wedlock.

- First, article 828, first alinea BCC states that heirs whose relationship with the deceased has been established only after the latter's death and who did not demand their inheritance rights within six months from the opening of the estate, cannot question the validity of acts performed in good faith by other inheritors, nor can they demand their share in assets regarding property that has been alienated or distributed by the other inheritors after the six-month period has elapsed. According to the second alinea of article 828, these heirs may demand their share in value (compare with the German *Erbersatzanspruch*).
- Based on article 837, first alinea BCC, the surviving spouse or descendants of a marriage during which adultery was committed, may demand that a child of an adulterous relationship who has not been raised in the family dwelling be excluded from inheriting hereditary assets. The descendants of the marriage have no such right if the marriage was dissolved before the opening of the succession (article 837, third alinea BCC). The child of the adulterous relationship will receive his share in value (article 837, second alinea BCC).

3.34 The status of an adopted child differs according to the form of adoption. In the case of simple adoption (*adoption simple*) the child retains all his inheritance rights in his natural family; he has the same succession rights in the estate of the adapter as an ordinary legitimate child, except as regards the relatives of the adopter (article 365 BCC). In the case of full adoption (*adoption pleinère*) the child loses all inheritance rights in respect of his natural family, but is completely assimilated into his adoptive family (article 370 BCC).

3.35 (2) The second category of privileged collaterals and privileged ascendants (parents) if they come up with privileged collaterals.

3.36 (3) The third category of ascendants (including parents if there are no privileged collaterals).

(4) The fourth category of ordinary collaterals. 3.37

Degree

The method of calculating the degree of proximity is determined by articles 737 and 738 of BCC. When considering the direct line, there are as many degrees as there are generations of persons. In the collateral line degrees are counted by reference to the number of generations from the deceased up to but not including the common ancestor, and from the latter down to the other relatives. 3.38

The deceased is related in the first degree towards his parents and his children; in the second degree towards his grandparents, grandchildren, brothers and sisters; and to the third degree towards his great-grandparents, great-grandchildren, uncles and aunts. 3.39

The inheritance rights of the ordinary collaterals are restricted to the fourth degree, except where relatives at a further degree inherit by representation (article 755 BCC) (see paras **3.43–3.46**). There is no restriction by degree in the other categories of heirs. 3.40

Devolution

To determine the hereditary rights of blood relatives, it is necessary to look first at the categories. Heirs who are members of the first category exclude all others. Heirs from the second category exclude members of the third and fourth category, and so on. However, the technique of *splitting* will correct this basic rule in some cases. 3.41

Secondly, to determine the rights between the heirs in the same category, the degree will be decisive. The nearest degree will exclude all other heirs who are in a further degree related to the deceased. Here, the technique of *representation* will operate as a correction. 3.42

First corrective mechanism: representation

A first correction is obtained through the technique of representation. The rule of representation permits a potential heir to step into the shoes of and so receive the share which his predeceased ascendant would otherwise have inherited (article 739 BCC). This is a legal fiction that allows an heir to take the place of his ancestor who is already dead at the moment the succession has fallen open. The conditions for application of representation are to be considered both as to whose place can be taken, and who can take the place. 3.43

It is possible only to take the place of a person: 3.44

- who predeceased (not someone who renounced the succession);
- who had capacity to inherit (not unworthy);
- who was a descendant, brother or sister, uncle or aunt of the deceased.

That place can be taken only by a person: 3.45

- who is a descendant of the person whose place is taken (he may have renounced the succession of the latter);
- who has capacity to inherit.

3.46 If two or more persons are inheriting through representation they inherit *per stirpes* (as opposed to *per capita*). This means they inherit as one person, in lieu of the one person they represent, so that they will have to divide, in equal shares, the portion of the predeceased heir whom they represent.

Second corrective mechanism: splitting

3.47 In some circumstances the succession is split into two lines: the paternal and the maternal line. One half of the succession then goes to heirs who are blood related through the father, the other half to heirs who are blood related through the mother.

3.48 The technique of splitting must be applied if there are heirs from the third or fourth category. A limited application of splitting is made in the second category if there are half brothers or half sisters (see para **3.53**).

3.49 The one-half part of the succession going to one line is inherited by the heir who is the nearest in category and degree within that line (article 733 BCC). However, if there is no heir in one of the lines, the property devolves entirely upon the other line (article 755 BCC).

INTESTATE DEVOLUTION IN THE ABSENCE OF A SURVIVING SPOUSE

3.50 The principles set out above can be applied in an example, given below.

First category

3.51 If the deceased, X, had two children, A and B, and one of them, B, predeceased, leaving two children, c and d, at the moment of death of the deceased, the devolution will be as follows:

- category – first;
- degree – A in first degree; c and d in second degree;
- devolution without representation – A inherits everything;
- correct devolution (with representation) – A gets one half; c and d each receive one-quarter, thus sharing the one half part of B by way of representation (inheriting *per stirpes*).

Second category

3.52 One possibility is that parents are sharing with brothers and sisters. In this case each parent gets one-quarter, and the other half is shared equally between the brothers and sisters (*per capita*), eventually corrected through application of representation. If one parent died, three quarters go to the brothers and sisters. If both parents die, everything is divided between brothers and sisters.

3.53 If there are half brothers or half sisters, having only one parent in common with the deceased, a limited splitting is to be applied. The succession is divided in a paternal and a maternal line, each receiving one half of the succession. Half brothers or half sisters inherit only in the line of their common parent. Full brothers and sisters inherit in both lines.

Third category

If the parents are not sharing with brothers and sisters, or if only ordinary ascendants are present, the third category applies, and splitting is relevant. One half of the succession goes to the paternal line; the other goes to the maternal line. In each line, the nearest category will exclude all others. Within that category, the nearest degree will inherit. 3.54

If there are two parents, each gets one half (third category; first degree). If the father is still alive and the grandmother from the mother's side, each receives one half. The father is the nearest in the paternal line; he cannot, however, inherit in the maternal line. In that line, everything goes to the grandmother, who is the nearest (third category; second degree). 3.55

If the father is still alive, and the nearest person in the maternal line is an aunt (fourth category; third degree), both receive one half of the succession. This may seem somewhat inequitable, but it is a consequence of the splitting technique, implying that one parent can never receive more than half of the succession. However, if a parent from one line is sharing with an ordinary collateral from the other line, the parent will receive one-third of that collateral's share in *usufruct* (life interest) (article 754 BCC). 3.56

Fourth category

In the fourth category splitting must also be applied. One very important restriction is that it is impossible to inherit further than the fourth degree. However, an exception exists where, through representation, a person of a further degree is brought close enough to take the place of his ancestors. 3.57

INTESTATE DEVOLUTION IF THERE IS A SURVIVING SPOUSE

General observations on marital property law[1]

Introduction: marital property law comes before succession law

In order to understand the property rights of a surviving spouse it is necessary to take into account the spouse's marital property regime. A fundamental principle is that marital property comes first, followed by succession. Therefore, if 3.58

1 Selected bibliography (in addition to the general bibliography in sections 1–3): Casman, H, *Huwelijksvermogensstelsels*, Antwerp: Kluwer, loose-leaf; Gerlo, J, *Handboek Huwelijksvermogensrecht*, 2nd edn, Bruges, 1992; Raucent, L, *Les Régimes Matrimoniaux*, 3rd edn, Brussels/Louvain-la-Neuve, 1988; Verbeke, A, *Leading Principles of Private Law: Family Property Law*, Leuven, 1991; Verbeke, A (general reporter) and Cretney, Grauers, Malaurie, Ofner, Savolainen, Skorini-Paparrigopoulou, van der Burght, 'European Property Law Survey 1988–1994', *European Review of Private Law*, 1995, pp 445–482.

community property exists, which is automatically dissolved in case of death of one of the spouses, this community must be settled, liquidated and distributed before one can deal with succession. Even if there is separation of property, the marital property situation must be settled first. One should not forget that spouses who are married with separation of assets, very often have joint property, which must be divided between them.

Marital property law and marital property regimes

3.59 In Belgian law, as in all continental legal systems, the concept of marital property law refers to that set of specific rules dealing with the patrimonial consequences of a marriage. Two different regimes may be discerned in Belgian marital property law.

3.60 First, the *basic marital property system or primary regime* defines the mutual rights and obligations of husband and wife. It contains basic rules both on the personal and patrimonial level, and applies to all marriages, whether or not there is a marital contract (articles 212–224 BCC). Patrimonial rules are, for example, that the family home may not be sold without consent of the other spouse, that spouses are jointly liable for household debts, and that a gift *inter vivos* or personal security given by one spouse may be declared null and void if requested so by the other spouse before a certain date and if proven to endanger the family interests.

3.61 The *secondary regime* regulates the patrimonial aspects of marital life, both during and upon dissolution of the marriage. This regime may be chosen by the spouses through a *marital contract.* If the spouses do not make such a choice, a statutory system is applied, which is called the *legal regime.*

The Belgian legal regime of community of marital gains

3.62 The Belgian legal regime is a system of community property limited to the marital gains. Thus, besides the community property, there are two other patrimonies, ie the separate property of the husband and of the wife (article 1398 BCC). Community property is not a legal entity, a partnership, or a situation of joint ownership. It is an estate *sui generis* with a specific purpose, namely to bear the expenses arising out of the marriage.

Assets

3.63 To determine which goods belong to which patrimony, three criteria are used: the time criterion, the source criterion and the nature criterion.

Separate or personal property

3.64 According to the time criterion, all assets and credits acquired before the marriage are the separate property of the spouses (article 1399, first alinea BCC). Thus, it seems, at least in the application of this criterion, that everything acquired during the marriage is community property. However, this conclusion is not correct, since it is necessary also to apply the source and nature criteria to the property acquired during the marriage.

3.65 According to the source criterion, assets and credits acquired during the marriage by way of gift *inter vivos*, legacy or inheritance, are the separate property of the spouses (article 1399, first alinea *in fine* BCC). The nature criterion designates certain goods, whatever the time of acquisition, as separate property. An exhaustive list of these goods is found in articles 1400 and 1401 BCC. Article 1400 does not exlude compensation for payment of these assets using money from the community property, upon dissolution of the marriage. This article lists, inter alia: accessories to separate property; goods and rights acquired in exchange for separate property; tools and other instruments needed in a professional activity; and rights to personal insurance subscribed to by the beneficiary which accrue to him upon the death of the spouse or the dissolution of the marriage. Upon liquidation of the regime, no compensation will be due for separate property listed in article 1401 BCC. This article lists: clothes and other objects of strictly personal use; literary, artistic or industrial property rights; the right to compensation for a personal wrong, either corporal or moral; the right to pensions, life annuities or allotments which by their nature belong only to one spouse; and the membership rights of certain common shares.

Community property

According to the time and source criteria, everything acquired during the marriage for consideration is community property. In addition, the spouses' professional revenues and the revenues, fruits and interests from separate property received during the marriage belong to the common patrimony (article 1405, §§ 1 and 2 BCC). Property given to both spouses jointly or to one spouse with the stipulation that it shall be common, is community property (article 1405, § 3 BCC). All property that is not proven to be separate property is presumed to be community property (article 1405, 4 BCC). 3.66

Evidence

The rules of evidence concerning separate property are laid down in article 1399, second and third alinea BCC. The second alinea deals with the evidence with regard to third parties. Only certain documents may be accepted as proof. The third alinea provides that proof of ownership between the spouses may be given by any lawful means, including testimony, presumptions and even by common repute. In fact, there is a double presumption in favour of community property. First, all property that is not included in the exhaustive determination of separate property is community property. In addition, property alleged to belong to the category of separate property must be proven to be separate property, according to the evidence rules of article 1399 BCC. 3.67

Debts

Between the spouses: separate and common debts

The question whether a debt is separate or common is relevant mainly in the internal relationship between spouses. This issue arises at the end of the marriage upon dissolution of the marital property regime. It concerns the final settlement of the negative side of things: the *contributio.* 3.68

In principle the rules concerning debts are the mirror image of the positive side: *Ubi emolumentum, ibi onus.* Therefore, debts contracted before the marriage and debts that burden gifts, legacies and inheritances are separate debts (article 1406 BCC). Furthermore, according to article 1407 BCC, separate debts include: debts contracted in the exclusive interest of separate property; debts resulting from a personal or real surety contracted in an interest other than that of the community 3.69

property; debts incurred from the exercise of a profession forbidden by virtue of article 216 BCC, or debts resulting from acts that a spouse could not perform without his partner's consent or a court authorisation; and, finally, debts arising out of a penal sentence or a tort committed by one of the spouses. Separate debts are listed exhaustively in articles 1406–1407 BCC.

3.70 Again, there is a double presumption in favour of the community. Debts which are not proven to be separate according to articles 1406 and 1407 BCC are common debts (article 1408 *in fine* BCC). Thus, the list of common debts in article 1408 is not restrictive. For example, debts contracted by both spouses together in the same capacity or jointly are common. In addition, debts contracted by one spouse may be common: article 1408, for example, mentions debts contracted by one spouse for the needs of the household and the education of the children, or debts contracted by one spouse in the interest of the community property.

Creditors' rights

3.71 Third parties such as creditors are not, in principle, interested in the definitive classification of a debt. They simply want to know out of which property they can recover their debts. This issue (the *obligatio*) arises during the marriage. There are two simple rules of thumb.

3.72 (1) Debts contracted by both spouses together, even if on different bases, will allow maximum recovery from all three patrimonies: both spouses' separate property as well as the community property (article 1413 BCC).

3.73 (2) Debts contracted by one spouse may be presumed by the creditor to be common debts allowing recovery of the entire debt out of all three patrimonies, unless the opposite is proved by the spouses. This proof may be that (a) the debt is separate or (b) that it is a common debt not allowing maximum recovery out of all patrimonies. Thus, in rebutting this presumption, the question whether a debt is separate or common is relevant. Upon such proof, the recovery rights of the creditor will vary accordingly.

3.74 The principle is that a separate debt can only be recovered from the separate property and the revenues of the debtor (article 1409 BCC). There are, however, some exceptions to this rule. The first exception is based on the principle of unjust enrichment (articles 1410 and 1411 BCC). Insofar as the community property has taken advantage of the separate property, it has to share in its debts. A second exception arises from debts resulting from a penal sentence pronounced against one spouse or from a tort committed by one of the spouses (article 1412 BCC). If the debtor's separate property is insufficient to pay the debt, payment may be enforced on the community property, up to the amount of half of its net credits.

3.75 A common debt may, in principle, be recovered from all three estates: the community property and both the spouses' separate property (article 1414, first alinea BCC). This rule is also subject to an important exception. Certain common debts may not be recovered from the separate property of the non-contracting spouse. There are four types of such common debts, listed in article 1414, second alinea BCC. Examples are professional debts and debts contracted for the needs of the household and the education of the children, if they involve excessive charges with regard to the family's means of existence.

Management

Article 1415, first alinea BCC defines management rights as the power of administration, enjoyment and disposition of property. The reform of 1976 has introduced the principle of equality of husband and wife. 3.76

Since both spouses are equal, they manage their separate property alone and independently (article 1425 BCC). This is the principle of exclusive management. However, the primary regime restricts this freedom to a certain extent in some particular areas such as the role of the family home (article 15 § 1 BCC) and gifts and personal securities (224 BCC). 3.77

As to the management of community property, unlike separate property, complete independence of both spouses is impossible because of the common nature of this estate. Therefore, a certain amount of interdependence is involved here. Article 1415, second alinea BCC states that the spouses manage the community property in the interest of the family. This fixity of purpose is the expression of the solidarity component of the law. 3.78

As a general principle, concurrent management allows each spouse to exercise the powers of management alone (article 1416 BCC). Each spouse is also responsible for taking into account the acts of management performed by his partner. This means that the chronologically first performed act is binding upon the other spouse. To this general principle there are two exceptions. 3.79

In the first exception, one spouse obtains exlusive management rights over community property. This is the case where one spouse exercises a professional activity alone. He can perform alone all acts of management necessary for his professional activity (article 1417, first alinea BCC). 3.80

In a second exception, management rights must be exercised jointly. The interdependence and solidarity of a man and wife is clearly expressed by the rule that for certain important acts a spouse may not act alone, but must obtain the consent of his partner to act validly. This occurs in three situations. 3.81

Article 1417, second alinea BCC provides that when both spouses exercise a professional activity together, the co-operation of both is required for acts other than acts of administration, which should be construed broadly in this context, taking into account the circumstances of the professional activity. 3.82

Article 1418 BCC requires the consent of both spouses for several important acts, such as the sale of real estate or loaning money. Article 1418 applies without prejudice to the provisions of article 1417. This means, for instance, that an act mentioned in article 1418 which is necessary for the professional activity exercised solely alone by one spouse, may be performed by this spouse without his partner's consent. 3.83

Article 1419, first alinea BCC requires the partner's consent for gifts *inter vivos* regarding community property. 3.84

Dissolution – settlement – distribution

Upon divorce or death of a spouse, the community property is dissolved automatically. After settlement of the community property, the net result must be 3.85

divided in two equal shares (article 1445 BCC). This principle of equal distribution may be modified contractually (see further).

Contractual regimes

General principles

3.86 Belgian law respects the parties' contractual freedom. Spouses may regulate their matrimonial agreements as they see fit (article 1387 BCC). Besides the usual general requirements of consent, object, cause and capacity in order to create a valid contract, there are some specific requirements, both as to the content of the contract and to its formal aspects.

3.87 The marital contract cannot contain provisions contrary to public policy and good morals (article 1387 BCC) or depart from the rules regarding the couple's mutual rights and obligations (ie the primary regime), the rules relating to parental authority and guardianship or the rules determining the legal order of succession to estates (article 1388 BCC).

3.88 A foreign system cannot be adopted by mere reference to it. It must be described in detail, unless both spouses are foreigners (article 1389 BCC). Nor can a couple adopt abrogated legislation by mere reference to it. All marital agreements entered into before the marriage takes place, and all changes therein, must be done by notarial act (article 1392 BCC).

3.89 The spouses may change their marital regime during the marriage, at any time. There are no expiry dates or waiting periods, nor are there limitations as to the number of changes. They can make any changes they deem fit and may even change their matrimonial regime entirely (article 1394, first alinea BCC). They do not have to justify any changes. However, there are some material (interests of the children and third parties) and formal (notarial act, court approbation, publications) requirements for a change of matrimonial regime to be valid.

Marital contract of community property

3.90 Marital contracts adopting a community property system are agreements modifying the legal regime, since the latter is itself a community property system. The freedom of contract is limited in that spouses adopting a community property regime may not derogate from the management rules of the legal regime (article 1451 BCC) nor from the rules regarding creditors rights. In addition, the supplementary function of the legal regime is emphasised, since spouses remain subject to its rules, from which their contract must not derogate (article 1451, *in fine* BCC).

3.91 Two types of modification of the legal regime are possible. First, the definition of the three criteria designating the size of the community property can be changed. The size of the common patrimony as defined in the legal regime (articles 1452 to 1456 BCC) can be expanded, or the community property can be limited. However, there is a limit in that revenues received during the marriage out of a professional activity must fall automatically and immediately into the community property. If they do not, such contract may not be qualified as a system of community of property, but as a separation of assets (see further).

Secondly, it is possible to modify the fifty-fifty partition rule of community property (article 1445 BCC) in principle in case of dissolution of the marriage by the death of one of the spouses. This may be executed directly by changing the equal partition rule into an unequal partition (articles 1461 to 1464 BCC). Therefore, spouses can provide in their marital contract that the surviving spouse will receive a larger share of the community than one half or will even receive the community in its entirety. The surviving spouse could also be awarded a right of *preciput* (articles 1457 to 1460 BCC), which enables the beneficiary spouse to take by preference from the common patrimony, before any partition, either a certain sum, certain property in kind, or a certain quantity or percentage of a specific category of property (article 1457, *in fine* BCC). The remainder is then divided equally. 3.92

Marital contract of separation of property

Spouses may stipulate in their marital contract that their property will be separate, in which case the management of their patrimony will also be separate. Each spouse alone has the powers of administration, enjoyment and disposition (article 1466 BCC). However, the spouses must take into account the rules of the primary regime that are binding on them (see para **3.77**). 3.93

In a system of separation of assets, spouses may have undivided or joint property. In principle, the common rules of private law will apply to such joint property, except for imperative rules following from the primary regime. 3.94

Inheritance rights of surviving spouse[1]

Marital property law comes first

In the case of death, the marital property system must first be settled. In the case of community property, one half of the community (subject to any contractual modification) goes to the surviving spouse by virtue of marital property law, and has nothing to do with succession law. The other half of the community property passes under the law of succession. In the case of separation of property, all property of the deceased belongs to his estate, including his share in co-owned property. 3.95

The surviving spouse is a regular and full heir

The trend towards solidarity of the spouses, which was an important objective of the marital property law reform of 1976, is also evident in other fields of family property law. In 1981 the Belgian inheritance law was reformed in a revolutionary way. Previously, the basis of inheritance law was always the blood relationship between the deceased and his heirs. The new law, however, introduces a regular and full heir who is not a blood relative of the deceased, namely the spouse. The surviving spouse is a regular statutory heir who enjoys the *saisine* (see para **3.12**). By virtue of the new law, the regular heir, including the surviving spouse, enjoys the rights and claims of the deceased. However, he is also required to pay the debts of the estate (see para **3.6**). 3.96

1 Selected bibliography (in addition to the general bibliography in sections 1–3): Bourseau, R, *Les Droits Successoraux du Conjoint Survivant*, Brussels, 1982; Casman, H and Vastersavendts, A, *De Langstlevende Echtgenote. Erfrechtelijke en Huwelijkvermogenrechtelijke Aspectem*, Antwerp, 1982; Verbeke, A, *Leading Principles of Private Law: Family Property Law*, Leuven, 1991.

3.97 Only a spouse who, at the time of the death of the deceased, was still married to the latter, is considered to be a surviving spouse (article 731 BCC). Divorced or judicially separated spouses cannot qualify to inherit from their former partner. If the spouses lived, in fact, separately at the time of death, in principle the surviving spouse will inherit. However, it is possible for the decedent to disinherit his spouse through a will, if certain conditions are met (see paras **3.143–3.144**).

Intestate rights of the surviving spouse

Rights of the surviving spouse

3.98 By article 745*bis* § 1 BCC the intestate inheritance rights of the surviving spouse vary according to what other heirs are present. Three situations may be discerned.

3.99 The first situation occurs when the decedent leaves descendants, adopted children or their descendants. The children do not necessarily have to be born of the marriage of the deceased with the surviving spouse. In this case, the surviving spouse will receive the *usufruct* (life interest) in the entire estate (article 745 *bis* § 1, first alinea BCC).

3.100 Secondly, if the deceased leaves no descendants but other inheritors, the surviving spouse receives full ownership of the share of the predeceased in the community property (if any) and *usufruct* in the deceased's separate property (article 745*bis* § 1, second alinea BCC). Thus, the surviving spouse receives full ownership of the entire community property, half of which is obtained by virtue of marital property law (see above), and the other half by virtue of inheritance law. This rule clearly favours spouses married under a community property regime. If a house was community property, the surviving spouse will be full owner for the entirety; if a house was joint property in a regime of separation of assets, the surviving spouse will be full owner of his own half share, and only have a right of *ususfruct* in the other half belonging to the inheritance, in which he will have to tolerate the rights of the deceased's blood relatives.

3.101 Thirdly, if the deceased leaves no other inheritors the surviving spouse receives full ownership of the entire estate (article 745*bis* § 1, third alinea BCC).

Consequences for other heirs

3.102 The inheritance rights of the surviving spouse have resulted in a decline of the traditional inheritance rights of the descendants of the deceased, who have to await the death of the surviving spouse before they will have full ownership of the estate.

3.103 For other inheritors, the situation is even worse. They lose their rights to the community property, and only receive an interest in the separate patrimony of the deceased which only matures on the surviving spouse's death.

Specific rules concerning the right of* usufruct *of the surviving spouse

3.104 The division of inheritance rights in *usufruct* and bare ownership during the *usufruct* may cause some practical problems. Often, heirs prefer full ownership. Notwithstanding any stipulation to the contrary, an heir receiving bare ownership may require that for all property subject to *usufruct* an inventory of real property and a list of personal property be made. He may also require that the sums of money be invested and that bearer securities be, at the choice of the surviving spouse, converted into registered securities or deposited in a joint bank account (article 745ter BCC). Moreover, the law makes it possible to convert *usufruct* either into full ownership of the goods burdened with *usufruct*, cash, or a price-indexed and guaranteed annuity (article 745*quater* § 1, first alinea *in fine* BCC).

Who can ask for conversion?

If the bare ownership belongs to the deceased person's descendants, adoptive 3.105
children or their descendants, total or partial conversion of *usufruct* may be demanded both by the surviving spouse and by one of the bare owners (article 745*quater* § 1, first alinea BCC). A child conceived during the marriage by the decedent and a person other than the surviving spouse does not enjoy the right to demand conversion of *usufruct* (article 745*quater* § 2 BCC). Conversion may be demanded at any time. *Usufruct* applying to real property serving as the principal family dwelling at the time of the opening of the estate and to the furnishings equipping this realty (the so-called 'preferential assets'), may not be converted without consent of the surviving spouse (article 745*quater* § 4 BCC).

If heirs other than those mentioned in article 745*quater* § 1 BCC receive bare 3.106
ownership, it is, in principle, the exclusive right of the surviving spouse to demand conversion within a period of five years from the opening of the estate (article 745*quater* § 2, first alinea BCC). However, the court may, if it deems it to be equitable because of the particular circumstances of the case, grant a demand for conversion by the surviving spouse after this five-year period (article 745*quater* § 2, fourth alinea BCC). Moreover, the surviving spouse may, at any time, demand the conveyance of the bare ownership, against payment in cash, of the real property serving as the principal family dwelling on the day of the opening of the estate, and of the furnishings therein (article 745*quater* § 2, second alinea BCC). In principle, the bare owners (other than those mentioned in article 745*quater* § 1 BCC) may not demand conversion of *usufruct*. However, the court may, if it deems it to be equitable because of the particular circumstances of the case, grant a demand for conversion by one of these bare owners (article 745*quater* § 2, fourth alinea BCC). The court may refuse the conversion of *usufruct* and the granting of full ownership if this would seriously harm the interest of an enterprise or a professional activity (article 745*quater* § 2, third alinea BCC).

The right to demand conversion of *usufruct* or the award of full ownership of the 3.107
preferential assets is personal and non-transferable. It may not be exercised by the creditors of the holder (article 745*quinquies* § 1, second alinea BCC).

What property may be converted?

The right to demand conversion of *usufruct* or the awarding of full ownership of 3.108
the preferential assets applies to any *usufruct* of a surviving spouse, whether it is received by law or by testament, or results from a marital contract or contractual inheritance provision (institution contractuelle; see para **3.150**) (article 745*quinquies* § 1, first alinea BCC).

Valuation of usufruct

The *usufruct* is valued on the day of conversion. Elements for valuation are, 3.109
according to the circumstances, inter alia the value of the property, its revenues,

debts and charges and the probable life-expectancy of the *usufructuary* (article 745*sexies* § 3 BCC).

3.110 If the surviving spouse inherits together with descendants of the deceased by a former marriage, and conversion is demanded by one of these parties, the surviving spouse is presumed to be at least 20 years older than the eldest of the descendants of the preceding marriage (article 745*quinquies* § 3 BCC).

Procedure

3.111 If all parties are adults and legally competent, they may at any time proceed by common accord to convert *usufruct* or to convey bare ownership of property serving on the day of the opening of the estate as the principal family dwelling and the furniture therein (article 745*sexies* § 1, first alinea). If one of them is a minor or otherwise legally incompetent, the procedure of article 1206 of the Judicial Code must be followed (article 745*sexies* § 1, second alinea BCC). In default of agreement, the court will decide the matter according to article 745*sexies* § 2 BCC.

3. WILLS

TYPES OF WILLS

3.112 Under Belgian law, there are three valid forms of will: the holograph will, the public will, and the international will (article 969 BCC). However, irrespective of form, two conditions apply to all wills:

(1) a will must be in writing;
(2) a will may only contain the wishes of one individual.

3.113 Article 968 BCC prohibits joint wills. This will apply where the form of a will is joint – for example, where two separate testamentary dispositions made by two different testators are nevertheless contained in a single document. This is merely a formal rule. Identical 'mirror' wills are, in general, considered to be valid, as long as there are two separate documents (in compliance with article 968 BCC) and as long as there is no clause indicating that the wills are so connected that they are interdependent to such extent that none of the wills may be revoked unilaterally. Such wills are materially joint wills and are invalid because they violate the fundamental principle of revocability of wills, rather than because of the formal rule under article 968 BCC.

Holograph will

3.114 A holograph will is one which is entirely hand-written, dated and signed by the testator (article 970 BCC). For the will to be valid, the person making it must write it himself. A typed will is void, as is one drawn up by someone else.

The will must be dated in order to determine the testator's capacity when the will was made and to determine which will should take priority if there are several wills. If it is not explicitly stated in the later document, the latest will shall at least impliedly revoke all dispositions in previous wills that are not compatible with the most recent document.

Until recently, the signature requirement was applied restrictively, demanding that the will was signed with the testator's usual signature. For the last 10 years, the Cour de Cassation, Belgium's highest court in matters of private law, has accepted a more flexible interpretation. The court now allows as a valid signature any sign that may be considered to prove the intention of the testator effectively to sign the will. If it is established that the testator clearly intended to sign the document as his will, such signature is valid, even if it would not be his usual signature but a signature used only on this 'special' occasion. 3.115

The testator may retain a holograph will himself or he may give it to a notary to be stored in a safe until the testator's death. The existence of the will may be registered in the central register of wills (*registre central des testaments*). Rather than merely keeping the will in a safe, the notary may draw up a notarial act of deposition of the will, which certifies the date of the will. At the same time, the testator may witness his writing and his signature. In that case existence of the will must be registered in the central register of wills. 3.116

Public will

The will made by public deed is one which is written down by a notary in the presence of two witnesses, or by two notaries. Certain general conditions which apply to any notarial act must be satisfied. In addition, some particular formalities regarding the witnessing, signing and form of the will must be satisfied (see articles 971 to 975 BCC). 3.117

The witnesses must sign the will. They must be adult, physically and intellectually capable of attesting, and able to sign. 3.118

The testator must dictate his wishes to the notary and, accordingly, a dumb or deaf and dumb testator may not make a will in this manner.

The will must be hand-written by the notary himself and must be read over to the testator. If the testator is deaf only, it is accepted that he may read the will himself. The will must contain a provision confirming compliance with all these formalities. It must be signed by the testator, or contain the testator's declaration that he is unable to sign. In addition, the two witnesses and the notary (or notaries) are required to sign. 3.119

Again, the existence of the will must be registered in the central register of wills.

International will

This was introduced into Belgian Law by the Law of 2 February 1983 (*Moniteur Belge*, 11 October 1983), thereby enacting the Treaty of Washington on a uniform law concerning the form of an interestional will (26 October 1973). The international will consists of both a private document and a notarial act. 3.120

The private document

3.121 The will may be written by the testator or by someone else and may be handwritten or typed in any language. However, it may not contain testamentary dispositions by two or more persons (see article 968 BCC).

3.122 The testator declares in the presence of two witnesses and a notary that the document is his will and that he knows the contents of it. In the presence of these persons the testator signs the will or acknowledges his signature. The international will is invalid if signed by a person other than the testator.

The notarial act

3.123 The purpose of the notarial act is to prove that the formalities have been complied with. Article 10 of the Law of 1983 determines its form and subject matter.

Hence, the existence of the will should be registered in the central register of wills.

LIMITS ON FREEDOM OF DISPOSITION

Reserved portion and disposable share

Principle

3.124 The freedom of a person to dispose of his assets by will is limited in most continental legal systems through the traditional mechanism of reserved portion. This is a kind of forced heirship right guaranteed by the legislature to certain heirs (children and ascendants), because of their close bood relationship with the deceased. In Belgium, in addition to blood relatives, since 1981 the surviving spouse is also entitled to a reserved portion which, in principle, cannot be taken away from her.

3.125 The reserved portion is a share of the inheritance, of which these heirs may not be deprived and therefore protects them against all excessive gifts by the deceased. This protection extends only to those who have inheritance rights and, accordingly, an unworthy heir or a person who has renounced is not protected.

The reserved portion is determined as a fixed share of the succession, varying according to the protected heir, the number of heirs, and the other heirs present.

Reduction

3.126 However, before explaining these shares, it is necessary first to determine on what basis this reserved portion must be calculated. This is not done on the basis of the assets present upon death, but on the basis of a fictive hereditary mass, which must be established mathematically. Therefore, all gifts *inter vivos* done by the deceased are added to the existing assets. After deduction of the debts, the net result constitutes the fictive hereditary mass. On this basis the fixed share of forced heirship must be calculated. The remaining part of the succession is disposable. To that disposable part, first, the gifts which have been made and, secondly the testamentary dispositions, are imputed. If the total figure would exceed the disposable portion, it must be reduced. The heirs with a reserved portion may then enter a claim for reduction of testamentary dispositions or gifts *inter vivos.*

Finally, the legacies are reduced and then the gifts, beginning with the latest one (article 923 BCC).

Restitution (hotchpot)

This mechanism of reduction should not be confused with the mechanism of restitution or bringing into account of gifts. 3.127

In principle, every gift made to a person who has inheritance rights on the donor's death is presumed to be a simple advance of his inheritance. On the death of the donor or testator the heir who has received the gift is obliged to make restitution or bring it into account. Through this process of bringing into account, the law tries to put all the heirs on the same footing before division of the estate. However, the donor may expressly exempt an heir from the obligation to make restitution. 3.128

Reserved portion of blood relatives

Blood relatives with a reserved portion are, first, the children (and their issue if coming up through representation) (articles 913 and 914 BCC). Their protected heirship and the free disposable shares vary according to the number of children (article 913 BCC). 3.129

Where a child predeceases leaving issue, that issue will inherit his share *per stirpes*. 3.130

No of children	*Global reserve*	*Individual reserve*	*Disposable share*
1	1/2	1/2	1/2
2	2/3	1/3	1/3
3	3/4	1/4	1/4
4	3/4	3/16	1/4

Secondly, the ascendants also enjoy a forced heirship (article 915 BCC), except against a surviving spouse (see further para **3.141**). This applies only if the ascendants are called to the succession; for the parents this might be in the second category; for other ascendants it applies only from the third category on. This reserved portion for ascendants is one quarter of the succession for each line where ascendants are participating as heirs. In such line, the nearest ascendant is protected. 3.131

The ascendants of an adopted child in full adoption (*adoption pleinière*) (article 370 § 1) and the ascendants of a child born out of wedlock, whose parentage has been established (article 334 BCC) have a right to the same reserve. However, in the case of a simple adoption (*adoption simple*) the adopting ascendants, not the ascendants of origin, have the right to a reserve (article 366 BCC). 3.132

It is important to note that ascendants cannot claim a reserved portion against the surviving spouse (article 915, second alinea BCC). However, if the deceased has no descendants, the ascendants who are in need at the time of his death may claim maintenance from his estate up to the amount of the inheritance rights which they lose because of gifts to the surviving spouse (article 205*bis* § 2 BCC). 3.133

Reserved portion of the surviving spouse

3.134 In the Belgian Parliament, a controversy arose concerning a reserved portion for the surviving spouse. Advocates argued that this right was inevitably connected with the recognition of the surviving spouse as a full and regular heir. Opponents found this reserved portion to be impractical and technically unrealisable. Moreover, the adversaries argued, it imposed a new and undesirable limit on a married person's freedom to dispose of his assets by testament as he wishes.

3.135 A compromise was found. The surviving spouse enjoys a reserved portion, but it is merely analogous with his intestate right, *usufruct*, and not a real reserved portion in full ownership (see para **3.126**). Moreover, unlike the reserved portion of others, the deceased or a judge may, under strict and limited conditions, deprive the surviving spouse of this right (see paras **3.143–3.146**).

Abstract and concrete reserved portion

3.136 (1) The surviving spouse may enjoy an abstract or concrete reserved portion, whichever he chooses. The abstract or quantitative reserved portion is the right to *usufruct* in half of the property of the estate (article 915*bis* § 1 BCC). The concrete or qualitative reserved portion is the *usufruct* in the real property serving on the day of opening of the succession, as principal family dwelling and the furniture therein (article 915*bis* § 2 BCC).

3.137 (2) Both rights are a minimum. If the principal family dwelling and furniture would represent more than 50 per cent of the estate, the protected *usufruct* rights over these preferential assets will stand (see article 915*bis* § 2, third alinea BCC). If these assets would be valued at less than half the estate, *usufruct* rights over other assets will be added in order to obtain the abstract reserved portion, being the *usufruct* in one half of the estate.

3.138 (3) If the surviving spouse shares with other heirs who benefit from a reserved portion, the spouse's reserved portion will proportionally burden the heirs' reserved portion and the disposable portion (article 915*bis* § 4 BCC). Example: Jim dies. He leaves his wife Rose and two children Mildred and Jacob. He left a will giving the entire disposable portion of his estate to his friend Michael. The preferential assets are 30 per cent of Jim's estate. Who receives what out of Jim's estate?

3.139 (4) Let us first examine the situation if Rose were not there:

- Reserved portion for Mildred: one-third full ownership
- Reserved portion for Jacob: one-third full ownership
- Disposable portion for Michael: one-third full ownership

Rose's reserved portion is the *usufruct* in half of the estate. The other reserved portions and the disposable portion must be burdened proportionally with it:

- Reserved portion for Mildred: one-sixth full ownership and one-sixth bare ownership
- Reserved portion for Jacob: one-sixth full ownership and one-sixth bare ownership
- Disposable portion for Michael: one-sixth full ownership and one-sixth bare ownership.

(5) If Jim would like to give as much as possible to his wife Rose, then he would give her the entire disposable share, one-third in full ownership. Unless Jim explicitly disposes otherwise, this gift or legacy does not imply that Rose would lose her intestate *usufruct* right over the entire estate. Thus, already receiving one-third in full ownership, she would receive *usufruct* over the other two-thirds of the estate. The children's reserved portion must entirely tolerate the burden of the mother's *usufruct* rights (see article 1094 BCC). 3.140

Number of children	*Maximum amount of gifts or legacies to surviving spouse*
1	1/2 in full ownership
	1/2 in usufruct (over the children's reserved share)
2	1/3 in full ownership
	2/3 in usufruct (over the children's reserved share)
3 or more	1/4 in full ownership
	3/4 in usufruct (over the children's reserved share)

In competition with all his spouse's other relatives (ascendants or collaterals), the surviving spouse may inherit the whole estate, because the ascendants lose their right to the reserve as against the surviving spouse (see para **3.131**). 3.141

Divestment of the reserved portion

Unlike other reserved portions, the reserved portion of the surviving spouse may be taken away. However, the surviving spouse who is in need at the time of the death of his partner, may invoke article 205*bis* § 1 BCC and claim maintenance from the latter's estate. 3.142

Divestment by the deceased

The surviving spouse may be disinherited by the deceased under the following conditions, laid down in article 915*bis* § 3 BCC. 3.143

First, the deceased must write a will divesting the surviving spouse of his reserved portion. Secondly, the spouses must have lived separately; in fact, on the day of death for more than six months. Thirdly, the deceased must have requested a separate residence before his death, by legal action, either as plaintiff or defendant. Finally, the spouses may not have resumed living together after that legal action. If these conditions are met, the surviving spouse is automatically disinherited. The judge has no discretionary power. 3.144

Divestment by judgment

If article 915*bis* § 3 BCC cannot be applied, the surviving spouse invariably receives his abstract reserved portion. However, his concrete reserved portion (*usufruct* over preferential assets) may still be lost in the case of factual separation. In this hypothesis, the *usufruct* in principle applies to the real property in which the spouses had established their last conjugal residence and the furnishings therein, but only if, first, the surviving spouse continued living there or had been prevented against his will from living there and secondly, the awarding of *usufruct* is equitable (article 915*bis* § 2, second alinea BCC). In this situation the surviving 3.145

spouse is not automatically disinherited. The judge has discretionary power and will determine whether or not it is equitable to award *usufruct.* The court will examine which one of the spouses is guilty of the factual separation.

3.146 Thus, in case of factual separation, if the surviving spouse is living in the last family dwelling, he will enjoy his concrete reserved portion, unless the descendants can prove that this is not equitable. If the surviving spouse does not live in the last marital residence, he will obtain his concrete reserved portion only if he proves that he left the home involuntarily, and that it is equitable to award him such *usufruct.*

Prohibition of agreements regarding future inheritance rights

General principles

3.147 An individual may not by any deed or agreement dispose *inter vivos* of any right or asset which will or may form part of a future estate (article 1130 BCC). An agreement regarding succession to a living person's estate is forbidden if that agreement purports to renounce merely contingent rights in such a future estate, or parts thereof.

3.148 Agreements concerning future inheritance rights are considered contrary to public policy (*ordre public*) and are, in principle, ineffective. Some examples of prohibited agreements are an agreement by which one appoints an heir; a legacy or promise of a legacy made by a contract in return for some consideration; a deed (unilateral or bilateral) by which a presumed heir renounces his future hereditary entitlement.

3.149 Belgian law does, however, provide for some exceptions to the rule prohibiting agreements on future inheritance rights. The most important are as follows.

Formal nomination of an heir

3.150 The formal nomination of an heir (*institution contractuelle*) is an agreement otherwise than for valuable consideration by which one disposes of all or part of the assets of one's estate for the benefit of another person. Such nomination is permitted only in the following cases:

3.151 (1) A third party may make a nomination in favour of one or both of the future spouses in a marriage contract (article 1082 BCC).

3.152 (2) The spouses themselves may make such a nomination in the marriage contract (article 1093 BCC). These gratuitous nominations may be modified or revoked by the spouses by agreement, in accordance with the formalities applying to the modification of marriage contracts (articles 1394 to 1396 BCC) (see para **3.88**).

3.153 (3) During the marriage such a nomination may be made by the spouses in a deed modifying the matrimonial regime or by a simple notarial act. It is advisable that such nomination be undertaken by separate deed in order to ensure its revocability in the event of later doubts (article 1096 BCC).

Share-out by ancestors (articles 1075 to 1080 BCC)

3.154 Parents and other ancestors may make a distribution and division of their assets to their children and remoter issue. This distribution may be undertaken by *inter vivos* and *mortis causa* deeds under the conditions and according to the rules prescribed for *inter vivos* and testamentary gifts. Where such distributions are made *inter vivos* they may only involve existing assets.

Succession agreements under article 918 BCC

Both the sale and the gift with reservation of *usufruct* rights or any other life interest contracted by the deceased with one of his descendants must be taken into account in ascertaining the estate's disposable share for the entire full ownership value of the property. However, the other heirs with a reserved portion may explicitly agree with and intervene in such act, thereby waiving their rights to claim the eventual reduction of such transaction, because of infringement of their protected heirship rights. 3.155

4. PRIVATE INTERNATIONAL LAW[1]

CONFLICT RULES

Basic principles

Belgian private international law does not designate one single *lex successionis* or material law applicable to the succession. A distinction is made between succession law governing movable property and succession law governing immovable property. 3.156

(1) The law of the place of physical location of the assets, the *lex rei sitae*, governs succession to immovable property. 3.157
(2) The law of the last 'domicile' of the deceased governs succession to movable property everywhere in the world.

It follows that an international estate may be subject to several different legal systems so that there can be a plurality of succession rules. 3.158

In order to define the concept of domicile as a connecting factor, one must refer to article 102 BCC. According to that article, 'domicile' is the place of the principal establishment of a person. Those words must be widely interpreted. They concern the place where the person has at the same time situated his residence, the centre of his affairs, the seat of his wealth, and the affections of his family. 3.159

(Other Belgian concepts of domicile are sometimes given in international treaties concerning diplomats or international officials.) 3.160

1 Selected bibliography: Rigaux, F, *Droit International Privé I: Theorie Generale*, 2nd edn, Brussels, 1987; Rigaux, F and Fallon, M, *Droit International Privé II: Droit Positif Belge*, 2nd edn, Brussels, 1993; Van Hecke, G and Lenaerts, K, *International Privaatrecht*, 2nd edn, Brussels, 1989; *Répertoire Notarial*, Brussels: Larcier, loose-leaf. See also the regularly updated and very substantial case-law chronicles in such law journals as *Tijdschrift voor Privaatrecht*, *Revue Critique de Jurisprudence Belge* and *Journal des Tribunaux*.

3.161 Belgian case-law consistently takes the view that the law of the forum determines whether assets are to be classified as movable or immovable.

Succession law applicable to transmission of succession

3.162 The *lex successionis* applies to the option (see para **3.5**) of persons entitled to succeed and governs its scope, the relevant time periods, the form it should take and its effects. Since it is quite feasible that several laws will control the same succession, it is accepted that an heir can make different choices within the legal systems concerned. The option must be exercised in all the countries in which the law controls part of the succession to the deceased's estate, 'succession' including administration of estates.

3.163 According to the majority opinion it is also the *lex successionis* which determines the law applicable to transmission of possession and administration where estates have an international character.

3.164 This solution permits the same person to be legally responsible for the transmission of all the assets and paying the debts.

3.165 As far as transmission of possession and administration of immovables is concerned, succession law and the law of the location of the assets coincide. The latter will determine where *saisine* is conferred and will designate, where necessary, the persons who can intervene to administer the immovable property.

3.166 Transmission of possession and administration of movable property is subject to the law of the last 'domicile' (in the sense of principal residence) of the deceased. If a foreign law is applicable and by that law a foreign administrator is appointed, this administrator will be allowed to take possession of movable assets situated in Belgium to the extent that his appointment is recognised as valid in Belgium.

3.167 If required by the succession law, the Belgian court will issue an order for possession (*envoi en possession*). In the case of an order for possession sought by a universal legatee (see para **3.13**), the court will check the regularity of the will and will judge its effectiveness. A similar formality which has been accepted by a foreign authority seems to be sufficient. The succession law controls the delivery of the legacy.

Renvoi

3.168 In general, Belgian law accepts the application of *renvoi* in the first degree in matters of personal status, succession law and matrimonial regimes. This means that if the foreign conflict rules referred to by the Belgian conflict rules lead back to Belgian law, then Belgian law will be applied. The mechanism is often used in Belgian notarial practice, as much for succession to movables as to immovables. Application of *renvoi* sometimes enables one to have resort to a single law controlling the whole succession.

The right of levy (prélèvement)

Article 912 BCC provides that in the case of division of an estate comprising assets situated in a foreign State, co-heirs who are not nationals of that foreign State may levy against the assets situated in Belgium a portion equal to that proportion of the foreign property from which they would be excluded, on whatever grounds, by virtue of local laws and customs. This complicated disposition has been criticized almost unanimously and is applied very rarely. 3.169

Public policy

The definition of international public policy was established by the Belgian *Cour de Cassation* in Cass, 4 May 1950, Pas I, p 624: A law of internal public policy (*ordre public*) is only one of international public policy to the extent that the legislator has intended to create, by the provisions of that law, a principle which he considers essential to the established moral, political or economic order. 3.170

In general it is accepted that the exception of international public policy can be an obstacle to the normal application of the foreign law when the latter clashes with the fundamental principles of public policy of the forum, qualified as international public policy. 3.171

Since public policy is a concept which varies in time and space it is impossible to determine what foreign law is considered incompatible with Belgian international public policy. In any case, before the exception of international public policy can be invoked, the following must apply: 3.172

(1) there must be a serious incompatibility of the foreign law with the essential principles of Belgian law;
(2) the effects claimed in Belgium by the application of the foreign law must be 'aggressive' from the point of view of the *lex fori*;
(3) the succession link to Belgium must be sufficiently strong to justify the eviction of the foreign law.

INTERNATIONAL JURISDICTION

According to the terms of article 635, 4 of the Judicial Code: 'foreigners may be brought before the court of the kingdom, either by a Belgian or by a foreigner, if the action concerns a succession opened in Belgium'. In principle, therefore, the court has jurisdiction if the succession process was opened in Belgium. 3.173

That will be the case if the last 'domicile' of the deceased was in Belgium because the succession process is deemed to open at the deceased's last 'domicile' (see para 3.1). The meaning of 'domocile' has been dealt with above: it is the place where the deceased has his principal establishment.

In addition, the Belgian court has jurisdiction when succession to immovables is involved and the immovable is situated in Belgium (article 635, 1 of the Judicial Code). 3.174

3.175 The international jurisdiction of the Belgian courts can equally depend on the 'domicile' of the plaintiff being situated in Belgium (articles 638 and 636 Judicial Code).

5. SOME PRACTICAL PROBLEMS

PROBLEMS

3.176 The problems most likely to be encountered by British practitioners will be those arising when someone who is domiciled (in the British sense) in England or Scotland or Northern Ireland dies leaving assets (whether movable or immovable) in Belgium.

MOVABLES

3.177 As mentioned above (para **3.155**), according to the Belgian conflict rules, succession to Belgian movables will, in these circumstances, be in accordance with the law of domicile in the Belgian sense of principal residence. This should limit problems where British residents die leaving Belgian-situated movables, which will pass under the testator's will or intestacy, in accordance with English, Scottish or Northern Irish law.

IMMOVABLE PROPERTY

3.178 According to the Belgian conflict rules, however, Belgian law will always regulate the succession to Belgian immovable property. This means that the restrictions on freedom of testamentary disposition set out at paras **3.124** *et seq* and **3.147** *et seq* above will apply.

3.179 In particular, where there are children or descendants they will be entitled to reserved shares. Where there is a surviving spouse this will mean that it will not be possible to leave personal property to that spouse outright: the maximum that the surviving spouse will be entitled to receive will be a one half interest outright (if there is only one child) and *usufruct* over that child's reserve.

3.180 Where there is no spouse, the restrictions are more severe. A single person without children who has both parents alive and who wishes to leave his Belgian immovable property to a friend will only be able to do so to the extent of a half-share in the property. Not merely may this frustrate his wishes, but it will be inefficient from the point of view of UK inheritance tax.

STRUCTURING PURCHASES

Before Belgian immovable property is purchased, it is wise to consider these restrictions and to ensure that, so far as possible, the purchase is structured in the best manner possible to take account of these restrictions. 3.181

Taking into account that British citizens are usually married under a system of separation of assets, one might consider a purchase in joint names (the same in the case of unmarried joint purchasers). This will at least mean that on the death of the first joint owner, only one half of the property will be affected. This will involve a purchase *en indivision* which is broadly similar to an English 'tenancy in common', ie where each joint owner has an undivided share to pass under his will or intestacy without it automatically accruing to the survivor. 3.182

Following a purchase, it makes sense for the owner or owners to make a Belgian will which confers, to the greatest extent possible under Belgian law, the maximum interest on those whom it is desired to benefit. Although it is legally possible for an English [Scottish or Irish] will to be accepted under Belgian law, for practical reasons it may be wise to consider having a Belgian will to deal with Belgian assets only. The reason for this is not that a foreign will would not be valid *formally*, but simply that a Belgian notary or legal counsellor is more familiar with Belgian law than an English solicitor. Therefore, an English will where the clauses related to Belgian assets have been drafted upon the advice of, and have been checked by, a Belgian notary or legal counsellor could be a good alternative. Although, concerning a Belgian will, the holograph will seems to be the easiest form to use, the international will is preferable since it ensures legal correctness and the safekeeping of the document. This kind of will is especially fit to be used in international succession cases. 3.183

If one chooses two wills, an English and a Belgian one, it should be made clear in each will that the wills are separate and limited geographically (ie in the case of Belgium, limited to Belgian–situated [movable and] immovable assets) and that neither will revokes the other. 3.184

PURCHASE *EN TONTINE*

A purchase of a fixed asset *en tontine* offers the possibility of circumventing the reserved shares of the inheritance. 3.185

A purchase *en tontine* is a form of joint ownership in respect of which it has been determined by deed that the total ownership will pass to the last survivor. 3.186

It should be noted that it is also possible to leave only the *usufruct* in its totality to the last survivor. This should be considered if one of the owners has children from a previous marriage or relationship. 3.187

3.188 This method circumvents the reserved share of the inheritance and it can circumvent at least part of the taxes to be paid. Although this mechanism of *tontine* is still accepted by case-law and by the fiscal administration, some authors warn that it may be a 'trick' to be ignored.

PURCHASE BY A COMPANY

3.189 When an immovable property is purchased by a company whose shares are owned by an individual then, instead of owning immovable property, the individual owns movable property (shares in the property owning company). Thus the law of the last domicile of the deceased is applicable. This method can, for example, be used by a person living in the United Kingdom and owning property in Belgium in order freely to dispose of this property by will. One should however consider the possible tax disadvantages.

3.190 This method is also used by people living in Belgium in order to secure the anonymity of the owners in so far as the company is a limited company with anonymous shares. Such shares may also be transferred to the next generation by way of a special kind of gift *inter vivos*, which, under some circumstances, will even be free of both gift and succession taxes.

CHAPTER 4

THE BRITISH ISLES†

1. INTRODUCTION

A good deal of confusion can arise on the subject of exactly what territory is meant when words such as 'England', 'Great Britain', 'the United Kingdom' and 'the British Isles' are employed in a legal context. In this work the usage followed will be that set out in *Halsbury's Laws of England* (4th edn), which is as follows: 4.1

> 'England' includes both England and Wales which have the same legal system. Therefore all references to 'England' or 'English law' include Wales. 4.2
>
> 'Great Britain' means England (including Wales) and Scotland, but this is more of a geographical than a legal concept and will not generally be used in the following chapters.
>
> 'The United Kingdom' means Great Britain (comprising England, Scotland and Wales) and Northern Ireland. While for succession purposes, England, Scotland and Northern Ireland each have their own laws, for tax purposes reference is made to 'the United Kingdom' because the fiscal regime is usually consistent throughout the jurisdiction.
>
> 'The British Isles' means the United Kingdom, the Channel Islands (Jersey, Guernsey, Alderney and Sark) and the Isle of Man. Jersey, Guernsey and the Isle of Man are independent jurisdictions both for succession purposes and for tax purposes. Alderney and Sark are dependencies of Guernsey.

From the above it should be clear that 'the British Isles' is really a loose geographic description which embraces several legal systems. This chapter will begin with England and Wales and will then have sections covering Scotland, Jersey and the Isle of Man. 4.3

All of the jurisdictions within the British Isles have certain aspects in common concerning the administration of estates. However, some of the jurisdictions such as Scotland and Jersey also have points in common with civil law systems. To avoid constant repetition of the same concepts (such as an explanation of a grant of probate), the two opening sections on administration and succession in England include explanations of concepts which all the systems have in common. 4.4

The individual sections on other jurisdictions do not repeat or explain at any length those aspects of law which are similar to the law in England, but will concentrate on the differences. 4.5

---

† This introduction was written by James Denker, Solicitor and Partner in Rowe & Maw, Solicitors, 20 Blackfriars Lane, London EC4V 6HD, tel 0171 248 4282.

4.6 As this is a book on succession and not on tax, the fiscal regimes of the various jurisdictions will not be set out in any detail, although a brief summary is included at the end of each section. However, it should be stressed that it is only the UK which imposes inheritance tax: this tax is therefore not applicable to the Channel Islands or to the Isle of Man, which have their own less strict tax regimes. There is a flat rate of tax for UK inheritance tax irrespective of the consanguinity of heirs, so that the tax is not a true inheritance tax as understood in civil law systems.

ENGLAND†

1. ADMINISTRATION OF ESTATES

INTRODUCTION

This section focuses upon an explanation of the English system of administering estates for practitioners from civil law countries. Practitioners from common law countries will be familiar with most of the concepts mentioned in this chapter, although the actual rules may vary somewhat from those of their own jurisdictions. 4.7

As mentioned in the introduction to this book, an important distinction is made in common law countries between the administration of the gross estate and the eventual succession rights to the net assets. The persons entitled to administer an English estate are not necessarily the same persons who will eventually inherit the assets. Unlike civil law countries, where the heirs inherit the assets immediately on the death of the deceased, in England there is a two-stage process: first the estate is administered and then the beneficiaries receive the assets remaining after administration. 4.8

This section will deal solely with the administrative process, and the following section will deal with the rights of succession to the assets.

GRANT OF ADMINISTRATION

In order to make title to and gain control of the assets of a deceased person, it is necessary to obtain an order from the court which is referred to as a 'grant of representation'. Where the matter is non-contentious this is an administrative matter not requiring any appearance before a court official. Without this document, it is not possible to deal with the deceased's land, bank accounts, stocks and shares or, indeed, any other assets, except sometimes tangible movable property ie chattels. This type of document will exist in all common law countries, although the categories may vary and the grant of representation may have different names. In England there are two types of grant of representation. 4.9

---

† This chapter was written by James Denker, Partner in Rowe & Maw, Solicitors, 20 Blackfriars Lane, London EC4V 6HD, tel 0171 248 4282, fax 0171 248 2009. For detailed authority see Williams, Mortimer & Sunnucks, *The Law of Probate* (16th edn), Parry & Clarke, *The Law of Succession* (9th edn).

4.10 First, there is *the grant of probate* which is what the grant of representation is called when the deceased left a will which names specified people as executors, and those executors exhibit the will to the court and apply for a grant. Executors can be individual persons or in some cases institutions (such as banks) authorised to administer estates. A testator can appoint a sole executor.

4.11 Secondly, there is the grant of *letters of administration* which is what a grant of representation is called in all other circumstances, and there are several varieties of this type of grant. When there is a will but it does not name executors or the named executors do not prove the will, then the grant is of 'letters of administration with will annexed' and beneficiaries under the will are entitled to apply for the grant.

4.12 Where there is no will, then there is an order of priority governing the right to apply for a grant of letters of administration. Each category may only apply if all higher categories have been 'cleared off' (ie there is no-one in a higher category who wishes to apply for a grant). Within a category all applicants are equal, and one or more may apply for the grant:

(1) the surviving spouse of the deceased;
(2) the children of the deceased and the issue of any deceased child who died before the deceased;
(3) the father and mother of the deceased;
(4) the brothers and sisters of the whole blood of the deceased or the issue of the deceased brothers and sisters of the whole blood;
(5) the brothers and sisters of the half blood of the deceased or the issue of deceased brothers and sisters of the half blood;
(6) the grandparents of the deceased;
(7) the aunts and uncles of the whole blood of the deceased or the issue of deceased aunts and uncles of the whole blood;
(8) the aunts and uncles of the half blood of the deceased or the issue of the deceased aunts and uncles of the half blood;
(9) the Crown;
(10) creditors.

4.13 When there is a grant of probate the personal representatives are called 'executors' and in all other circumstances the personal representatives are called 'administrators'. In this chapter, the term 'personal representatives' will be used, because the powers of executors and administrators are very similar. There are some differences, and one in particular should be mentioned. If there is a will naming only one executor, that executor will have full power to deal with all assets. If, however, there is a situation where there are administrators rather than executors, then in certain circumstances there will be a requirement that there should be at least two administrators (such as for the sale of immovable property). Furthermore, where a residuary beneficiary is a minor or has a life interest, the court will always require at least two administrators.

4.14 It is noteworthy that a person named as an executor in a will always has the right to renounce probate or indeed to take no steps at all to administer the estate. A person who has the right to be an executor or an administrator and who chooses to take no steps will not have any liability. However, if an executor 'intermeddles' with the assets of the estate by taking any step that an executor or administrator would be expected to take then he will have taken on the responsibility of an executor and cannot subsequently renounce this obligation. Furthermore, any person not lawfully appointed executor or administrator and without title to a grant, may by reason of his own interference with the affairs of a deceased person, be treated for some purposes as having assumed the executorship: the person in this situation is referred to as an executor *de son tort* and this expression would apply whether the deceased had a will or had died intestate.

Most significantly a personal representative is liable only for the debts of the deceased up to the value of the assets that come under his control. The civil law concept of 'accepting' or 'rejecting' the succession is unknown to English law. Neither the personal representatives nor the beneficiaries of the estate can be liable for the deceased's debts for an amount which exceeds the deceased's assets except that a personal representative may be liable up to the amount of the deceased's assets he should have obtained but for his own breach of duty. 4.15

ASSETS NOT COVERED BY THE GRANT OF REPRESENTATION

Although the grant of representation is the document needed to make title to the deceased's assets situate in England, there are certain assets which devolve independently and which therefore do not come under the control of the personal representatives. The main categories for which the grant of representation is not the document of title are set out below. 4.16

Jointly held assets

In England it is possible if two or more persons own an asset for them to choose to designate the asset as 'joint property'. If an asset is designated as joint property and one of the owners should die, then the surviving owner (or owners) automatically becomes entitled to this asset immediately upon the first death. Not all assets held in the name of more than one person are necessarily joint property, so this must always be checked. While this concept bears some similarity to the French concept of the *tontine*, it is not identical in that joint property is a form of property ownership, whereas the tontine is a contractual arrangement. The latter can only be terminated by mutual agreement, whereas the former can be terminated unilaterally. 4.17

Assets held by a trust

The deceased may have enjoyed the income or use of assets held on trust for him by trustees, in which case the assets will not devolve as part of his estate but will be controlled by the trustees and will devolve in accordance with the terms of the trust. Although a trust is not an independent legal entity with its own personality like a company, assets held by trustees rank as a separate estate independent of the private estate of the trustees: see Articles 2 and 11 of The Hague Trusts 4.18

Convention 1985. While assets comprised in a trust will in many cases be aggregated with the deceased's own assets for purposes of calculating the rate of inheritance tax payable on the deceased's death, the trust assets will devolve entirely separately from the deceased's estate.

Assets situate outside England

4.19 The grant of representation is a document of title only in respect of assets under the control of the English court (ie situate in England). In many cases the grant will be recognised with little or no extra formalities in other jurisdictions, particularly other jurisdictions within the UK. In each case, advice will need to be taken about local law.

Certain pension and insurance benefits

4.20 Very often a sum of money will become payable on a person's death by reason of a pension scheme provided by his employer or by reason of special insurance policies which he took out during his lifetime. Usually, to avoid inheritance tax, these benefits will be held under the terms of a trust document and will therefore devolve in accordance with those terms for the benefit of the deceased's family rather than pass to the deceased's personal representatives.

FORMALITIES FOR THE GRANT OF REPRESENTATION

4.21 There are very strict formalities in applying for the grant of representation, and these in turn will depend on whether the deceased was domiciled in England or was domiciled outside England. The concept of domicile (as understood under English law) has been fully dealt with in paras **1.7** *et seq.* The procedures for applying for a grant are as follows.

Where the deceased was domiciled in England

4.22 (1) The personal representatives must prepare a document for the tax authorities called the Inland Revenue Account. This document lists all the deceased's assets and debts, and in many cases it must also list assets which will not come under the control of the personal representatives but which were enjoyed by the deceased eg by virtue of a trust or a joint tenancy. In cases where specific assets have not come under the control of the personal representatives, there are rules for apportioning the inheritance tax between the personal representatives and the other persons who have control of assets (such as persons who inherit assets by reason of the joint property rules).

4.23 (2) If there is a will, the intending personal representatives must 'prove the will', which means that they must satisfy the court that the will is valid. This process is purely administrative where matters are non-contentious, not requiring any appearance before a court official. Unless the validity of the will depends on the law of a foreign territory (see para **4.29**) the validity of the will depends on the rules set out below.

No will is valid unless:

(a) it is in writing, and signed by the testator, or by some other person in his presence and by his direction; and
(b) it appears that the testator intended by his signature to give effect to the will; and
(c) the signature is made or acknowledged by the testator in the presence of two or more witnesses present at the same time; and
(d) each witness either –
    (i) attests and signs the will; or
    (ii) acknowledges his signature,
    in the presence of the testator (but not necessarily in the presence of any other witness), but no form of attestation is necessary.

(3) The intending personal representatives must swear what is called either 'the executors' oath' (if they are going to be executors) or 'the administrators' oath' (if they are intending to be administrators). This is a document (delivered to the Probate Registry), in which the intending personal representatives swear that they will administer the estate according to the terms of the will (if there is one) or intestacy and will take all the necessary steps required by law and account to the court if required to do so. Although the court has ultimate jurisdiction over the administration of all estates, it is not usual for the personal representatives to be required to present a formal accounting to the court during the course of the administration or at the end of the administration. 4.24

(4) There are special rules, which will not be discussed in this chapter, governing the administration of estates where there is a contentious aspect, such as disagreement over whether a will is valid or whether a particular person has the right to administer an estate. There are also procedures whereby the court can appoint an administrator to deal with circumstances where the assets need to be protected pending litigation or the resolution of other problems. 4.25

Where the deceased was domiciled outside England

(1) The personal representatives must complete the Inland Revenue Account, but they are only required to list the assets and debts of the deceased situate in the UK. They must make a formal application to the Capital Taxes Office to establish that the deceased was not domiciled in the UK for tax purposes, and this may involve giving a history of the deceased's life and his intentions as to permanent residence. 4.26

(2) If the deceased died domiciled in Northern Ireland or Scotland, then a grant of representation made by the court in Northern Ireland or a 'confirmation' given by the court in Scotland is treated as a grant of representation made by the English court. 4.27

4.28 (3) Where there is already a grant of representation from a court in a British colony or certain former British colonies then there is often a special procedure by which such grant can be 'resealed' so that it will be validly recognised in England.

4.29 (4) If the above requirements are not met and if there is a will, then it will be necessary to establish the formal validity of that will, and the rules for this are laid down by the Wills Act 1963 (though there are additional rules relating to wills made before 1 January 1964). The court will recognise a will as properly executed if its execution conformed to the law in force in any one or more of the following:

(a) in the territory where it was executed;
(b) in the territory where the testator was domiciled, either at the time of its execution or at the time of his death;
(c) in the territory where the testator had his habitual residence either at the time of its execution or at the time of his death;
(d) in a State of which, either at the time of its execution or at the time of his death, he was a national;
(e) in the territory where immovable property is situate, so far as that particular property is concerned.

4.30 The UK is a signatory to the 1961 Hague Convention relating to the form of testamentary dispositions, which also contains the above provisions.

4.31 If there is a will in a foreign language, then it will be necessary to have a certified translation of that will. If the personal representatives are relying upon the will being valid in the deceased's country of habitual residence or domicile, then it will often be necessary to obtain an affidavit of law from a qualified person from that jurisdiction. However, if there is already a grant of representation from the jurisdiction in question (such as a State in the USA) then an affidavit of law will not usually be necessary.

4.32 (5) If there are persons clearly named in the will as executors then they will usually be entitled to administer the estate situate in England. Failing that, it will be necessary to prove to the court the identity of the persons already entrusted by a foreign court to administer the estate in the country of domicile (if such persons exist, which will be more likely in a common law country than in a civil law country). Failing that, it will be necessary to prove to the English court the identity of the persons entitled to administer the estate in the country of domicile or (which is often the case in civil law countries) the identity of the persons who are the heirs.

4.33 A similar procedure will apply when there is no will. The document presented will usually be either a certificate of heirship from a local notary or a document issued by the local court. For example, a document of proof which would be acceptable would be an *acte de notoriété* sealed by a French *notaire* which would set out the heirs of the deceased and their entitlements. Certified translations will need to be provided for any documents not in English. If there are no notarial or court documents available from the jurisdiction of the deceased's domicile, it will be necessary to file both an affidavit of fact (giving all relevant information and in particular why there is no court or notarial document) and an affidavit of law usually from a person qualified in the local jurisdiction (confirming the legal position on heirship and administration in the jurisdiction of domicile in the existing circumstances).

(6) It is almost always necessary for foreign personal representatives or heirs to obtain an English grant of representation before they can gain control of assets situate in England. A foreign personal representative who, without an English grant, meddles in the English estate will become liable as an executor *de son tort*. Although a person (or institution) having control of assets in England could release the assets to people who appear to be the rightful heirs, this would be taking a great risk because the person releasing the assets could be personally liable if it turned out that the apparent heirs were not entitled. It is only upon seeing the grant of representation that a person or body can safely hand over assets to the people named in the grant or register them as the new owners of shares or land. 4.34

PROCESS OF ADMINISTRATION

Collecting the assets

Once the personal representatives have obtained a grant of representation, they are in a position to collect the assets of the deceased, other than the assets which do not come under their control (see paras **4.16** *et seq*). They obtain complete control of all assets in the deceased's sole name including immovable property. They can thus sell land and give a valid receipt for the proceeds: the signatures of the beneficiaries of the estate are not needed to sell immovable property. A purchaser will only need to see the grant of representation to satisfy himself as to the correct persons who can sign all sale documents. 4.35

Payment of debts and taxes

The personal representatives are responsible for paying all valid debts of the deceased and the inheritance tax payable by the estate as a result of the death. As mentioned above, the personal representatives are only liable for the deceased's debts up to the value of the assets which come under their control or should have come under their control but for their breach of duty. Before they can safely distribute these assets to beneficiaries, they must take all proper steps to ascertain the debts. Furthermore, they will wish to protect themselves by placing statutory notices (announcements of the deceased's death and the fact that creditors can contact the personal representatives) in at least two publications. They are only protected against creditors if they wait at least two months after publishing these notices before distributing the assets, although in most cases the administration of an estate will take longer in any event. 4.36

There are special rules which govern the administration of estates which are insolvent, but these are outside the scope of this chapter. 4.37

4.38 It should be stressed that personal representatives have very serious responsibilities to the beneficiaries. They must take all reasonable steps to obtain control of and protect the assets of the deceased and to obtain the best possible price for assets which are sold. They must seek the best professional advice which they can obtain and if it is necessary for them to litigate to collect or to protect the assets of the estate then they must do so (and if in doubt as to whether to incur the expense or risk of litigation then there is a procedure whereby they can apply to the court for directions). There are special rules relating to the rights of beneficiaries to bring proceedings against personal representatives who fail to discharge these responsibilities to a high standard.

Application for inheritance tax clearance

4.39 At the end of an administration, the personal representatives must apply to the Capital Taxes Office for clearance that all inheritance tax has been paid. They are then given a certificate of discharge.

Preparation of accounts and distribution of net assets

4.40 The final stage of the administration procedure is the preparation of accounts and the distribution of assets in accordance with the will or intestacy. The rights of the beneficiaries are dealt with in paras **4.42** *et seq.*

JURISDICTION

4.41 If the deceased left property in England, the English courts have jurisdiction to make a grant of representation. Such a grant unless restricted to English property will theoretically extend to all his property wherever it is situated, though in practice foreign local law will determine who is entitled to the deceased's local property. A grant can even be made although there is no property in England but only in very exceptional circumstances will such a grant be made, eg where the court of the country where the property is situate requires an English grant in respect of the estate of a person of English domicile or British nationality. Where an English grant of probate covers English property then matters of administration will be governed by English law.

2. SUCCESSION TO ESTATES[1]

INTRODUCTION

4.42 For the purposes of English succession law, the most important concept is that of the domicile of the deceased. As seen, (paras **1.7** *et seq*) the concept of domicile under English law is very different from that of many civil law countries, in that it

1 For detailed authority see *Theobald on Wills* (14th edn); Parry & Clark, *The Law of Succession* (9th edn); Dicey & Morris, *The Conflict of Laws* (12th edn).

means something much more than residence. The concept of domicile is not defined by statute, and therefore it can appear as rather vague. Briefly, domicile means the jurisdiction where a person has his permanent base and where he intends to live for the rest of his life. Under English law everyone has a 'domicile of origin' (the domicile of their father at the date of their birth if they are legitimate) but this can be displaced by a 'domicile of choice'. There is a large body of case-law on domicile, and advice should always be sought whenever there is any doubt. It is important to understand that the rules defining domicile for the purposes of the general law (including succession) are different from the broader rules governing domicile for purposes of inheritance tax: tax must always be regarded as a separate issue.

It is noteworthy that English law does not have the equivalent of marital regimes or marital contracts which exist in many civil law countries, and therefore married couples always hold property under English law in a manner similar to the 'separation of property' concept known in countries with marital regimes. Nevertheless, foreign marital regime arrangements can be relevant when a deceased person has died domiciled outside England or with property outside England.[1] Furthermore, if the parties to a marriage had a non-English matrimonial domicile at the time of their marriage which involved a statutory marital regime or the signing of a marriage contract, then in most circumstances the property rights imposed by that regime or contract would be recognised by the English court even if the parties to the marriage subsequently changed their matrimonial domicile. Thus expert advice should always be sought if the original marital domicile of the parties to a marriage was not English. 4.43

Because the most important concept governing succession is that of domicile, this section will deal first with the rules governing devolution of assets where the deceased died domiciled in England and secondly with the rules of devolution where the deceased died domiciled outside England. 4.44

DEVOLUTION OF ASSETS WHERE THE DECEASED DIED DOMICILED IN ENGLAND

Distinction between intestate succession and testate succession

Intestate succession

(1) The rules governing intestate succession (where the deceased did not leave a valid will) are complicated and depend to a large extent on the monetary value of the estate. These rules provide for inheritance primarily by a surviving spouse and issue, or if there are no such persons, by the parents or brothers and sisters of the deceased or their issue. A table showing how these rules operate is annexed at the conclusion of this chapter. 4.45

---

1 See J G Miller, '*Family Provision on Death: The International Dimension*' (1990) 39 ICLQ 261.

(2) If there are no living persons entitled to inherit under the intestacy rules, then by virtue of prerogative right (and not as successor under succession law) the Crown will obtain the ownerless estate as *bona vacantia.*

(3) In some circumstances it is possible for there to be a 'partial intestacy'. This can arise when there is a valid will but the will fails to dispose of all the assets in the estate, eg because a beneficiary predeceased the testator.

Testate succession

4.46 (1) Where there is a will, the personal representatives are responsible for ensuring that the assets devolve in accordance with the terms of that will.

(2) There are different categories of beneficiaries, and the main distinction is between legatees (persons to whom sums of money or specific assets have been gifted) and residuary beneficiaries (persons who inherit all or a stated proportion of the residuary estate after payment of legacies and specific gifts). It is usual for a will to specify whether legacies or specific gifts should bear their own inheritance tax or whether the personal representatives should pay the tax relating to those gifts out of the residuary estate before dividing the residuary estate amongst the residuary beneficiaries.

(3) A gift to an attesting beneficiary or his spouse is ineffective, though the will otherwise remains valid.

Distinction between movable property and immovable property

Movable property

4.47 Under English law all movable property of a person who died domiciled in England devolves in accordance with the rules of English law (either under the terms of a valid English or foreign will or under the English intestacy rules). However, if property is physically situate outside England (eg shares in a German company) and is under the control of a local court, then it may well be subject to local rules (eg if the deceased were a German national or if a German matrimonial property regime applied to the German shares). In those circumstances the English court will be obliged to accept a determination of a local court even if the position would be different under the rules of English succession law.

Immovable property

4.48 (1) If such property is situate in England then it will devolve according to English law (either under the terms of a valid English or foreign will or under the English intestacy rules if there is no will).

(2) If the property is situate outside England, it will devolve in accordance with local law, which may or may not recognise the provisions of an English will or the English law of intestacy depending on the local rules governing conflicts of law in these situations.

The Inheritance (Provision for Family and Dependants) Act 1975

4.49 While there are no rules of forced heirship in England and the members of the family of a deceased person have no automatic rights of inheritance, the above Act will apply if the deceased person died domiciled in England. This Act provides that a spouse, a cohabitant (as defined by the Act), a child of a deceased person or, indeed, anyone who was dependent on the deceased person for financial provision can apply to the court for provision from the estate on the basis that the deceased 'failed to make reasonable financial provision' for him. There is no fixed definition as to what is 'reasonable financial provision' (which is measured either by the surviving spouse standard or alternatively by the lesser maintenance standard) because this will always depend on all the circumstances of the case: the size of the estate, the needs and assets of the person making a claim (taking account of provision made for him by the deceased in his lifetime, eg under trusts), the needs and assets of persons who would be prejudiced by the claim, the earning power of the claimant, etc.

Thus, it is clear that a minor child of the deceased will usually succeed in receiving provision from the estate, whereas an adult able-bodied child of the deceased in gainful employment will probably not have much success. There is a large body of case-law relating to this Act and advice should always be sought as to whether a claim would succeed or not. It should be mentioned that it is not possible to negative the powers of the court under this Act by contract during the deceased's lifetime, and indeed ante-nuptial contracts as known in the USA and other jurisdictions are not usual in England and would not override the powers of the court under this Act or the Matrimonial Causes Act 1973 (dealing with divorce). 4.50

DEVOLUTION OF ASSETS WHERE THE DECEASED DIED DOMICILED OUTSIDE ENGLAND

If the deceased died intestate

Movable property

Under English law, all movable property will devolve according to the law of the deceased's domicile, even if that property is situate in England. Therefore evidence will be taken if necessary as to the rules (including conflicts of law rules) of devolution of the country of the deceased's domicile. 4.51

Immovable property

If the property is situate outside England, it will devolve according to the law of the *situs* whereas if the property is situate in England it will devolve according to the English rules of intestacy. 4.52

If the deceased died testate

The rules governing the formal validity of wills (ie whether or not they would be recognised as wills by the court) are dealt with in the chapter on administration. However, even though a will may be formally valid and accepted by the court, it will not necessarily govern the devolution of all assets. This is because the material or essential validity of wills may be governed either by the law of the testator's domicile at the date of death or by the *lex situs* of property, depending on the nature of the property in question. 4.53

Movable property

4.54 Under English law, the material or essential validity of provisions governing the devolution of movable property is determined by the testator's domicile at the date of death. Therefore, a will may be formally valid under English law and be recognised by the court, but some or all of its provisions may not be operative if they are provisions to which the law of the deceased's domicile might not give effect. For example, in respect of movable property, the English court will recognise the forced heirship requirements (other than 'clawback') of certain civil law countries and the personal representatives will have to administer the estate accordingly, notwithstanding that there might be a valid will in English form which attempts to distribute the assets in a different manner.

Immovable property

4.55 In respect of immovable property English law specifies that the material or essential validity of dispositions is governed by the law of the *situs* of the property. Thus two different situations should be noted.

(1) If the property in question is situate in England, a valid foreign will is recognised but it cannot create interests unknown to English law.
(2) If the property is situate outside England then the law of the *situs* will always operate although sometimes the law of the *situs* may refer the matter back to England under the rules of *renvoi* (see paras **1.38** *et seq* and below).

JURISDICTION AND CONFLICTS OF LAW ASPECTS

4.56 The above outline sets out the basic provisions of English law on succession to estates. It is outside the scope of this work to give a full treatise[1] on the conflict of laws on succession and related matters, but some important points should be noted in this area.

4.57 (1) Wherever more than one legal system is involved, there will often be an inter-play between succession rights including forced heirship rights and discretionary statutory inheritance rights and related matters such as rules concerning *inter vivos* transfers of property, marital community of property rights and joint property rights. This is a difficult area of the law because not all of these matters strictly come under the heading of 'succession' and therefore the laws of different jurisdictions may be applicable to different aspects of the problem. Indeed, one jurisdiction may characterise D's transfer of property to X five years before D's death as pertaining only to the law of property, while another jurisdiction may characterise it as pertaining to the law of succession.

4.58 (2) When the laws of more than one jurisdiction are involved, there will often be an aspect of *renvoi* whereby one jurisdiction looks to the laws of another jurisdiction to determine the answer to a question. For example, the court of the jurisdiction in which an asset is situate may look to the laws of the

1 See Dicey & Morris, *Conflicts of Law* (12th edn); Cheshire & North, *Private International Law* (11th edn).

deceased's nationality to determine succession rights. The court in the country of the deceased's nationality may in turn look to the laws of the country in which the deceased died domiciled (often the country in which the asset is situate) which results in what is called a 'double *renvoi*'. In each instance, it will be necessary to determine which jurisdiction will 'accept the *renvoi*' so that the matter can be finally determined.

3. MINIMISING PROBLEMS WHERE FOREIGN ELEMENTS ARE CONCERNED

It is sometimes advantageous, from a purely administrative point of view, to have a separate English will dealing with English assets. This arrangement can be particularly helpful when a deceased person's main will is situate in a foreign country where it must be delivered to a local notary who may take many months to provide a certified copy which can be used for the English probate procedure. However, when preparing more than one will for a testator, it is extremely important that both wills define clearly which property they govern, that neither will cancels the other in whole or in part and that neither will can cause problems in any of the jurisdictions with which the testator was connected. **4.59**

Because English immovable property is governed solely by English law there can be no forced heirship rights in such property regardless of the domicile of a deceased person. Furthermore, the court will have no discretionary powers under the Inheritance (Provision for Family and Dependants) Act 1975 if the deceased person was not domiciled in England. **4.60**

As mentioned earlier, the concept of forced heirship is unknown to English law although an English court will enforce such provisions in the case of the movable property situate in England of a deceased person who died domiciled in a forced heirship jurisdiction. Various techniques are sometimes employed by foreign domiciled people who have assets in England and wish to defeat the rights of heirs. For example, a person who has assets in England and wishes to defeat future forced heirship claims might place his English movable property in joint names with someone else during his lifetime so that the property will not form part of his estate (ie his succession) at the date of his death but will devolve by survivorship. Similarly, with the same purpose in mind, he might place his English movable property in an English trust so that on his death the property will not form part of his estate but will devolve according to the terms of the trust. In both of these examples, it is likely that English conflict of law rules relating to succession would not lead to the application of a foreign succession law since the assets in question would have been effectively alienated by the deceased during his lifetime and would not form part of his estate at the time of his death: see paras **1.62** *et seq*. These points have not yet been tested in the English courts but it is true to say that these techniques (involving the law of property and not the law of succession) are often used in practice and remain unchallenged. **4.61**

4.62 It should be noted that these techniques will be less effective if the deceased also leaves property in a jurisdiction which recognises forced heirship provisions. In such cases the heirs could apply to the court in that jurisdiction to request that court to give them a greater share of the assets under its control in compensation for the assets situate in England which they will not receive. Such claims are likely to be successful, thus partly or completely defeating the intention of the deceased.

4.63 In the case of an English trust the heirs of the foreign settlor may also be able to trace any trust property that is transferred to a trust beneficiary resident in the same jurisdiction as the heirs (or invested in such jurisdiction) and claim to satisfy their forced shares out of such property.

4. TAXES ON DEATH

INTRODUCTION

4.64 This section is intended to give a very brief outline of the basis on which inheritance tax is payable on the estates of deceased persons. It should be mentioned at the outset that references in this section will be to 'the UK' rather than to 'England' as inheritance tax is imposed throughout the UK, although there are some minor areas where Scottish law differs from English law.

4.65 Inheritance tax in the UK differs from taxes payable on death in many other European jurisdictions in that inheritance tax is based on the value of the entire estate of the deceased person, which for tax purposes also includes other assets which must be aggregated for this calculation (such as assets in certain trusts or assets which were jointly owned by the deceased together with one or more other persons). Thus the calculation is based on the value of the entire net estate and other aggregable assets, rather than on the value received by a particular recipient or on that recipient's relationship to the deceased. With the exception of assets passing to a surviving spouse, which are usually entirely exempt from inheritance tax, the relationship of the beneficiary to the deceased is not relevant to the amount of tax payable.

THE BASIS OF THE TAXABLE ESTATE

4.66 Inheritance tax is based on the principle that when an individual makes a transfer of value which results in a reduction in the value of his estate, inheritance tax is charged on the amount of that reduction. It is therefore necessary to calculate the open market value of the deceased's assets at the date of death together with assets in any trusts in which the deceased enjoyed what is called 'an interest in possession' (basically the right to the income or lifetime enjoyment of the assets in the trust). The deceased's share of any jointly owned property must also be aggregated, as well as certain gifts made within seven years of the deceased's death (there are special rules relating to such gifts). The deceased's debts owing at the date of death can be deducted from these totals to produce a net value which is the basis for the inheritance tax liability.

Insofar as the assets were the deceased's sole property, his personal representatives are liable to pay the inheritance tax before distributing assets to beneficiaries under the deceased's will or intestacy. If the assets were held in a trust then the trustees are liable for the relevant portion of the inheritance tax liability, and likewise if assets pass to joint owners then the joint owners of the particular assets are liable to pay their proportionate share of the total inheritance tax. 4.67

RATES OF TAX

In recent years, calculation of inheritance tax has been greatly simplified. The first £215,000 of taxable assets fall within the 'nil rate band' and are not taxable, but it should be noted that certain lifetime gifts may have used up all or part of the nil rate band. This must always be checked in detail. Above the nil rate band figure, tax is payable at a flat rate of 40%. 4.68

EXEMPT TRANSFERS

Certain transfers are exempt from inheritance tax either in whole or in part. These are as follows: 4.69

(1) transfers between spouses (except in the unusual circumstance that the transferor was domiciled in the UK but the transferor's surviving spouse is not in which case only the first £55,000 of the transfer is exempt);
(2) gifts to charity;
(3) gifts for certain national purposes;
(4) gifts to funds for the maintenance of certain heritage property;
(5) gifts into certain trusts for the benefit of employees;
(6) gifts to political parties;
(7) gifts to housing associations;
(8) gifts for public benefit.

Certain lifetime gifts are also exempt, but otherwise gifts made within seven years of death come within the tax net.

CHARGEABLE LIFETIME TRANSFERS

Normally transfers are exempt from inheritance tax if they are made more than seven years before an individual's death, and within the seven-year period these gifts are referred to as 'potentially exempt transfers' ('PETS'). There are special rules relating to these, and it should also be noted that certain lifetime transfers to particular types of discretionary trusts may be immediately chargeable to tax regardless of how long the donor does or does not survive after making the 4.70

transfer. In such cases the rate of tax is half the rate payable upon an individual's death.

RESERVATION OF BENEFIT

4.71 It should be noted that there are special rules which relate to situations where an individual purports to make a gift of property but then retains some form of benefit from that property (particularly if he should give away the property and retain the right to income from that property or the right to use the property during his lifetime). The reservation of benefit rules are complicated, but the basic principle is that if the donor reserves a benefit, then on his death this property will be treated for tax purposes as part of his taxable estate.

SPECIAL RELIEFS FROM TAX

4.72 There are special reliefs relating to certain agricultural and business property and certain shares in private companies. There are very technical rules relating to these reliefs but they are an important part of tax planning when agricultural land or business property or assets are involved.

THE INTERNATIONAL ELEMENT

4.73 From an international point of view, inheritance tax is based not on the citizenship of the individual but on his domicile at the date of his death. The concept of domicile is discussed earlier in this chapter, but for inheritance tax there is an additional aspect which must be noted.

4.74 By reason of s 267 of the Inheritance Tax Act 1984, an individual is treated as having a domicile in the UK if he was resident in the UK for tax purposes in not less than 17 out of the 20 years of assessment ending with the year of assessment in which the chargeable event occurs (that event usually being his death). Also by reason of s 267, an individual who was domiciled in the UK within three years immediately preceding the chargeable event will be treated as being domiciled in the UK at that date (this being particularly important in respect of individuals who have left the UK). Section 267 relates only to inheritance tax, and the artificial domicile acquired by reason of s 267 is often referred to as a 'deemed domicile' even though this term does not appear in the legislation.

4.75 References to 'domicile' in this section therefore include the concept of 'deemed domicile'. This is important because an individual can have a non-UK domicile for the purposes of succession law or income tax but have a 'deemed domicile' in the UK for the purposes of inheritance tax only.

4.76 The importance of domicile for inheritance tax is as follows.

(1) If an individual dies domiciled in the UK, inheritance tax will be payable on his worldwide assets (subject only to relief which may be given by a particular double taxation treaty or unilaterally in respect of tax paid to a foreign government in respect of certain foreign assets).

(2) If an individual dies domiciled in a jurisdiction outside the UK, inheritance tax will only be payable in the UK in respect of chargeable assets situate in the UK (as the term 'situate' is defined under UK tax legislation). For such persons even certain UK situate property is treated as excluded property (ie non-taxable) if it is within the list of special assets covered by the legislation. There are also special rules relating to trust assets.

THE VARIATION OF WILLS

Inheritance tax legislation provides for special rules whereby the beneficiaries of an estate can agree to vary the terms of the deceased's will or intestacy within two years of his death. Where the requirements of the legislation are complied with, the terms of the document of variation will be treated for inheritance tax purposes as if they were the terms of the will or intestacy at the date of the deceased's death. 4.77

COLLECTION OF TAX

The personal representatives of a deceased person are required to deliver an 'Inland Revenue Account' to the Capital Taxes Office. This document sets out details of the deceased's assets and liabilities and the amount of tax payable as a result of the deceased's death. The Inland Revenue Account must also include the value of aggregable property (certain trust assets and joint property as mentioned above) as well as the value of certain lifetime gifts. All of this information is needed to calculate the overall inheritance tax liability, although the personal representatives are usually only liable to pay the tax in respect of the assets actually owned by the deceased. The tax payable in respect of aggregable trust assets is payable by the trustees of the relevant trusts, and the tax in respect of joint property is payable by the surviving owners of that property. 4.78

Interest is payable on inheritance tax which is not paid within six months of the last day of the month in which the deceased died. 4.79

It should be noted that the personal representatives cannot obtain a grant of probate or letters of administration until they have filed an Inland Revenue Account and paid the inheritance tax shown as being due from them in respect of that account. For certain types of property, tax may be paid in instalments. 4.80

SCOTLAND†

1. INTRODUCTION[1]

4.81 Scots law is a 'mixed' legal system, a hybrid whose rules of succession (as of other areas of law) derive from both the common law and civilian legal traditions. Some aspects, such as its conflict of law rules, closely resemble English law, while tax law is (with very minor exceptions) identical. This chapter stresses particularly those aspects where Scots law differs from English.

Several major features are noteworthy.

4.82 (1) Scots executry procedure, like English, is a two-stage process: the estate is first administered by an *executor* and then distributed to *beneficiaries*. Until 1964 immovables – 'heritage' in Scottish terminology – passed under a separate procedure directly to the heir, but that is normally no longer the case.
(2) Unlike England, Scotland gives the deceased's spouse and children protected rights of inheritance known as *legal rights*. These cannot be defeated by will, but apply only to moveable[2] property.
(3) Scots and English law differ considerably as regards the required formalities.

4.83 The Scottish Law Commission has recently proposed major changes to the law. It is uncertain when they will be enacted (if at all), but they are noted where appropriate in the text.[3]

2. GRANT OF ADMINISTRATION

4.84 To allow the executor to obtain and administer the estate of a deceased person, he must obtain a court order of *confirmation* of his title to act. This is analogous to a grant of representation in England. In non-contentious cases this is an administrative procedure; in contentious cases (as where a question arises as to the validity

---

† This chapter was written by Ross Macdonald of the Department of Law, University of Dundee.

1 For further reading see: (generally) Macdonald, *Succession* (1994); Meston, *The Succession (Scotland) Act 1964* (4th edn, 1993); (executry administration) Currie, *Confirmation of Executors* (8th edn, 1995); Wilson & Duncan, *Trusts Trustees and Excecutors* (2nd edn, 1995); Anton, *Private International Law* (2nd edn, 1990) (all published by W Green, Edinburgh).

2 In Scots law, movable and immovable are spelled as moveables and immoveables, moveables bearing a precise meaning.

3 Report no 124 (1990).

of a will or of the executor's entitlement to act) supporting documents and written affidavits will be required but personal appearance is not necessary.

Without confirmation the executor has no title to deal with the deceased's property. Any such dealing will be an illicit 'vitious intromission' and the executor may incur unlimited liability for the deceased's debts. After confirmation he is normally liable only up to the value of the deceased's assets received by him or which he should have obtained but for his own neglect or default. **4.85**

Confirmation, like a grant of probate in England, has the effect of declaring a will formally valid and genuine. If the will was attested, this declaration is immaterial because the will is automatically presumed valid by virtue of attestation; but it is important in the case of non-attested wills to which this presumption does not apply. Confirmation does not conclusively prevent a later challenge to the validity of the will, but such a challenge would require very strong evidence to be successful. The court may also set a will aside on other grounds such as undue influence. **4.86**

There are two usual types of executor (detailed below): an *executor-nominate* and an *executor-dative*, corresponding to the English executor and administrator respectively. (More rarely a creditor of the deceased may appoint an *executor-creditor* to enforce his claim against the estate.) Both types have largely identical powers and duties, except that an executor-dative may not, without court authority, resign or appoint a new executor to act along with him or in his place. In either case, it is permissible (though sometimes unwise) for there to be one sole executor instead of several acting jointly. **4.87**

(1) An *executor-nominate* is usually expressly named by the deceased in his will. Alternatively, if the deceased has named a trustee or has left his whole estate to a beneficiary, that trustee or beneficiary is entitled to apply for confirmation as executor-nominate. **4.88**

(2) An *executor-dative* is appointed by the court. This is necessary if there was no will, or it named no executors, or those named as such decline to seek confirmation as executor. There is a statutory order of preference for appointment: each category has preference over those lower in the list. An applicant must show that there are no other applicants from higher-ranked categories (because they do not exist or have declined appointment); within each category, anyone may seek appointment alone or jointly with other members. The usual categories are as follows: **4.89**

   (a) the deceased's spouse is exclusively entitled to appointment if he inherits the whole estate by virtue of 'prior rights' under the rules of intestacy. If the estate exceeds that sum, he is entitled equally along with (b);

   (b) those who inherit the deceased's 'free estate' under intestacy, such as children or parents. Those who inherit in their own right have priority over those who inherit by 'representation' (ie because they are the issue of someone who died before the deceased but who would have inherited had he lived);

   (c) the deceased's creditors;

(d) legatees who receive a specific legacy or life interest under the deceased's will;
(e) a *judicial factor* whom the court had appointed to look after the deceased's affairs (eg because he was insane).

4.90 An executor-dative must apply by petition to the court for appointment. The petition must set out (a) his entitlement to appointment – evidence of the relationship to the deceased is not normally required; and (b) the deceased's domicile – if this was outside Scotland, the applicant must lodge an expert opinion that he is entitled to be executor under the law of that place. Any documents referred to in the petition (such as a will) must also be produced.

4.91 After appointment, the executor-dative must find 'caution' for his acts; only then can he apply for confirmation. This is a guarantee that he will perform his duties honestly: the guarantor must not be a beneficiary, and is invariably a court-approved insurance company in Scotland. Caution is not needed if a surviving spouse inherits the whole estate by 'prior rights' under intestacy.

4.92 An executor may be an individual or (in the case of an executor-nominate) an institution with power to administer estates. He must be aged 16 or over, but may be bankrupt. He need not be resident or domiciled in the UK; in that case, he can grant someone in Scotland a 'power of attorney' to apply for confirmation and administer the estate on his behalf, but confirmation will be granted in his name and not the attorney's.

ASSETS NOT COVERED BY CONFIRMATION

4.93 Confirmation is the executor's title to deal with the deceased's assets. Whoever holds them can insist on seeing it; if the holder chooses not to, and pays the wrong person, the true confirmed executor will still be entitled to demand payment.

In some cases confirmation is not required, and the claimant must instead simply produce proof of the deceased's death. Nevertheless the assets must be entered in the Inland Revenue account for purposes of inheritance tax unless the Inland Revenue has certified the estate as free of tax.

4.94 (1) *Jointly held assets.* 'Joint property' in the English sense, whereby an owner's share passes automatically to other co-owners on his death, is virtually confined to trusts and unincorporated associations. Instead, Scots law recognises two different types of co-ownership.

4.95 (a) *Common property*, whereby co-owners own in equal shares: in particular, this includes movable assets (except for cars, domestic animals, money and securities) bought by spouses for joint use in their matrimonial home.[1] Each co-owner can dispose of his half-share while alive or by will; it does not automatically pass on death to the other co-owners, but (failing a will) devolves to the owner's heirs as part of his intestate estate.

1 For matrimonial property see Thomson, *Family Law in Scotland* (Butterworths, 3rd edn, 1996).

But note that, if the assets are situated in a place outside Scotland (such as shares in an English company), the Scottish courts may regard them as joint property under the law of that place.

(b) The title deed to an asset may include a *special destination* stating that, on a co-owner's death, his share devolves to the surviving co-owners or (less often), to some other named person. If the destination is to surviving co-owners, they inherit automatically without the need for confirmation. This device is common where spouses co-own a house, but may be used for movable assets (eg shares in a Scots company). However, it cannot apply to bank accounts in joint names, because the account documents are not legally title deeds; the funds are not co-owned but belong to whoever contributed them, and devolve on death to that person's beneficiaries under his will or intestacy. 4.96

(2) The deceased may, while alive, have made a *mortis causa* donation of assets. This is a gift made in contemplation of death; it is immediately effective though revocable by the donor until he dies, and the asset therefore belongs at once to the donee. 4.97

(3) The deceased may have *nominated* someone to receive funds on his death. On proof of death the nominee may obtain the funds without confirmation. Nomination applies only to certain forms of small savings; special formalities are required, which vary according to the type of fund in question. 4.98

(4) Assets held under a *trust* form a separate legal estate, even though the trustees are regarded as their full owners subject to the trust terms. If the deceased was *beneficiary* under a trust, eg he had the lifetime use of the property, the assets devolve according to the trust terms and, except for purposes of calculating inheritance tax, are not included in his estate. If he held them as *trustee*, they pass automatically to any other co-trustees. But if he was sole trustee, the executor should include them in a note appended to the confirmation: this prevents the trust lapsing and enables title to be conveyed at a later stage to beneficiaries or new trustees. 4.99

(5) The treatment of *pension and insurance benefits* depends on the terms of the deceased's pension scheme or insurance policy. If payable to his estate confirmation is needed. More commonly, to avoid inheritance tax, they are held in trust for members of his family; in that case they are payable directly to them and do not form part of his estate on death. 4.100

(6) *Banks and companies* may permit funds or shares to be transferred without confirmation, provided a death certificate is exhibited. They may also insist on Inland Revenue certification that no inheritance tax is due on the asset. This applies only to small holdings (there is no uniform maximum sum for all assets), and is at the institution's discretion in each case. 4.101

(7) *Assets situated outside Scotland.* In principle, confirmation only gives the executor title in respect of assets situated within Scotland. Note, however, that if the deceased was domiciled in Scotland it may include property situated within England, Wales and Northern Ireland, and no separate grant of probate or administration is needed. (Conversely, English etc grants of probate or administration carry Scottish estate without the need for separate confirmation, provided the deceased was domiciled in the place where the 4.102

grant was issued). In Commonwealth countries and Eire, confirmation may be recognised with extra formalities, but property elsewhere will require a separate local grant of administration.

FORMALITIES FOR CONFIRMATION

4.103 The precise formalities of the application for confirmation depend on whether the deceased was domiciled in Scotland or elsewhere. In the case of an executor-dative this is a two-stage procedure, with the application being preceded by a separate petition to the court for appointment as executor. An executor-nominate appointed under the deceased's will can simply proceed directly to the application.

Deceased domiciled in Scotland

4.104 The executor must prepare an Inland Revenue account. As it performs a dual function of enabling inheritance tax to be levied and title to be obtained to the estate, it is submitted first to the Inland Revenue and then to the court for confirmation. It comprises three parts:

4.105 (1) The *inventory* of the deceased's estate. This includes assets in Scotland, England and Wales, and also elsewhere. In addition the executor must list: (a) the deceased's debts, and (b) assets which devolve without confirmation, such as property subject to a trust or a special destination, because although they are outside his control they may be subject to inheritance tax.

4.106 (2) The *executor's oath*, sworn by him that the inventory and the associated details are correct. In addition, it must specify the executor's authority to act, be it a will or a court decree appointing an executor-dative. It is sworn before a notary public (a type of solicitor) or certain types of judge or court official, who must not be in partnership with the executor or benefit under the will. Only one executor need swear.

4.107 Alternatively he may grant someone else (such as a solicitor) a written power of attorney to swear on his behalf; this is particularly useful where the executor lives abroad, but the grant of confirmation is still made in the executor's own name. The power should preferably be in Scots form (attested by one witness); it may also be effective provided it meets the formalities required by the law of the place of execution but, in that case, he must also lodge an expert affidavit confirming its validity.

4.108 (3) The inheritance tax *account*, calculating the tax due. This must be paid in full (or in part if it relates to immovable assets) before confirmation can be granted.

4.109 If there was a will, the original or an official court copy must also be lodged in court. Other supporting papers may be required depending on the form of will. An attested will is automatically valid and its genuineness is presumed, so nothing else is needed. With other wills, genuineness is not presumed but must be proved by a written affidavit from someone who can swear that the testator wrote it. In rare cases where it is doubtful whether the will is formally valid, a more complex procedure (equivalent to probate in solemn form) is used. The procedure is administrative and generally non-contentious, with no personal appearance in court required.

For small estates there is a simpler one-stage procedure which requires no submission to the Inland Revenue or (for executors-dative) separate petition for appointment. 4.110

Deceased domiciled outside Scotland

The executors must prepare an Inland Revenue account, which will include only the deceased's assets and debts within the UK. They must satisfy the Capital Taxes Office that the deceased was domiciled outside the UK for tax purposes. 4.111

If the deceased died domiciled in England and Wales or in Northern Ireland, a grant of representation made there is automatically treated as a Scottish grant of confirmation. If the deceased was domiciled elsewhere, such a grant has no effect in Scotland and separate confirmation is required. 4.112

If a grant of representation has already been made in a British colony or former British colony, it may often be 'resealed' by the Scottish court so as to be treated as equivalent to confirmation. The deceased need not have been domiciled in the country where representation was granted. 4.113

In all other cases, it is necessary to apply afresh for confirmation in Scotland. The Scottish court will grant confirmation to the person entitled to administer the estate in the country of the deceased's domicile; in some countries, he may be a different person from anyone nominated by the deceased, eg an heir. The applicant for confirmation must lodge either: (a) a grant of representation made in that country; or (b) if no grant has been issued, an expert affidavit from someone qualified under the local law detailing the relevant facts (such as the applicant's relationship to the deceased) and stating that he would be entitled to administer. 4.114

Further documentation may have also to be lodged. 4.115

(1) The deceased's will, if he left one. If there has already been a grant of representation, a copy of the will certified by the local court may suffice. If the will is in a foreign language, a certified translation is also required. If the deceased was domiciled in a country where the will is deposited with a notary and grants of probate are not made, a notarial copy may be lodged. In these cases the affidavit already referred to must state that the will (or, as appropriate, notarial copy) is legally valid under the local law.
(2) If the executor grants a power of attorney to someone in Scotland to swear the executor's oath on his behalf, and the oath is not in Scots form, he must lodge an affidavit that it is formally valid under the law of the place where it was executed.

4.116 The form of confirmation, ie as executor-nominate or executor-dative, follows Scots law. This means that, unless the applicant was nominated as executor in the deceased's will, he must petition for appointment as executor-dative, find caution for the estate situated in Scotland, and then seek confirmation.

THE PROCESS OF ADMINISTRATION

The executors' duties

4.117 Executors have similar powers and duties to trustees. In particular they must take all reasonable care to collect the deceased's estate and distribute it to the correct beneficiaries; in doing so, they should obtain professional advice and conduct any necessary litigation. Furthermore, they are under a fiduciary duty not to profit at the expense of the estate: so they are not entitled to payment unless the testator authorised it in his will. If, through negligence, they breach these duties, they will be liable to compensate the beneficiaries for the resulting loss to the estate.

Collecting the assets

4.118 Confirmation gives the executors title to collect the assets of the deceased comprised in it. Even beforehand they can raise court actions for payment of any debts owed to the deceased, but cannot enforce a court decree until confirmation has been issued.

Payment of debts and taxes

4.119 The executors must pay all debts of the deceased and inheritance tax arising from the death. Provided confirmation has been obtained and due care taken in collecting all assets, their liability is limited to the value of the estate confirmed to. If debts exceed assets, the executors should have the estate declared insolvent, and special procedures then apply; unless they take this step they may be liable for all the deceased's debts without limit.

4.120 Care should be taken correctly to ascertain all debts, by advertisement if necessary: this is not always necessary but is prudent if their total value is unknown. If there is doubt whether a debt is valid the executors may insist that the creditor establishes it by litigation.

4.121 Debts are usually borne by the movable estate as a whole; the same applies to inheritance tax. In some cases they fall on one particular asset (eg because the will so requires or the asset is security for a debt). The executors must check the point carefully.

4.122 Debts have a legal order of priority. All debts in each class should be paid in full (or funds should be reserved for the purpose) before any from the next in order, unless it is quite clear that assets exceed total debts. The order is as follows:

(1) the costs of the funeral, obtaining confirmation, and executry administration have first priority;
(2) certain taxes and employees' wages, to specified limits;

(3) other debts. None of these should be paid until at least six months after the deceased's death unless (a) and (b) have been fully provided for.

Distributing the estate

If the estate is solvent the executors may start distribution 12 months after the death; sooner if, after due inquiry, they are satisfied that all debts have been paid or provided for. Depending on the will, or agreement with beneficiaries, they may transfer assets to beneficiaries or sell them and transfer the proceeds. Anyone buying in good faith from the executors gets an unchallengeable title even if they were, by selling, breaching the terms of the will. 4.123

If an illegitimate beneficiary appears after the estate has been distributed, the executors are not liable to compensate him provided that they did not know (and should not have known) of his existence. 4.124

If the beneficiary is a child under 16, the property may (subject, for large sums, to the approval of the Accountant of Court) be paid over to the child's guardian to hold on the child's behalf until age 16. Alternatively, the will may authorise the executor to hold the property until the child is 16. 4.125

Inheritance tax clearance

Once administration is complete the executors must obtain a 'clearance certificate' from the Capital Taxes Office stating that all inheritance tax due has been paid. 4.126

Preparation of accounts

Beneficiaries are entitled to see an account up to the end of the executry setting out the executor's dealings with the estate. In return he can ask them to give him a written discharge for his actions, acknowledging that they have received their entitlement from the estate. 4.127

JURISDICTION

If the deceased had Scots domicile, the Sheriff Court in the area where he lived has jurisdiction; if domiciled abroad, it is Edinburgh Sheriff Court. In either case, the court at present will not grant confirmation unless the deceased left some confirmable assets situated within Scotland.[1] If there were none, representation must be applied for in the jurisdiction where they are located. 4.128

1 This will change under the Commission's proposals.

3. FORMALITIES FOR WILLS

FORMALITIES FOR EXECUTION

4.129 The will must be in writing, but no particular form of words is required. In all cases, it must be clear that the testator understood the meaning and effect of the document, and intended by his signature that it should have effect as a completed statement of testamentary intention. He must be aged 12 or over.

Types of formality: pre-1995 wills

4.130 There are three main methods of execution:

(1) An *attested will.* To be valid:
   (a) the testator must sign personally at the foot of every page;
   (b) two witnesses (preferably, but not essentially, both present at the same time) must see the testator sign or acknowledge his signature to them. They must be aged 16 or over. They may be related to the testator or benefit under the will, though either factor may sometimes make it easier subsequently to challenge the will on the ground of possible undue influence on the testator;
   (c) the witnesses must sign at the end of the will.
(2) A *holograph* will. All the essential provisions are in the testator's own handwriting, and he must sign at the foot of the last page.
(3) A will may be '*adopted as holograph*'. The document is typed or printed; at the end the testator writes that phrase in his own handwriting and signs below it.

4.131 While all methods are valid, (1) has the advantage that the will is *probative*: that is, it is automatically presumed genuine without further proof. By contrast, (2) and (3) require proof by an affidavit from someone who can confirm that the testator's writing and signature are genuine; this must be supplied when the executor applies for confirmation. Conversely, (2) and (3) have the advantage that no witnesses are required.

4.132 Printed will forms are often used, the testator completing the blanks in his own writing. These should be signed and attested as in (1). If not, the printed words or in some cases the whole document may be invalid.

Types of formality: post-1995 wills

If the will was executed on or after 1 August 1995, different rules apply.

4.133 (1) Any will is valid if in the testator's handwriting and signed by him at the foot of the last page. Unless attested, however, its genuineness needs (as before) to be proved.
(2) An attested will requires only one witness. As before, attestation confers a presumption of validity without a further court declaration being necessary.

Defects in execution

A will may be valid although the above procedures have not been correctly followed. 4.134

(1) In some cases the court has power to declare it valid, eg where the testator has not signed on every page.
(2) Another, formally valid, will may contain a clause *adopting* it as valid.

If the solicitor drafting the will fails, negligently, to give effect to the testator's intentions, intended (and thus disinherited) beneficiaries have no claim for compensation against the solicitor. Nor can the court retrospectively correct the drafting error to implement the testator's wishes. 4.135

Other methods of execution

(1) If the testator is blind or cannot write, the will may be *notarially executed.* Another person, usually a solicitor, signs on his behalf following a specified procedure. The signatory must receive no benefit under the will; if he does, it is totally invalid. 4.136
(2) A will executed *abroad,* or by someone domiciled outside Scotland, may be valid if it complies with the Wills Act 1963. (For details see para **4.29** on English law.) In addition, the Administration of Justice Act 1982 establishes a new form of 'international will' which is valid for purposes of internal Scots law and recognised by any state which has signed and ratified the 1973 Convention providing a Uniform Law on the Form of an International Will. 4.137

Note that Scots law distinguishes between formal validity and essential validity of a will. Though formally valid, the provisions in a will may still be challenged on the grounds: 4.138

(1) that the testator lacked the necessary testamentary intention, eg because of insanity or undue influence exercised over him;
(2) that they breach some substantive rule of law, eg the family protection rules of *legal rights.*

REVOCATION OF WILLS

The testator may usually revoke a will during his lifetime without specific formalities. He may do so by: (a) destruction; (b) alteration of the document (but special formalities apply to authenticate the changes); (c) explicit or implicit reference in a subsequent will. Special rules govern revocation of special destinations in title deeds to property. 4.139

A will can also be revoked by operation of law. This may occur if a child is subsequently born for whom it makes no provision. The rule only applies if the child in question chooses to invoke it; it may be against his interests to do so (since intestacy may result) and he should take advice in each case. A will is not revoked by the subsequent marriage or divorce of the testator. Under Law Commission 4.140

proposals: (a) divorce will usually revoke legacies between spouses; (b) the birth of a child will not revoke a previous will.

4. DOMESTIC LAW OF SUCCESSION

INTESTATE SUCCESSION

The intestate estate

4.141 The rules of intestate succession apply to any estate, whether movable or immovable, which is not validly disposed of by will. Intestacy may be total or partial, eg where a legacy is ineffective because the beneficiary predeceased the testator. If partial, special rules apply to set off the surviving spouse's 'prior rights' against any legacy he receives.

4.142 Intestacy may also arise if a beneficiary disclaims a valid legacy. If the beneficiary is a surviving spouse, it may be in his interests to disclaim the legacy, because he can then inherit by 'prior rights' which (unlike legacies) have priority over the 'legal rights' of surviving children. The value of prior rights depends on the type of assets available in each case, and disclaimer is only beneficial if the estate is small.

The order of dividing the estate

After paying the deceased's debts the executors should distribute the estate in the following order:

4.143 (1) *Prior rights* in favour of the surviving spouse. Unlike *legal rights* these only apply in intestacy and so can be defeated by will. There are three.[1]

(a) The deceased's dwelling-house, if, when he died, the surviving spouse ordinarily lived there. In some cases the spouse gets a cash sum instead, eg if the house exceeds £110,000 in value.
(b) Furniture and belongings of the deceased, to a maximum value of £20,000, if situated in a house where the surviving spouse lives. Heirlooms are excluded.
(c) A cash sum from the estate remaining after (a) and (b) have been satisfied. This is £35,000 if the deceased left surviving children; £50,000 if he did not.

If any estate remains, the claim with next priority is:

4.144 (2) *Legal rights* in favour of the surviving spouse and children. These are an automatically protected right of inheritance which cannot be defeated by will; they are described in detail later. It is open to the beneficiaries all to agree that specific assets are transferred in satisfaction of their claims, but

1 To be replaced by a single cash sum under Law Commission proposals.

(failing agreement) the executors will give them a cash sum instead.

Movable and immovable property Legal rights apply only to movable property, not immovables ('heritable property' in Scottish terminology). For this reason, the executors must take care to deduct debts and prior rights correctly from the value of movable and immovable property as appropriate. This may be complicated, eg because in Scots law certain types of asset may be heritable or movable in different circumstances. Once legal rights have been paid, the heritable and movable estate can be aggregated together. **4.145**

(3) The *free estate*: assets remaining after (1) and (2) are satisfied. The order of priority is: **4.146**

- (a) children;
- (b) parents *and* brothers or sisters (if someone survives from both classes); each class takes half the estate;
- (c) brothers or sisters (if no parents alive);
- (d) parents (if no brothers or sisters alive);
- (e) surviving spouse;
- (f) uncles and aunts, maternal and paternal;
- (g) grandparents;
- (h) grandparents' brothers or sisters;

and so on until a relative is found. The whole estate goes to the first category in which a relative survives. If none can be traced, the estate goes to the Crown by prerogative right.

Unlike in England, courts have no discretionary power to award provision to the deceased's dependants. Cohabitants thus have no rights of intestate succession. **4.147**

Under both (2) and (3), if a potential claimant predeceased the deceased leaving issue who survive, the issue inherit in his place by 'representation'. For instance, grandchildren can succeed under (3)(a). The exception is that the issue of the deceased's parents or spouse cannot represent them: thus stepchildren do not inherit from step-parents. There are complex rules to subdivide the estate between members of any category, eg where children and grandchildren both survive. **4.148**

There are statutory rules in both intestate and testate succession to determine a presumed date and order of death if (a) someone has disappeared for seven years, or (b) he and others are known to have died (eg in a plane crash) but it is uncertain exactly when or in what order. **4.149**

Adopted people inherit from their adoptive relatives. Illegitimate and legitimate people have the same rights of succession. **4.150**

RESTRAINTS ON TESTAMENTARY DISPOSITION

Legal rights

General rules

4.151 Scots law gives the deceased's spouse and children protected rights to inherit a share of his estate, known collectively as *legal rights*. They are automatic rather than discretionary, and no court application is necessary. They cannot be evaded by will. If the deceased's will leaves less to his spouse or child than the protected entitlement, that person can claim legal rights instead. This does not invalidate the will, but the legacies in it are reduced to provide for the claim.

4.152 Conversely, legal rights only apply to movable property belonging to the deceased. He can therefore evade them by: (a) transferring them to someone else while alive, or into a trust (but inheritance tax may arise as a result); (b) converting movable property into immovable, either physically (by annexation as a fixture) or by simply replacing them. In addition, (c) if he dies intestate, the spouse takes prior rights; these have priority over legal rights and, if the estate is small, may exhaust it completely.

4.153 Legal rights consist of:

(1) *ius relictae* (or *relicti*) in favour of the widow/widower: one half of the movable estate if no children or their issue survive, one-third if they do;

(2) *legitim* in favour of the surviving children or their issue: one half (between them) if there is no spouse, one-third if there is. (Under Law Commission proposals: (a) these proportions will be changed; (b) the right lapses unless expressly claimed from the executor in two years after the death.)
If someone claiming *legitim* received assets in advance from the deceased before his death, he may have to set off their value against his claim: this is known as 'collation'. The calculation is complex and ensures he does not benefit at the expense of other claimants. Heritable (immovable) property and sums paid over for his education need not be collated.

Election

4.154 One cannot usually claim legal rights out of a testator's estate and also take a legacy under his will; one must elect – choose – between them. If one claims, one forfeits the legacy and vice versa. For the choice to be valid and binding it must be made freely and in full knowledge of the alternatives available. The executor should therefore inform potential claimants that they are entitled to claim; insist, if possible, that they obtain independent legal advice; and, if they then opt for the legacy, obtain an express discharge of their claim. A child can elect if aged 16 or over, but (if aged 16 or 17) can subsequently (up to age 21) ask the courts to re-open the election and set it aside. The executor may therefore pay the legacy at once (if the will permits) but should retain sufficient funds in case the child later opts for *legitim* within these time-limits.

4.155 A legal rights claim is *extinguished* by:

(a) a valid and binding election for a legacy;

(b) in intestacy, a simple disclaimer. The effect depends on its timing: if made before the deceased dies, the claim passes to any other claimants; if after, it lapses and the sum goes to the free estate;
(c) failure to claim within 20 years;
(d) a spouse's marriage contract (but this cannot affect the children's right to *legitim*).

Accumulation

A testator may not direct that the executor is to retain the estate and accumulate the income indefinitely. Accumulation cannot usually go on for more than 21 years, calculated under various statutory formulae; thereafter the income must be distributed to beneficiaries. Similarly there are time-limits on the creation of successive life interests in an asset, after which it must pass to a beneficiary as outright owner. 4.156

Public policy

In rare cases the court may declare a legacy invalid because it breaches rules of public policy. For instance, it must not be immoral, or motivated by the testator's vanity without conferring some obvious benefit on an individual or a section of the public. 4.157

DISQUALIFICATION FROM INHERITANCE

Unworthy heirs

On grounds of public policy, Scots law will debar a murderer from inheriting from his victim, being appointed executor of the estate, or benefiting under an insurance policy as a result of the death. In other cases of unlawful killing – 'culpable homicide', the Scottish equivalent of manslaughter – the court has discretion to set this rule aside to some extent: eg the killer may be allowed to inherit if he was provoked by the victim. The killer must petition the court within three months after the death. 4.158

Divorce

Divorce does not usually invalidate a legacy to the testator's spouse or a special destination in a title deed. The former spouse can, of course, no longer inherit under intestacy. Also, if a wife is judicially separated from her husband (though not divorced), her husband's right to inherit from her if she dies intestate is restricted. 4.159

There is no bar on an executor or a witness to a will taking a legacy under it. A solicitor who prepares the will should not do so: the court may set it aside on the ground that he abused a position of trust and exercised undue influence over the testator in making the will. Someone who notarially executes a will must never benefit under it: if he does, it is totally invalid. 4.160

TESTATE SUCCESSION

4.161 There are various classes of legacy: specific (of a specified item); general (of a certain quantity or value of generic goods or money); and residue (the remainder of the estate). This has two effects:

(a) if the available estate is insufficient to pay all legacies (because the testator has miscalculated or legal rights must be provided for), they 'abate' (ie are reduced) in reverse order, residue first;
(b) unless the will says otherwise, debts and taxes are paid primarily out of the residue.

In principle a legacy lapses if a legatee predeceases the testator. But the will may name an alternative legatee to inherit in that event – a 'destination-over'; or the law may allow the legatee's issue to inherit in his place.

5. PRIVATE INTERNATIONAL LAW ASPECTS

4.162 Scottish and English rules of private international law are similar. This section covers the substantive law; details of executry administration are dealt with in paras **4.84** *et seq* above.

GENERAL PRINCIPLES

4.163 General principles are:

(1) 'Domicile' has the same meaning in Scots as English law.
(2) To characterise a problem as (say) one of inheritance, property law, or executry administration, the Scots courts will apply Scots law as the *lex fori*. For instance, they treat protected 'legal rights' as a matter of inheritance, not matrimonial property. But the status of property as movable or immovable is referred to the *lex situs*: eg Canadian law for assets situated in Canada.
(3) There is no uniform approach to the problem of *renvoi*. But under the Wills Act 1963, the Scots courts exclude *renvoi* by treating formalities of execution as purely a matter for the appropriate foreign domestic law.

INTESTATE SUCCESSION

4.164 Intestate succession to movables is governed by the law of the deceased's domicile at date of death; to immovables, by the *lex situs*. So Scots law applies to immovables within Scotland if the deceased was domiciled elsewhere.

There are now no protected legal rights of inheritance in respect of immovables in Scotland. As for 'prior rights', labelling them as movable or immovable can cause difficulties in some cases.[1] Finally it seems that, because of its wording, the Scots courts cannot make orders under the Inheritance (Provision for Family and Dependants) Act 1975 if the deceased had English domicile and left immovables in Scotland. **4.165**

TESTATE SUCCESSION

The formalities for a will are detailed elsewhere. As regards essential validity, capacity to make a will, and interpretation of a will, the deceased's domiciliary law or the *lex situs* apply according as the will relates to movables or immovables; but the Law Commission proposes that the domiciliary law should apply to both. However, if a movable asset is situated somewhere outside Scotland (eg a share in an English company) and the provision in the will is to take effect there, the Scots courts tend to make a pragmatic exception and apply the local *lex situs*. With legacies to a person's 'heirs' or 'issue', that person's domiciliary law identifies the heirs or issue. **4.166**

EXECUTRY ADMINISTRATION

The question who is entitled to be appointed as executor is referred to the deceased's domiciliary law. In purely procedural and evidentiary matters, Scots law applies as the *lex fori*. **4.167**

6. MINIMISING PROBLEMS WHERE FOREIGN ELEMENTS ARE INVOLVED

The advice given in relation to English law applies also in Scotland, with one main difference. 'Joint property' in the English sense does not apply to assets owned by individuals. While the same practical outcome may arise with a 'survivorship destination' contained in the title deed to a movable asset, this device is really relevant only to company shares; in any case, it may be treated as a matter of succession (not property law) because the asset still forms part of the estate on death. **4.168**

It will be convenient for a foreign executor to grant a power of attorney to someone in Scotland to obtain confirmation and administer the estate on his behalf. Framing this in Scottish form avoids the need to obtain an affidavit certifying that it is valid under the law of the place where it was executed. **4.169**

---

1 See Leslie, 'Prior Rights in Succession: the International Dimension', (1988) *Scots Law Times* (News) 105.

4.170 If the legatee is less than 16 years old and is domiciled outside Scotland, the executor may have problems obtaining from the legatee's guardian a discharge (for payment of the legacy) which is effective in Scotland.[1]

1 Wilson & Duncan, *op cit*, p 447.

JERSEY†

I. INTRODUCTION

Jersey originally formed part of the Duchy of Normandy. When Duke William of Normandy conquered England and became the King of England, England and Normandy became united for approximately 150 years until Normandy was lost to the English Crown. The Channel Islands then became the last outpost of the Duchy of Normandy left in the possession of the English Crown, but the Islands were never incorporated into the English system of government and from this they derive their present internal independence and a legal tradition which owes much to their Norman heritage. 4.171

Although much of Jersey law has arisen out of Norman French customary law, it has also inevitably over the centuries been much influenced by English law as Jersey lawyers studied in England and brought back with them English legal ideas. In the last two centuries, statute law, often based on English models, has become increasingly important. Nevertheless, the influence of Norman customary law remains strong and aspects of both English and Norman law can clearly be seen in Jersey succession law, so that both common law practitioners and civil law practitioners will find elements which are familiar to them. 4.172

On 1 September 1993, the Wills and Succession (Jersey) Law 1993 (the 1993 Law) came into force on the Island. The 1993 Law made wide-ranging changes to the rights of heirs both on an intestacy and where a valid will has been made and affects both movable and immovable estates. The main changes are set out in the third section of this chapter. However, the Law does not materially affect the rights of the non-Jersey resident. 4.173

The first section of this chapter will deal with the Jersey law of administration of estates, and the second section will concentrate on the actual law of succession. 4.174

---

† This chapter was written by Steven Meiklejohn (partner Ogier & Le Masurier, Jersey Advocates & Solicitors, St Helier, Jersey, tel 01534 504000, fax 01534 35328).

2. ADMINISTRATION OF ESTATES

MOVABLE AND IMMOVABLE PROPERTY

4.175 The first important distinction Jersey law makes is between movable property and immovable property. Succession to movable property situated in Jersey is governed as a matter of Jersey law by the *lex domicilii* whereas the succession to immovable property is governed by the *lex situs*.

4.176 Broadly speaking, immovable property consists of land, buildings and their fixtures and fittings and certain rights in and over land.

4.177 Movable property consists of everything else, and apart from obvious movable tangible property, also includes such items as intangible assets, cash, shares, insurance policies, and legal rights.

4.178 In the case of tangible movable property there will usually be no doubt as to where it is situated, but there are instances where the location of the assets may not be so obvious. For example, a debt will be regarded as situated where the debt is repayable, and if this has not been specified, this will usually be taken as the place where the debtor is resident.

4.179 Where shares of a company are in registered form, they will be deemed to be located where the register is maintained. So, if the share register of a Panamanian company is maintained in Jersey, the shares in the company will be deemed to be property situated in Jersey. This will be so even if the certificates are held in some other country altogether. Equally, if share certificates relating to shares in English incorporated companies are held in Jersey, and the share register of those companies is maintained in England, then the shares will be deemed to be property situated in England.

4.180 On the other hand, bearer shares and securities are deemed to be situated where the certificates are physically held, irrespective of where the company is incorporated.

4.181 In relation to movable property, Jersey law in practice follows very much the same procedures as in England in maintaining a distinction between the persons who have a right to administer the estate and the ultimate beneficiaries. It is necessary first of all, for the persons entitled to administer the estate to establish legal title to the assets comprised in the estate, to settle the debts of the estate, and then to pass legal title in the assets to the beneficiaries ultimately entitled.

4.182 However, in the case of immovable property (real estate) Jersey law is quite different from English law because ownership passes by operation of law to the persons entitled either by will or on intestacy without the need for any person to establish a separate right to administer the estate.

4.183 The process by which legal title in immovable property passes to the beneficiaries will be considered in the second section dealing with succession, and in this section only the law of administration of estates in relation to movable property will be considered.

DOMICILE

At this stage, it is important to examine the concept of domicile. Jersey broadly follows the same rules as England in determining the location of a person's domicile but with some differences. Practitioners from common law countries will probably be familiar with the concept of domicile, but practitioners from civil law countries will often find it difficult to grasp the Anglo-Saxon concept of domicile because they may well use the same terms themselves to describe a different concept. In civil law countries, domicile will usually describe the concept of permanent residence. 4.184

In Jersey, as in other common law countries, the concept of domicile can be quite detached from that of residence. It is possible for a person to be resident for many years in one jurisdiction whilst remaining domiciled in another jurisdiction. The concept of domicile in Jersey is also quite distinct from the concept of nationality, and indeed it is based on an association with a territory having its own legal system rather than an association with a particular sovereign State. Thus, within the British Isles, a person might be domiciled in England and Wales (which form a joint jurisdiction) or in Scotland, Northern Ireland, the Isle of Man, Jersey or Guernsey all of which territories have their own courts and legal systems. Similarly, in countries having a federal system, such as Spain or the USA, a person would be domiciled in an individual State rather than in the sovereign country itself. 4.185

A person of full age, (which in Jersey is 20) and mental capacity may acquire a domicile of choice by establishing permanent residence in a jurisdiction *with the intention of remaining there permanently or indefinitely*. It is important to note that establishment of permanent residence in a new jurisdiction without the intention of remaining there indefinitely will not establish a new domicile, and, correspondingly, if a person establishes an intention of settling in a new jurisdiction, he will not establish domicile there until he actually takes up residence there. 4.186

A married woman living with her husband will acquire a domicile of dependence which will follow that of her husband. Here Jersey law differs from the law of England and the Isle of Man, where a married woman may have a different domicile from that of her husband even if she is living with him. 4.187

A child will also have a domicile of dependence determined by the domicile of one or other of its parents according to circumstances. 4.188

The law of domicile is quite complex and technical as seen in paras **1.7** *et seq*, and the foregoing is only a very brief outline. Where questions of domicile arise professional advice should always be sought. 4.189

GRANT OF REPRESENTATION

In theory, the principal heir takes possession automatically of all movable property of the deceased on the death of the deceased by operation of customary law. 4.190

4.191 However, under the Probate (Jersey) Law 1949, in order to make title to and to gain control of the movable assets of a deceased person situate in Jersey, it is necessary to obtain an order from the court which is referred to as a 'grant of representation'. In Jersey, it is in fact a criminal offence punishable by imprisonment or fine to 'intermeddle' in the estate of a deceased person, without having first obtained a grant of representation. There are two types of grant of representation.

4.192 If the deceased left a will, it will usually appoint one or more persons to act as executors of the will. If the executors accept the appointment, their first duty will be to prove the will, which means lodging the will at the court to establish its validity. Therefore, when the executors *prove* the will they will receive a *grant of probate*. Once a grant of probate is obtained the will becomes a public document and can be inspected by any member of the public upon request. Executors can be individual persons or trust corporations registered and recognised as such by the Royal Court.

4.193 Where a person named in a will as executor obtains a grant of probate he is referred to as the executor nominate. Where a will fails to appoint an executor, or the executor named by the will does not wish to accept the appointment or is incapable of acting, then it will be necessary to apply to the Royal Court to appoint another person as executor who will be referred to as the executor-dative. The executor-dative will normally be the principal heir but in special circumstances the court has power to appoint anybody whom it sees fit. The executor-dative will be required to provide a bond to the value of twice the personal estate that he will execute the will and faithfully discharge his office; he may also have to provide sureties.

4.194 Where there is an intestacy, a grant of letters of administration must be applied for. Where the deceased was domiciled in Jersey, it will be the principal heir who is entitled to apply for such a grant. However, where by virtue of the 1993 Law, the whole of the movable estate devolves upon the surviving spouse, it will be the surviving spouse who is entitled to apply for the grant. Where the deceased died domiciled outside Jersey, then it will be the persons entitled to administer the estate under the law of the domicile who will be entitled to apply for the grant.

4.195 As has been pointed out above, bearer securities are deemed to be situated in the place where the actual certificates are physically held. It quite frequently happens that bearer securities, for example, Eurobonds, are acquired through a Jersey bank or broker, who is then asked to hold the bonds for the purchaser. In practice, instead of taking physical delivery of the bonds, the Jersey bank or broker will usually arrange for them to be held by a sub-agent, in the case of Eurobonds, usually one or two clearing houses both situated in Luxembourg, Euroclear and Cedel. Because the bonds are not physically held in Jersey, they will not form part of the Jersey estate if the purchaser dies, and therefore their value should not be included when computing the amount of stamp duty payable on applying for a grant of representation (see below).

It follows that the Jersey bank or broker could properly insist upon the production of a grant or equivalent documentation from Luxembourg, where the bonds are situate, but in practice the banks in Jersey will probably deliver the bonds to the order of the person producing a Jersey grant of representation. 4.196

GRANT OF PROBATE

Testators domiciled in Jersey

A grant of probate can only be obtained by personal application before an officer of the Royal Court, normally the Judicial Greffier or Greffier substitute. The applicant must swear the executor's oath to execute the will and well and faithfully discharge the duties of his office. The executor's oath is subject to stamp duty at the rate of approximately ½% of the declared value of the estate up to £50,000 and approximately ¾% thereafter. The oath is made in written form, and must state the value of the estate in Jersey. The stamp duty is paid by purchasing stamps to the required value and affixing them to the executor's oath. If it is not possible for the executor to attend the court in person, he may appoint an attorney executor who will attend the court to swear the oath and the grant of probate will then be issued in the name of the attorney executor. 4.197

The court will need to satisfy itself that the will is valid in accordance with Jersey law and the usual requirements for formal validity are as follows: 4.198

(1) the will must be in writing and signed by the testator, or if incorporated by some other person in his presence and by his direction; and
(2) it must appear that the testator intended by his signature to give effect to the will; and
(3) the signature must be made or acknowledged by the testator in the presence of two or more witnesses present at the same time; and
(4) each witness must either attest and sign the will or acknowledge his signature in the presence of the testator and in the presence of at least one other witness; and
(5) the witnesses must be over 20 years of age, and must not be beneficiaries under the will.

To avoid problems arising when applying for probate these formal requirements should be reflected by the form of attestation to the will.

It is, however, also possible in Jersey to make a valid holograph will. That is a will entirely written, dated and signed by the testator, and such a will is regarded as valid even though the other formalities have not all been met. However, the use of a holograph will is not recommended as there may be evidential problems in establishing its validity. 4.199

A will is regarded as invalid if it is shown that it was executed by the testator under duress or undue influence. A testator who is not of full age (which is 20 in Jersey) or of full mental capacity is not capable of making a valid will and there are certain 4.200

other circumstances where a person is regarded as 'under the control of another person' and thus lacking testamentary capacity.

4.201 The executor is not obliged to distribute the estate for a year and a day from the death of the deceased. Under the 1993 Law, the *année de jouissance* by which rule the executor was entitled to keep the income arising from an estate during the year and a day period has been abolished. Equally, the right under the customary law of the principal heir to interpose during the year and a day period and demand possession of the movable estate from the executor by paying into the hands of the executor the amounts of the debts, legacies and costs of administration, has been abolished. However, the 1993 Law makes it clear that estates of persons dying before 1 September 1993, when such Law came into force, shall continue to be administered in accordance with the law and procedure in force prior to that date.

Testators domiciled outside Jersey

4.202 The procedure here is very much the same, except that in determining the validity of the will, the Jersey court will not be at all concerned as to whether the formal requirements of Jersey law outlined above have been complied with, but as to whether the will is a valid document in accordance with the law of the testator's domicile at the date of his death. In practice, in these cases the testator's principal assets are likely to have been situated outside Jersey, and the most usual procedure will be first to obtain a grant of probate of the will in the country where the testator was domiciled, or whatever the equivalent procedure is.

4.203 The original will is normally retained by the court of the country where it has first been proved, and the Jersey court will be satisfied by the production of a copy of the original will which has been both sealed and certified by the court where it was first proved, together with a sealed and certified copy of the grant of probate by that court. The grant of probate of the foreign court will normally state where the deceased died domiciled, and the fact that the foreign court has granted probate of the will is normally sufficient evidence for the Jersey court as to the validity of the will in accordance with the law of the testator's domicile.

4.204 However, if for any reason it is decided to make the first application for probate in Jersey, then it will be necessary to produce an affidavit sworn by a practitioner qualified in the law of the jurisdiction of the deceased's domicile and stating the basis as to why the deceased should be regarded as domiciled in the jurisdiction in question and confirming that the will would be regarded as valid in accordance with the law of the deceased's domicile.

4.205 It sometimes happens that a foreign domiciled testator will leave one will in relation to his assets situated in the jurisdiction of his domicile and another will for his assets situated in Jersey. In this case, it will be necessary to make a first application for probate of the will relating to the Jersey estate in Jersey, and accordingly the application will need to be supported by an affidavit of foreign law as detailed above. However, it should also be noted that if, from the face of the Jersey will, it is apparent that it is not the only will of the testator, then the Jersey court will probably demand a court-sealed and certified copy of the other will so that it can make sure that there is no inconsistency between the two wills.

It therefore follows from what has been said that if under the law of his own domicile, the testator would not have had capacity to dispose of his property by will, for example where under the law of domicile a testator's heirs have indefeasible rights of succession, then he will not necessarily be able to overcome this incapacity by leaving a will purportedly disposing of his assets in Jersey. The will may be challenged by the heirs. 4.206

Where this problem exists, the testator would be well advised to create an *inter vivos* settlement under Jersey law. A recent amendment to the Jersey Trusts Law specifically states that if a person domiciled outside Jersey transfers or disposes of property during his lifetime to a trust, he shall be deemed to have had capacity to do so if he is at the time of such transfer or disposition of full age and of sound mind under the law of his domicile, and that no rule relating to inheritance or succession, including forced heirship or similar rights of the law of his domicile or any other system of law, shall affect any such transfer or disposition or otherwise affect the validity of such trust. (Forced heirship describes the situation where the law restricts the testamentary powers of disposition of the deceased in such a way that the rights of the heirs to inherit cannot be defeated.) The testator should, however, take into account the possibility of his heirs seeking to set aside the trust in the jurisdiction of the testator's domicile. Advice should be taken on this matter. 4.207

GRANT OF LETTERS OF ADMINISTRATION

Deceased domiciled in Jersey

If the deceased has not left a will, it is necessary to apply for a grant of letters of administration. Letters of administration are normally granted to the eldest son or next principal heir in order of priority, subject to the surviving spouse's right to apply where the whole of the movable estate devolves upon the surviving spouse by virtue of the 1993 Law. 4.208

If the principal heir does not wish to take out a grant of administration, he may renounce his right and the next heir in order of priority will then have the right to take out a grant. If there is no heir willing to take out a grant, the court will appoint an administrator who will advertise for heirs. This will usually be a court official known as the Viscount. 4.209

The person applying for a grant of letters of administration must appear personally before the Judicial Greffier, as in the case of an application for a grant of probate. He must swear the administrator's oath to the effect that he will administer according to law all the personal estate of the deceased and will render a just and true account thereof to the court whenever required by law so to do and certify the net value of the estate. Again, court stamps must be affixed to the administrator's oath to the appropriate value. In addition, administrators must execute a bond binding themselves and their heirs or successors in title to the 4.210

value of twice the amount of the estate faithfully to discharge the office of administrator.

4.211 In most cases, the bond must be attested by a Notary Public or some other suitable witness, but this requirement is dispensed with in the case of trust corporations and certain other administrators. Administrators must, in general, also provide sureties to the bond, but no sureties will be required where the administrator is the principal heir or a trust corporation or in certain other instances.

4.212 As in the case of a grant of probate, a person obtaining a grant of letters of administration is not obliged to distribute the movable estate of the deceased for a year and a day from the date of death of the deceased.

Deceased domiciled outside Jersey

4.213 In establishing who has the right to apply for a grant, the Jersey court will look to the law of the deceased's domicile.

4.214 In practice, a grant of letters of administration, or equivalent, will often have been first made in the jurisdiction where the deceased was domiciled, and if this is the case, it will be necessary to produce to the Jersey court a copy of the grant of letters of administration, or equivalent, sealed and certified by the court where the original grant was obtained. The administrators who obtained the original grant in the jurisdiction where the deceased was domiciled will not normally find it convenient to travel to Jersey to make a personal appearance before the Judicial Greffier to swear the administrator's oath; this problem can be overcome if they appoint an attorney administrator to attend before the Judicial Greffier and swear the oath on their behalf. The attorney administrator will also have to give the administrator's bond referred to in the foregoing section.

4.215 In jurisdictions where there is no equivalent to the procedure of a grant of administration and the heirs take the deceased's property automatically by process of law, the Jersey court will wish to satisfy itself as to who in practice has the right to administer the estate. Accordingly, if for example a number of heirs are each entitled to a certain portion of the estate and they receive these portions automatically by operation of law, it will be necessary for all the heirs to join together in applying for a grant of letters of administration because it would require all the heirs to act together in order to deal with the legal title to the whole estate.

CONTENTIOUS MATTERS

4.216 Where there is a dispute or a potential dispute as to who may be entitled to apply for a grant of probate or letters of administration, it is possible for an interested party to enter a caveat. This can be done on payment of a small fee to the Judicial Greffier, and this will then prevent a grant of probate or letters of administration being made to any person until the matter can be considered by the court or the caveat has expired or been withdrawn. A caveat will expire after six months, but can be renewed indefinitely for further six-month periods.

The Judicial Greffier may, on his own initiative, refer applications to the court for directions, and in such a case the court may either issue the appropriate directions to the Judicial Greffier, or it may simply forbid the Judicial Greffier to take further proceedings, in which case the person applying for the grant must apply to the court by means of an *ex parte* application. Upon any such *ex parte* application, the court may order such persons to be convened, such evidence to be taken and such enquiries to be made as the court deems necessary and may make such order as the circumstances require. 4.217

Where any legal proceedings touching the validity of the will of a deceased person or for obtaining, recalling or revoking any grant are pending, the court may place the estate in the possession of an officer of the court known as the Viscount who will act under the direction of the court. 4.218

CASES WHERE A GRANT OF PROBATE OR ADMINISTRATION IS NOT REQUIRED

Small estates

Until very recently, if a deceased person, wherever domiciled, left any portion of their estate situate in Jersey, no matter how small, it was necessary to obtain a grant of representation in Jersey before the Jersey estate could be dealt with. Any person who dealt with any part of the estate without a grant having been obtained was guilty of intermeddling in the estate which is a criminal offence and renders the intermeddler liable on conviction to a fine not exceeding £1,000 or to imprisonment for a term not exceeding 12 months. 4.219

The growth of Jersey as a finance centre has, however, meant that it frequently happens that people die domiciled in other parts of the world leaving some small portion of their estate in Jersey in the form of a bank account or some shares in a Jersey based unit trust or mutual fund. Sometimes the amount of the Jersey estate is very insignificant and the legal costs involved in applying for a grant of representation could exceed the value of the Jersey estate. With this problem in mind, the Probate (Amendment) (Jersey) Law 1990 was passed which allows the release of Jersey assets in some circumstances without a grant of representation in Jersey. The concessions made by this law apply only to the assets of a person who dies domiciled outside the Island. A Jersey grant is always required for the estates of persons domiciled in Jersey. 4.220

The new law provides that a person in the Island who holds any personal estate situated in the Island and forming a part or the whole of the estate so situated of a deceased person who died domiciled in any place outside the Island, may release assets without the production to him of a Jersey grant of representation provided that the value of the assets held by that person is not more than £10,000. This sum is not the overall limit but applies to each person. The person holding the assets, provided the foregoing conditions are met, may release them on the application of any person to such person or persons as appear to him to be entitled to receive them under the terms of the will, if any, of the deceased person or under the law 4.221

relating to intestate succession in force in the place in which the deceased person was domiciled at his death. The person concerned will, of course, wish to satisfy himself that the persons claiming the delivery of the Jersey estate are, in fact, the persons properly entitled under the law of the deceased's domicile, and this means that he will normally require production of the appropriate foreign grant of probate or letters of administration or equivalent.

4.222 It should be noted that this law is only an enabling law, enabling persons, such as banks or fund managers to release assets without the production of a Jersey grant without the risk of criminal prosecution. The bank or fund manager does not obtain legal protection from a potential civil claim unless he pays out to a person with a Jersey grant, and consequently, if someone else does subsequently successfully obtain a Jersey grant the bank or fund manager could be compelled to pay out for a second time. Accordingly, nobody can be forced to pay out without production of a Jersey grant and it will be necessary in each case to persuade the relevant bank or fund manager to dispense with this requirement. In practice, the banks and fund managers usually do pay out in these circumstances on the production of a foreign grant but will usually require the applicant to provide an indemnity.

4.223 There is also a potential technical problem in the wording of the law in relation to certain types of asset. It is difficult, for instance, to say that a company registrar 'holds' shares in a Jersey company registered in the name of a deceased person and arguably therefore he would not be protected by the new law if he registered a transfer of those shares without production of a grant. On the other hand, the registrar would probably be covered if the shares were redeemable preference shares which could be redeemed by the company and the proceeds paid to the applicant.

Property owned jointly

4.224 Where property was held by the deceased jointly with another person or persons, ownership in the property passes automatically to the survivor or survivors by virtue of the *jus accrescendi*, and there will be no need to apply for a grant of representation. However, it should also be noted that property in Jersey can be owned by two or more persons in common as distinct from jointly, and, in fact, the presumption in Jersey is in favour of ownership in common, so that express words are needed for joint ownership to be created. Where ownership in common exists, each co-owner is treated as having an individual share in the property, which he can dispose of during his lifetime or by his will or which will pass to his heirs on an intestacy, and the survivor will not have the *jus accrescendi*.

Property subject to a trust

4.225 Property subject to a trust in which the deceased had a life interest or any other interest does not form part of the deceased's estate, and accordingly no grant of representation is necessary.

3. JERSEY LAW OF SUCCESSION

IMMOVABLE PROPERTY (REAL ESTATE)

The law of domicile is not relevant in the case of immovable property situated in Jersey. The rules governing succession to immovable property situated in Jersey are governed by Jersey law as the *lex situs.* 4.226

Where there is a will

It is usually recommended to make a separate will in relation to immovable property situate in Jersey. Special rules apply to the execution of a will of immovable property. For example, the will must be read out loud and, if signed on the island, one of the witnesses must be an advocate or solicitor of the Royal Court, or one of a limited number of other categories of witness. If the will is made outside the island, one of the witnesses must be a notary. An advocate or solicitor of the Royal Court should always be consulted when making a will of Jersey immovable property. 4.227

There is no need to apply for a grant of probate of a will of Jersey real estate. On the testator's death, the will is registered in the Royal Court, and this registration automatically evidences ownership of the property by the beneficiary. 4.228

A testator can leave his Jersey immovable property by will almost entirely as he wishes except that, in the case of a married man, his widow will have a right of 'dower', that is a life interest in one-third of his immovable property at the date of his death, that will rank in priority to any dispositions made by the will. In addition, in the case of a married woman, her widower will have a *droit de viduité,* that is a life interest in the whole of the immovable property of his deceased wife providing a child has been born alive of the marriage. However, this life interest is lost if the husband remarries. If there have been no children of the marriage then the widower is not entitled to any interest at all in his wife's immovable property. Subject to the widow's right of dower and the widower's right of *viduité,* the heirs have no right to challenge or set aside any gifts of immovable property made by the testator by will, and they can accordingly be totally disinherited as regards immovable property. 4.229

It should be noted that by virtue of the 1993 Law, the prohibition on legacies of immovable property to churches or other religious bodies has been abolished. However, it is still not possible to create a trust of Jersey immovables whether by will or otherwise. 4.230

Immovable property on intestacy

The Jersey law of succession to immovable property has been changed significantly following the coming into force of the 1993 Law on 1 September 1993. The previously somewhat arcane rules, based strongly upon Norman customary law, have been abolished. 4.231

4.232 Under Article 4(i) of the Law, the immovable estate as to which a person dies intestate devolves equally between the heirs at law, and such heirs take as tenants in common. It is still the position in cases of succession to immovable property that there is no administrator and title to land passes to the heirs immediately by operation of law by virtue of the death.

4.233 Under Article 5 of the Law, where a spouse dies intestate as to the matrimonial home, unless under the provisions of Articles 6 or 7, the surviving spouse is entitled absolutely to the matrimonial home, the surviving spouse shall be entitled to a *usufruit* (life enjoyment) of the matrimonial home. Article 6 of the Law states that where a spouse dies intestate as to immovable property, the surviving spouse shall be entitled absolutely to the whole of the immovable estate where there is no issue of the deceased's spouse, and to an equal share of the whole of the immovable estate with each of the surviving children of the deceased's spouse where the deceased's spouse leaves issue.

4.234 Article 6 also states that where a spouse dies intestate as to immovable estate, the surviving spouse shall not be entitled to dower or *viduité* in any immovable estate as to which the deceased spouse died intestate.

4.235 Article 8 of the Law sets out, however, that the provisions relating to surviving spouses referred to in the two preceding paragraphs shall not apply where at the date of death the deceased spouse and the surviving spouse were not living together, and either the surviving spouse had deserted the deceased spouse without cause and the desertion was continuing, or a decree of judicial separation with respect to the surviving spouse had been granted. Instead, the immovable property of the deceased spouse devolves as if the surviving spouse had died immediately before the deceased spouse.

4.236 Where there are no heirs in direct line for either a man or woman, immovable property passes to be divided amongst the nearest blood relations according to the customary rules.

4.237 Under Article 19 of the Law, the customary law whereby aliens (save EU nationals) were incapable of inheriting property in Jersey, whether movable or immovable, has been abolished.

4.238 At customary law illegitimate children have no rights of inheritance on intestacy, but this disability has been partially removed by statute to the extent that an illegitimate child can now inherit from its mother but not from its father. The Law does not further alter the position. Adopted children are treated in the same way as natural legitimate children.

The legal position before the coming into force of the Law

4.239 Because the old rules will continue to govern the administration of estates of persons who died before 1 September 1993, the old law will continue to be important for some time to come. Under the old law, there was always a principal heir. Where the deceased left children the principal heir would always be the eldest son, or where there were no sons, the eldest daughter. Where the eldest son had died before the deceased leaving children himself, then his eldest son (or eldest daughter if there were no sons) would be the principal heir in precedence to any other sons or daughters of the deceased. On an intestacy, the deceased's immovable property would pass immediately to the principal heir by operation of law by virtue of the death. The principal heir would have the responsibility of ensuring that the claims of the other heirs to their respective entitlements were duly satisfied. To the extent that the heirs and the widow or widower could not reach agreement between themselves, the old law provided an extremely complex procedure for determining the entitlements of the heirs to share in the immovable property of the deceased.

Under the old law, the widow's right of dower and the widower's rights of *viduité* **4.240** applied where a spouse died intestate as to immovable property. As is still the case, where there were no heirs in direct line for either a man or woman then immovable property passed to be divided amongst the nearest blood relations according to the customary rules.

MOVABLE PROPERTY

Persons domiciled outside Jersey

Where there is a will

It will be necessary to obtain a grant of probate in respect of the will, and the Jersey **4.241** court will need to be satisfied that the will is formally valid in accordance with the law of the deceased person's domicile. If the deceased person has made a will and purported to dispose of property in Jersey which he did not have power to dispose of freely under the law of the domicile because, for example, under the law of his domicile he would not be free to leave property away from his legal heirs, then application for a grant of probate could be opposed on those grounds by his heirs.

Furthermore, even if a grant of probate has been given, it would still be open to **4.242** any person having an interest to challenge the will on the grounds that the dispositions made by the will are not valid in accordance with the law of the deceased's domicile, because for example, the heirs under the law of the domicile cannot be dispossessed.

However, one must bear in mind that once an executor who is not resident in **4.243** Jersey has obtained a grant he will be able to establish legal title to any assets situate in Jersey and to remove those assets from the jurisdiction of the Jersey courts.

If any action is brought touching the validity of a Jersey will the Jersey court will **4.244** hear evidence as to what the law in the place of domicile of the deceased is and will decide the case accordingly. Here, there will be the opportunity for the doctrine of *renvoi* to apply. If, for example, the law of the deceased's domicile would look to the *lex situs* to decide the law applicable to property situate outside the jurisdiction of the deceased's domicile, then it is thought that the Jersey court would apply the Jersey law of succession to assets situate within its jurisdiction.

4.245 Once a grant of probate has been given in Jersey to the person named as executor in the will, then that person will be able to establish legal title to all the assets in Jersey and thus distribute them in accordance with the terms of the will. If an attorney executor has been appointed, he will be responsible for delivering the movable estate into the control of the executor named in the will, or in accordance with his instructions.

On an intestacy

4.246 The law of succession will be governed by the law of the deceased person's domicile. The Jersey grant of letters of administration will be made to the person or persons entitled under the law of the deceased's domicile (see para **4.214**) and that person will be responsible for transferring title in the movable assets situate in Jersey to the heirs entitled thereto in accordance with the law of the deceased's domicile.

Persons domiciled in Jersey

Where there is a will

4.247 By virtue of the 1993 Law, the ability of persons domiciled in Jersey to dispose of their movable property is restricted in that where a person is survived by a spouse and issue, he or she will only have completely free power of disposition by will over one-third of his or her net movable estate. The surviving spouse will have an indefeasible claim to the household effects (as defined in the 1993 Law) and one-third of the rest of the net movable estate, and the issue (legitimate only in the case of a man) can claim a one-third share divisible between them in equal shares *per stirpes.* The respective shares of the surviving spouse and the issue are known as the *portion legitime.*

4.248 The expression *per stirpes* means literally 'through that root' so that where a child of a deceased person has predeceased that person himself leaving descendants, then those descendants collectively stand in the shoes of that child and divide that child's portion between themselves, if necessary applying the *per stirpes* rule again, if for example a grandchild has also died leaving great-grandchildren and so on.

4.249 Where a person leaves issue but no spouse, then he or she will still only be entitled to dispose freely of one-third of his or her movable property and the issue shall be entitled to claim as legitime two-thirds of the net movable estate between themselves in equal shares *per stirpes.*

4.250 Where a person leaves a spouse but no issue, the surviving spouse is entitled to claim the household effects and two-thirds of the rest of the net movable estate. The person has free power of disposition over the other third.

4.251 A will by which a testator or testatrix purports to dispose of more than that to which he or she is entitled by way of freely disposable portion is not automatically invalid or void, but merely liable to be challenged by the widow or the heirs on the grounds that their *portion legitime* has not been satisfied. A will must be challenged within a year and a day, if either the widow or any of the issue are seeking to claim their *portion legitime.* In the event that the will is not challenged within the year and a day from the date of the grant of probate, the will is fully valid and effective. It is in fact quite common for persons to execute wills which do not recognise the strict interests of the heirs or widow in the hope and expectation that the wills will not be challenged. Because of the possibility that a will might be challenged within a year and a day, the executors will not usually distribute any assets to the beneficiaries during this time.

It should be noted that in Jersey a *donation à cause de mort* – a lifetime gift made in expectation of death during an illness which is expected to be terminal – is regarded as a testamentary disposition. Consequently, the gift only takes effect on the death of the donor, and the gift is open to challenge if it involves the diminution of the *portion legitime*. 4.252

On an intestacy

Article 7 of the Law states that where a spouse dies intestate as to movable estate leaving a surviving spouse but no issue, the surviving spouse shall take the whole of the net movable estate. Where the deceased spouse leaves a surviving spouse and issue, the surviving spouse shall be entitled to the household effects, other movable estate to the value of £30,000 and half of the rest of the net movable estate and the issue shall take the other half of the rest of the net movable estate. The provisions excluding the surviving spouse's rights referred to at para **4.235** apply in respect of movable estates, both testate and intestate, and intestate immovable estates. 4.253

Where a person dies leaving neither a surviving spouse nor issue, then the movable estate goes to that person's nearest blood relatives in equal shares *per stirpes*. If there are no heirs, then the heirs' share falls to the Crown. 4.254

The legal position before the coming into force of the Law

Prior to the coming into force of the Law, the rules, both when there was a will and on intestacy, differed in respect of both men and women. 4.255

Where a man made a will

A married man leaving issue had completely free power of disposition by will over only one-third of his movable property. His widow had an indefeasible claim to a one-third share, and his legitimate issue could claim a one-third share, divisible between them in equal shares *per stirpes*. Where a man left legitimate issue but no widow, then he would still only be entitled to dispose freely of one-third of his movable property, and in that case the legitimate issue would be entitled to divide two-thirds of the movable estate between themselves in equal shares *per stirpes*. 4.256

Where a husband left a widow but no issue, then the widow would be entitled to claim one half of the estate and the husband would have free power of disposition over the other half. 4.257

Where a woman made a will

Where a woman left issue (whether legitimate or not), the issue would have been entitled to claim two-thirds of her movable estate, and she would have had free power of disposition over the remaining third. Where a woman left no issue, she could have disposed of the whole of her movable estate by will in any way she 4.258

pleased and in those circumstances her widower would not have any claim on her estate.

Where the intestate was a man

4.259 Where a man left a widow and legitimate issue, the widow would take one-third of his estate outright and his legitimate issue would take the remaining two-thirds outright in equal shares *per stirpes*. Where a man left legitimate issue but no widow, the legitimate issue would take all the estate outright in equal shares *per stirpes*.

4.260 Where a man left a widow but no legitimate issue, then the widow was entitled to half of the estate and the remaining half went to his nearest blood relatives, relatives of the same degree taking in equal shares *per stirpes* but heirs of the whole blood taking double portions against heirs of the half blood. Where a man left neither widow nor legitimate issue, then the whole estate went to his nearest blood relatives in equal shares *per stirpes*. If there were no heirs, then the heirs' share fell to the Crown, although an application could have been made to the Crown to waive its rights in favour of the widow.

Where the intestate was a woman

4.261 Where a woman died leaving issue (whether legitimate or not), then the issue would take the whole of her movable estate in equal shares *per stirpes*, whether or not she left a husband. The husband would have no claim at all on the estate. If, however, the widow left a husband but no issue, then the surviving husband took the whole of the estate, and the woman's blood relatives had no claim on the estate.

4.262 If a woman died leaving neither issue nor husband, then her estate went to her nearest blood relatives in equal shares *per stirpes*. As in the case of immovable property an alien who is a national of a non EU country, or any person claiming through him, was not able to inherit on an intestacy movable property of a person who dies domiciled in Jersey.

Survivorship

4.263 Under Article 9 of the Law, it is now possible to apply to the court for an order that persons, who died in circumstances rendering it uncertain as to which of them survived the other, shall be deemed to have died simultaneously, or as the case may be, declaring that one or more of those persons survived the other or others. Article 10 of the Law goes on to provide that where a court has made an order declaring that persons shall be deemed to have died simultaneously, the estate, movable and immovable, shall be dealt with in the way it would have been had no other deceased persons named in the order survived that deceased person. In other words, where two people are deemed to have died simultaneously their respective estates are to be distributed as if neither had survived the other. However, the 1993 Law does not prevent a testator from specifying in his will what should happen in the event of simultaneous deaths or death in the same accident of the testator and any beneficiary under the will.

4. CONFLICT OF LAWS

This chapter has so far been concerned mainly with Jersey domestic law. Clearly, conflict of law questions can arise and some of these have been touched upon. There is not a great deal of judicial authority in Jersey on conflict of law matters, but the probability is that the courts would find the English and Irish approach persuasive. 4.264

5. MINIMISING PROBLEMS WHERE FOREIGN ELEMENTS ARE CONCERNED

SEPARATE WILLS

It may be considered advantageous from an administrative point of view to have a separate will dealing only with Jersey assets. However, when preparing more than one will for a testator, it is extremely important that both wills define clearly which property they govern, and that neither will cancels the other in whole or in part, and that one will is not inconsistent with the other, and that neither will can cause problems in any of the jurisdictions with which the testator was connected. 4.265

It should, however, be borne in mind that where it is apparent on the face of the Jersey will that another will is in existence, the Jersey court may require a sealed and certified copy of the other will in order to satisfy itself that there are no inconsistencies between the two wills, and that one will has not been revoked by the other. 4.266

INTER VIVOS SETTLEMENTS

Where a person domiciled outside Jersey owns substantial assets in Jersey, the creation of an *inter vivos* settlement is strongly recommended. This will have the following advantages on the death of the settlor. 4.267

(1) *Continuity.* The trustees of the settlement continue in possession of the trust assets, and accordingly there is no delay in establishing control over the assets, such as, inevitably, results from the need to apply for a grant of probate or letters of administration. 4.268

(2) *Stamp duty.* Because there is no need to apply for a grant of representation the cost of the ½%–¾% court stamps is avoided. Also the legal fees in connection with the application for a grant of representation are avoided. 4.269

(3) *Flexibility.* A trust document can be set up in a very flexible way, so as to give the settlor power to vary the dispositions during his lifetime by means of a power of appointment. Alternatively, a discretionary trust can be set up where the trustees are given a discretion as to how they should distribute the trust fund and its income amongst beneficiaries. In practice, the trustees are guided in the exercise of this discretion by a letter of wishes from the settlor, which although not binding 4.270

on the trustees is usually followed by them, provided that it is not inconsistent with the terms of the trust or the proper exercise of their discretion. The letter of wishes can be amended at any time during the settlor's lifetime without the necessity for the formalities required for execution of a will.

4.271 (4) *Forced heirship.* As has been pointed out at paras **4.206** and **4.241**, a foreign domiciled person cannot leave Jersey movable property by will in such a way that the rights of his heirs under the law of his domicile would be defeated, since Jersey law will look to the law of the deceased's domicile to see who would be entitled to his movable estate. If, however, such a person transfers assets during his lifetime to trustees of a Jersey trust, he will be regarded in Jersey as having effectively alienated this property during his lifetime, and the Jersey court will not recognise the claims of the heirs upon these assets.

4.272 For the avoidance of doubt on this point the recently enacted Trusts (Amendment) Jersey Law 1989 specifically provides that:

> 'if a person domiciled outside Jersey transfers or disposes of property during his lifetime to a trust
> (a) he shall be deemed to have had capacity to do so if he is at the time of such transfer or disposition of full age and of sound mind under the law of his domicile; and
> (b) no rule relating to inheritance or succession (including, but without prejudice to the generality of the foregoing, forced heirship, "*legitime*" or similar rights) of the law of his domicile or any other system of law shall affect any such transfer or disposition or otherwise affect the validity of such trust.'

4.273 For detailed knowledge of trust law in Jersey, reference should be made to Matthews and Sowden, *The Jersey Law of Trusts*, 3rd edn (1994).

Disadvantages of a settlement

4.274 The disadvantages of establishing a settlement are that the settlor loses the control of the administration of his assets, which will now be vested in the trustees, and that additional expenses are incurred in respect of the administration of the trust and the payment of trustee fees during the lifetime of the settlor. For the latter reason, a settlement will usually be justified only if the assets situate in Jersey are of sufficient value.

4.275 It should also be noted that the creation of a Jersey settlement may not be entirely foolproof in defeating the claims of the heirs in the country of domicile, because if there are other assets situated in the country of the deceased's domicile, it is possible that the heirs in that jurisdiction could apply to their own courts to rule against the validity of the transfer to the Jersey settlement and to compensate them out of the other assets situate in the jurisdiction of the deceased's domicile.

4.276 Furthermore, if following the death of the settlor the trustees transfer trust assets to a beneficiary resident in the jurisdiction where the settlor was domiciled, it is possible that the dispossessed heirs might bring an action in the courts of that jurisdiction against that beneficiary to compensate themselves for the shares to which they would have been entitled under the law of the domicile.

JOINT OWNERSHIP

An alternative method of avoiding some of the problems associated with applying for a grant of representation in Jersey would be to have the Jersey assets vested in two or more names jointly. On the death of any of the persons in whose joint names the assets are vested, the share of the deceased person would automatically accrue to the survivor or survivors by virtue of the *jus accrescendi* without any need for a grant of representation. 4.277

Note that clear words are required to create joint ownership which confers the *jus accrescendi* on the survivor, as opposed to ownership in common which does not. See para **4.224** in the foregoing section dealing with the administration of estates. 4.278

Furthermore, whereas under English law a beneficial joint tenancy can be severed unilaterally by a joint tenant this is not possible under Jersey law. Joint ownership of Jersey property can only be converted into ownership in common by agreement of the joint owners, except that under Jersey insolvency law the court can sever the ownership into equal or unequal shares upon the insolvency of a joint owner. Careful consideration is needed, therefore, before placing property into joint ownership because of the problems if the joint owners subsequently fall out with each other. 4.279

6. TAXES ON DEATH

The only tax levied in Jersey is income tax. The standard rate of income tax is 20% which has been enforced since 1940. Since 31 December 1983, it has been the only rate when the reduced rate of 10% for the first £250 of taxable income was abolished. 4.280

Income tax is charged on Jersey resident individuals, partnerships, companies and trustees in respect of worldwide profits and income, regardless of whether such profits or income are remitted to Jersey. There is statutory relief in the case of individuals who are resident but not ordinarily resident in Jersey so that foreign income not remitted to Jersey escapes taxation. Domicile is irrelevant. 4.281

Non-residents are taxed only in respect of Jersey source income but, by concession, Jersey bank interest paid to non-residents is not taxed. This concession now applies to an attorney of an Executor of an estate of a deceased non-resident in respect of interest which arose from the date appearing on the Grant of the Jersey Probate to the date of distribution of the estate. This concession applies only where the death of the non-resident falls after 31 December 1992. 4.282

Special rules apply to companies incorporated in Jersey but which are in the beneficial ownership of non-residents. Since 31 December 1988, all companies incorporated in Jersey have been resident in Jersey for tax purposes but collective investment funds and companies in the beneficial ownership of non-residents have been able to elect for exempt company status on payment of a fee of £500 and the effect of that election is to make them non-resident for Jersey income tax 4.283

purposes. They are still liable to income tax in respect of Jersey source income other than bank interest. Subject to these rules, there is no separate system for the taxation of Jersey resident companies.

4.284 Capital gains are not subject to tax in Jersey. Any attempts to artificially turn income into capital will probably be challenged by the Comptroller under the blanket anti avoidance provisions. There is no value added tax in Jersey and no inheritance tax or gift taxes are chargeable either. There is no stamp duty in Jersey other than in respect of immovable property or in respect of the obtaining of a Grant of Probate or Letters of Administration as is referred to in para **4.197** above.

4.285 This chapter is believed to contain a correct summary of the law as it stands at the time of writing (April 1997). However, this chapter is only intended as a brief guide, and is not intended to be a complete exposition of what is a complex and involved subject.

ISLE OF MAN †

1. INTRODUCTION

The administration of estates in the Isle of Man is in a number of respects similar to that in England. Practitioners should not fall into the trap of believing that the law in the Isle of Man is exactly the same because it does differ from English law in a number of material ways. 4.286

As in England, the estate of a deceased person vests in his personal representatives rather than in the persons who inherit the estate. The personal representatives are responsible for administering the estate (collecting the assets, paying debts and taxes, etc). On completion of the administration the beneficiaries are entitled to receive the remaining assets. 4.287

Jurisdiction in relation to wills and the administration of estates is vested in the High Court of Justice of the Isle of Man (Common Law Division, Testamentary Jurisdiction). This Court also has authority to grant probate. 4.288

The first part of this chapter deals with the administration of the estate and the second part deals with succession rights in the Island.

In this chapter, the term 'personal representatives' will refer to either the 'executors' of a deceased person's will (the person appointed by the will to administer the estate) or the 'administrators' of a deceased person's estate (a person appointed by the court to administer the estate where there is no will or where the executors appointed by the will do not prove the will). 4.289

In Manx law, the first duty of an executor is to deal with the funeral arrangements. 4.290

2. GRANT OF REPRESENTATION

If a person dies leaving a valid will, he is classified as dying 'testate' and the executors apply to the High Court for a 'grant of probate', ie an order of the court confirming their authority to make title to and gain control of the assets of a deceased person. If there is no dispute in relation to the estate, then the court 4.291

---

† This chapter was written by Neil Morris of Eversheds, Senator House, 85 Queen Victoria Street, London EC4V 4JL, tel 0171 919 4500, fax 0171 919 4919, with the assistance of John Wright of Simmocks, Douglas, Isle of Man.

performs a purely administrative function without requiring any appearance by the executors in court.

4.292 If the deceased does not leave a will, he dies 'intestate' and in this case the court grants 'letters of administration'. A grant of letters of administration is also issued if the deceased has left a will but there are no executors (eg because the deceased has failed to appoint executors or because the appointed executors have died or are unwilling to act). This is known as a 'grant of letters of administration with the will annexed'.

4.293 Grants of probate and letters of administration are referred to in this chapter as grants of representation.

4.294 Where there is a valid will and it is uncontested, the appropriate procedure is for a petition to the court to be lodged and dealt with by the Chief Registrar. Where a will is contested, or if a *caveat* has been lodged in the court which is still subsisting, the will must be proved in 'solemn form' before the Deemster (the Isle of Man term for Judge). No grant of representation can issue within seven days of the death.

4.295 The documents which must be submitted to the court are:

(1) the petition,
(2) an affidavit in support setting out details of the deceased, and the amount of the estate,
(3) an oath sworn by the applicant verifying the facts stated in the application,
(4) an undertaking by the applicant to perform the duties of an executor, and
(5) the original will (exhibited to the oath). In addition, the death certificate must be lodged in court together with such other papers as the court may require.

4.296 The probate papers if sworn in the Isle of Man must be sworn before a Commissioner for Oaths or a Justice of the Peace. If they are signed outside the Isle of Man, the papers have to be sworn before a notary public or other person authorised to administer oaths.

4.297 The entitlement to a grant of representation depends on whether or not the deceased died 'domiciled' in the Island. The concept of domicile is the same as under English law (see paras **1.7–1.14**) except that the date after which a married woman is able to have a separate domicile from that of her husband is January 1975.

CASES WHERE DECEASED DIED DOMICILED IN THE ISLAND

4.298 Where the deceased left a will, the person entitled to apply for a grant of probate is the executor. His duty is to 'prove' the will which means he must satisfy the court that the will is valid.

If for any reason the person named as executor in the will does not prove it, a 'grant of letters of administration with the will annexed' may be applied for by any person who has any interest under the will, by a creditor of the deceased or by any person having no interest under the will but who would have been entitled to a grant of letters of administration if the deceased had died intestate. 4.299

If more than one executor is appointed by the will and not all executors named wish to prove the will, the non-proving executor can either renounce probate or a grant of probate can be issued to the executors who wish to act (the proving executors) with power reserved to the non-proving executor to prove the will in the future if circumstances so require. The application must state that notice of the application for probate has been given to the named executor to whom power is reserved. 4.300

Where the deceased does not leave a will, the persons who wish to administer the estate make an application to the court for a grant of letters of administration. The application must be made with notice to all persons within the Island who take beneficially under the law of intestacy. If no person has a beneficial interest in the estate the Attorney-General is entitled to apply for a grant if he claims the estate on behalf of the Treasury. A creditor may also apply. 4.301

In granting letters of administration the court must have regard to the rights of all persons interested in the estate of the deceased. Until letters of administration are issued the estate vests in the Treasury. When the grant is issued the estate vests in the administrators by operation of law. 4.302

The court in granting administration may require one or more sureties to guarantee that they will make good within a limit imposed by the court any loss which any person interested in the administration of the deceased's estate may suffer if there is a breach by the administrator of any of his duties. Any guarantee given will be for the benefit of any person interested in the estate although no action can be brought in respect of the guarantee without the leave of the court. Normally, the surety is an approved company trading in the Island or two suitable individual persons. 4.303

When the person entitled to apply for the grant of administration is resident outside the Island, it is possible for a grant to be taken by an attorney administrator with the will annexed for the use and benefit of the executor or administrator, provided that, where the person entitled is an executor, administration is not granted to an attorney without notice to the other executors. 4.304

CASES WHERE DECEASED WAS DOMICILED OUTSIDE THE ISLE OF MAN

Where the deceased was domiciled outside the Isle of Man, the court may order that a grant of representation be issued to the person entrusted with the administration of the estate by the court having jurisdiction at the place where the deceased died domiciled. If there is no such person, then the court may issue a grant to the person beneficially entitled to the estate by the law of the place where 4.305

the deceased died domiciled or, if there is more than one beneficiary, to such of them as the court directs. Alternatively, if circumstances so require, the court may issue a grant to such other person as it directs.

4.306 In any event, where probate has been issued in another jurisdiction and where the will is in the English language, probate can be issued to the executor named therein. In addition, if the will describes the duties of a named person in terms sufficient to constitute him as an executor according to the tenor of the will, then probate can be issued to that person.

4.307 If the only estate in the Island is immovable property, a grant limited to such property can be made in accordance with Manx law as if the deceased had died domiciled in the Island.

4.308 In all cases where the deceased was not domiciled in the Island at death, it is necessary to establish that the will is formally valid and an affidavit to support its formal validity will have to be produced to the court. The Wills Act 1985 provides that a will will be treated as property signed if its signature conforms to the law in force in any one or more of the following:

(1) the territory where it was signed;
(2) the territory where at the time it was signed or of the testator's death he was domiciled or had his habitual residence; or
(3) a state of which at the time of the signature of the will or of the testator's death he was a national.

4.309 If the will is in a foreign language, it will be necessary to have a certified translation of the will. If the personal representatives claim that the will is valid in the country of the deceased's habitual residence or domicile, it will be necessary to obtain an affidavit of law from a qualified person from that jurisdiction unless there is a grant of representation from the jurisdiction in question when an affidavit of law will not usually be necessary.

4.310 If the will is proved in any court outside the Island and the original cannot be produced to the High Court, an office copy of the will sealed and certified by the foreign court must be produced to the High Court instead.

3. THE WILL

4.311 Under Manx law, any person who is aged 18 years or more and who is of sound mind may make a will. The will must be in writing and signed by the testator (the person making the will) or by some other person in his presence and by his direction. It must appear that the testator intended by his signature to give effect to the will and his signature must be made or acknowledged by him in the presence of two or more witnesses present at the same time who must sign and attest the will or acknowledge his signature in the presence of the testator. There are special rules for soldiers' and sailors' wills.

The Isle of Man has adopted the International Wills Convention relating to international wills and the persons authorised to act in connection with international wills in the Isle of Man are Manx advocates. International wills which are made under the convention must be accompanied by a certificate in support of it in the form set out in Article 10 of Schedule 2 to the Wills Act 1985. 4.312

4. ASSETS NOT COVERED BY A GRANT OF REPRESENTATION

As in England, certain assets do not vest in the personal representatives. 4.313

(1) *Joint assets.* The surviving owner(s) of jointly held assets automatically become entitled to the assets following the first death. In each case, it is necessary to check that the asset held in the name of more than one person is actually 'joint' property (as distinct from property held in separate shares). There is a presumption of Manx law in favour of property held in separate shares. Unless a conveyance of land to joint owners has the phrase 'as joint tenants and not tenants in common' it is likely that ordinary domestic property will be owned as tenants in common (property held in separate undivided shares).

(2) *Trust assets.* If the deceased was a beneficiary of a trust then the assets themselves will be held in the name of or on behalf of the trustees. The assets do not form part of his estate as they devolve in accordance with the terms of the trust. 4.314

(3) *Assets outside the Isle of Man.* The Manx grant of representation will only apply to assets under the control of the Manx Court. It will usually be necessary to obtain a separate grant of probate in other parts of the world including the United Kingdom if the deceased owned assets outside the Isle of Man. In each case, advice must be taken on local law. 4.315

(4) *Life policies.* Often, life policies are written in trust for a named person and as such the proceeds do not become payable to the personal representative of the deceased: the Manx grant of representation will not be a document of title to such assets. Similarly, under the terms of some companies' pension schemes, death in service benefits are payable to dependants of a deceased employee and these assets do not form part of the deceased's estate and will be paid to the ultimate beneficiaries without production of a Manx grant of representation. 4.316

5. ADMINISTRATION OF THE ESTATE

After the grant of representation is issued, the personal representatives are under a duty to collect and get in the assets comprising the movable and immovable estate of the deceased, and to administer them in accordance with the law. Provided the estate is solvent, this involves settling all liabilities of the deceased and payment of all administration expenses, payment of legacies and distributing 4.317

the net residue of the estate to those persons entitled under the terms of the will or under the law of intestacy.

COLLECTION OF ASSETS

4.318 The personal representatives have full power to deal with the deceased's assets both movable and immovable situate on the Island. They can operate bank accounts, buy and sell shares or land or any other assets of the estate. They can give good receipts and settle disputes relating to the estate. Persons dealing with the personal representatives only have to see the grant of representation to satisfy themselves as to whom they should be paying monies due to the estate and who should be signing sale documents in relation to the disposal of assets in the estate. The personal representative cannot be held responsible for any assets other than those which come into his hands or which would have done so but for his default.

PAYMENT OF DEBTS

4.319 The assets of the deceased are available for the payment of his debts and liabilities of the estate. Any provision in the will directing that particular assets are not to be available to meet debts and liabilities is void as against the creditors of the deceased.

4.320 The personal representatives are responsible for paying all valid debts to the extent of assets which come into their hands or which should have come into their hands but for their own breach of duty. The personal representatives should be careful to ensure that they have ascertained details of all debts before they can safely distribute assets to beneficiaries. Section 26 of the Trustee Act 1961 provides that if a notice to claimants against a deceased's estate is given in two newspapers circulating in the Isle of Man, stating that the estate will be distributed two months after the date of the notice having regard only to those claims of which the personal representatives had notice at that date, then if a proper claim arises after the assets have been distributed the creditor cannot hold the personal representatives personally liable, although they can follow the estate assets into the hands of the beneficiaries. The creditor retains this right until the statutory period for limitation of actions elapses.

4.321 The Administration of Estates Act 1990 contains detailed provisions governing the administration of estates which are insolvent but these are outside the scope of this work.

4.322 The personal representatives have serious responsibilities to both creditors and the beneficiaries of the estate. They must take all reasonable steps to collect in the assets of the deceased and protect them and they must obtain the best price they can for assets which are sold. Personal representatives should seek professional advice and if it is necessary to litigate to collect or protect assets they are legally obliged to do so. Executors are liable to the beneficiaries of the estate if they fail properly to carry out their duties.

Personal representatives have power to appropriate assets to the interest of a particular beneficiary of the estate provided they do not prejudice any specific gift made in the will of the deceased. For the purpose of appropriation, the personal representative may fix the value of the respective parts of the estate and the liabilities of the deceased as he thinks fit but he is well advised to employ a qualified valuer in any case where that may be necessary. Once an asset is appropriated it can be conveyed or assented to the beneficiary. The person receiving the appropriated asset must consent to the appropriation. 4.323

Many of the powers given to the personal representatives may be varied by the terms of the will and this should always be checked. When the administration of the estate is complete it is usual for the personal representatives to prepare a full set of estate accounts which provide details of the assets of the deceased at death together with liabilities and administration expenses, and of the distribution of the estate. 4.324

6. PROBATE JURISDICTION

The Manx court has power to grant representation to a deceased person's estate even if there was no estate subsisting in the Isle of Man at the date of death, although there would have to be a good reason why probate should be issued in these circumstances. Unless the grant of probate is restricted to Manx property or to specific assets such as immovable property, the wording of the grant is wide enough to extend to worldwide estate. In practice, local law in many countries requires that a separate grant of probate be obtained in those countries. 4.325

7. SUCCESSION TO ESTATES

As in England, domicile is the crucial factor determining devolution to a person's movable estate. Manx law does not have the concept of community of property and spouses own their own property under Manx law. Foreign law is often relevant where the person dies domiciled outside the Isle of Man. 4.326

WHERE THE DECEASED DIED TESTATE

Where there is a will the personal representatives are responsible for ensuring that the assets of the deceased devolve in accordance with the terms of the will. Where the deceased died domiciled in the Isle of Man, Manx law will govern devolution of worldwide movable property and of immovable property situate in the Isle of Man, and the terms of the will should be followed in relation to such property. If immovable property is situate outside the Island, it will devolve in accordance with the law of the country where it is situate (although sometimes that law will recognise the provisions of the Manx will or the Manx law of intestacy). 4.327

4.328 The distinction between movable and immovable property is the same as in England. Broadly, land and buildings are immovable and all other assets are movable. Immovable property subject to a contract of sale is movable property.

4.329 Where the deceased died domiciled outside the Island, devolution of movable property is governed by the law of the country of domicile of the deceased at death. Such foreign law may or may not recognise the provisions of a Manx will. In any event, devolution of immovable property situate in the Island is governed by Manx law irrespective of the domicile of the deceased. Accordingly, any rights to forced heirship (rights given to stated relatives of a deceased to a fixed part of the estate) will be defeated in relation to such immovable property if they do not accord with the terms of the will or the Manx law of intestacy.

4.330 Under Manx law, there is complete freedom of testamentary disposition and any person can benefit under the terms of a will. It is possible to set up trusts in a will which benefit individuals or charities, as well as setting up purpose trusts. There are detailed guidelines relating to purpose trusts which need to be followed. There are no specific statutory requirements that any particular part of the estate must be bequeathed or devised to surviving spouse or issue. However, a person who witnesses the will or whose spouse witnesses the will cannot take any benefit under it unless the will is validly executed without the attestation by such beneficiary.

4.331 Although there is complete freedom of testamentary disposition, the Inheritance (Provision for Family and Dependants) Act 1982 does allow certain family members and dependants to make a claim for reasonable provision from the estate of a testator or an intestate person, who dies domiciled in the Isle of Man. The protected class includes any spouse or child of the deceased or any former spouse of the deceased who has not remarried. The measure of provision for a spouse is higher than for any other claimant. There is no fixed level of provision for any class of claimant because the court has to take into account a number of factors including the financial resources and needs of all applicants and beneficiaries of the estate, any obligations and responsibilities the deceased had towards the applicant, the size of the estate and any disability of any party.

4.332 Any claim must be made within six months from the date of the grant of representation unless the court extends this time-limit. In considering the estate for the purposes of this Act the court can include any gift made by the deceased immediately before and in contemplation of death and any property jointly held prior to death. The operation of this Act cannot be negated by will or by a lifetime contract.

4.333 A will is automatically revoked if the testator subsequently marries, although any disposition in a will exercising a power of appointment takes effect notwithstanding the marriage unless the property appointed would pass to his personal representatives but for the appointment. An exception to this is where the will was made in contemplation of the marriage. Similarly, if a disposition in a will made by a person expecting to be married is intended to survive the marriage it will do so. Wills may also be revoked by a subsequent valid will, by writing declaring an intention to revoke the will, executed in a similar manner to a will or by burning, tearing or other destruction by the testator or some person in his presence at his direction. A will is not revoked by the mere intention of the testator that it should be because of a change in circumstances.

Where a testator is divorced or his marriage is annulled after a will is signed, the will takes effect as if the former spouse had died on the date of the divorce or annulment. Thus any appointment of the former spouse as executor, trustee or guardian will be ineffective, and any gift to the former spouse will pass as if the spouse had died before the testator, unless there is a contrary intention expressed in the will. This does not prejudice in any way the former spouse's right to apply for financial provision under the Inheritance (Provision for Family and Dependants) Act 1982. **4.334**

WHERE THE DECEASED DIED INTESTATE

Manx law provides a detailed code as to who can inherit the estate. The devolution of movable property is in accordance with the law of the country of the deceased's domicile whereas Manx intestacy law applies to devolution of Manx immovable property. The order in which an estate devolves on intestacy under Manx law for deaths after 1 April 1994 is as follows: **4.335**

(1) if the deceased leaves a spouse who survives him by 14 days, but no issue, the whole of the estate passes to the surviving spouse; **4.336**

(2) if the deceased leaves a spouse who survives him by 14 days and issue (lineal descendants) then the surviving spouse takes the following assets: **4.337**
  (a) personal chattels;
  (b) the first £125,000 of the estate (before 1 April 1994, £75,000) free of duties and costs and one half of the residuary estate. The other half is held on statutory trusts for the issue. The legacy of £125,000 carries interest currently at a rate of 6% (before 1 April 1994, 9%) from the date of death until the date of payment;

(3) if the deceased leaves issue but no spouse the whole estate is held on statutory trusts for the issue; **4.338**

(4) if there is no spouse and no issue the estate passes to the parents of the deceased or the surviving parent outright; **4.339**

(5) if there is no spouse, issue or parent, the estate passes in the following order: **4.340**
  (a) on statutory trusts for the brothers and sisters of the whole blood of the deceased and, if none
  (b) on statutory trusts for the brothers and sisters of the half blood of the deceased and, if none
  (c) for the grandparents of the deceased and, if none
  (d) uncles and aunts of the whole blood of the deceased and, failing them, uncles and aunts of the half blood of the deceased and, if none
  (e) great-aunts and great-uncles of the whole blood of the deceased and, failing them, great-aunts and great-uncles of the half blood of the deceased.

4.341 If there are no living relatives as listed above, then the estate passes to the Treasury as *bona vacantia*. The Treasury is, however, empowered to provide from the estate for dependants of the deceased or for persons for whom the deceased might reasonably be expected to make provision.

4.342 The distribution of the estate under the law of intestacy is of course subject to any claim which may be made under the Inheritance (Provision for Family and Dependants) Act 1982. Where part or all of the estate is held on statutory trusts, it is held in equal shares for the child or children of the deceased who attain 18 years or marry under that age and for the issue of any such child or children living at the death of the intestate who attain 18 years or marry under that age if the child of the deceased pre-deceased him. No issue is permitted to take any part of the estate if his parent is alive at the death of the deceased. Children of the deceased must bring into account assets received from the deceased in his lifetime or settled by the deceased on the child by way of advancement or on marriage, when their interest in the estate of the deceased is distributed unless any contrary intention is expressed by the deceased or inferred from the circumstances of the case.

4.343 There are provisions under Manx intestacy law which enable the surviving spouse who is resident at the time of death of the deceased in a house comprised in the estate of the deceased to notify the personal representatives in writing within one year of the issuing of the grant of representation that he/she wishes the personal representatives to appropriate to her or him the interest of the deceased in the house as part satisfaction of the £125,000 statutory legacy. This right ceases on the death of the surviving spouse within the 12-month period. This right is not available where the deceased owned a tenancy in the property which had less than two years to run from the date of death of the deceased or where the interest was a tenancy which the landlord could terminate by notice within two years of death. In certain circumstances, the consent of the Manx Court is required.

4.344 In any event, during the first 12 months following the death of the deceased, the personal representatives cannot dispose of the deceased's interest in the house (except in the course of administration owing to want of other assets) without the written consent of the surviving spouse.

4.345 In some cases a partial intestacy arises where a valid will fails to dispose of all the assets of the deceased. If this arises where a spouse and issue survive the deceased the surviving spouse must bring into account any benefit received under the will in computing the legacy of £125,000 given to her.

8. CONFLICTS OF LAW

4.346 This chapter has been concerned mainly with Manx domestic law. Conflict of law questions clearly can arise in relation to such matters as community of property, forced heirship and *renvoi*. The law in this area is not well developed in the Isle of Man but one can be reasonably confident that the approach of the Manx courts will be the same as in England and Ireland.

9. MINIMISING PROBLEMS WHERE FOREIGN ELEMENTS ARE INVOLVED

The comments made in paras **4.59** to **4.63** in relation to English law apply equally to the Isle of Man. 4.347

10. TAXES ON DEATH

There are no death duties or capital taxes arising in the Island on or by reason of death. There may, of course, be such taxes in other jurisdictions, but actions for the recovery of these taxes will not normally be entertained by the Manx courts. 4.348

11. RULES OF INTESTACY

where the deceased was domiciled in England and Wales

	Distribution of Estate	Those who can apply for a Grant of Letters of Administration†
Surviving spouse AND		
No children or remoter issue, parent, brother or sister of the whole blood or their issue.	All to surviving spouse.	Surviving spouse.
Children or remoter issue and estate not exceeding £125,000.	All to surviving spouse.	Surviving spouse.
Children or remoter issue estate exceeding £125,000.	Surviving spouse takes personal chattels, £125,000 free of Inheritance Tax and costs with interest at 6% until paid and income of half the residue for life. The children take half the residue absolutely and if more than one in equal shares and the other half of the residue on the surviving parent's death.*‡	Surviving spouse and a child.
No children or remoter issue but parents, brothers or sisters of whole blood – estate exceeding £200,000.	Surviving spouse takes personal chattels, £200,000 free of Inheritance Tax and costs with interest at 6% and one-half of residue absolutely. The other half goes to parents absolutely or if no parents, to brothers and sisters of the whole blood in equal shares.*‡	Surviving spouse.

No Surviving Spouse AND		
Children or remoter issue.	Children (including illegitimate children) or remoter issue in equal shares on attaining 18 years or marryng under that age.*	Children (including illegitimate children).
No children or remoter issue but father or mother.	Father or mother.	Father or mother.
No children or remoter issue but father and mother.	Father and mother in equal shares.	Either or both father and mother.
No children or remoter issue and no parent.	1. Brothers and sisters of the whole blood in equal shares;*‡ but if no person takes interest then 2. Brothers and sisters of half blood in equal shares;*‡ but if no person takes interest then 3. Grandparents in equal shares; but if none survive then 4. Uncles and aunts who are brothers and sisters of a parent*‡ but if no person takes interest then 5. Uncles and aunts who are brothers and sisters of the half blood of a parent.*‡	A person entitled to share in the estate.

No person with an interest under these Rules	ALL TO CROWN (which may waive its rights in the face of a particularly strong moral claim by some person – eg 'common-law' wife of long standing or stepchildren). OR to the Duchy of Cornwall if the deceased died resident in Cornwall.	Treasury Solicitor Solicitor for Duchy of Cornwall or
	OR to the Duchy of Lancaster if the deceased died in any area belonging to the Duchy.	Solicitor for the Duchy of Lancaster

Notes

* If a member of a class marked in this way predeceases the intestate leaving children, those children take between them the share which their deceased parent would have taken.

‡ The inheritance of a member of a class marked in this way fails if he or she does not attain 18 years or marry under that age.

† Creditors may apply for a Grant if all persons having a prior right to the grant have renounced or been cleared off.

Unless the contrary appears in the table, the inheritance is absolute, not conditional or for life.

Where a beneficiary under these rules is under 18, his share is held on statutory trusts until he attains 18.

To inherit under these rules a person need be alive only at the intestate's death (not when the estate is wound up), and 'alive' includes conceived but not yet born (except a child born dead). The exception to this rule is that of the surviving spouse, who must survive the intestate by a period of 28 days in order to benefit. If the surviving spouse does not survive for 28 days, the rules operate as if he or she had not survived the intestate.

If the deceased left a will which did not effectively dispose of all his assets, these rules apply to the undistributed part as if there were no other estate and he had died completely intestate.

Where the estate falls to be divided between a class of people with the same relationship to the deceased the estate is divided equally between all the members of that class.

Deeds of Variation or Disclaimer can be used on intestacies to avoid or lessen Inheritance Tax by rearranging the distribution of the estate.

CHAPTER 5

DENMARK†

1. INTRODUCTION

Originally, Danish inheritance law only allowed relatives to inherit because it did not allow wills or inheritance by spouses. However, rules gradually developed allowing a spouse to inherit and allowing property to be disposed of on death by will. The '*Austerische Bürgerliche Gesetzbuch*' from 1811 was adapted in 1845 as Danish inheritance law and modified until the present Inheritance Act of 31 March 1963. Under the new Act, as amended, the only heirs who are entitled to a reserved minimum part of the deceased's estate are descendants and the spouse who often also has a right of '*usus fructus*' as well, ie a usufruct. 5.1

A new Act on Probate was adopted on 22 May 1996 with effect from 1 January 1997. No automatic transmission of title to the heirs occurs: they obtain title from the estate which is considered an independent entity. The estate must file an opening balance and an account from the date of the death until the distribution of the assets, whereupon a balance has to be made showing the distribution between the heirs. Further, estates over DKK 1,000,000 (approx) are subject to tax and have to file tax returns. Denmark applies unity of succession and, accordingly, the estate comprises all the assets of the deceased if he had 'venue' in Denmark which for practical purposes may be considered as habitual residence. Danish law does not distinguish between 'domicile' and 'residence' as under English law. 5.2

2. MATRIMONIAL PROPERTY REGIME

Because it is only the assets of the deceased that pass on to his successors, it has to be established which assets were owned by the deceased and, accordingly, the matrimonial property regime is important if the deceased was married upon his death. If a married deceased did not make a marriage contract, community of property exists between the spouses. Within such community of property are all assets acquired by the spouses before and during the marriage. Upon death the community of property has to be dissolved. Each spouse's assets, less liabilities, form his net part of the community of property. A positive net part is divided equally between the spouses. This way of accounting is relevant only if one spouse's net assets are negative, since it then has the effect that the other spouse is not liable for the liabilities of the first mentioned spouse. In the event that both 5.3

† This chapter was written by J Qviste of Ronne & Lundgren, 1 Midtermolen, PO Box 889, DK–2100 Copenhagen, Denmark, tel (45) 39 25 25 35, fax (45) 35 25 25 36.

spouses have positive net parts, half of the community of property belongs to the deceased.

5.4 A spouse may renounce the right to half of the net part. The renunciation is not subject to formalities, but may be invalid if the renouncing spouse was not able to evaluate the consequences.

5.5 Outside the scope of the community of property are assets belonging to the spouses by virtue of a marriage contract between them or by the decision of a testator or donor in connection with inheritance or gifts. A marriage contract can be set up both before or during the marriage. The marriage contract has to be registered in the Central Register of marriage contracts which is situated at the court of Aarhus. Matrimonial contracts entered into between spouses not resident in Denmark made under foreign law remain valid when the spouses take up residence in Denmark. However, they are only valid against third parties if registered within one month of the spouses having taken up habitual residence in Denmark or, if registered later, only from the time of registration.

3. TYPES OF MARRIAGE CONTRACT

5.6 The spouses may decide by marriage contract that part or all of the assets shall not form part of the community of property but remain the separate property of the relevant spouse. The contract may provide that separate property shall only be applicable in the event of marriage dissolution by divorce: this is called 'divorce' separate property. Thus on death, applying the rules mentioned above, it becomes possible for the surviving spouse to take over the estate as undivided estate (dealt with in s 5 below). It is also possible to agree that property will be separate whether the marriage is dissolved by divorce or by death: this is called 'complete' separate property. 'Complete' separate property and 'divorce' separate property may be combined: it may even be agreed that the belongings of the surviving spouse are going to be 'divorce' separate property, thus making it possible for the surviving spouse to keep his assets while the deceased spouse's assets are subject to probate and considered community of property, so giving the surviving spouse a right to keep half of it before the remainder is divided.

5.7 The marriage contract may apply to all assets or specified assets as well as a fraction of the net assets and may be limited in time.

5.8 As described above, it is possible by a marriage contract to reduce the effect of the rules of forced minimum parts which apply only to assets not excluded from the deceased's estate by virtue of a marriage contract. Most gifts between spouses have to be made by a marriage contract which is registered in the court and available to the public as described above.

4. THE SURVIVING SPOUSE

Assets that have served exclusively for the personal use of the surviving spouse or children may be distributed to the surviving spouse in advance of probate in the case of small estates. Children under 21 have the right to an amount to secure maintenance and education if it is required. Unless otherwise provided for in the deceased's will, the surviving spouse has first right to specific items and real estate. If their value exceeds his or her inheritance part, such spouse is entitled to pay the difference. The spouse is always entitled to at least DKK 150,000. 5.9

5. DANISH INHERITANCE LAW

According to Danish law, the world-wide assets of a deceased pass irrespective of the location of the movable and immovable property. The Danish legal system is concerned with the manner of administration and distribution of the estate. However, if the deceased left immovables abroad which under the *lex situs* are not distributed according to Danish law, Danish law will accept the application of the foreign system. 5.10

Insurance policies of whatever kind are as a main rule included in the estate when calculating the inheritance parts unless the beneficiary designated by the deceased in the insurance policy has been appointed as the beneficiary or is a descendant or spouse of the deceased. 5.11

An estate of a deceased individual without habitual residence in Denmark may apply to the Ministry of Justice for permission to deal with the estate – fully or partly – if the deceased was a Danish citizen and the relevant assets are not being dealt with abroad. The Ministry will refer the estate to the most appropriate court of probate. If the deceased was not a Danish resident then the authorised person under the relevant *lex successionis* (eg the executor of an English domiciliary) can deal with the Danish part of the estate without seeking any permission or any Danish probate. 5.12

Currently, children born within or outside marriage inherit as do adopted children, the latter thereby losing their legal right to inheritance from their biological parents. Different provisions still apply for adoptions and children born out of marriage more than a generation ago. 5.13

Upon registration two persons, of the same sex, may apply the rules applicable to married couples with regard to matrimonial regime and to inheritance law. 5.14

CONDITIONS FOR INHERITANCE

The heir must be alive at the time of the death of the deceased in order to inherit from him. An unborn child inherits if born alive. Where two persons inheriting from each other die and it cannot be decided who predeceased the other, neither are deemed to have survived the other. 5.15

5.16 An heir convicted of killing the deceased may, according to the decision of the court, lose his right to inheritance and a man does not inherit from his child if he is convicted of a rape that led to the child's birth.

5.17 Legally separated or divorced spouses do not inherit from each other.

DISTRIBUTION RULES ON INTESTACY

5.18 If a married person dies intestate without leaving issue, the spouse will be the only heir. In the event that the surviving spouse dies without leaving issue the estate is divided in two equal parts, each part being attributed to the heirs of each spouse. In the event that only one spouse leaves heirs they inherit the entire estate. If the deceased only leaves issue, they inherit from him in equal shares *per stirpes* (ie in the event that an heir has died before the deceased, the descendant of such predeceased heir will take his place as heir).

5.19 If the deceased leaves spouse and issue the spouse will inherit one-third of his estate and his children will inherit two-thirds in equal shares *per stirpes.*

5.20 If the deceased was unmarried and leaves no descendants, each of his parents will inherit half of his estate. If one of his parents has died the inheritance of such parent will be distributed among his descendants *per stirpes.* If one of the parents has predeceased and leaves no descendants, the other parent or his descendants will inherit everything.

5.21 If both parents have died without leaving descendants, the estate is divided in four parts and allocated to the grandparents. In the event that one grandparent has died his share is distributed between his children but not his grandchildren. If he has not left any children, his share is allocated to his spouse or his spouse's children or if they are deceased the other grandparents and their children. In default of the above rules, the state will inherit the estate. By long-term concession the state may renounce its right in favour of individuals close to the deceased.

Minimum inheritance parts

5.22 In the event that an individual leaves a spouse or issue he may only dispose of 50% of his estate by will. Otherwise no limitation exists. The term for the part of the spouse and/or descendants inheritance part which the deceased cannot allocate in his discretion is the 'minimum inheritance part'. These minimum inheritance parts are distributed in the same way as the intestacy parts mentioned above. In the event that no descendants are left the deceased may reduce the spouse's inheritance from 100% to 50%, and if no spouse is left the descendants' part from 100% to 50%. If both spouse and descendants are left the spouse's part may be reduced from one-third to one-sixth and the descendants' part from two-thirds to one-third.

5.23 The minimum inheritance of the descendants is divided in equal shares *per stirpes* and the minimum inheritance part may not be divided otherwise by will.

Concerning community of property, a spouse may not without the consent of the other spouse dispose by will of the matrimonial home and its appurtenant movables or real estate and tools forming part of the business of the other spouse. 5.24

In calculating the minimum inheritance parts no regard is paid to life-time gifts considered gifts completed *inter vivos*. 5.25

In case the deceased by will infringed upon the rights of the descendants or the surviving spouse to receive their mandatory portion, the offended party will upon challenging the will receive his minimum inheritance part and the necessary amount is deducted from the other heirs according to the understanding and interpretation of the will. 5.26

The surviving spouse's usufruct in the 'undivided estate'

In the event that the deceased was married and not separated and leaves common issue with the surviving spouse, he may postpone probate having '*usus fructus*' to the total community property and 'divorce' separate property of the estate which is called 'undivided estate'. In the event that the deceased leaves separate issue, the surviving spouse may only include their inheritance part in the undivided estate with their prior consent. The 'complete' separate property of the deceased is divided upon death. 5.27

The surviving spouse must not be bankrupt or unable to pay his debts as they fall due. 5.28

The surviving spouse may dispose *inter vivos* as an owner of all assets included in the undivided estate and has to assume the liabilities of the deceased. 5.29

The deceased may by will exclude the surviving spouse's right to undivided estate regarding the part of the estate of which he may dispose by will (one-quarter of the community of property). In the event that the intention of the testator cannot be construed from the will it is considered not to prejudice the right of the surviving spouse to take over the estate as undivided estate. The surviving spouse may by agreement renounce the right to undivided estate. 5.30

Succession in respect of undivided estate

The surviving spouse may submit the estate to probate. The undivided estate has to be submitted to probate in the event that the other heirs prove that the surviving spouse has materially reduced the estate by abusing her right of disposal in good faith, eg if she bought an excessive life annuity or made an excessively large gift. Further, it has to be divided in the event the spouse remarries. 5.31

Distribution of the assets of the undivided estate

In the event that the undivided estate is submitted to probate while the surviving spouse is alive, the estate of the deceased spouse is divided according to his will or the rules of intestacy between the heirs living at the time the estate is submitted to probate. In the event that the estate is submitted to probate after the death of the surviving spouse, no inheritance share is allocated to the surviving spouse, the 5.32

estate being divided into two equal parts and distributed between the heirs of the two spouses. In the event that the surviving spouse does not leave heirs the heirs of the predeceased spouse inherit the entire estate.

5.33 The surviving spouse may by will dispose of half of the community of property including individual items not disposed of by the deceased spouse. However, the right of disposal may be extended by the will of the deceased spouse.

6. WILLS

FORMAL VALIDITY: THE HAGUE CONVENTION

5.34 Denmark is party to the Hague Convention on wills and accordingly recognises foreign wills under that convention, ie if the will is formally valid according to the jurisdiction where the testator made the will, or according to the law of the state of which the testator is a citizen at the time of the will or when he died, or according to the law of the land where he had his habitual residence or domicile according to the *lex situs* definition of the 'domicile' at the time of his will or when he died, or according to the *lex situs* for real property.

FORMAL VALIDITY: DANISH LAW

5.35 Two forms of will exist under Danish law; the notary will and the witness will. Amendments to wills are sometimes called codicils. The same rules apply to codicils as to wills regarding validity. The title of the document is in itself immaterial. Two or more individuals may draw up a joint will without being related or necessarily inheriting from each other (mutual will).

5.36 A will is construed according to the intent of the testator, not necessarily giving the words their usual legal meaning.

Notary will

5.37 The notary will must be signed or acknowledged in front of a Danish notary. In each county jurisdiction the judge also serves as notary. In Danish embassies abroad a person is usually authorised as notary.

5.38 A copy of the will is kept in the central register of wills from which it can be acquired if the original will cannot be found for some reason. Unless otherwise proved, it is assumed that the will has not been revoked even though it cannot be found.

5.39 The other distinguishing feature of the notary will is that the testator is assumed to be mentally capable, and anybody claiming otherwise must satisfy the burden of proving otherwise.

Witness will

The will must be signed (or be acknowledged) in front of two witnesses who must be present and know that they are witnessing the signature of a will which should be written on the will above the witnesses' signatures. Excluded from being witnesses are heirs and their close relatives. 5.40

Emergency wills

These types of wills are only accepted in the event of illness or emergency where it is not possible to make a notary will or a witness will: they consist of the oral will and the holographic will. 5.41

The oral will can be told to two witnesses present at the same time who must as soon as possible write down the will and sign it. The holographic will must be written and signed by the testator lacking the possibility of calling in witnesses. 5.42

These two types of wills become null and void automatically if the testator for three months or more has had the possibility of making a notary or witness will. 5.43

CAPACITY

Competent to draw up wills are persons over 18 years or married if they are mentally capable. 5.44

INVALIDITY

A will can be fully or partly invalid if it contains illegal or obscene provisions, if the testator has been subject to threats of violence, fraud or the like in connection with the execution of the will, or he has been subject to a decisive misunderstanding in connection with provisions in the will. 5.45

REVOCATION

Unless otherwise agreed, a will may be revoked. No formality is required to revoke a will. In order to prove the revocation, it might be done in the presence of a notary who will keep a copy of the revocation in the Central Register of Wills. 5.46

A revocation of a joint will is only valid if the other testators are informed of the revocation. 5.47

In the event that spouses have made a mutual joint will without a provision for revocation the surviving spouse may dispose of half of the community of property. 5.48

RESTRICTED DISPOSITIONS

5.49 Danish law explicitly prohibits any *fideicommissum*. Prohibited *fideicommissa* are dispositions by which the testator leaves the estate or part of it to an heir on condition that the assets upon his death will pass to a specified successor. These dispositions are, however, allowed if they concern only one unborn generation.

TRUSTS AND DANISH LAW

5.50 The concept of trust is not part of Danish law. In some situations, however, Danish law allows arrangements which in many ways are similar to trusts. For instance it is possible to withhold the inheritance from the heir, making only the income from the inheritance available to the heir. However, the heir may upon his 25th birthday demand the minimum part of his inheritance. A bank has to be used to manage the investment of the minimum part of his inheritance, though any inheritance in excess of such part may be managed by someone other than a bank.

Denmark is not party to the Hague Convention on Trusts.

7. CONTRACTS REGARDING INHERITANCE

RENUNCIATION OF INHERITANCE

5.51 An individual may renounce all inheritance rights with or without reserving the inheritance rights of his issue. The renunciation has to be made to the testator. It can be made with or without consideration. The renunciation may be in favour of a spouse who has taken over the estate as undivided estate.

AGREEMENTS NOT TO MAKE OR REVOKE A WILL

5.52 A testator may agree (with or without consideration) not to revoke or not to draw up a will. The agreement has to be in the form of a will and has to be brought to the knowledge of the heir or an individual acting in the interest of the heir.

DISPOSITIONS OF INHERITANCE

5.53 An heir may not validly dispose of his inheritance including his share in an undivided estate until after the death of the person from whom he is inheriting.

8. GIFTS

As described above, life-time gifts are not included in the estate. A gift may be agreed to be an advance of an heir's inheritance, in which event it is added to the estate in calculating the inheritance parts and deducted from the inheritance part of the heir. 5.54

If the donor does not intend to give effect to the gift until after his death, or in the event the gift is made at a time when the donor knows his death is imminent, the gift will have to be made in the form of a will. 5.55

9. PROBATE

The estate is considered an independent entity for all purposes and may sue and be sued. Accordingly, there is no direct transfer of ownership from the deceased to the heirs. 5.56

The probate may be a private administration or an administration under an administrator (no longer called an executor). 5.57

The heirs, or in an undivided estate the surviving spouse, must make an announcement in the Official Gazette inviting claims by all creditors, with the effect that creditors who do not make a claim within eight weeks are precluded. 5.58

In order to legitimate the heirs as owners of the deceased's assets, a transcript from the court of probate has to be produced; and a final balance showing the distribution of the inheritance and an account from the deceased's death concerning income and expenditure have to be submitted to the court of probate when the inheritance has been distributed. 5.59

UNDIVIDED ESTATE

The surviving spouse submits the request to the court of probate which issues a declaration concerning the undivided estate. The surviving spouse then has to submit a list of assets and liabilities of the undivided estate within six months from the death. 5.60

10. PRIVATE INTERNATIONAL LAW

The law applicable to succession to the estate will be the law at the last 'venue' of the deceased being his habitual residence at the time of his death. One must, however, note that the heirs may unanimously choose Danish law for the probate. Denmark does not accept *renvoi* and accordingly Danish private international law does not refer to private international law of foreign countries. 5.61

5.62 In the event that the deceased left property abroad and it is divided according to special rules prescribed by the *lex rei situs* Danish law accepts this division. Private international law on the form of the will is governed by the Hague Convention on wills.

5.63 Danish law will not accept the creation of a *fideicommissum* of Danish real estate or property which will be kept in Denmark. It does have the concept of a family foundation (which has separate legal personality and a board of directors) but in the foundation one cannot provide a succession of beneficiaries for more than one generation.

5.64 Agreements concerning inheritance are subject to the same law as the inheritance. However, such an agreement might be upheld if it was valid by the law of the deceased's habitual residence at the time it was entered into.

5.65 Denmark has entered into a treaty with Norway, Sweden, Iceland and Finland concerning the estates' choice of law and jurisdictions.

JURISDICTION OF DANISH COURTS IN MATTERS OF SUCCESSION

5.66 The Danish court has jurisdiction over the world-wide estate in the event that the deceased had habitual residence in Denmark at the time of his death. In the event the deceased was a Danish national, it is possible to refer the estate to the Danish court of probate as already mentioned. The Danish court of probate will recognise a foreign probate even though the foreign probate only provides for the private distribution of the estate without any public authority intervening, as long as it complies with the rules of the country of probate.

II. DOMESTIC SUCCESSION LAW

5.67 Danish law recognises unity of succession, so that if a deceased dies habitually resident outside Denmark (eg in England) it will apply the foreign *lex successionis*. If this foreign law, like English law, is schismatic, applying the *lex situs* to foreign immovables, like Danish real estate, an old Danish decision is authority for rejection of any *renvoi* to Danish law and for rejection of any forced heirship claims under Danish Law. There is no problem over foreigners acquiring or inheriting Danish real estate although, because the trust concept does not exist in Danish law, there are serious problems where persons holding title to Danish property are supposed to be trustees. Strictly speaking, a separate Danish will for Danish assets is not crucially important but it can simplify and expedite matters if there is such a will in the Danish language using Danish terminology and avoiding the use of foreign legal concepts.

12. TAXES ON DEATH

INHERITANCE TAX

Transfers on death are subject to tax according to the Estate and Gift Tax Act (*Afgift af dødsboer og gaver*). Estate tax is payable when the estate is subject to probate in Denmark either because the deceased was domiciled in Denmark at the time of death or because the heirs have applied for probate in Denmark. 5.68

Property inherited from an estate abroad is not subject to tax in Denmark, apart from immovable property situated in Denmark which is always subject to estate tax upon the owner's death even if he was not resident in Denmark. 5.69

TAXABLE BASE

Estate tax is calculated on the net value of the estate. If the deceased was a resident of Denmark, all property of the deceased, wherever situated, is taxable property. However, a tax reduction or exemption may be granted with respect to foreign-*situs* immovable property if inheritance tax has been paid abroad. 5.70

If the deceased died resident outside Denmark, Danish estate tax is due only with respect to Danish-*situs* immovable property, including equipment and capital represented by property forming part of a permanent establishment in Denmark. 5.71

The general principle of Danish law is that estate tax is calculated on the fair market value of the property. Valuations are generally moderate. The authorities accept the official valuation for tax purposes ±15% for real estate. 5.72

RATES

The estate tax is calculated as 15% of the net value of the death estate. Assets received by the spouse of the deceased are exempt from estate tax provided the spouses were not separated at the time of death. 5.73

An additional estate tax of 25% is calculated on the values received by persons other than: 5.74

(1) the descendants of the deceased including adopted children, stepchildren and their descendants;
(2) the parents of the deceased;
(3) the spouse of the children or stepchildren of the deceased, irrespective of whether the child is alive or dead;
(4) persons who have shared the deceased's home in the two years preceding the death or before the deceased moved to an institution, such as an old people's home;
(5) the separated or divorced spouse of the deceased;

(6) children who have been supported by the deceased but not adopted and who have been living with the deceased continuously for at least five years (subject to certain other conditions).

5.75 The estate tax of 15% is calculated on the net value of the estate reduced by approximately 200,000 Dkr. Assets received by persons other than the above are subject to an additional estate tax of 25% of the total net value received by these other persons reduced by the estate tax of 15% resulting in an effective estate tax of 36.25%. No other reduction is granted. Certain payments from pensions and insurance policies are exempt from estate tax.

INCOME TAXATION ON THE ESTATE

5.76 Estates subject to probate in Denmark are regarded in Danish tax law as legal entities and are subject to estate income tax. The estate must use the same accounting year as the deceased. A tax return must be filed. The taxable base for a deceased's estate is the same as for individuals. The income tax rate is 50% (flat rate). The estate is entitled to a monthly relief of approximately 5,000 Dkr.

5.77 Estates with a value less than approximately 1,000,000 Dkr are not subject to estate income tax.

CHAPTER 6

FINLAND†

1. INTRODUCTION

Finland is a civil law country with a codified legislation. Much of the legislation concerning wills and inheritance can be traced back to the Swedish codified law of 1734.[1] Then codified law was divided into chapters (*balkar*), and that division has been maintained to the present day. The chapter on inheritance and wills has been amended several times. The present law (as amended) dates from 1966. 6.1

Most provisions are found in the chapter on inheritance and wills, but some are found scattered elsewhere in the legislation. Such provisions are for the most part special stipulations relating to a specific field of activity. In particular, one should note the tax laws relating to inheritance and gifts, in which the tax regime is set out and which therefore is of major importance. 6.2

The structure of the chapter on inheritance and wills is set out in an organised way with the provisions relating to the death of a person first, with subsequent provisions leading to the provisions dealing with the final disposition and division of the deceased's estate. 6.3

2. INTESTATE SUCCESSION

The legal rights of an heir commence with the death of a person and normally end when the property of the deceased has been legally divided. 6.4

The heirs are part owners of the deceased's estate, which comes into being at the death of a person. In addition to the heirs, participants in the estate may include the widow or widower and a universal successor. The estate is not in itself a legal person. The assets of the deceased do not pass into the ownership of the estate, but pass to the estate only in order to be managed by the participants in the estate. 6.5

The heirs may either administer the estate jointly or apply for a court appointee to become the administrator. They may also apply for a person to be authorised to divide the estate between the participants. Thus the administrator administers the estate and the appointee for the division of the estate divides the estate between the participants. It is sufficient that one of the participants decides that an administrator or person authorised to divide the estate be appointed. If, after such 6.6

---

† This chapter was written by associate professor G O Z Sundström of the University of Helsinki and the senior partner in the law firm of Nordic Law, Helsinki, tel 358 0 648711, fax 358 0 605043.

1 Finland was then one of the *landskap* (districts) of the Swedish Kingdom.

an appointment has been made, the heirs and participants in the estate wish to resume the administration or to divide the estate by voluntary agreement, this requires the consent of all the participants.

6.7 The right to succeed to a person's estate is not dependent on nationality. In this regard a foreigner in Finland has the same rights as Finnish citizens. However, an heir or a successor without right of domicile in the Åland Islands may not acquire ownership of real property situated on the Åland Islands unless he obtains an authorisation from the provincial government. This restriction does not concern direct heirs or a widow/widower. They can inherit real property even if they do not have a right of domicile in the Åland Islands.

6.8 If at the time of his death the deceased was a citizen of a Nordic country (ie Denmark, Finland, Iceland, Norway or Sweden) the law of the country in which he had his domicile (in the sense of habitual residence) at the time of death will be applied. There are some exceptions to this rule. In other cases, the law applicable is the law of the nationality of the deceased. In this event, the law applicable to the division of the estate is the law of nationality of the deceased.

ORDER OF SUCCESSION

6.9 In order to inherit from the deceased, it is a precondition that the participant be alive at the time of the deceased's death. However, if a child has been conceived but not yet born at the time of death of the deceased, the child is eligible to inherit.

6.10 The right to inherit is based on a specific order of succession and on the degree of consanguinity. The only exceptions relate to the position of the widow or widower and any adopted children. If no one in one group in the order of succession inherits, the right to inherit passes to the next group of blood relatives. The order of succession is given below.

Direct heirs

6.11 Direct heirs are those who are in direct line to the deceased. According to recent law, this includes adopted children. If a child died prior to the person whose estate is in question, the right to inherit passes to the issue of the deceased child. If there is no survivor in one line of heirs, the other lines of direct succession divide the property which would otherwise have gone to the extinct line of issue in equal parts.

Widows or widowers

6.12 A widow or widower is second to the direct issue of the deceased. If there is no direct issue, the widow or widower inherits alone. With some exceptions, if divorce proceedings have been commenced prior to the deceased's death the widow or widower is not entitled to inherit. A marital right to half the property of the married couple is not a precondition of the right to inherit.

The right of a spouse to inherit is subject to certain limitation. When the surviving spouse dies, any property remaining from the estate of the first spouse normally reverts to the successors of the first spouse. The property of the surviving spouse is thus divided between the relatives of the surviving spouse and the relatives of the first spouse with a secondary inheritance right. If there are no living members of one or other of the groups of persons entitled to inherit, the other group inherits the entire property. It is to be noted that during the lifetime of the surviving spouse, such spouse is normally entitled to dispose of the property inherited from the first spouse. **6.13**

Parents and siblings

The parents and siblings of the deceased make up the third group of persons entitled to inherit. A parent who has died is replaced in the order of succession by the brothers and/or sisters of the deceased and their issue. In this group, the right to inherit in place of someone who has already died is unlimited with regard to subsequent issue (ie later generations). If there are no brothers or sisters, but one or other of the deceased's parents are still alive, that parent will be the sole heir. If neither parents nor siblings are alive, but only step-sisters and step-brothers, the entire property falls to them. **6.14**

Grandparents

The fourth group of persons in the order of succession consists of the grandparents of the deceased and their issue. In this group, the right of succession is limited to the grandparents' children, not to their grandchildren. **6.15**

The right of the state

If no one is entitled to inherit in the above order of succession, in the absence of a will the State inherits the entire property of the deceased. **6.16**

3. EXCEPTIONS TO THE NORMAL ORDER OF SUCCESSION

THE RIGHT TO DEPRIVE SOMEONE OF THE RIGHT TO INHERIT

In Finland, the freedom to dispose of one's property by will is limited only by the so-called 'legal share' (see para **6.21**). However, in exceptional cases it is possible to deprive a direct descendant of his right to inherit. In order for someone to be deprived of his legal share, the matter must be stipulated in a will, and can only be effected if certain preconditions laid down in the statute exist. In practice it is rare for anyone to resort to this measure. If, however, someone is deprived of his right to inherit, the persons that would be next in line will inherit the share instead. **6.17**

LOSS OF THE RIGHT TO INHERIT

6.18 The law stipulates that a person who has through a criminal act caused the death of another person placed in the order of succession above him, either as heir or a universal successor, loses the right to inherit from that person. A court may also stipulate that a person who has wilfully destroyed or concealed a will must lose the right to inherit, whether as heir or as universal successor. If someone loses the right to inherit, the person next in line will be entitled to inherit instead.

GIVING UP THE RIGHT TO INHERIT

6.19 A person entitled to inherit may give up the right to the inheritance either prior to a person's death or subsequently, provided that he has not begun administration of the estate. It is not possible to give up the right to inherit in favour of someone else.

4. THE SIZE OF THE INHERITANCE

6.20 As a rule, heirs in the same group of persons in the order of succession inherit in equal parts. This rule is subject to exceptions for a number of reasons. The deceased may have limited the share of the inheritance which would otherwise fall to someone in a direct line (ie his legitimate issue) to half of what it should be, thus leaving his legitimate issue with only the legal minimum ie his legal share. Potential heirs within the order of succession, other than direct issue of the deceased, may by means of a will, be left completely without any inheritance.

COMPULSORY LEGAL SHARE

6.21 Direct issue of the deceased have a statutory right to a share in the deceased's estate, with only a few exceptions. The legal share is half the normal share of the deceased's direct issue. It is not normally possible to violate the statutory right by means of a will provided, of course, that the entitled person wishes to invoke his or her right. Persons who have received so-called advance inheritance or gifts which may be equated with inheritance through a will may have to compensate a son or daughter of the deceased's estate if the legal share cannot be paid out of what remains of the property.

ADVANCE INHERITANCE

6.22 If, prior to his death, a deceased has given gifts to his direct issue, those gifts are presumed to be a part of the inheritance unless the deceased has otherwise directed or the circumstances show that an advance inheritance was not intended. The assumption that a gift is part of the inheritance given in advance of the donor's death does not apply to so-called 'normal' gifts or benefits, nor to contributions to living expenses or costs for studies if such expenses are reasonable.

If it is determined that someone has received property or benefits which are to be viewed as an advance on the inheritance, that advance will be added to the value of the deceased's estate. The value of the statutory share is then also calculated on the resulting value of the estate. Any heir has the right to demand that a gift or benefit be taken into account in calculating the share of another heir as an advance on his inheritance right. However, the person in receipt of a gift or benefit is not obliged to return its value to the estate over and above the value which is deductible from his share of the inheritance unless the donor so stipulated. 6.23

CONTRIBUTIONS

So-called contributions may substantially influence the division of the deceased's estate. The principle of granting contributions is based on equitable considerations. Contributions are usually deducted from the estate before it is finally divided. 6.24

The deceased's direct issue, ie his children, have a right to receive contributions to cover their living and schooling expenses until they are 21 years of age. Payment is made in a single payment based on the estimated need. 6.25

If the deceased has left children or parents who, because of sickness or infirmity, are unable to care for themselves, such persons are entitled to an estimated lump sum based on need from a universal successor or other beneficiary under a will. Such a sum is, however, limited to the value of the estate. 6.26

The right to reasonable living expenses may also be accorded to the widow or widower, or even to a person who has been engaged to be married to the deceased if such contribution is necessary. In the case of a widow or widower, this right is limited by the right of the spouse to continue to reside in the matrimonial home of the couple, even if the home constitutes part of the estate. 6.27

COMPENSATION FOR WORK DONE

An heir has the right to demand that he receives reasonable compensation for work done for the deceased, even if there is no agreement or contract to that effect. Such compensation is paid out of the estate before final division. Such compensation may not encroach on the legal share, but it takes precedence over any will or bequest. 6.28

There are two limitations on the right to claim compensation: 6.29

(1) there is no right to compensation if the work has been only occasional; and

(2) the right is limited to work done in the last five years (assuming that it was carried out after the heir reached 18 years of age), and not earlier than ten years before the death of the deceased.

5. THE WILL

6.30 Any person over the age of 18 may draw up a will as a means of disposing of his property. A person aged 15 or over may make a will dealing with property which he or she possesses. A married person of any age may make a will.

6.31 A will may transfer property in three ways:

(1) *Without limitations on ownership.* In practice, this is the most common. Through a will of this type the deceased confers full ownership on the recipient of the stipulated property.
(2) *Limited as to ownership in some respects.* This is a will in which it is stipulated that someone else will have the right of ownership of the property after the death of the first heir or successor.
(3) *It may only give a right to use property.* This ensures that the recipient has the right to use the property and to dispose of any income that may be generated.

MAKING A WILL

6.32 A will must be drawn up in writing and in the presence of two independent witnesses. The following categories of person may not be witnesses:

(1) a person under the age of 15;
(2) persons not of sound mind;
(3) the spouse of the testator;
(4) persons directly related to the testator, either directly ascending or descending;
(5) adopted children;
(6) siblings or their spouses;
(7) any person in direct descent to or ascent from such persons;
(8) any person in whose favour a will is made or anyone related to such person.

6.33 When a person has drawn up a will or acknowledged that the signature on the will is his, the witnesses must testify to the identity of the testator by appending their own signatures. Often they will also testify to the testator's soundness of mind and other aspects surrounding the procedure. However, it is only necessary that the witnesses know that the document they are signing is a will and who the testator is. They do not have to know the contents of the will. The word 'will' does not have to be included in the document.

6.34 In exceptional circumstances, Finnish law permits the making of an emergency will. Such an emergency might be a severe illness or injury, or some other serious reason. An emergency will may be made orally in the presence of two witnesses, or without witness if handwritten (holographic will), signed by the testator.

An emergency will remains in effect for three months following: 6.35

(1) the end of the emergency condition which prompted its making; and
(2) the opportunity for the testator to make a normal will.

REVOCATION OF A WILL

The maker of a will may revoke it at any time. No special formal procedures attach to revocation of a will. 6.36

BENEFICIARIES

A will may not validly be made in favour of a person not yet born or conceived (and later born alive) at the time of death of the testator. However, it is possible to bequeath property with full ownership rights to the children of a beneficiary under a will even if such children have not yet been born or conceived. The property would come into the ownership of such children at the latest when their parents die or, if ownership rights are exercised by third parties, when such rights are terminated. 6.37

NOTIFICATION OF A WILL

In order for a beneficiary to pass on what he has received as his own, he must notify the heirs in such a manner as can later be used as evidence. Each and every one of the heirs must be notified separately. There are no specific time-limits on notification, but the right to contest the will is limited to six months from the time when notice was given. 6.38

6. AVAILABLE REMEDIES

CONTESTING A WILL

As stated above, the heirs have six months to question the validity of the will from the time when they are notified of its existence. This remedy is available for next of kin. It is personal, and the benefits of any court proceedings will therefore accrue only to the person commencing the action. 6.39

The validity of a will may be questioned on the following grounds: 6.40

(1) that a formal error in the drafting of the will has occurred;
(2) that the testator was of unsound mind and incapable of making dispositions of his property; or
(3) that the deceased did not intend to make a will.

ACTION TO DECLARE A WILL NON-EXISTENT

6.41 This remedy may be available, for example, because of a forgery. There is no statute of limitations on this remedy, nor are the benefits of taking an action limited to the person who commenced the procedure.

ACTION TO REINSTATE A WILL

6.42 An heir or beneficiary under a will may commence an action to have a will which has been revoked reinstated. There is no statute of limitations on this remedy, nor are the benefits of taking an action limited to the person who commenced the procedure.

ACTION FOR DETERMINATION OF THE TESTATOR'S COMPETENCY

6.43 In the event that the testator included property belonging to another in his dispositions, it is possible to bring an action to determine the ownership of such property. There is no statute of limitations on this remedy, nor are the benefits of taking an action limited to the person who commenced the procedure.

ACTION TO OBTAIN INTERPRETATION OF A WILL

6.44 An action may be commenced by anyone whose rights are in issue to have the courts interpret the will. There is no statute of limitations on this remedy, nor are the benefits of taking an action limited to the person who commenced the procedure.

7. THE POSITION OF THE SURVIVING SPOUSE

6.45 In addition to the right of the surviving spouse to inherit, which takes second place only to the rights of the deceased's direct issue, the position of the surviving spouse is safeguarded against the demands of the direct issue of the deceased. The surviving spouse thus has the right to undisturbed possession of the property which the deceased has left. This protection subsists only so long as the heirs or other beneficiaries remain inactive. If they demand that the property be divided, the protection of the surviving spouse is limited to the right to continue to reside in the matrimonial home, unless he has a suitable dwelling elsewhere. The rules concerning marital property may modify the above.

8. MARITAL PROPERTY

The Finnish system of marital property is based on the principle of separation of property. Such property as a spouse had when entering the marriage continues to belong to him. Also, such property as has been acquired during the marriage is normally regarded as belonging to the spouse in whose name it is held. Of course, joint property may be acquired in the name of both spouses, and so is regarded as joint property. If it is not possible to identify the spouse to whom property belongs, it is regarded as joint property. 6.46

The same principles apply to debts. On principle, only debts incurred in relation to living expenses are regarded as joint liabilities. 6.47

Regardless of the rules about ownership of property, both spouses are entitled to half of the other's property. Thus the spouse is entitled to half of the net marital property when the marriage is dissolved, either through divorce or death. 6.48

A spouse may own property which is not marital property and thus is not taken into account when calculating what the net marital property might be. Property which is not marital property may have come into existence either by specific stipulation to that effect in connection with a gift, or the stipulation may be included in a will or a marital contract between the spouses. Some limited rights to this effect also exist by virtue of the law, such as author's rights. 6.49

A marital contract may be made either before the marriage or at any time thereafter. However, registration of the contract may only be made when the marriage is concluded. Such a contract may stipulate that certain property shall not be subject to the marital property rule, or that none of it be so subject. 6.50

A marital contract must be made in writing, dated and signed by both spouses, witnessed by two independent persons and registered with the local court. It is possible to register a marital contract at any time prior to the death of the other spouse or the dissolution of the marriage. 6.51

If neither spouse is domiciled in Finland, the competent court is the Helsinki court. 6.52

9. PRIVATE INTERNATIONAL LAW

LEX SUCCESSIONIS

The *lex successionis* is the law of the deceased's nationality at the time of his death unless the deceased was a citizen of a Nordic country (Denmark, Finland, Iceland, Norway or Sweden). In such a case, the *lex successionis* will be the law of the Nordic country in which he was domiciled at the time of death, provided that he was domiciled in that country for at least the previous five years. If less, an alternative nationality principle may come into play if a person entitled to make a demand to 6.53

this effect makes such a demand.[1] Thus a Finn who dies domiciled[2] in any country other than a Nordic country[3] will have the succession to his estate governed by Finnish law. Within the limits given above, a Finn domiciled in another Nordic country will have succession determined according to the rules in the Nordic Convention. A foreign national other than a Nordic national will have succession determined according to his *statuta personalia* applying the nationality principle (*lex patriae*).[4]

6.54 While Finnish law makes very little distinction between movables and immovables[5] and has statutory shares, it will accept the application of a foreign *lex successionis* which makes such distinction and has no statutory shares.[6]

DOCTRINE OF *RENVOI*

6.55 As a rule, the doctrine of *renvoi* is viewed negatively. However, it has some application in certain international convention-based legislation. The whole issue of *renvoi* is uncertain in Finnish jurisprudence.[7] Because Finland is basically a nationality state, save for the compromise made on this principle in the Nordic Convention on Inheritance, Wills and Deceased's Estate, with unity of succession for movables and, except for agricultural land, for immovables, it is likely that if, for example, an English national dies domiciled in England but owning a Finnish immovable, Finnish law, like Spanish law, will not apply its rules on statutory shares[8] to the immovable, but will treat the immovable as subject to English

---

1 See the Convention between Finland and Denmark, Iceland, Norway and Sweden on Inheritance, Wills and Deceased's Estates of 31 May 1935/253.

2 The term 'domicile' must be understood as in the footnote to para **6.57**.

3 In addition, the Conventions with the Netherlands (Treaty Series 48/1956), the United States (Treaty Series 18/1952), France (Treaty Series 25/1959) and Switzerland (Treaty Series 9/1957) contain principles which may deviate from the main rule for tax purposes.

4 The Law on the Determination of Paternity of 1976 (13 August 1976/673) will in some instances cause modifications to the nationality principle otherwise applicable. *Ordre Public* viewpoints relate to the determination of paternity. Also worthy of note is the Nordic Convention on private international law relating to Marriage, Adoption and the Representation of Minors of 18 December 1931/413, which has an impact on the *statuta personalia*. The latter Convention has not been modified to correspond accurately with the paternity legislation. Finland and Sweden apply the nationality principle or *lex patriae*, while Norway and Denmark apply the *lex domicilii*. A short and clear overview is given by M Bogdan, *Svensk internationell privat-och processrätt* Kristianstad 1987, p 111. See for an overview of private international law G O Z Sundström, *Om normkollision vid fartygs sammanstötning*, Borgå 1965.

5 See, however, chapter 25 in the Code dealing with agricultural land.

6 If a statutory share is due as a matter of legal right to someone domiciled in Finland, the Internal Revenue may take the position that in terms of tax liability the person is deemed to have received the statutory share which the laws in Finland would accord and rule on tax accordingly. However, there is no certainty about this in practice.

7 There is no unreserved acceptance in Nordic jurisprudence of the doctrine of *renvoi*. Recent articles and books dealing with the theory and practice of private international law tend to take a pragmatic approach to conflicts and the application of foreign law involving a certain amount of interaction between the *lex fori* and the *lex causae*. See further Sundström, *op cit* p 52 (English summary, p 469).

8 See the observation made in the footnote to para **6.57**.

internal law governing succession to movables. However, this position is not without problems in Finnish jurisprudence.[1]

The form of a will in private international law is governed by the Hague Convention on Form of Wills of 5 October 1961.[2] 6.56

Finland's somewhat uncertain position on the doctrine of *renvoi* specifically and on the private international law of succession generally[3] is to a degree offset by very specific rules on taxation which the Finnish Internal Revenue seeks to apply. The conclusions to which a Finnish court may come in terms of the *lex successionis* do not necessarily correspond to decisions made by the Internal Revenue on taxation. A brief summary of the existing rules of taxation is therefore included in paras **6.68–6.73**. 6.57

REFORM

Since there is no codified legislation concerning international succession law, the Ministry of Justice has made a proposal for new legislation in this field inspired by the Hague Succession Convention. The intention is to add provisions concerning international succession law to the already existing chapter on inheritance and wills. At this moment, the Finnish international law of succession is mainly based on case-law and doctrine. 6.58

It is important to bear in mind that the contents of this proposal might change during its preparation and during parliamentary proceedings. The main change will be that the habitual residence of the deceased will constitute the determining factor instead of his nationality. As has been stated above in para **6.53** the *lex successionis* is now the law of the deceased's nationality at the time of his death. It is now suggested that habitual residence instead of nationality should determine the *lex successionis*. This means that the law in the state in which the deceased is habitually resident at the time of his death determines the *lex successionis*. If the deceased, however, had been habitually resident in another state as well, the law of the latest habitual residence will apply only if the deceased was either a national of that country or had been habitually resident there for at least five years prior to his death. 6.59

The nationality principle should, according to this proposal, be a secondary point of reference and be applied when the habitual residence, according to what has been said above, does not apply. The nationality principle will, however, not apply when the deceased, all circumstances considered, has a stronger connection to any other state. 6.60

---

1 Thus agricultural land under chapter 25 of the Code is likely to be dealt with in accordance with Finnish law stipulating unity of such land.

2 Brought into Finnish law on 25 May 1976/835.

3 Note for example that the term 'residence, domicile and habitual residence' may take on different shades of meaning in the general international private law of Finland as well as in the Nordic Convention (see footnote 3 to para **6.53**) compared with the meaning ascribed to such terms in other legal systems.

6.61 *Lex successionis* shall according to the proposal be applied to the whole inheritance regardless of where the property is situated (there are some exemptions to this rule concerning real property).

6.62 This new legislation is intended to include a provision on the right to make a choice of law. A choice of law has to be made according to the same formal requirement as a will. The choice of law can also be included in a will. The law chosen has to have some connection with the deceased. This connection can, for instance, be habitual residence or nationality at the time when the will is drawn up or habitual residence or nationality at the time of death.

6.63 In the proposal, it is suggested that certain material provisions in the Finnish legislation should apply even though foreign law generally is applied to the estate. It is suggested that, for instance, the Finnish provision concerning the right of the spouse to continue to reside in the matrimonial home should be such a provision (see para **6.45**). This provision will apply only if it results in a reasonable solution.

6.64 In the proposal, it has also been suggested that Finnish procedural law always applies when the Finnish authority is the competent authority. The Finnish authorities are considered to be competent when the deceased at the time of his death was habitually resident in Finland. The Finnish legislation will be applied to the estate administration and to the distribution of the estate, while the question of who inherits and how much is decided according to the *lex successionis*.

6.65 Another essential provision in the proposal is the suggestion that the doctrine of *renvoi* should not apply to the international law of succession (see para **6.39**). It is further suggested that a specific provision on *ordre public* should be included amongst the new provisions on international succession law.

10. MINIMISING PROBLEMS WHERE FOREIGN ELEMENTS ARE INVOLVED

6.66 Although the position is not certain, on balance it seems that a non-Finnish national, who is not a Nordic citizen who dies resident in Finland, can die owning Finnish residential land without Finnish statutory shares affecting such immovables.

6.67 Dealing with property situated in Finland will be facilitated if the testator makes a Finnish will using Finnish concepts and takes care that no other non-Finnish will revokes the Finnish will. If a foreign will is made to deal with Finnish property, it should be worded as simply as possible to avoid mistranslation of legal terminology. Taking note of the tax aspects outlined in paras **6.68–6.73** will help the draftsman of the will to avoid clauses in the will which may attract tax disputes under the rules applying in Finland.

11. TAXES ON DEATH

Immovable property situated abroad attracted neither inheritance nor gift tax in Finland until the law was amended from the beginning of 1996 (1995/1561). 6.68

As a consequence of the amendment, the law has been changed to require that if the successor (recipient) resides in Finland at the time of the death of a person resident in Finland, all movable property, even when situated abroad, attracts inheritance tax (with the exception of the special Nordic regime or the regime of the treaties with the countries listed in para **6.53**, footnote 3, insofar as it concerns immovable property or movables abroad).

When the successor resides abroad at the time of death of a person residing in Finland, all Finnish immovable and movable property is taxed in Finland (with the exception of the special Nordic regime or the regime of the treaties with the countries listed in para **6.53**, footnote 3). When in addition the deceased was residing abroad, all immovables situate in Finland are taxed in Finland, but movables are free of tax in Finland even if they are situated in Finland. 6.69

Since the question of residence assumes importance in the above instances, it is useful to note the Finnish view on when a person is deemed to be resident in Finland.[1] 6.70

According to the new provisions of s 4.3 of the Finnish Estate and Gifts Tax Act, which came into force in 1996 (1995/1561), a person is resident in Finland if he has his ordinary residence and abode in Finland. This provision differs from earlier legislation on the subject.[2] 6.71

The inheritance tax law also differs from the general law on taxation in that its criteria for residence are narrower. The general law on taxation applies *inter alia* as its criterion 'essential ties to Finland', which in many instances relating to general tax cases makes a person resident and taxable in Finland even when, according to the Estate and Gifts Tax Act the person is clearly resident abroad. 6.72

If according to the above rules inheritance tax has been paid on property located abroad, the Estate and Gifts Tax Act stipulates that the tax so paid abroad can in certain circumstances be deducted from the inheritance tax payable in Finland. On the other hand, if the property is located in Finland, no deduction can be made in Finland for tax paid abroad. 6.73

---

1 In the presentation of tax aspects, guidance has been taken from the Internal Revenue's looseleaf handbook *Kansainvälisen verotuksen käsikirja* no 621, s 9, published in Helsinki by the Internal Revenue and last updated in March 1996.

2 The so-called 6-month rule which existed in earlier legislation has been removed from the present Act.

CHAPTER 7

FRANCE†

I. INTRODUCTION

7.1 In French law, succession and *inter vivos* gifts constitute headings I and II respectively in the third book of the *Code Civil*. During the last few decades, the 3 July 1971 Act has produced greater equality between co-inheritors while the 3 January 1972 Act has extended this idea of equality, although with some limitations, to the rules governing the succession rights of legitimate and of natural relatives. A review of the law of succession, intending to simplify the administrative procedures, has been in progress for many years, but has, as yet, not been concluded.

7.2 In French law, devolution of a deceased's estate primarily depends on the closeness of blood relationship with the deceased. However, the testator may create a different result through manifesting his contrary intentions, either in the form of a will by which he nominates one or several legatees to receive all or part of his estate, or by gifts by which he gratuitously disposes, *inter vivos*, of certain of his possessions. Nevertheless, this power of free will has significant restrictions which result from the existence of the *réserve héréditaire* (the indefeasible reserved share of the inheritance for close heirs) and the prohibition of *pactes sur succession future* (agreements on succeeding to someone's future estate) (art 1130).

7.3 French law reserves an untouchable right to a fraction of the deceased's estate for the direct-line inheritors, whether descendants or ascendants. This is the *réserve héréditaire*. The non-reserved part, which can be freely disposed of, is called the *quotité disponible*. Those entitled to the reserved portion are protected against the deceased making *inter vivos* gifts or testamentary dispositions to third parties or co-inheritors.

7.4 Dispositions which exceed the freely disposable fraction of the estate and so affect the reserved portion are reduced. The purpose of the reserved portion is to maintain equality between co-inheritors and to assure the permanence of certain family possessions. Only the descendants and ascendants of the deceased are reserved inheritors. The reserved descendants are the children and their descendants, whatever their filiation. A child's reserved portion is a half if there is one child, a third if there are two children, a quarter if there are three children (art 913). Beyond the third child, the freely disposable portion is fixed at a quarter. A child born out of wedlock is also a reserved inheritor, but, if there are any legitimate children, the reserved portion is equal to only half what he would

† This chapter was written by Marie L Revillard, Docteur en droit, Juriste Consulte au Cridon de Lyon, 10 place d'Helvétie, 69452 Lyon, Cedex 06.

have received if all the children, including himself, had been legitimate (art 915 al 1). The remaining half can benefit only the children of the marriage affected by the adultery which produced the illegitimate child. In the absence of descendants the reserved inheritors are the deceased's ascendants whether legitimate or natural. Their reserve portion is a half if there are ascendants from both lines and a quarter if there are only ascendants from one line. The surviving spouse has no reserved portion.

7.5 In principle the devolution of the estate cannot be affected through a contract. The *Code Civil* prohibits any agreement relating to the division of a deceased's estate before his death. However, there are numerous exceptions to the principle forbidding agreements on succeeding to someone's future estate.

2. CONDITIONS FOR A VALID WILL

7.6 > 'A will is an act by which the testator disposes, for when he will be dead, of all or part of his possessions, and which he can revoke.' (art 895)

7.7 To be valid a will must comply with precise conditions of form and content.

FORMAL VALIDITY

Rules common to all wills

7.8 A will must be in writing. An oral will is not valid. There are, however, exceptions to this principle. Although the inheritors are not bound by a verbal legacy or by any will made invalid through faulty execution, in such cases an *obligation naturelle* is placed upon the inheritors. Case-law accepts that an inheritor can confirm an oral legacy after the testator's death. Another exception from the requirement of writing arises if the will is destroyed or disappears against the testator's wishes.

7.9 *Testaments conjonctifs* (joint wills) made by two or more people are prohibited. Two or more people cannot make a will by the same instrument, whether for a third party beneficiary or for their reciprocal and mutual benefit (art 968). Case-law, however, limits the scope of this rule: two wills can be created by the same instrument followed by two signatures.

7.10 The Hague Convention of 5 October 1961, concerning testamentary formalities, is in force in France. The dominating policy of the Convention is in favour of making wills valid so that it is exceptional for the form used by the testator not to conform with one of the wide selection of available laws offered by the Convention. Therefore, few difficulties are met in this area.

Types of testaments

7.11 > 'A will may be handwritten, or drawn up in a public instrument, or created and kept secret.' (art 969).

Testament olograph (handwritten will) (art 970)

This is the most common type of will in France. It is completely written, dated and signed by the testator. The will must be entirely written by the testator so it must not be typed. The choice of alphabet is free, the will can be written in any language, in ink or in pencil. A shorthand will does not fulfil the conditions of validity necessary for a holograph will and is void even if the author attests by an added written and signed statement that he is in fact the author. The onus of proof regarding the veracity of the handwriting and signature rests on the beneficiary. 7.12

Dating the will is essential to the validity of a handwritten will. This necessity helps to monitor the testator's capacity at the moment of writing and also determines the priority of wills if the testator has written several. In principle the date must include three elements: date/month/year. However, it is not necessary to indicate the place where the will was drawn up. 7.13

The will must be signed by the testator's hand, whether or not it is his customary signature. It is not essential that the signature be placed at the end of the text, but this is the recommended practice. There is no requirement for any witnesses. 7.14

In order to preserve a handwritten will, the most usual precaution is to deposit it with a notary. This step is optional before death and obligatory after death. The deposit of the will with a notary before death prevents the will's destruction by dishonest beneficiaries. After death the handwritten will *must* be deposited with a notary who then institutes the formal 'opening' or commencement of the succession process, recording this in his official minutes and preserving the will in his archives (art 1007). This obligation to deposit the will with a notary is binding on all persons in possession of a will in France. The notary must send a certified copy of the will to the greffier of the *Tribunal de Grande Instance* for the area where the succession process was 'opened'.[1] 7.15

Testament authentique (formal will by public deed) (arts 971–975)

This instrument must be received by two notaries or one notary assisted by two witnesses. It requires strict formalities to be observed. The second notary or the witnesses must be present during the time it is drawn up for it to be valid: ie when it is dictated, written, read and signed. The witnesses must be French and over 18 and be able to sign and enjoy all their civil rights. A *testament authentique* must be dated and state the place where it was drawn up. The testator must dictate his testamentary dispositions in full: he can express himself in a foreign language or in any idiomatic form but only if the notary and witnesses understand the language or idioms used without the aid of an interpreter.[2] 7.16

The testator does not write the will. The will is written by hand or typed out by the notary or one of his clerks under the testator's dictation. Shorthand is therefore allowed. All these formalities must be carried out or the will becomes void. 7.17

---

1 For international succession see: M Revillard, *Droit international privé et pratique notariale*, Répertoire Defrénois, 3ème éd (1993) no 258.

2 Cass Civ, 18 Décembre 1956, J C P 1957.II.9718 note C Jaquillard.

7.18 The evidentiary certainty of a *testament authentique* is much stronger than a *testament olograph* and is presumed valid until proved fake. Other particular types of *testament authentique* exist for exceptional circumstances (art 981) – military wills, wills drawn up in certain conditions of isolation, naval wills (art 988).

Testament mystique (secret will) (arts 976–980)

7.19 The notary draws up an *acte de souscription* stating the date of delivery. The *testament mystique* has the advantage of secrecy present in the *testament olograph* and benefits from the intervention of the notary as in a *testament authentique.* However, this form of will is rarely used (a French notary can only participate in one *testament mystique*) owing to the risks of annulment due to complicated formalities.

Testament international

7.20 The Washington Convention of 26 October 1973, creating a uniform rule concerning the form of a *testament international* has been in force in France from 1 December 1994 (d. 8 November 1994 OJ 16 November 1994, p 16219).

7.21 This Convention has been in force from 9 February 1978 in a certain number of states (eg Belgium, Italy, Portugal, Equateur, Provinces anglaises du Canada, Chypre, Libya, Niger, Slovenia, Bosnia Herzegovina, ex Yugoslavia). The Law of 29 April 1994 (OJ 30 April 1994, p 6327) designates the persons entitled to act: the notaries in France and the French diplomatic and consular agents for French residents abroad.

7.22 The *testament international* is a simplified secret will. The will may be written by the testator or by someone else and may be handwritten or typed in any language. The testator declares in the presence of two witnesses and a notary that the document is his will and that he knows the contents of it. In the presence of these persons the testator signs the will or acknowledges his signature.[1]

7.23 The 'attestation' or notarial act is to prove that the formalities have been complied with. Article 10 of the Convention determines its form and subject matter.

Types of revocation

7.24 A will only comes into force after the testator's death. A will is essentially revocable. Moreover, certain events taking place after the will's creation, but before the testator's death, can cause legacies to fail.

7.25 Revocation by the testator can be express or implied. An express revocation must take the form of a regular will, or a binding legal act (art 1035). An oral revocation is invalid. A revocation can arise from a later will expressly revoking an earlier will but without making any new dispositions. A corresponding form need not be adopted so that a *testament authentique* can be revoked by a *testament olograph.* An express revocation can equally arise from an act in front of the notary declaring a change in intention and this revocation is not submitted to the formalities for a *testament authentique.*

---

1 M Revillard, Une nouvelle forme de testament: le testament international, Defrénois 1995 art 36021; l'entrée en vigueur de la Convention de Washington portant loi uniforme sur la forme du testament international, JDI 1995, 585.

Implied revocation arises from the creation of a new will incompatible with the first (art 1036) or the alienation of the subject matter of a testamentary gift. The decision as to what constitutes an incompatible disposition leading to revocation has created abundant case-law.[1] The testator would be better advised to revoke by means of an express revocation. 7.26

Case-law accepts that the destruction of a will results in revocation if it was carried out by the testator voluntarily. In case of doubt over the reason for the destruction of a will the destruction itself does not give rise to an automatic presumption of revocation of the will. A later rectification of the terms of the will constitutes a revocation if it is by the testator's own hand, dated and signed. In French law the marriage or divorce of a testator does not constitute an automatic revocation of his will nor does the disposition in favour of the now-divorced spouse fail. 7.27

Revocation can occasionally occur irrespective of the testator's wishes. Dispositions can be revoked by the court if the beneficiaries do not carry out duties imposed on them, or through the beneficiaries' 'ingratitude' as set out in article 1046. 7.28

A disposition will fail if its subject matter has ceased to exist during the testator's lifetime (art 1042 al 1). If the destruction is only partial, the failure is partial. Loss of the subject matter covers not only its material destruction but its alienation: the mechanism of subrogation does not apply here; so that a legacy of property that is sold is not transposed into a legacy of the proceeds of sale of the property. A testamentary disposition is void if the legatee has predeceased the testator (art 1039). Finally, incapacity can make a gift fail. 7.29

When the will is totally revoked, the testator dies intestate and the heirs under the intestacy rules receive his property. When only certain dispositions are revoked, such dispositions will accrue in favour of the heirs under the intestacy rules or the universal beneficiary or the beneficiary under a universal title as the case may be. The disposition accrues in favour of surviving co-beneficiaries if it was made in favour of a number of people together (arts 1044–1045). These principles can be ignored if a contrary intention is expressed by the testator as where he designates another legatee in the form of a simple substitution for the original legatee. 7.30

CENTRAL REGISTER OF TESTAMENTARY DISPOSITIONS

In order to avoid ignorance or belated knowledge of a will, a central register of wills was created in France from 1 January 1975, based on the Basle Convention of 16 May 1972. This Convention creates within Member States of the Council of Europe a uniform regime in the international sphere for the registration of wills. It is now in force in Cyprus, Spain, Luxembourg, France, Turkey, Belgium, Netherlands, Portugal and Italy. The aim of the Convention is to create a system 7.31

1 Terré et Lequette, *Précis Dalloz de droit civil, les successions, les liberalités,* 3rd edn, 1997, No 401 and notes.

allowing the testator to register his will, so avoiding it being ignored by facilitating its discovery after his death. In France the system is run by the central register of testamentary dispositions – A.D.S.N. 13770 Venelles Cedex. An international liaison organisation – in France *le Conseil Supérieur du Notariat* – is designated by each State involved, which enforces the necessary registration in other States and receives requests for information originating from national agencies in other States.

7.32 The registration system covers:

- *testaments authentiques* drawn up by a notary, public authority or other competent body;
- private wills which have been the subject of official deposit with an authority;
- *testaments olographes* which, if so permitted by the national legislation of the State have been handed over to a notary or a public authority without any official act of deposit being effected.

Also registrable is the revocation of a will if in a form which would lead a will in such form to be registrable.

7.33 The testator cannot prevent the registration of a *testament authentique* or a private will officially deposited with an authority. However, he can prevent the registration of a *testament olograph* simply delivered to a notary or to a public authority if no official document of deposit has been drawn up.

7.34 By virtue of article 6(1), registration does not depend upon the nationality or place of residence of the testator. All wills must be registered in France when they are drawn up by a French notary or deposited officially in his archives.

7.35 In France, a will is registered at the request of the notary concerned with the will. Registration in other States is provided for (art 6 al 2). It may be in the interests of the testator for his will to be known in all countries where he owns property. If these countries are Member States, a French notary at the testator's request can contact the liaison agency, *le Conseil Supérieur du Notariat*, which will in turn proceed to carry out the registration in the register of the other State. All notaries involved in succession to a deceased's estate are under an obligation to consult the central register.

ESSENTIAL VALIDITY

7.36 A will, like other acts, is subject to certain substantive rules originating from substantive rules common to all transfers of property and also has special rules of its own to cope with specific problems.

The mind of the testator

7.37 All transfers require a knowledgeable consent not vitiated by any defect. 'In order to make an *inter vivos* gift or a will one must be of sound mind' (art 910). This requires the knowledgeable intention of the donor: proof of insanity renders a will void. The onus of proof is upon the inheritor. The defects which can affect the testator's knowledgeable involvement are mistake, fraud, blackmail or misdirection.

Capacity

Legal capacity is required when the will is made. If the testator did not then have capacity the will is ineffective, regardless of whether the testator had capacity when he died. 7.38

A minor under 16 is incapable of making a valid will. Upon reaching the age of 16, he can dispose by will of half the estate of which an adult could dispose (art 901). An adult under *sauvegarde de justice* and *en curatelle* can make a will as if of full legal capacity. An adult under *tutellage* has no legal capacity because a will made under *tutellage* is void (art 502). However, a will made before *tutellage* remains valid unless after the start of *tutellage* the subject matter is no longer the testator's to dispose of (art 504). Finally, under article 36(I) of the *Code Penal*, prisoners condemned to life sentences cannot make a will. 7.39

Certain incapacities only exist between certain people due to their reciprocal relationship. Some incapacities are inspired by the desire to protect the testator against any undue influence by the would-be beneficiaries. A minor, even over 16, cannot dispose in favour of his tutor (art 907); an invalid cannot dispose in favour of his doctors, pharmacists or religious minister who may have assisted him during an illness from which he later died (art 909). In the above cases, the incapacity will lead to an annulment of the disposition. If the testator resorts to pretences or to a third party to make a disposition to someone incapable of receiving it then it is void (art 911). 7.40

Lawful ascertainable objects

The disposition must have an ascertainable lawful purpose. It cannot be for objects outside the meaning of *commerce* under article 1128 of the *Code Civil*. A disposition whose purpose is illegal or immoral is void. Although dispositions between cohabitees at one time created legal problems such a disposition is no longer considered immoral with the development of cohabitation. 7.41

The contents of the will

A will can include simple non-detrimental wishes in favour of the inheritors and can express non-dispositive intentions. It can forbid human organs to be extracted from the deceased. If the will is *authentique* it can recognise an illegitimate child. A testamentary tutor can be designated by the mother or father of a minor. A testator can nominate an executor, who in French law, possesses powers limited to a year and can only deal with chattels (art 1026). A testator can make provisions for his burial and his sepulchre. 7.42

Dispositive intentions can be effected by legacies or devises. They are not subject to any particular formality or set form of words. A will can deal with all or part of the testator's estate. The legatee must be ascertained or ascertainable. If the 7.43

designation of a legatee is incomplete or imprecise, the courts can specify what in their discretion was the testator's intention.

7.44 The *Code Civil* specifies three types of testamentary gifts:

- *universel*;
- *à titre universel*;
- *à titre particulier*.

7.45 A *legs universel* is a gift conferring entitlement to the whole of the testator's estate (art 1003). The existence of a *legs universel* is not dependent on any set form of words. Case-law recognises as a *legs universel*:

- a gift of all the movables and all the immovables or of the whole estate of the testator;[1]
- a gift of all the testator's disposable property or all his freely disposable fraction;
- a gift of all the testator's remaining property;
- a gift of the bare legal title to all his property.

7.46 A *legs à titre universel* confers entitlement to part of the testator's estate, eg where there is a gift of all movables, or of all immovables, or of a portion of movables or immovables (art 1010) or of a usufruct in part or all of the estate. Article 1010, para 2 states that all other dispositions are only dispositions *à titre particulier*.

7.47 A *legs à titre particulier* is a gift conferring entitlement to one or more specific possessions of the testator.

7.48 Important practical consequences flow from this classification. A person with a *legs universel* has title and the immediate right to possession of the testator's property if there is no relative entitled to a reserved share of the estate (*un héritier réservataire*) (art 1006). However, if the will is *mystique* or *olograph* he will have to seek the assistance of the courts to gain full possession (art 1008). If he is faced with a relative entitled to a reserved share or a legatee *à titre universel* or a legatee *à titre particulier*, he must deliver their entitlements to them (for the right to intermediate income see arts 1005, 1014).

7.49 The legatee *universel* and legatee *à titre universel* have to pay the debts and charges payable on the deceased's death proportionately to the value of their interests. The legatee *à titre particulier* is not liable for such debts or charges.

1 But the mention of the country where the assets are situated changes the legacy into a *legs particulier*: legs de tous les biens situés en France, Cass Civ I, 13 February 1973, Rev Crit 1974, 338 note Droz DS 1973, 686 note Bredin; Droz et Revillard, Jcl droit int fasc, 557 B 1er cahier No 121.

3. DOMESTIC SUCCESSION LAW

SOME IMPORTANT FEATURES

Unity of succession is insisted upon by the French *Code Civil*, ie one law must apply to the whole of succession to a person's estate. Article 732 states that the law does not consider the nature or origin of possessions in its regulation of succession to a deceased's estate. The nature (movable or immovable or separately owned or co-owned) is irrelevant. However, this unity can be broken by the principle of French private international law, which subjects immovables to the law of the place where the land is situate and movables to the law of the deceased's last place of habitual residence. Moreover, the nature or origin of certain possessions can be taken into account in determining their devolution in the case of exceptional or abnormal succession, as with possessions which after the testator's death must revert to their original donor (art 368–1 *Code Civil*). Other exceptions exist due to the intellectual character of certain property (literary or artistic property) or due to personal considerations (letters etc). The important development in preferential treatment *vis-à-vis* family interests and family property also means taking into account the nature of the possessions and so limits the unity of succession (art 832). For moral reasons family memorabilia, jewels documents, medals, arms, portraits fall under the heading of specific transmission. Finally, a law of 12 July 1909 for the benefit of the family allows the constitution of a protected immovable property called *bien de famille* governed by its own special rules. 7.50

Property subject to the rules of succession law includes only the assets and liabilities which had been part of the deceased's estate even if only for an instant when he died. Excluded from such property are amounts of money given to a close relative by third parties following the deceased's death such as life insurance, social security benefits and tortious damages received due to fatal injury. 7.51

There is a special relationship between **succession law and the deceased's matrimonial regime**. Prior to the application of succession law a problem will arise as to the winding up of the matrimonial regime if the deceased was married at the time of his death. This winding up process is effected in order to determine the estate's true assets. On the practical level the winding up of the matrimonial regime and the application of the succession law are carried out in a single act performed by the notary. The French legal regime being one of community of assets, the winding up can lead to complex calculations of compensation in order to separate the assets. Only after this winding up process can the assets and liabilities of the estate be established. Of course if the couple were married under a regime of separation of estates, the operation of winding up the spouses' interests is simplified. 7.52

For a person to be a beneficiary, he must have been alive at the time when the deceased died (art 725). A child in the womb can succeed if born alive. We have already seen that certain other persons are incapable of inheriting. In order to inherit one must not be unworthy (*indigne*) as set out in article 727 of the *Code Civil*. 7.53

7.54 The **droit de prévèlevement successoral** is a special rule of devolution. Article 2 of the Law of 14 July 1819 states that, in the case of division of the same estate between French and foreign co-inheritors, the former can receive an amount of the possessions in French territory equal to that which they would be excluded from claiming in the foreign country due to local laws and customs. If this rule is interpreted widely, case-law has created a conflict of laws rule. It permits the taking of French possessions not only when a French person is barred by foreign succession law from foreign possessions, but also when a French person receives a lesser benefit through foreign law when he would have received more under the French regime. According to Batiffol's formula:[1]

7.55 'all French inheritors can claim out of the possessions in France the part which French law would have given them regardless of the actual law applicable.'

This rule creates a privilege based on nationality in favour of French inheritors. This principle, criticised by the majority of legal writers due to its archaic character and the complications it creates in the liquidation of the estate, more importantly goes against the spirit of private international law. The elimination in the name of French public order of all discrimination based on race, sex or religion cannot easily be reconciled with a shockingly biased discrimination purely based on the French nationality of the inheritors. Though the suppression of this principle is desired by many legal writers, it nevertheless remains very active in practice.[2]

DEVOLUTION ON INTESTACY

7.56 This is regulated by the *Code Civil.* In order to inherit, one must be closely related to the deceased. The *Code Civil* sets out a hierarchy of inheritors based on the rules 'of order and degree'. (The degree, which is the term for each generation succeeding to the deceased's estate, is taken into consideration to choose representatives of the same order, the nearest degree to the deceased inheriting first.) It classes inheritors in a priority order, relatives of one order being favoured over relatives of a subsequent order even if the former are in fact of a more distant degree of parentage than the latter (see arts 733 and 742). Each order is preferred over a subsequent order as follows:

(1) descendants;
(2) privileged ascendants (mother/father) and privileged collateral parents (brother/sister and their descendants);
(3) ordinary ascendants (other than mother/father);

---

1 Batiffol et Lagarde, *Droit international privé* T II No 647 p 410.

2 T G I Lyon, 7 Octobre 1971 Clunet 1972, 597 note Ponsard; Reims 1ère ch, 14 Janvier 1971 Clunet 1975, 323 ch P Kahn; Cass Civ I, 1er Février 1972 Rev Crit 1973, 313 note Droz, D S 1973, 59 note Lagarde; J C P 1973.II.17406 note Malaurie; Cass Civ I, 20 Mars 1985 Rev Crit 1986, 66 note Lequette, J C P 1986.II.20630 note Boulanger; Cass Civ I, 4 Février 1986 Defrénois 1987 art 33837 p 42 note Revillard, Rev Crit 1986, 685. TGI Paris, 2ème ch Sect 2, 21 Mai 1993 cts de Bourbon Parme: J C P 1994 éd G 22265 p 215 note L Ruet. Confirmée Paris 2e Ch A, 26 Novembre 1995 J C P 1996 ed G 22745 note L, Ruet; Paris 1e ch Sect C 16 Mai 1995 JDI 1996. 83 note M Revillard, confirmée Cass Civ, 3 Juin 1997 J C P 1997 ed G lab jur no 1599.

(4) spouses;
(5) ordinary collateral parents (other than sister/brother and their descendants).

However, in addition to this system of preference there exists a corrective element, in that the surviving spouse when faced with descendants, ascendants or privileged collateral parents nevertheless has a usufruct in quarter or half of the estate. The first order of descendants inherits in equal shares. Since the reform in the law of *affiliation* of 3 January 1972, French law has introduced the principle of equality in matters of succession (in the case of legitimate, legitimised, natural or adopted children (see arts 760–762). Privileged ascendants (father/mother, legitimate or natural) and privileged collateral relations (brother/sister, legitimate/natural as well as their descendants) are inheritors of the second order. When the two categories composing this mixed order are present, each parent has a right to one-quarter of the estate (art 748). The remaining half or three-quarters is divided between the privileged collateral relations in equal shares if they are from the same marriage. If they issued from different marriages, then one must first divide the property into as many shares as there were marriages that produced children. 7.57

When only the privileged collateral relations are present, then ordinary ascendants and ordinary collateral relations are excluded (art 750). When only privileged ascendants are present the succession is divided between father and mother (art 746). If the deceased only leaves one privileged ascendant, then this inheritor must share the estate with those from a lower priority order. 7.58

The surviving spouse has had inheritance rights on an intestacy only since the 23 December 1958 Act. The share of such a spouse is clearly insufficient if one compares it with that allotted in other legal systems. Furthermore, the surviving spouse is not a reserved inheritor so that the deceased can exclude the spouse from succeeding to any of the estate. Sometimes, the spouse takes a life interest, sometimes an absolute interest. If there are descendants, the spouse is entitled to a life interest in one quarter of the estate. This life interest is in one half if the deceased leaves only privileged collateral relations, ascendants or natural children, born out of wedlock. In one case (arts 759 and 766), the survivor's spouse takes the whole estate: this is where there are only ordinary collateral relations (art 765). Inheritors, if unanimous, can force the spouse to convert a life interest in particular property into an annuity. This is left to the courts' discretion in case of conflict. The surviving spouse, if in financial difficulty, has *droits alimentaires* (rights to maintenance payments) if the spouse makes a claim within one year of the deceased's death (art 205). 7.59

In the absence of the above heirs or a surviving spouse, the deceased's estate passes to the State. 7.60

DEVOLUTION BY WILL, GIFT OR CONTRACT

7.61 Instead of leaving his estate to be governed by the intestacy rules, a testator may dispose of his estate by virtue of making a will or a gift or a contract. *L'institution contractuelle, la donation entre époux, la donation partage* are contractual dispositions frequently used in French law. However, in general the *Code Civil* forbids agreements on succeeding to someone's future estate and prohibits certain substitutions. It does not contain the trust concept so that there cannot be testamentary or lifetime trusts under French domestic law. However, the Government intends to introduce a concept similar to a trust to be known as *la fiducie.*

Donation entre époux

7.62 Gifts between spouses during marriage, contrary to the general rule concerning gifts, are always revocable by express or implied wish of the donor alone. In order to respect this revocability, case-law makes disguised gifts void even if they do not exceed the donor's freely disposable estate (*quotité disponible*) (art 1099).

L'institution contractuelle (or donation de biens à venir)

7.63 This is a contract by which the donor agrees to leave his estate or a share of his estate or specific property to the donee. It constitutes an exception to the rule forbidding agreements on succeeding to someone's future estate. The donor does not immediately divest himself of his property but he undertakes not to dispose of it gratuitously. It is generally part of a marriage contract and is thus irrevocable. Outside the marriage contract, it is only allowed between spouses and is thus revocable *ad nutum.* The gift of future property between spouses is very widespread and is often suggested to spouses following the purchase of real estate in France.[1] The advantage of this procedure is to favour the surviving spouse, who, under French law only benefits from a reduced share of the succession and has no reserved share as *héritier réservataire.* The same result can also be obtained through the use of a will. Gifts of future property between spouses may be revoked at any time. The gift between spouses of future property will be treated as a legacy and will follow the rules for the reduction of the *quotité disponible speciale* between spouses when the succession is regulated by French law (arts 1094, 1094-1, 1094-2).

Donations sous condition potestative (contingent gift)

7.64 To comply with the requirements which flow from the rule that *donner et retenir ne vaut* (to give and keep back is invalid) and the special irrevocability of gifts, all contingent gifts are forbidden: any gifts *inter vivos* subject to conditions the effectiveness of which depends upon the sole will of the donor are void (art 944).

---

1 On the problems of *donations entre époux* in private international law see Droz et Revillard, Jcl droit int fasc, 557 B 2ème cahier No 63 *et seq*; M Revillard *op cit* No 260.

The exclusion of all conditions which depend upon the will of the parties does not prohibit all conditions. Those which remain valid are gifts subject to a condition which depends on chance and over which the parties have absolutely no control (art 1169). It is the same with gifts subject to a mixed condition depending both on the will of the donor as expressed in a legal document and also on the will of a third party (art 1171). 7.65

Substitutions

A *substitution* is a method of disposal whereby the settlor imposes on the donee a duty to preserve the property which he has given or left him so as to be able to hand it over to a designated third party (*l'appelé*). In principle, *substitutions* are forbidden (art 896, para 2) and made void.[1] Exceptionally, they are allowed (arts 1048 *et seq*) if the settlor names as primary donees his children or his brothers and sisters and the *substitution* is to be made in favour of the donee's existing or future children as a class. When the donee is the child of the settlor only the *quotité disponible* can be subject to the *substitution*. 7.66

Le partage d'ascendant (sharing out by ancestors)

The *partage d'ascendant* is an operation whereby the mother, father or other ancestors share out their property between their presumptive heirs (art 1075 *et seq*). This constitutes an exception to the prohibition upon agreements disposing of estates. This operation allows a great degree of latitude in the organisation of a family settlement whilst at the same time assuring equality between the heirs and their security from economic fluctuations. The *partage d'ascendant* may be established either by *donation partage* (lifetime gifts to presumptive heirs) or by a *testament partage* (testamentary gifts) and the rules as to appropriate formalities apply. 7.67

The *donation partage* is the most commonly used method. It is subject both in its substance and in its form to the rules applying to gifts and is established by a notarial deed. Initially limited to ascendant–descendant relationships, a *donation partage*, since the Law of 5 January 1988, may benefit people other than descendants. It operates only on direct lines of descendants, having to be made by the father or the mother in favour of their issue. It requires several descendants whatever their filiation. The gift may be *conjonctive*, that is to say, made by parents who merge their property into a single mass, so as to share it, or *cumulative*, that is to say, made by the survivor and taking account of both the property of the survivor and that of the deceased. To ease the passing on of companies, the legislature has allowed the donor to name people other than descendants (art 1075, para 3); but this possibility presupposes several descendants and that the third party only receives the title to certain types of property. The donation can only comprise presently possessed assets but it can take account of anterior gifts. 7.68

---

1 This is the reason why French law treats as valid some concepts similar to *la substitution* such as 'le legs précatif ou fidéicommis sans obligation de rendre, le legs de residuo nommé fidéicommis sans inalienabilité, le legs alternatif ou double legs conditionnel, dispositions en usufruit et nue-propriété'.

7.69 In theory, the *donation-partage* must be a division of goods between all the donor's descendants, but it can be carried out for the benefit of only a certain number. The share-out is now valid even if one or more children are omitted or refuse to take their share. It is only required that the dispositions benefit at least two descendants or even, since 1988, in the case of several descendants, one of these and a third party. The omission, or the refusal, of a child allows such child to exercise *l'action en reduction* if at his ancestor's death there is not sufficient property outside the donation to provide him with his *réserve*. This action must be started within five years of the death.

Joint tenancy and the tontine

7.70 Joint tenancy is a form of co-ownership in which the survivor becomes sole owner of the co-owned property. It generally arises where spouses own property, particularly the matrimonial home and they choose to own the property as joint tenants and not as tenants in common. In its effects, it comes close to *la tontine* in French law. The *tontine* agreement is a special mode of acquisition of property which depends upon the contract of sale. When immovable property is situated in France it is possible to acquire ownership in the form of a *tontine* or an accretion clause (*clause d'accroisement*) because French law recognises the validity of such a stipulation. The mechanism is as follows. Two or more people together acquire property, generally immovable property, and agree that the acquisition is made for the survivor of them. He is considered to have been the sole owner of the property from the date of the purchase, the predeceasing persons supposedly never having had any rights of ownership over the acquired property. Such an agreement does not constitute a gift but a contract with an element of chance for valuable consideration.[1]

7.71 Persons living in countries, like England, whose domestic legislation does not contain the concept of the indefeasible share of heirs (*réserve héreditaire*) can use this *tontine* mechanism so that it will allow the survivor of co-purchasing spouses to become sole owner of the house and not become co-owner with their own children or children of a previous marriage. However, such a purchase in *tontine* by spouses is only possible if the spouses are married under a marriage contract of the separation of property type, since the principle of immutability of the matrimonial regime does not allow the conclusion of a *tontine* settlement between spouses married under the community of property matrimonial regime. If from the point of view of civil law the insertion of a *tontine* provision is satisfactory in a common act of purchase by spouses, from the tax point of view the operation will only be advantageous if the value of the real estate, which is the principal residence of the spouses at death, is less than 500,000 FF and if the survivor has undertaken to keep it as his principal residence for a minimum period of two years. It is only if these conditions are fulfilled that the surviving spouse will take

1 However, under the guise of a contract for value containing an element of chance the survivorship clause can conceal a gift. This will be the case if the purchase price was paid by only one of the co-owners. The gratuitous character of the operation can also result from an important difference in ages or in health of the co-owners. Further see B Abry, *L'immobilier et la famille* (Masson, 1991) 75–88.

over the other's share, paying the low taxes applicable to the transfer of goods for valuable consideration. If these conditions are not satisfied, it is the higher taxes applicable to the gratuitous transfer of goods which will be levied on the other's share and the rate will be that applicable between spouses with tax-free allowances.

Trust and *fiducie*

The testamentary trust of Anglo-Saxon legal origin[1] is a means of providing for succession to all or part of one's estate. For a long time, French legal practice was at quite a loss to know how to deal with trusts. The Hague Convention of 1 July 1985 concerning the law of trusts and their recognition now gives the civil lawyer a better understanding of this legal institution.[2] Whilst awaiting the future ratification of this convention by France, it is possible to note that an adaptation of the trust is already taking place in France in resolving issues concerning deceased's estates with international dimensions.[3] The problem of carrying out a testamentary trust validly established under foreign law, involving property in France, frequently arises when British, American, or Canadian testators die. 7.72

When the succession to an estate is regulated by English law, it is possible to give effect to a trust of movable assets in France, the movables in France being handed over to the trustee, the person qualified to receive them by English law. In practice, the notion and powers of foreign administrators in respect of succession to foreign movables are recognised in France. It does not matter very much that the trust creates a method of ownership without an equivalent under French law, because fundamentally the issue is more a matter of powers than of ownership.[4] 7.73

On the other hand, to what extent may a trust be carried out in France when the transfer of movables or immovables is governed by French law? A testamentary trust even if validly constituted under English law, which recognises trusts, cannot call into question rules of public policy of French law concerning the *réserve*. The carrying out of a testamentary trust where the *lex successionis* is French raises a delicate problem where there are *héritiers réservataires*. It frequently happens that the testator gives the trustee the power to sell the testator's property and to invest the proceeds of sale with a duty to pay the income to the beneficiaries and to defer to a later date the transmission of the capital. The *héritiers réservataires* can demand their mandatory share in kind, without any restriction upon their right to its disposal and so the trust cannot be performed so far as the assets situated in France are concerned.[5] It therefore has to be accepted that for the time being a 7.74

---

1 See D J Hayton, *The Law of Trusts* 2nd edn (Sweet & Maxwell, 1993).

2 Hague Conference on Private International Law, Proceedings of the Fifteenth Session – vol II: Trusts – Applicable Law and Recognition 1985. However, as far as the qualification of trust is concerned see: Cass Civ 1ère ch 20 Février 1996 *Zieseniss*, D 1996 Ch 231 *et seq.* Y Lequette; Rev Crit 1996, 696 note Droz, J C P éd G 22647 M Behar-Touchais.

3 M Revillard, *Droit international privé et pratique notariale*, 2ème éd Defrénois 1989 p 182 *et seq* examples 105 and 106; 3ème éd 1993 p213 *et seq* examples 128 and 129.

4 Cass Civ, 3 Novembre 1983 Rep Not 1984 art 33325 et Rev Crit 1984 338 note Revillard, Clunet 1985 115 note B Ancel.

5 Paris, 10 Janvier 1970 Rev Crit 1971 518 Droz; Clunet 1973 107 Loussouarn D 1972 122 note Malaurie.

testamentary trust in Anglo-American law cannot operate according to its own law and affect the heirs' rights under the French law of succession.[1] However, if all the interested parties agree, French notarial practice manages to make the trust function without deforming its nature too much. Those with rights under the French succession law may put the trustee in charge of the administration of the succession and so conform to the wishes expressed by the deceased. It is even possible to find instances where the trustee has been written in as such in certain mortgage transactions so that he appears on the land register.[2] In the absence of unanimous consent of the interested parties to the carrying out of a trust, the trust will only be able to be performed within the limit of the testator's freely disposable portion (*quotité disponible*). The trustees will thus take part in the sharing of the estate along with the *héritiers réservataires* and once the shares have been determined will administer the trust's share.

7.75 In practice, the trust's purpose is usually to ensure the proper management of the deceased's estate and the *héritiers réservataires* often have an interest in accepting its execution. All will depend therefore on the position taken by these *héritiers réservataires.* They will either put the management of the assets in the hands of the trustees and conform to the trust provisions, or they will want to take their *reserve heréditaire* immediately in kind. There is no doubt that the adaptation to trusts will be able to take place with more ease once the Hague Convention on trusts is ratified and in force in France or if a similar concept known as the *fiducie* is introduced into French domestic law.

7.76 A draft bill concerning the *fiducie* has been prepared by the Ministries of Justice and of Finance. The text aims to transpose into the *Code Civil* the essentials of the trust as described by the Hague Convention. The project contains provisions relating to succession law aiming to bring the text into line with other provisions of the *Code Civil* relating to forbidden substitutions or agreements on future succession to estates and the protection of *héritiers réservataires.* Article 2 of the draft Bill provides that the *fiducie* may not cause prejudice to the rights of *héritiers réservataires.* When the aims of the fiducie give it the character of a gratuitous disposition the fiducie may only concern the *quotité disponible.* The Bill implementing the *fiducie* has been suspended indefinitely.

7.77 On a practical level, the establishment of qualification as heirs by those claiming rights under succession law is done in the form of an *acte de notoriété* by a French notary who certifies the transmission of the deceased's property under the intestacy rules or the rules of testamentary or contractual succession. *Actes de notoriété* drawn up in France are recognised abroad in relations between countries having a similar notarial procedure. An *acte de notoriété* drawn up abroad will only be recognised in France in as much as it was established in a mode close to that of French law.

1 Droz, Rev Crit Dr Int Pr 1977, 329 *et seq*; Motulsky, Rev Crit 1948, 466.
2 Droz et Revillard, Jcl dr int fasc 557 B 2ème cahier No 104.

ADMINISTRATION OF THE ESTATE

Once the heirs are known and the extent of their claim is established, then the transmission of the deceased's estate may take effect. In French law, transmission of a deceased's estate takes effect fully for the benefit of the heirs. However, it is not imposed on an heir who has an option, retrospective to the date of formal opening of the succession. The option is to choose between three possibilities: straightforward acceptance, acceptance with the benefit of an inventory or renunciation. 7.78

The heirs' option

The heir may renounce his rights if it appears that the debts are manifestly greater than the assets. The renunciation is made by declaration to the office of the clerk of the *Tribunal de Grande Instance* of the place where the succession was formally opened (art 784). If the heir accepts his entitlement purely and simply then the estate of the deceased and of the heir become one and the deceased's debts become his own debts, for which all his assets can be made liable. The potential liability takes him beyond the limits of the deceased's estate. His acceptance may be explicit, or implicit if he should commit an act which necessarily requires his intention to accept (eg he takes steps to dispose of some asset of the deceased), or even forced if he has misappropriated the assets of the deceased. Finally, when there is doubt as to the deceased's solvency, acceptance subject to an inventory restricts the heir's liability to the deceased's assets. This type of acceptance requires certain formalities: a declaration to the Tribunal clerk's office and the drawing up of an inventory. 7.79

In an international context, if the law governing the succession is French law, it covers the conditions, the form and effects of the heir's option, but the interest of any third party must be taken into account. The declaration of the Tribunal (of the place where the succession was formally opened) is therefore mandatory because French succession law requires it. Since the acceptance or rejection by the heirs directly affects the deceased's creditors, it is advisable for the heir to respect the formalities of the law of the locality of the assets so as to avoid the possibility of being sued personally.[1] It is also to be noted that if the deceased was resident abroad and had immovables in France, the option should be exercised before the Tribunal clerk's office in the place where the immovable is situated and, if there are several, in the locality of the most valuable property. 7.80

Administration of the succession[2]

The heir having made his choice, it becomes necessary to ascertain and collect the estate of the deceased, to manage the assets and to settle his debts. The totality of the operations is known as the *administration of the succession* and may be carried 7.81

1 Répertoire Dalloz de droit international privé Vo successions par P Lagarde 140; Droz et Revillard, Jcl dr int fasc 557 A No 188 *et seq.*

2 M Goré, L'administration des successions en droit international privé français, Economica 1994.

out under one or two major legal systems. According to the theory of 'succession to property' the estate of the deceased retains its identity, there being no direct transmission of the deceased's assets and liabilities to the heirs who ultimately receive the net assets of the estate. Succession to the deceased's estate is subject to judicial control. The deceased's goods are entrusted to an executor chosen by him or to an administrator chosen by the judge, applying specific priority rules of entitlement to become administrator. The function of the executor or administrator is to collect the assets and to pay the debts before sharing the balance between the heirs. This is the system in common law countries.

7.82 According to the theory of 'continuity of the person', the heirs become directly entitled to and responsible for the goods, rights and liabilities of the deceased at the moment of his death. His estate becomes one with that of his heirs who will administer it as their own estate. Their powers and, as a consequence, their responsibilities are limited. It is here that the notion of the *saisine* (directly taking over the assets and liabilities of the deceased) appears in all its complexity. This is the system in French law and in countries such as Belgium, Switzerland, Italy, Spain and Germany.

Obtaining title or possession

7.83 Certain heirs have *la saisine* and may exercise the role of heir without any preliminary formalities and without obtaining any authorisation. Others are required to ask for judicial authority to enter into possession or to deliver legacies to legatees.

7.84 Without any restrictions the legitimate and illegitimate heirs of the deceased and the surviving spouse have *la saisine* (art 724). In the case of testamentary succession the *legataire universel* has *la saisine* when he is not in competition with the *héritiers réservataires* (art 1006). However, notwithstanding his immediate vested interest, he must be confirmed in his possession by a ruling of the president of the *Tribunal de Grande Instance* when his entitlement arises either by virtue of a handwritten (*olograph*) will or a secret (*mystique*) will (art 1008). This ruling is given after checking that the will seems genuine and not to have been tampered with. The heir may then take possession immediately of the deceased's property and benefit from it. He may bring personal or proprietary actions that the deceased could have brought if still alive and stand in the shoes of the deceased as a defender of actions concerning the deceased. (Saisine is indivisible and applies to all the inherited assets; if several heirs are entitled each one of them can exercise saisine in respect of all their undivided inheritance.)

7.85 The State is an irregular successor in that it does not have *la saisine* before being awarded possession (art 724, para 2). The following also do not have *la saisine*: the *legataire universel* when he is faced with an *héritier réservataire*, the legatee *à titre universel* and the legatee *à titre particulier*. They must ask the heirs or *universel* legatee with *saisine* for their entitlement (art 1004) and in the case of refusal, the *Tribunal de Grande Instance* of the place where the succession was opened.

7.86 When an international succession is opened, a conflict may arise in relation to the transmission of the assets if two laws are capable of applying to part of the deceased's property, one conferring immediate *saisine* upon the heirs, the other organising a judicial administration of the estate. French law characterises the whole class of inheritance problems relating to *la saisine* mentioned above, as matters of succession law, whereas some other states consider that these questions are procedural matters governed by the *lex fori*. The competent succession law governing entitlement to the deceased's estate does not necessarily apply to the administration of the estate as is the case in French law.

7.87 In practice, the problem of entering into possession of French immovables does not give rise to practical difficulties, even if a foreign succession law is applicable and no succession was formally opened in France, because the law of succession blends with the French *lex situs*. If immovables are situated in France, when French law requires a confirmation of title such must be obtained in France from the tribunal in the locality of the immovable. Conversely, if confirmation of possession of real estate situated abroad is sought of a French tribunal it will declare this is outside its jurisdiction.

7.88 A problem in obtaining possession only arises for French movables. Consider a foreigner who dies abroad but whose estate includes property deposited in a French bank and a bank balance in this bank. Does the accession to title of the heir or the legatee depend on the foreign succession law or the French *lex situs*? Take a British citizen who has just died in Oxford and his estate includes a portfolio of investments deposited in a French bank. His personal representatives (whether executors or administrators) in conformity with English law claim the property on the grounds that English law entitles them to take the property. On the other hand, the French *lex situs* holds that the lawful heirs alone have *la saisine* and only they can take over the movables in France. In conformity with French law there are grounds for considering that *la saisine* comes under succession law in the broad sense that encompasses administration of estates, so that the English personal representatives can take all the deceased's movables.[1]

7.89 A particular problem is raised by the grant of possession (*envoi en possession*) in article 1008 of the *Code Civil* referred to above, which has frequent practical effects upon private international law. When will a grant of possession be required in France when a foreign national died whilst living abroad? If the foreign law (or French law) requires a grant of possession and if this has been given by the foreign tribunal which normally has jurisdiction, then it may receive *exequatur* in France and so be recognised. If the foreign succession law does not require a 'grant of possession' and if the legatee directly presents the original copy of the testament with the intention of having effect given to it, it is necessary to submit it to the granting of possession procedure under article 1008 to verify the authenticity of his title. On the other hand, if foreign succession law does not require a 'grant of possession' and if the *universel* legatee shows title already verified abroad and brings sufficient proof of his right there is no reason to require the 'grant of

1 Cass Civ 22 Décembre 1970 Rev Crit 1972, 467 note A P; J Not 1971 660 note Droz; Droz et Revillard, Jcl dr int fasc 557 A No 200 *et seq*.

possession' procedure. If a British citizen dies in England (with no *héritier réservataire*) designating a *legataire universel* and leaving immovables in France, there will be no need to ask for a grant of possession in France once a grant of probate has been issued by the High Court certifying the authenticity of the testament, which is the aim of article 1008. The French notary will have a copy of the grant of probate given to him so as to give effect to the provisions of the will in France.[1]

4. ASPECTS OF PRIVATE INTERNATIONAL LAW

CONFLICT OF LAWS

Connecting factors: normal rules

Distinction between immovables and movables

7.90 French law distinguishes between immovables and movables because succession to immovables is governed by the *lex situs* and succession to movables is governed by the law relating to the deceased's habitual residence. This rule of conflict of laws applies whether the deceased died testate or intestate. Relying on article 3, para 2 of the *Civil Code*, which provides that immovables are governed by French law even when owned by foreign nationals, case-law consistently subjects succession to immovables to the *lex situs*. This solution has the advantage of having one simple rule for transmission of ownership to immovables and for solving problems of *indivision* and *partage* but there can be as many different succession laws applicable as there are immovables situated in different countries. French immovables owned by a British national will devolve according to French law. English immovables owned by a French national will devolve according to English law. On the other hand, case-law consistently subjects succession to movables to the deceased's last habitual residence.

7.91 The effect of French private international law is, in most cases, equivalent to the application of French domestic law, as it suffices for French domestic law to apply that the deceased, even if he be a foreign national, should have died resident in France or should have left immovables in France. These conflict of laws rules are simple and effective. The proposed change of the conflict of laws rules under the Hague Succession Convention of 1 August 1989, so that one law governs succession to movables and immovables, normally being the law of the deceased's last habitual residence, will no doubt lead to a more frequent application of foreign laws, notably for the devolution of secondary residences owned by foreign nationals in France.

---

1 Trib Gr Inst Paris, 22 Avril 1976 Rev Crit 1977 324 Droz; Droz et Revillard, Jcl dr int fasc 557 B 1er cahier No 131 *et seq.*

With one law currently governing movables and another law or laws governing immovables, it is crucially important whether an asset qualifies as a movable or an immovable. Under the general rules of French conflict of laws, the question of characterising an asset as movable or immovable is determined by the *lex fori*. A frequent practical example of the characterisation of property by the *lex fori* concerns shares in a company which confer a right to enjoy occupation of an immovable owned by the company: such shares have the character of movable property. This may provide a surprise for those foreigners who consider such shares as immovables. Characterisation by the *lex fori* is also crucial in the case of 'time-shares' relating to immovables. French law characterises them as movables. 7.92

Problem with French immovables

It is important when a foreigner purchases a French immovable to make clear to him that the property will be subject to French succession law. An Englishman living in London will be surprised to learn that the *réserve héreditaire* limits his freedom to dispose of his French immovables when the concept of indefeasible reserved shares is unknown to Anglo-Saxon Law (except for Scotland and then only in respect of movables).[1] Conversely, if he purchases shares in an immovable-property-owning company he will have to be informed that because they are movables their devolution will be governed by English law if this is the law of his domicile. 7.93

To avoid having succession to his estate governed by more than one law, it could be suggested to an Englishman living in England, where most of his estate is situate, that he set up a French or foreign property-holding company to which the French immovables can be transferred. At his death, the shares in the company will be distributed as movable property governed by the English law of his domicile. The setting up of a property-holding company will thus allow the deceased legitimately to avoid the ill effects of having different parts of his estate governed by different rules of succession.[2] 7.94

Whilst there have been cases accepting the conversion of immovable property to movable property by means of a fictional sale of French immovable property to a foreign company the shares in which were transferred to trustees of a trust, one must be aware that a similar manoeuvre in the *Caron* case, which was carried out as an obvious fraudulent manipulation of conflicts of law rules so as to try to deny the rights of a daughter to her reserved share, was held to be ineffective.[3] 7.95

Habitual residence

The French connecting factor of the habitual residence of the deceased must be determined according to French law. It is a question of fact and the estimation of 7.96

1 In the case of international estates the réserve héréditaire is calculated separately on each part of the estate which is governed by a different succession law. The héritiers réservataires can retain the totality of the réserve héréditaire given by the French succession law applicable to French immovables (Cass Civ 1ère, 4 Decembre 1990, Clunet 1991, 391 note Revillard, Rev Crit 1992, 76 note Droz).

2 Lequette, Ensemble législatif et droit international privé des successions, Trav comité fr D I P 1983 1984 p 170.

3 Aix, 9 Mars 1982, Rev Crit 1983 282 note Droz et Cass Civ, 1ère, 20 Mars 1985, Rev Crit 1986, 66 note Y Lequette; J C P 1986.II.20630 note F Boulanger; Clunet 1987, 80 note M L Niboyet-Hoegy.

the factual circumstances is solely within the power of the trial judge. The elements of residence are provided by article 102 onwards of the *Code Civil* so that a person is resident where he has his principal home with a certain permanence. In the course of settling succession to many estates with an international dimension, it is noticeable that the determination of this residence at the time of death does not raise many difficulties. The problem arises more on a taxation level particularly when trying to give estate planning advice in the course of preparing a will.

Connecting factors: corrective rules

7.97 The application of French conflict of law rules may be affected by the doctrines of *renvoi,* public order, or fraudulent manipulation of the law, or the exercise of the *droit de prélèvement* that favours French persons over foreigners as already seen in para **7.54**.

Renvoi

7.98 The doctrine of *renvoi* developed in connection with succession to movable property. It arises from the application of two divergent conflict rules to the same juridical situation. There may be a positive conflict or a negative conflict. If each connecting factor makes its own internal law the governing law, there is a positive conflict as where a Frenchman is domiciled or resident in England and on a particular issue by French law the connecting factor is nationality so French internal law applies while by English law the connecting factor is domicile or residence so English internal law applies. There is a negative conflict where each connecting factor rejects the jurisdiction which the other gives it, as where an Englishman is domiciled in France and on a particular issue by French law the connecting factor is nationality so English law applies while by English law the connecting factor is domicile so French law applies.

7.99 This negative conflict raises the *renvoi* problem. English law refers back to French law the jurisdiction that the latter attributes to it. Will a French court accept this *renvoi* application of the English conflicts of law rule? Such *renvoi* was accepted in the famous *Forgo* case[1] which dealt with the succession to movable property of a Bavarian who had lived and died in France without having acquired a French *domicil* so that he remained domiciled in Bavaria. According to French private international law, Bavarian law as the law of his legal residence governed the matter, but Bavarian law referred the matter to French law as the law of his actual residence. The *Cour de Cassation* accepted the *renvoi* from Bavarian law to French Law. The decision has been followed on numerous occasions in matters of succession to movable property.[2] Considered legal opinion favours the general application of *renvoi* in the first and second degree (see para **1.38**). Without entering into doctrinal controversies caused by *renvoi,* it has to be accepted that *renvoi* usefully permits a certain amount of co-ordination of conflict of laws rules in the resolution of succession matters involving international estates.

1 Cass Civ 24 Juin 1878 S 1879.1.156; Req 22 Février 1882 D 1882.I.301;

2 Arrêts: Soulié 9 Mars 1910, Ben Attar 7 Novembre 1933, de Marchi 7 Mars 1938; Jcl dr int fasc 557 A No 68 *et seq.*

Renvoi is also applicable where succession to immovable property is concerned. Where the French conflicts of law rule makes a foreign *lex situs* applicable, it is possible that the conflicts of law rule of the *lex situs* refers the issue to the deceased's national law or to the law of the deceased's domicile. For example, such a *renvoi* will be accepted where a French national dies leaving immovable property in Italy, Italian law making the deceased's national law applicable. Similarly, where a French national died leaving immovable property in Spain so that Spanish law referred the matter to French law as the nationality law then the French court accepted this *renvoi*.[1] 7.100

Public policy

An inconsistency with French international public policy ousts the application of the otherwise applicable foreign succession law. French public policy ought to intervene to prevent any discriminatory condition of a religious or racial nature which would otherwise be valid under the relevant foreign law. Any incapacity based on non-adherence to a specific religious faith is deemed to be contrary to public policy.[2] The inequality of succession rights under Moslem law ought not to be allowed in view of international conventions aimed at eliminating sex discrimination. 7.101

Fraude à la loi

There is fraudulent manipulation of the law (*fraude à la loi*) where the interested parties have lawfully, but artificially, organised the circumstances attracting the application of a particular law with the sole aim of eluding the application of this law. Until the *Caron* case already mentioned, there was no application of *fraude à la loi* within the context of succession law. It is considered that there are grounds to restrict this decision to the exceptional case where the attempt to defraud an heir of his reserved share is blatant. The transfer or sale of French immovable property to a French or a foreign company cannot be presumed fraudulent in itself when the parties and their heirs are trying in the most equitable manner to settle certain economic, family or taxation problems. 7.102

Matrimonial property regimes and succession law

In French domestic law, the winding up of the matrimonial property regime and that of the deceased's estate are effected by the same *acte de partage* of the notary. Indeed, in the case of dissolution of marriage by death, the winding up of the matrimonial regime must first be done in order to determine the content of the estate governed by the *lex successionis*. However, although the law applicable to the matrimonial regime appears to have a unitary character in France, the property to which the regime applies may be situated in several countries having different conflicts of law rules dealing with succession matters or matrimonial property regimes. Even where the rules on matrimonial property regimes and succession to estates are closely related in domestic law, it is possible that the matrimonial 7.103

---

1 Aix, 19 Juillet 1906 S 1906 293; Rev Crit 1908 805; Tr Inst Lille, 28 Mars 1980, Rev Crit 1981 289 note Lequette.

2 Cass Civ, 17 Novembre 1964; J C P 1965.II.13978 concl Lindon; Rev Penant 1965.251 note Lampué; Rev Lois 1965.249 note Droz.

regime may initiate separation of property, while allowing the surviving spouse important succession rights, even though succession law neglects the succession rights of the surviving spouse by reason of the existence of an extended community of property system. If circumstances lead to applying two systems of opposing inspiration cumulatively, the surviving spouse will either receive too much or too little: see paras **1.24–1.29**.

7.104 To remedy the inequality of a property regime or a succession regime unfavourable to one of the spouses, they may grant each other advantages by marriage contract. In Belgian or French law, a clause attributing the joint estate to the survivor is often added to a contractual regime of general community of property. The execution of these clauses contained in a marriage contract subject to foreign law will, however, be subject to the retrenchment action of article 1527 of the French *Code Civil* which protects children of a first marriage from the moment that the law of succession is French law. If the agreed advantages are subject to the law of the matrimonial regime and not the *lex successionis*, article 1527 tends to extend the scope of succession matters so as to protect the children's reserved share.

7.105 The determination of the boundary between the rights arising from matrimonial property regimes and succession rights of the surviving spouse brings up another difficulty.

7.106 Some systems use the law of succession to give effect to the matrimonial regime's rules. An example is the *quarte* of the poor spouse in Maltese law, which attributes a certain share of a deceased spouse's estate to the matrimonial property regime. A similar situation arises in winding up a German matrimonial regime of community of additionally acquired property when French law governs succession; it will be necessary to find a system of adaptation aiming to solve the difficulties caused by German law.[1]

7.107 In dealing with international problems there is a clear tendency to territorialism in French notarial practice. The same attitude may be found outside France so that very often immovable property in France is not included in the winding up of a foreigner's matrimonial property regime.

CONFLICTS OF JURISDICTION

7.108 The divergences arising from the different legal systems that may be involved in sorting out succession to a person's estate require a considerable effort of adaptation which is effectively achieved in practice. Indeed, the affairs of a considerable number of estates with an international dimension are settled by French notaries without any judicial intervention. However, a dispute is always possible so one should consider the conflict of jurisdiction rules.

1 Droz, *Les régimes matrimoniaux en droit international privé comparé*, Rec cours La Haye, 1974, t. 143 No 113; M Revillard, *Doir international privé et pratique notariale* 3ème éd 1993 no 313.

Succession to movable property is subject to the jurisdiction of the tribunal where the succession was 'opened' and succession to immovable property falls within the jurisdiction of the tribunal where the property is situate. These rules are, however, subject to certain exceptions.[1] 7.109

In the case of succession to movable property, the tribunal with jurisdiction is that of the deceased's last habitual residence. French tribunals do not have jurisdiction if the succession procedure was commenced abroad and French national's rights are not concerned. In the case of immovable property the tribunal of the locality of the immovable has jurisdiction irrespective of the last residence of the deceased. If the immovable property is situated in France French tribunals are the only ones with jurisdiction. If immovable property is in different locations in France, the tribunal will be chosen that is in the interest of the good administration of justice. When immovable property is abroad French tribunals declare that they have no jurisdiction even if the last *domicil* of the deceased was situated in France. If the succession includes immovable property abroad and in France French tribunals only have jurisdiction over the immovable property in France. 7.110

One exception to these principles is the result of the privilege afforded by articles 14 and 15 of the *Code Civil* allowing French litigants to bring a foreign citizen in front of a French tribunal and allowing French or foreign litigants to bring a French citizen before a French tribunal. These provisions have a general effect extending to succession to movable property but they do not apply to proprietary claims to immovable property or to personal claims for the sharing out of immovable property abroad. 7.111

5. MEANS OF MINIMISING PROBLEMS WHERE FOREIGN ELEMENTS ARE CONCERNED

CHOOSING THE RIGHT NATURE OF PROPERTY

Some of the difficulties may be avoided at the outset by acquiring one sort of property rather than another sort. The purchase of immovable property in France will lead to the application of French law to the devolution of the property on death and may, in certain circumstances, lead to one law governing such property and other law(s) governing other property passing on death. The purchase of a movable asset will mean that it will be comprised within the movable estate succession to which will be governed by the law of the deceased's *domicile*. The nature of the property chosen is thus crucial: all purchasers should be warned of the succession implications of the particular purchase. If a purchaser wants to own a French immovable property without having succession to it governed by the French *lex situs*, then he can use a company to purchase the property so that the 7.112

1 Droz et Revillard, Jcl dr int fasc 557 A No 240 *et seq.*

shares in that company form part of his movable estate on death. Such a choice should not be considered a fraudulent manipulation of the law as already seen in para **7.102**.

TONTINE

7.113 Another solution is that of the *tontine*, particularly where spouses are concerned. This device will allow the survivor of two co-purchasing spouses to become sole-owner of immovable property on the death of the spouse instead of co-owner with their children or children of a previous marriage. This solution is subject to the qualifications already discussed in paras **7.71** and **7.104**.

CHANGING THE MATRIMONIAL PROPERTY REGIME

7.114 If spouses wish to escape the payment of tax that the purchase in *tontine* will give rise to, they may modify their matrimonial regime if they are already married under the regime of separation of property by adding to their regime agreement a clause attributing their joint property or the joint gains on their property to the survivor.

7.115 In private international law, the possibility of changing or modifying the matrimonial regime is subject to the law of that regime and spouses may change their matrimonial regimes only if that law allows it. Suppose spouses are married under a German marriage contract of separation of property and suppose that German law allows the regime to be changed. The spouses can then modify their regime by adding a clause constituting a community of property regime or a marital community of after-acquired property for property situated in France so that the survivor alone will take such property on the death of the other. However, where French law is the *lex successionis* (eg because immovable property in France is concerned) this solution is only possible if the spouses have no children from a first marriage because such children would have a right to claim their reserved shares under article 1527 as already seen in para **7.104**.

ESTATE PLANNING

7.116 Of course, the problems referred to above justify professional advice for a person making arrangements to pass his estate on after his death. Estate planning should provide the most equitable and if possible the least costly solution for the intended heirs taking account of civil and fiscal laws. Until the Hague Succession Convention of 1 August 1989 brings in one law to govern succession to a deceased's estate, lawyers and testators should try to arrange matters so that on the testator's death all matters of succession are governed by the same applicable law.

OBTAINING ONE LAW GOVERNING BOTH THE DECEASED'S ESTATE AND HIS MATRIMONIAL REGIME

The difficulties caused by the interaction between the law governing succession to a deceased's estate and the law governing his matrimonial property regime can be resolved if the spouses manage to make the law governing their matrimonial property regime coincide with the law that will govern succession to their estates. This was recognised by the Hague Convention of 14 March 1978 on the law applicable to matrimonial regimes. By a change in their matrimonial regime made easier within the framework of this Convention, the spouses will be able to make the matrimonial regime law coincide with the law applicable to succession to their estates. This Convention came into force for France, the Netherlands and Luxembourg on 1 September 1992.[1] By Article 6 the spouses can jointly change the law applicable to their matrimonial property regime to a new law. They can change either to the law of the State of which either spouse is a national at the time of designation or to the law of the State in which either spouse has his habitual residence at the time of designation. A separate choice of the *lex situs* of immovables can also be made. Furthermore, if the Hague Succession Convention of 1 August 1989 is adopted, then its introduction of the *professio juris* principle allowing the testator to choose as his *lex successionis* the law of his habitual residence or of his nationality should help to make it possible for spouses to have the *lex successionis* coincide with the law governing their matrimonial property regime. 7.117

Quite apart from taking advantage of some of the above suggestions, it is hoped that by making persons aware of the problems caused by foreign elements such persons will already be in a position to start to solve such problems. 7.118

6. TAXES ON DEATH

PRINCIPLES

Inheritance and gift tax apply to all assets ie the world-wide estate of a deceased or donor who is domiciled in France. The definition of fiscal domicile is contained in CGI article 4B. Inheritance and gift taxes apply to all non-residents located in France (CGI art 750 ter). France has signed double taxation treaties with many countries concerning inheritance taxes. 7.119

1 *Actes et Documents de la Treizème Session de la Conférence de La Haye de Droit Intertational Privé* (1976) T. II Matrimonial Property Regimes, Explanatory Report by A E von Overbeck; Revillard, *La Convention de la Haye du 14 Mars 1978 sur la loi applicable aux régimes matrimoniaux* (Répertoire Defrénois, 1992) art 35219 and *Droit International Privé et Pratique Notariale* 3ème éd (1993) no 110 *et seq*; Droz, *Les nouvelles règles de conflit françaises en matière de régimes matrimoniaux*, Rev Crit 1992, p 631 *et seq*. M Revillard, *Premier bilan d'application de la Convention de La Haye* du 14 Mars 1978 sur la loi applicable aux régimes matrimoniaux, E. pluribus unumliber amicorum G Droz, Martinus Nijhoff p 369 *et seq*.

GIFT AND ESTATE TAX

7.120 Rates of tax vary according to the relationship between the deceased and the beneficiaries, as shown in the following Table.

Value transferred (Francs)	*Rate (%)*
Between parents and children (CGI art 777) (after an allowance of F300,000 (CGI art 779))	
Up to 50,000	5
50,001–75,000	10
75,001–100,000	15
100,001–3,400,000	20
3,400,001–5,600,000	30
5,600,001–11,200,000	35
Over 11,200,000	40
Between spouses (CGI art 777) (after an allowance of F330,000 (CGI 779))	
Up to 50,000	5
50,001–100,000	10
100,001–200,000	15
200,001–3,400,000	20
3,400,001–5,600,000	30
5,600,001–11,200,000	35
Over 11,200,000	40
Between siblings (CGI art 777) (after an allowance of F10,000 for inheritance only)	
Up to 150,000	35
Over 150,001	45
Between relatives (up to fourth degree) (after an allowance of F10,000 for inheritance only)	
	55
Between other persons (after an allowance of F10,000 for inheritance only)	
	60

In addition, there is an allowance for each grandchild of F100,000 for gifts only (CGI 790B) (*Loi de 12 Avril 1996 JO 13 Avril p 5707*).

DOUBLE TAXATION TREATIES CONCERNING INHERITANCE AND GIFT TAX

7.121 France has signed tax treaties relating to inheritance tax with many countries. There are six treaties in force which cover both inheritance and gift tax, the co-signatories of which are: Austria, Italy, New Caledonia, St Pierre and Miquelon, Sweden and the USA.

The treaties which cover only inheritance tax are listed in the Table below:

Country	*Date of conclusion*
Algeria	17 May 1982
Austria	26 March 1993
Bahrain	10 May 1993
Belgium	20 January 1959
Benin	27 February 1975
Burkina Faso	11 August 1965
Cameroon	21 October 1976
Central African Republic	13 December 1969
Comoro and Mayotte	27 March and 8 June 1970
Congo	27 November 1987
Finland	25 August 1958
Gabon	21 April 1966
Italy	20 December 1990
Kuwait	7 February 1982
Lebanon	24 July 1962
Mali	22 September 1972
Mauritania	15 November 1967
Monaco	1 April 1950
New Caledonia	31 March and 5 May 1983
Niger	1 June 1965
Oman	1 June 1989
Qatar	4 December 1990
St Pierre and Miquelon	30 May 1988
Saudi Arabia	18 February 1982
Senegal	29 March 1974
Spain	8 January 1963
Sweden	8 June 1994
Switzerland	31 December 1953
Togo	24 November 1971
Tunisia	28 May 1973
United Arab Emirates	19 July 1989
United Kingdom	21 June 1963
United States	24 November 1978

CHAPTER 8

GERMANY†

I. INTRODUCTION

GERMAN CIVIL LAW SYSTEM

Since German reunification on 3 October 1990, there has been one law of succession in Germany. The law of the Federal Republic of Germany now applies to the area of the former Democratic Republic of Germany in respect of all deaths after 3 October 1990 in accordance with Article 230 EGBGB (*Einführungsgesetz zum Bürgerlichen Gesetzbuch*/Introductory law relating to the German Civil Code). There was previously another law of succession in the former East Germany which was changed substantially in 1976 before reunification. 8.1

There is a system of complete codified law (civil law system). The regulations regarding the national German law of inheritance are contained in the fifth book 'Inheritance' (*Erbrecht*) of the BGB (*Bürgerliches Gesetzbuch*/German Civil Code). Sections 1922 BGB to 2385 BGB regulate the law of inheritance. 8.2

The national German law of inheritance tax is likewise codified and is found in the ErbStG (*Erbschaftsteuer-und Schenkungsteuergesetz*/German inheritance tax law and gift tax law) in 37 sections. 8.3

German private international law is also regulated by statute and is contained in the EGBGB. Particular regulations with respect to the law of inheritance are contained in Articles 25 and 26 EGBGB. In addition there is the convention in respect of the form of last wills of 5 October 1961 (Hague Convention concerning the form of wills/*Haager Testamentsabkommen*). 8.4

With regard to international inheritance tax law, there are double taxation conventions with only five countries; there are no double taxation conventions between the Federal Republic of Germany and the UK and some other European countries. The existing double taxation conventions relate to Greece, Austria, Sweden, Switzerland and the USA. The national regulations with regard to the avoidance of double taxation are in force. Section 21 ErbStG provides under certain circumstances for credits for inheritance tax paid in a foreign country. 8.5

Automatic devolution

On the death of a person, all his assets and property pass to one or more persons as the heirs. Two or more heirs form a particular civil law partnership 8.6

---

† This chapter was written by Dr Karsten Kühne, Rechtsanwalt and German Notary Public, Berlin and London. kkuehne@compuserve.com

(*Erbengemeinschaft*). At the same time, it is stated in s 1967 BGB that all debts also pass to the heirs. The heir is in principle responsible for the estate liabilities. There is no scope for any executor (if not expressly appointed in a will).

8.7 This principle relating to the devolution of an entire estate applies whether the heirs become entitled in accordance with a will or whether they become entitled under the statutory law of succession in case of intestacy. On the death of the deceased, the inheritance passes automatically and directly to the heirs (*Direkterwerb*). The heir therefore becomes directly entitled to all rights and directly responsible for all obligations of the deceased. Inheritance takes effect (s 1942 BGB) in accordance with the law even without the knowledge and agreement of the heir. The deceased cannot exclude such law or make an inheritance in the case of intestacy dependent on a declaration of acceptance by the heir. The heir has, however, the opportunity to disclaim the inheritance. There are specific periods during which the heir may elect to disclaim or accept his entitlement (s 1944 BGB: six weeks from knowledge of death; six months for heirs abroad: see paras **8.52** *et seq*). At the end of the period the heir is deemed to have accepted his inheritance. Before the heir's final acceptance, no claim that is directed against the estate can legally be directed against him (s 1958 BGB).

Capacity to be an heir

8.8 A person can become an heir of a deceased if he is alive at the time of the deceased's death, or if at the time of the death he had already been conceived and is later born alive (s 1923 BGB). It is not possible for notaries, interpreters and trustees to be heirs if such people were involved in the certification of a will. For serious reasons a testator can however exclude, for example, a descendant from being an heir by will if, for instance, the descendant has attempted to take the life of the testator or of his spouse or any other descendant (s 2333 BGB). Such reasons not existing, the children, wife and parents of the deceased are guaranteed a statutory share of the estate: see paras **8.42** *et seq.*

2. INTESTATE SUCCESSION

ORDER OF INHERITANCE IN THE CASE OF INTESTACY

8.9 If there is a valid last disposition, this governs the order of inheritance. If there is no valid last disposition (whether a will, joint will or inheritance contract), the general rules of the statutory law of succession in Book V of the BGB prevail (see s 1922 BGB).

8.10 The heirs are divided into particular degrees (*Ordnungen*) which determine the order of the inheritance. The statutory heirs are the spouse, the children and certain relatives of the deceased. The spouse is not a relative and has a particular legal entitlement. With regard to the relatives, the existence of relatives of a lower degree prevents relatives of a higher degree from becoming entitled to the estate (s 1930 BGB). The degrees can be illustrated through a family tree. Statutory heirs of the first degree are the descendants of the deceased himself (s 1924 BGB). The statutory heirs of the second degree are the parents of the deceased and their descendants (s 1925 BGB). Statutory heirs of the third degree are the grandparents of the deceased and their descendants (s 1926 BGB). The system continues until there are no more eligible relatives. If at the time of the inheritance there is neither an eligible relative nor a surviving spouse of the deceased, then the Inland Revenue of the Federal State of the Federal Republic of Germany in which the deceased lived at the time of his death is the legal heir (s 1936 BGB). The Revenue as the statutory heir is unable to give up its inheritance. It can, however, like any other heir, limit its liability to the actual assets of the deceased's estate.

As far as the degrees are concerned, relatives effectively exclude relatives of the next generation in the degree. For example, a descendant living at the time of the deceased's death excludes descendants through him who are related to the deceased (s 1924 para 2 BGB). Inside the degrees themselves, the devolution passes according to stem, ie *per stirpes*. For example, descendants of a descendant who himself predeceased the testator or intestate take his share (s 1924 para 3 BGB). A testator, however, can under his last will exclude a spouse or an eligible relative from the statutory inheritance without inserting an heir (s 1938 BGB: see also para **8.26**). This exclusion from inheritance is limited by the statutory entitlement (*Pflichtteilsrecht*): see paras **8.42** *et seq*. There are no special rules for real property or businesses, all the assets of the deceased are treated the same way. 8.11

Inheritance entitlement of spouse and children on intestacy

The inheritance entitlement of the spouse is specifically regulated (ss 1931–1934 BGB) dependent upon the property regime of the marriage. The entitlement of the spouse consists of an inheritance element and a matrimonial element. The spouse's share is taken from the estate first and the rest is shared between the other heirs. The surviving spouse, generally speaking, and subject to the following, inherits if there are relatives of the first degree of the deceased (in particular children) one-quarter of the estate. If the nearest relatives are relatives of the second degree, generally speaking, the spouse again takes one-half of the estate (s 1931 para 1 BGB). If neither relatives of the first or second degree are alive, nor grandparents, then the surviving spouse receives the whole of the estate (s 1931 para 2 BGB). The full entitlement of the spouse ends when divorce proceedings have been commenced (s 1933 BGB); it is replaced by a reduced entitlement and a claim for maintenance. The surviving spouse receives in any event without it being calculated as part of his inheritance share the chattels belonging to the matrimonial home. This rule relates to those items which are necessary for the running of a reasonable household if the spouse inherits along with the children of the deceased (s 1932 BGB). 8.12

The inheritance share of the spouse is dependent upon the property regime agreed between the spouses. The statutory adjustments for the matrimonial property regime are made by an increase of the inheritance share of the spouse if the marriage ends due to the death of one of the spouses. In practice the following two matrimonial property ownership regimes are important in Germany. Insofar 8.13

as the spouses have not agreed anything else by a notarial agreement, the statutory rule of community of additionally acquired property applies (s 1363 BGB/ *gesetzliche Zugewinngemeinschaft*). The community of additional property implies a separation of the original property of the spouses during the marriage. The increase of their property which the spouses acquired during the marriage is normally divided in equal shares between the spouses at the time that the community of additional property ends (for example through the death of a spouse, divorce or the agreement of a different property arrangement). Gifts to a spouse, or lottery wins, are deemed not to be acquired and are not divided.

8.14 If the statutory community of additionally acquired property arrangement is ended by the death of a spouse, then the division of the additional property is dealt with by a binding legal presumption to the effect that the statutory share of the surviving spouse is increased by one-quarter of the estate. As far as this is concerned, it is irrelevant if and at what price the spouses have in their particular case acquired any additional property (s 1371 BGB). The otherwise usual calculation of the matrimonial acquisitions (difference between the final property and the property held at the beginning, s 1373 BGB) does therefore not take place but effectively leads in the case of a death to a lump sum adjustment at the ending of the matrimonial community of property through an increase in the inheritance of the surviving spouse.

8.15 If the statutory rule of community of additionally acquired property applies, the result in the case of a marriage with children is that the surviving spouse receives one-quarter of the estate as community property division (s 1371 BGB) and in addition a further one-quarter as the statutory inheritance (s 1931 BGB), a total of one-half of the estate. The children then share the remaining half equally between them.

8.16 An alternative applies if the spouses have chosen to enter into a marriage contract (s 1408 BGB/*Ehevertrag*) as a contractual legal basis for the separation of property ownership regime (s 1414 BGB/*Gütertrennung*). Such a marriage contract is usually published and registered in the property register of the district court of the area of residence of the spouses (s 1558 BGB and s 1562 BGB). The public may inspect this property register (s 1563 BGB).

8.17 In the case of separation of property regimes, the spouses have separate property and a division of acquired property does not take place after a death. Accordingly the spouse only receives a set statutory inheritance share. In accordance with statute, the surviving spouse where there are one or two children of the deceased who are statutory heirs, inherits together with the surviving children in equal shares. In the case of two children the surviving spouse therefore inherits one-third of the estate. If there are three or more children the surviving spouse is entitled as statutory heir to one-quarter as against relatives of the first degree (s 1931 BGB). The children inherit in equal shares (s 1924 para 4 BGB). In the case of three children, the spouse and the three children each inherit a quarter. In the case of over three children, one-quarter passes to the surviving spouse and the remaining three-quarters are divided between the children in equal shares.

In the case of a separation of property agreement, the inheritance entitlement of the surviving spouse could therefore indirectly be altered substantially and automatically. In the case of three children, the surviving spouse receives one-half of the estate where there is the statutory community of property. In the case of separation of property, he only receives one-quarter of the estate. These differences lead to different inheritance tax burdens too. Changing the property regime needs careful consideration. 8.18

Inheritance entitlement of children in the case of intestacy is regulated by statute so that children in principle inherit in equal shares (s 1924 para 4 BGB). The children are second in rank after the spouse whose entitlement has to be settled first. 8.19

Illegitimate children

Since 1970, illegitimate children, although not heirs, are in special cases put in the same position as legitimate children according to value through their inheritance substitution claim (s 1934a BGB/*Erbersatzanspruch*). The illegitimate child then receives the same amount as a legitimate child. The rule of the minimum entitlement under the statutory inheritance (*Pflichtteil*) also applies for the benefit of the illegitimate child (s 1934b BGB). If the illegitimate child receives together with the spouse or together with legitimate children of the deceased then he is legally entitled only to an inheritance substitution claim against the heirs (s 1934a BGB). The illegitimate child is therefore, in contrast to the spouse or the legitimate children, not an heir and has no entitlement in the estate. Rather he is entitled to a legal claim against the estate in respect of the value of his entitlement. This claim is to be paid over by the heirs as a liability of the estate. The intention of the law is to avoid friction between the heirs by excluding the illegitimate children. The inheritance entitlement of the illegitimate child can however be satisfied by a lump sum payment in cash during the lifetime of the father. The illegitimate child can demand this payment between his 21st and 27th birthdays. The division of the inheritance in this case is calculated according to a particular formula taking into account the average maintenance payments made before then (s 1934d BGB). (This part of West German succession law is generally speaking not applicable for illegitimate children born in the former East Germany.) 8.20

3. DISPOSITIONS ON DEATH

WILL (TESTAMENT, *LETZTWILLIGE VERFUEGUNG*), JOINT WILL (*GEMEINSCHAFTLICHES TESTAMENT*), INHERITANCE CONTRACT (*ERBVERTRAG*)

Non-delegable personal capacity to make a will

A person can, after attaining his 16th birthday, make a disposition to take effect on death and therefore regulate the inheritance after his death independently of the statutory intestacy regulations. German law provides for numerous disposition 8.21

possibilities. However, it is not possible to reduce beyond a given limit the statutory inheritance shares of the descendants, parents and spouse of the deceased who constitute the people entitled by law to a minimum provision from the estate (*Pflichtteil*). As a form of last will, there can be selected an individual will regulated by law under s 1937 BGB and s 2064 BGB, the joint will, a particular form regulated for spouses in s 2265 BGB, and an inheritance contract with any contractual partner regulated under s 2274 BGB. These dispositions on death can only be made personally: it is not possible for these to be done through a third party (s 2064 BGB and s 2274 BGB). The deceased has to decide the content of his will himself and cannot make a last will in a manner providing that a third party can decide whether a last disposition is to be valid or not and the deceased cannot leave to a third party the identity of a recipient or the amount of a legacy (s 2065 BGB). Only limited rights and powers can be given to an especially appointed executor (*Testamentsvollstrecker*), s 2197 BGB.

Formalities and revocation

8.22 A will can only be validly executed by means of notarisation by a public notary or by a personally written will (s 2231 BGB). The so-called 'public will' completed before a notary by means of notarisation need not be written out by hand (s 2232 BGB). The notary reads the (usually typed) notarial will to the testator who approves and signs it together with the notary. The holograph will must be entirely written by hand and signed or it will be void under s 2125 BGB. It does not have to be witnessed. It should contain the date and place of signature as well as the name and first names of the testator (s 2247 BGB). A joint will of spouses can either be completed by a notary or can be written by hand, in which case one of the spouses completes the will in the aforementioned manner and the other spouse in addition signs the joint declaration (s 2267 BGB). An inheritance contract can only be completed by a notary in the joint presence of both parties (s 2276 BGB). The valid document itself has the effect of a will.

8.23 A validly completed disposition on death can be revoked by the participants. A will of a single testator can be revoked at any time (s 2253 BGB). The revocation of a will can be through a subsequent valid will (s 2254 BGB) in which in testamentary form other different dispositions are made or a revocation is expressly declared. A will can also be revoked if the testator with the intention of revoking it destroys the will document or makes amendments to it through which his intention of revocation is apparent (s 2255 BGB). The taking back of a public will from official custody (see below) is also a revocation (s 2256 BGB). The revocation can itself be revoked (s 2257 BGB). Insofar as dispositions in joint wills and inheritance contracts are based on reciprocity so that the disposition of one contractual partner is a condition for the disposition of another contracting partner, such a disposition can only jointly and by agreement be revoked or set aside while both partners are still alive (s 2271 BGB).

Official safe custody and opening of will

8.24 Because only the original testamentary document has the effect of a will, it is absolutely essential to store the original in a safe place. For the security of last testamentary declarations, official safe custody is usual. Although the deposit of the document is not an essential requirement, the keeping of the document by a court is to be recommended. Sections 2258a to 2259 BGB provide specific rules as to how and as to which court the document should be delivered. The local courts are informed of all deaths by the German residence offices (*Einwohnermeldeamt*) and the courts will ensure that the last dispositions are taken into account. A handwritten will is taken into official custody on the request of the testator. The testator will then be given a so-called receipt certificate as confirmation (s 2248 BGB/*Hinterlegungsschein*). A testamentary disposition completed before a notary should be brought into official safe custody by the notary insofar as the testator does not direct otherwise (s 34 Certification Law/*Beurkundungsgesetz*).

The local courts (*Amtsgericht*) are responsible for the keeping of the document in safe custody. In the case of a notarially completed document, it should be given to the court of the area of the notary. The testator can, however, select a particular court (s 2258a BGB). In cases where last testamentary dispositions have not been brought into official custody prior to the death of the testator then, after his death, each person in possession of such a last will is required to deliver the document to the local court's Inheritance Section (*Nachlassgericht* s 2259 BGB). The court will determine a time for the opening of the will at which point the contents of the will will be made known. Those invited to the opening of the will are the legal heirs of the testator and others affected (s 2260 BGB). A person who makes a legal claim is entitled to see a will which has been opened and to require a copy of the will or of particular parts of it from the court (s 2264 BGB). In cases where a notarially completed will or, in particular cases, a will completed before a mayor as a matter of expediency, is taken from official safe custody by the testator, this taking back is classified as a revocation of the will (s 2256 BGB). The taking back of a handwritten will from official custody has however no effect on the validity of such a will (s 2256, para 3 BGB). 8.25

Many possibilities with regard to dispositions

Wills can contain many different types of contents, in particular the **declaration of heirs** (s 2087 BGB), the declaration of persons with interests in possession and reversionary beneficiaries (s 2100 BGB), legacies (s 2147 BGB), conditions and obligations (s 2192 BGB), the appointment of an administrative executor (s 2197 BGB), a negative content, eg merely the direction of a disinheritance (s 1938 BGB) or the revocation of an earlier will (s 2154 BGB). As a result of the automatic devolution to heirs of the indivisible rights and duties of the testator, it is in principle not possible to appoint heirs as particular heirs for certain items in the estate. If the testator leaves several heirs, the estate is classified as a unity of property (s 2032 BGB). Each heir can deal with his share of the estate but a co-heir is not able to deal with his share of individual items in the estate (s 2033 BGB). Nevertheless, the testator can give directions with regard to the division of the estate (s 2048 BGB). In such a division declaration the testator can direct that certain items in the estate shall go to one of the heirs. Alternatively, the testator can leave legacies. 8.26

Beneficiary with interest in possession and reversionary beneficiary

8.27 In the case of an estate where there is an interest in possession and a reversionary interest, the testator can declare a person to be an heir on the basis that this person only becomes the heir (reversionary beneficiary/*Nacherbe*) after another person has earlier become the heir (person with an interest in possession/*Vorerbe*) in respect of the same estate (s 2100 BGB). For example, spouses can ensure that the family property remains held for their descendants insofar as they give each other interests in possession and declare that on the death of the survivor of them, the reversionary beneficiaries are to be the children of the marriage equally. The person with an interest in possession is entitled to take the income (for example rent or interest) from the estate. He is also able to deal with the capital belonging to the estate with particular restrictions (s 2122 BGB). The person with an interest in possession cannot, as a general rule, deal with land (and ships), and he is unable to make gifts to the detriment of the estate (s 2113 BGB). The testator can limit the right of disposition of the person with an interest in possession in his will. Alternatively, he can free such a person from all limitations (s 2136 BGB) and limit the entitlement of the reversionary beneficiary merely to that part of the estate which remains when the reversionary entitlement arises (s 2137 BGB). This occurs when the person's interest in possession ceases and the estate passes to the reversionary beneficiary (s 2139 BGB). This can be at any time in accordance with the wishes of the testator. If the testator does not specify a particular time or event, the reversionary interest comes into force on the death of the person with an interest in possession (s 2106 BGB).

8.28 The person with an interest in possession and the reversionary beneficiary are classified as beneficiaries of the same testator: the reversionary beneficiary does not inherit from the interest in possession beneficiary. The capital estate can be subjected to a particular time-scale or condition, for example, a child can be included as an heir until a grandchild is born (also see s 2101 BGB) or, for example, a spouse can be limited to having an interest in possession for the period of ten years and thereafter the children become immediately entitled to the capital.

8.29 A disadvantage of such a disposition can be shown by a higher inheritance tax liability, because two transfers of assets are deemed to have taken place. It might be worth considering giving the assets to the children direct on condition that they grant only the use to the surviving spouse.

Legacy

8.30 By means of a legacy (*Vermächtnis*) certain items of value or particular chattels can be bequeathed to people, who through this gift do not become heirs. The legacy gives rise to a legal claim against the estate and, insofar as the testator does not declare otherwise, the heir is required to fulfil the legacy (s 2157 BGB). It can be used for all types of property, for example a particular cash sum, a life-long right of occupation or the income from property such as shares or residential property. Also with regard to tax considerations, a division of the estate between the heirs and the giving of an income entitlement to a legatee can be advantageous. It is, for example, possible through a legacy to leave a residential property to the children as heirs, but to give the spouse for the remainder of his life a right of occupation or right to income from the land.

Legacies can be given to heirs too. 8.31

Directions and conditions

The testator can set out directions (*Auflagen*) to be observed by the heirs (s 2192 BGB). Either the heir or a legatee can be required to carry out a task which is merely a moral obligation for him giving rise to no entitlement to performance (s 1940 BGB). The subject of a direction can be anything which could be the subject of a legal duty. Often the obligation involves the funeral arrangements or the care of the grave. The person who benefits by the task in a particular case has no right to require it to be performed, and therefore has no legal claim. The completion of the task is, however, secured on the basis that different or potential heirs have a legal claim against the heir if the heir fails to perform the task (s 2194 BGB). 8.32

The testator can strictly ensure the performance legally through making it a condition (*Bedingung*) of the benefit. In such a case, the heir will not obtain his inheritance if the condition is not observed. 8.33

Administrative executors

The testator in a will can appoint one or more administrative executors (*Testamentsvollstrecker*). The testator can cover the possibility that the named executor may not be available, whether before or after accepting the office and, as a precaution, name another executor (s 2197 BGB). An executorship by operation of law cannot arise. Executorships leave the heir his right of disposition. The heir at the time of the death becomes immediately the direct owner of the rights in the estate. On death, a common law trust is very different from a German executorship, which has the character of a guardianship. The task of the executor can be either to bring into operation the last wishes of the testator (s 2203 BGB) or the administration of the estate can be given to him for a particular length of time (s 2209 BGB). 8.34

The executor is entitled to take the estate into his possession and to deal with the estate assets. In entering into contracts he acts as representative of the heirs. The heirs' powers are limited in the disposition of the estate insofar as they are required to observe the control of the executor over the last instructions of the testator (s 2211 BGB). The executor is required immediately after taking up office to give a certificate to the heirs detailing the estate assets (s 2250 BGB) and he is required to administer the estate in a proper manner (s 2216 BGB). If he fails to perform his duties the executor is required to compensate the heirs in respect of the loss thereby suffered (s 2219 BGB). An executor can also be directed to manage a business for a particular period if, for example, the testator has made dispositions at the time of his death for minor children, so that such a child only takes over the business on attaining his majority. 8.35

Joint will

8.36 A particular legal possibility exists for spouses in that they can execute a joint will (s 2265 BGB/ *Gemeinschaftliches Testament*). A joint will can be executed through a notary or by hand. For the execution of a joint handwritten will, it is sufficient if one of the spouses writes out the will by hand and the other spouse signs the joint will by hand (s 2267 BGB). From the commencement of proceedings for divorce a joint will is automatically entirely revoked by law (s 2268 BGB). The most remarkable aspect of a joint will is that particular dispositions are only made if the other spouse for his part in return makes specific dispositions, these dispositions being described as 'mutual dispositions' (s 2270 BGB/ *wechselbezügliche Verfügungen*). The invalidity or the revocation of a mutual disposition automatically revokes the corresponding mutual disposition (s 2270 para 1 BGB). Mutual dispositions can only be revoked jointly by spouses. The right of revocation ends with the death of one spouse (s 2271 BGB). Thus a joint will can only be taken back by spouses jointly from safe custody (s 2272 BGB).

8.37 A standardised form of a joint will is the 'Berlin Will' (*Berliner Testament*). In a so-called 'Berlin Will' the spouses declare themselves to be heirs of each other with the addition that after the death of the survivor, the combined estate is to pass to a third party, usually the children (s 2269 BGB).

8.38 Such a will ensures the inheritance of the children but it does not protect the children in respect of dispositions of the surviving spouse during his lifetime. Not even an inheritance contract securing the heir's entitlement restricts the testator's right to dispose of his property legally during his lifetime (s 2268 BGB). A 'Berlin Will' can cause high inheritance tax liabilities because of the two successive transfers of assets involved.

Inheritance contract

8.39 A testator can conclude an inheritance contract (*Erbvertrag*) with a particular person in respect of his last testamentary dispositions. Such an inheritance contract can only be made in person and not in any way through a representative. It can only be completed through a notarisation by a notary in the joint presence of the parties (s 2276 BGB). In an inheritance contract, one or both of the parties can make a testamentary disposition. The dispositions binding on both sides are called 'contractual dispositions' (s 2278 *BGB/vertragsmässige Verfügungen*). These 'contractual dispositions' are comparable with the 'mutual dispositions' in a joint will: see para **8.36**.

8.40 On the taking on of a child in a business, the owner of the business can, for example, enter into a legally binding obligation to make the child his heir. The inheritance of the child as a result of a binding 'contractual disposition' is thereby secured. German law does not require any consideration to make such obligation binding. The inheritance contract does not, however, limit the right of the testator to dispose of his property during his lifetime (s 2268 BGB). The beneficiary under the inheritance contract therefore has no guarantee of the value of the estate which will be available at the time of the testator's death. Additional security measures may be necessary to protect the prospective heir.

An inheritance contract can be revoked by agreement of the parties who signed the inheritance contract: after the death of one of these people its revocation is no longer possible (s 2290 BGB). The testator can, however, unilaterally rescind the contractual disposition if the intended beneficiary carries out a criminal act which would enable the testator to exclude that person's statutory inheritance, for example, if the other party plots to kill the testator (s 2294 BGB and s 2333 BGB). 8.41

The statutory inheritance share

Children, parents and the spouse of the testator are in accordance with binding legal regulation entitled to their so-called statutory share (*gesetzlicher Pflichtteil*) as participants in the value of the estate. If a descendant, the spouse or the parents of a testator are excluded from the estate under a testamentary disposition then they are able to demand their statutory share from the heirs without prejudicing the validity of the will. The statutory share consists of one-half of the amount they would have received on an intestacy (s 2303 BGB). The person entitled to a statutory share is not an heir and is not involved in the heir's entitlement in the estate. The statutory share of one-half of the intestacy entitlement gives rise to a cash claim against the heir. Reference can specifically be made in a will to a statutory share. Such a disposition is in case of doubt (according to legal precedent) not to be interpreted as a declaration of an heir (s 2304 BGB). 8.42

To assess the value of the statutory share, the value of the fictitious intestate legal share has first to be established. In the case of a statutory community of property regime on the death of a spouse in a family with two children, the legal inheritance will pass to the spouse as to one-half and the two children will each receive a quarter. If, therefore, a child is specifically excluded from a will, then the statutory share of this child amounts to one-eighth of the estate. The calculation of the statutory share is based on the condition and value of the estate at the time of death of the testator (s 2311 BGB). The heir is required on demand to give details of the estate (s 2314 BGB). 8.43

The claim in respect of the statutory share arises on the testator's death (s 2317 BGB). A legal claim against the estate must be expressly claimed or the heir is not required to meet the obligation. The claim in respect of the statutory share must be made within three years of the time when the person entitled to the statutory share receives information of the death and the disposition affecting him. Irrespective of this, there is an overriding time-limit of 30 years from the death (s 2332 BGB). The claim itself is part of the estate of the entitled person (s 2317 BGB). 8.44

The person entitled to the statutory share has to bring into account in respect of the statutory share what is left to him under the will or what was given to him by the testator during his lifetime (s 2315 BGB). If the testator in the last ten years before his death has made gifts to third parties and therefore reduced his estate, the person entitled to the statutory share can require the heirs to increase the size of the statutory share as if the gifted property had formed part of the estate (s 2325 BGB). The statutory share can be given up by the entitled person (see paras **8.51** *et seq*), or could, in particular cases, be taken away by the testator. The statutory share 8.45

can only be taken away in a few and specialised legally determined cases by a last will (s 2336 BGB). For example, it can be taken away from a descendant if he tried to kill the testator, his spouse or another descendant (s 2333 BGB). The statutory inheritance can be taken away from the spouse if the spouse was guilty of serious physical mistreatment of the testator (s 2355 BGB) and the statutory share can be taken away from the parents if they deliberately ignored their maintenance obligations (s 2344 BGB).

8.46 The statutory share is always to be taken into account when a will is prepared. It might be possible to delay the payment of the statutory share by directing that part of the estate be sold and converted into cash to provide a legacy of an amount equivalent to the value of the statutory share and directing that such legacy be not paid out till some deferred future date.

4. CALCULATION OF ESTATE AND SHARES IN THE ESTATE

8.47 Due to the automatic devolution of the assets and debts the estate comprises all the assets and debts of the deceased.

8.48 If there are several heirs, however, calculation of their individual shares may lead them to receive different amounts. Sections 2050 BGB *et seq* provide rules for bringing into account lifetime gifts of the deceased to one of his heirs when the share of this heir is determined. Also, lifetime gifts on the occasion of the wedding of a child have to be added (s 2050 BGB) to the actual estate in order to establish a 'fictitious' estate. The shares of the heirs will be determined as shares of this fictitious estate, and an heir has to give credit for the relevant assets which he has already received before the death.

5. LIABILITY OF THE HEIR

8.49 In the context of the total transfer of rights and duties, the heir is in the first instance responsible for all estate liabilities (s 1967 BGB). This liability can, however, be limited by the heir to the assets of the estate if an administration of the estate or a liquidation of the estate to satisfy the creditors is ordered (s 1975 BGB/*Nachlassverwaltung, Nachlasskonkurs*). The heir should file an application immediately when he becomes aware of debts which cannot be met by the estate. Insofar as the costs required to carry out a liquidation of the estate are not to hand, then the application of the heir for a liquidation (s 1980 BGB) will probably be rejected because of the lack of assets (s 1982 BGB) and the heir can in such a case reject any settlement with the estate's creditors insofar as the estate is insufficient to meet the claims (s 1990 BGB). These rights are also available to the Revenue as statutory heir.

The inheritance court can set a time-limit for the heir to submit an inventory as to the value of the estate to an estate creditor; after elapse of such a time-limit the heir incurs unlimited liability for the estate liabilities if he has not earlier prepared the inventory with a list of the assets of the estate (s 1994 BGB). On the requirement of the estate's creditors the heir has to confirm by oath, in accordance with the requirements of the estate court, that he has given the details of the assets of the estate as fully as possible according to his knowledge; if he declines to take the oath, then the heir again becomes liable on an unlimited basis (s 2006 BGB). The giving of a false declaration by oath is a crime punishable with a fine or imprisonment. 8.50

6. WAIVER AND DISCLAIMER OF INHERITANCE

Heirs can, by means of a contract with the testator, waive (*Erbverzicht*) their entitlement in the estate and also their claim for statutory heirship. They are then excluded from the estate and have no right of statutory heirship (s 2346 BGB). A contract to give up an inheritance requires a notarial certification (s 2348 BGB), and, in particular, it requires clear advice to have been given by the notary with regard to the share being waived. 8.51

If the heir has not made any contract with the testator waiving his entitlement, and he establishes after the death of the testator that he does not want to accept the inheritance as an heir, whether under a will or on an intestacy, for example because of the insolvency of the estate, he can disclaim his entitlement in the estate (s 1942 BGB/*Erbausschlagung*). German law sets specific periods during which the disclaimer has to be made, eg six weeks from knowledge of death, six months for heirs abroad (s 1944 BGB). If the inheritance is disclaimed, then the share of the estate does not pass to the person disclaiming and the estate is administered as if the person disclaiming had not been alive at the date of the death (s 1953 BGB). Nevertheless, the person maintains the right to demand his statutory heirship (*Pflichtteil*, s 2306 BGB). 8.52

It is also possible (and often necessary) for the person who becomes the new heir through the disclaimer to disclaim his own new entitlement. The final heirs are the Revenue (s 1936 BGB, see para **8.10**) and the Revenue cannot disclaim (s 1942 BGB) but can limit their liability like any other heir (see para **8.49**). 8.53

The period, as mentioned previously, during which a disclaimer can be made amounts to six weeks from the date when the heir first knew of the death and his entitlement; the limitation period is six months if the deceased had his last place of residence abroad or if the heir is abroad when the period begins to run (s 1944 BGB). If an heir cannot be contacted within the limitation period and a public appeal to accept the inheritance does not bring him forward, then there is the presumption that the Revenue is the statutory heir (s 1964 BGB and s 1965 BGB). 8.54

7. CERTIFICATE OF INHERITANCE

8.55 The proof of inheritance entitlement is established through an *Erbschein*, ie a certificate of inheritance. This is only issued if the local court (*Amtsgericht*) which has jurisdiction as the inheritance court accepts the necessary facts of the establishment of the inheritance entitlement (s 2359 BGB). On an application by the heir, the inheritance court is required to issue a certificate of his heirship and if he is entitled only to a share of the estate, a certificate as to size of his entitlement in the estate. This certificate is the *Erbschein* (s 2353 BGB). The heir is required to make an application to the inheritance court (s 2354 BGB) in which he gives evidence of his entitlement through official documents or through an oath sworn before a notary (s 2356 BGB). The inheritance court officially confirms the facts given to it and goes through the evidence given to it relating to the heir (s 2358 BGB). If it transpires that a certificate of inheritance which has been issued is incorrect, then the inheritance court must retrieve it and then declare it to be invalid (s 2361 BGB). In the certificate of inheritance, any named executor must be mentioned (s 2364 BGB). The certificate of inheritance gives adequate grounds for proceeding on the basis that the person referred to in the certificate of inheritance is the person legally entitled and the person able to dispose of the property without any limitation (s 2365 BGB and s 2366 BGB).

8.56 If a German inheritance court only has restricted jurisdiction, that is to say in cases of the death of a person living abroad with German property, then as far as the property situated in Germany is concerned, a *gegenständlich beschränkter Erbschein* (limited certificate) can be issued with the validity of a full certificate of inheritance (s 2369 BGB) for assets in Germany.

8.57 The issuing of a certificate of inheritance is of great importance. It is the means of giving authority to the person entitled to it. In legal correspondence with authorities, banks etc, the certificate of inheritance is a necessary requirement for the acceptance of the entitlement of the heir to deal with the assets in the estate. As it might take some months to obtain a certificate of inheritance, the testator should consider giving additional powers of attorney to his appointed heirs during his lifetime. German law accepts enduring powers of attorney which will continue to be valid after the death of the testator. The heir can use this power of attorney until he receives his certificate of inheritance.

8. GERMAN INHERITANCE TAX AND THE USE OF COMMON LAW TRUSTS

8.58 The estates of German residents and assets in Germany are subject to German inheritance tax. With effect from 1 January 1996, German inheritance tax was changed substantially. On the one hand, new regulations for the valuation of assets came into force, which in many cases more than doubled the relevant tax values for land. The new tax values are supposed to reflect market values, whereas the former 'Standard Tax Values' (*Einheitswerte*) were regularly much lower than market prices. On the other hand, new and lower tax rates were introduced. There is a new inheritance tax scale which provides for tax rates between 7% and 50%. German inheritance tax is not borne by the estate for the value of the whole estate, but by the individual heir in respect of his share in the estate. It is therefore good practice to split the estate between spouse, children and even grandchildren in order to mitigate the inheritance tax burden.

There are three tax brackets, the tax rate increasing for heirs who are distant 8.59
relatives or who are not relatives of the deceased. Spouses and children come under tax bracket I; brothers, sisters and children-in-law as well as the divorced spouse come under tax bracket II; and tax bracket III catches everyone who does not come under brackets I or II. Obviously, the system is more complex and only some examples can be given. Each tax bracket is divided into tax bands, which are the same for all the brackets. There are seven tax bands, the lowest up to DM 100,000 and the highest starting at DM 50 million. In tax bracket I, the tax rate for the lowest band is 7% and for the highest 30%; in tax bracket II, 12% and 40%; and in tax bracket III, 17% and 50% respectively. The share of an heir is not assessed band by band, but the band is determined by the total value of the share. A share of more than DM 50 million is taxed at a rate of 30% in bracket I, which applies for the whole of the value of the share. There are preferential tax rates for business assets.

German international inheritance tax is governed by the national tax laws of the 8.60
countries involved. Double Taxation Treaties in respect of inheritance tax are only in force between Germany, Greece, Austria, Sweden, Switzerland, and the USA. German inheritance tax law allows credits for inheritance tax paid in other countries, generally speaking. The result, assuming that the other countries give credits as well, is often that the estate or the heir ends up paying the highest available tax in any of the countries involved.

For international estates with assets in different countries, it might be worth 8.61
considering the use of a common law trust. German civil law does not know the concept of the 'trust', the German *Treuhand* being a contract to provide certain services as asset manager. In recent precedents, the German Federal Fiscal Court (*Bundesfinanzhof* or BFH) has, however, accepted the structure of common law trusts as being tax-effective for German tax law, including German inheritance tax. However, German tax law does not accept trusts under which benefits can be directed by the settlor or third parties. In the latter case, German tax law would look to the settlor as the beneficial owner of the asset. For the time being, carefully structured trusts are effective in respect of German inheritance tax, subject, of course, to further approval by the German fiscal courts.

9. PRIVATE INTERNATIONAL LAW

According to German private international law (art 25 EGBGB), the devolution of 8.62
the movable and immovable estate of a person is dependent on the law of the country of which the testator was a national at the time of his death. Insofar as the private international law of this country refers the matter back to German law, this referral back is accepted under German law (art 4 EGBGB).

8.63 Under English private international law, the law of the deceased's last domicile governs succession to movables and the *lex situs* governs immovables. Germany accepts a referral back. As a result, succession to immovables in England or in Germany is governed by the domestic *lex situs*, irrespective of the deceased's nationality or domicile. However, German movables of a British national with English domicile will be governed by English law, while English movables of a person (whether British or German) domiciled in Germany will be governed by German law.

10. SOME SIMPLE MEANS OF MINIMISING PROBLEMS WHERE INTERNATIONAL ELEMENTS ARE CONCERNED

8.64 Establish separate wills for property in different countries ensuring that the proper formalities are observed, taking into account the 1961 Hague Convention on Form of Wills which Germany has implemented, so that it suffices if a will complies with the national law of the testator or the law of the place where the will was executed.

8.65 Provide for powers of attorney effected under German law that remain in force after the death of the deceased so that the attorney has capacity to dispose of the property covered by his power of attorney prior to the issue of the certificate of inheritance.

8.66 If a foreign person is about to acquire real property in Germany so that the German *Pflichtteil* rules become relevant it is possible to form a company (not necessarily in Germany) and have the company acquire for example, a house so that the person then owns shares, which are movables, rather than immovables subject to *Pflichtteil.* However, capital gains tax and further tax consequences upon the company subsequently selling the house may be such that it will be preferable to suffer the *Pflichtteil* consequences of the person owning the house directly. A structure like this might not be effective for a German resident as German law might regard him or her as the beneficial owner of the house.

8.67 It is not possible to avoid *Pflichtteil* consequences by *tontine* arrangements with a co-owner because German law does not allow such arrangements.

8.68 Currently, in 1997, it is possible to avoid some German inheritance tax problems through using an irrevocable discretionary common law trust. It seems that the trust assets will be sheltered from inheritance tax so long as the trustees do not make any payments or distributions and that the increase in the value of the assets in the trust will therefore only become subject to inheritance tax at the time of distribution. Revenue from the assets will be treated similarly in respect of taxes on income.

8.69 **Ask for the advice of an expert, especially so that tax issues can be properly considered.**

CHAPTER 9

GREECE†

1. INTRODUCTION

HISTORICAL OVERVIEW

Succession law is regulated in the fifth and last book of the Civil Code, which came into force on 23 February 1946. The other four books are: General Principles (arts 1–286); Law of Obligations (arts 287–946); Property Law (arts 947–1345); and Family Law (arts 1346–1709). 9.1

The roots of succession law can be traced back to the times of ancient Greece; indeed several of its basic concepts are to be found in the inheritance law of Athens.[1] Until the introduction of the Civil Code, succession law reflected the rules of Roman-Byzantine law, as the latter had evolved through the centuries. In the early parts of the twentieth century, a number of legislative attempts were undertaken to codify succession law. These attempts did not aim at producing a single comprehensive codification; they only succeeded in codifying specific issues of inheritance law.[2] Complete codification was achieved under the Civil Code. Book V produced many innovations and was to some extent influenced by the relevant provisions of the German (1896), French (1804) and Swiss (1907) Civil Codes. The Greek law of succession has been characterised as 'highly technical, formal and detailed [with an] often quite obscure structure'.[3] 9.2

---

† This chapter was written by KD Magliveras of Exeter College, Oxford. All references are to the Civil Code, unless otherwise mentioned.
References to the male gender imply the female gender as well and vice versa.
Abbreviations used: Code of Civil Procedure (CCP), Penal Code (PC), *Greek Justice* (journal published monthly in Greek).

1 Generally, see Caillemer, *Le Droit de Succession legitime a Athènes*, Ernest Thorin Paris 1879; MacDowell, *The Law in Classical Athens*, Thames and Hudson, 1978; Harrison, *The Law of Athens*, Vol I, Clarendon Press, Oxford, 1968, pp 122–162, Lane Fox, 'Aspects of Inheritance in the Greek World' in Cartledge and Harvey (eds), *Essays in Greek History*, Exeter, 1985, pp 208–332. Buechsenschuetz, Besitz und Erwebim griechischen Altertum, Scientia Verlag, Aalen, 1962; Biscardi, Dritto Greco Antico, Giuffra, 1982, pp 117–129; Todd, *The Shape of Athenian Law*, Clarendon Press, Oxford, 1995, pp 216–227. On litigious issues, see Bonner and Smith, *The Administration of Justice from Homer to Aristotle*, Vol II, AMS Press, New York, 1977, pp 97–116.

2 For example, the Act of 1911 on wills, and the Act 2310/1920 on intestate succession.

3 See Grammatikaki-Alexiou, 'The Law of Succession', in Kerameus and Kozuris (eds), *Introduction to Greek Law*, 2nd edn, Kluwer, 1993, p 161.

THE CONFLICTING INTERESTS IN SUCCESSION

9.3 The rules of succession law attempt to provide solutions that may reconcile the conflicting interests of the deceased and of those persons whose position is affected by his death. The following interests need to be taken into account:

(1) the interests of the deceased, who wishes his assets to be inherited but who also expects to be allowed to nominate his heirs and distribute his assets without any restrictions;
(2) the interests of the close family of the deceased, who demand not only a mandatory inheritance right but also to be protected by the law in case the deceased disinherits them without good cause (the notion of forced heirship; see arts 1825–1845);
(3) the interests of the heirs who wish to be free to choose whether to accept the inheritance or not, and, in the former case, to restrict their liability to an amount equal to the value of the estate's assets; in other words, they aim at avoiding unlimited personal liability, if they choose to accept the inheritance (benefit of inventory) (see arts 1901–1912);
(4) the interests of the creditors of the deceased, who fear that his death may result in their claims not being honoured and paid in full, and, in effect, expect that they should be able to demand payment from each and every heir;
(5) especially in cases of very large inheritances the interests of the economic life of the country dictating that the domestic impact of the deceased's death upon employment and the creation of wealth should be as little as possible;
(6) the interests of the state, which may in the last resort benefit as an heir (see art 1824), but which will in any event benefit by taking advantage of the excellent opportunity to increase its revenues by imposing taxes in respect of the deceased's assets passing to those who inherit them.
(7) the interests of the deceased's relatives, who, although they may not have contributed at all in the creation of his wealth, expect to inherit much of his wealth;
(8) the interests of the heir, who demands that for the proper calculation of inheritance shares, all donations made and all assets transferred to other persons be notionally added to the estate.

THE GENERAL PRINCIPLES OF SUCCESSION

9.4 The following principles can be distinguished and form the basis for reconciling the various opposing interests:

(1) the right of succession is recognised both in its active manifestation (ie a person may inherit assets from another person) and in its passive manifestation (ie a person's assets may be inherited by another);
(2) the freedom of a person to choose the destiny of his estate for the time after his death is acknowledged and accepted, albeit with certain restrictions;
(3) the family of the deceased is fully protected should the latter decide to deprive it of its active rights of succession;

(4) heirs at large, creditors, the economic life of the country and the interests of the state are all afforded a certain degree of protection.

2. THE WILL[1]

Wills are not a common phenomenon in contemporary Greek society. From a sociological point of view, it should be noted that the Greek family shares the characteristics of a typical Mediterranean family, the most important being the very close links that are developed between its members. If we add to this the fact that since World War II a typical Greek family has, on average, fewer than two children, it is not difficult to ascertain why testamentary succession is not very popular. 9.5

The Civil Code envisages two main types of wills: ordinary and extraordinary. The latter, as the name suggests, caters for specific and rather uncommon circumstances, which are of three kinds: wills made on a Greek-flagged commercial or war vessel while en route to her destination (arts 1749–1752);[2] 'military wills', which can only be drafted by members of the armed forces in war situations (arts 1753–1756); and 'blockade wills', which are made by persons residing in areas with restricted access, because of outbreaks of illnesses, war hostilities etc (art 1757). 9.6

ORDINARY WILLS

Ordinary wills are further divided into holographic, public and secret wills. It should be noted that all three types are considered to be equal in status and, in effect, a public will may be revoked by a holographic will and vice versa. 9.7

Holographic wills (arts 1721–1723)

Holographic wills are defined as wills, the whole text of which has been handwritten, dated and signed by the testator himself (art 1721(1)). They are considered to be private and not public documents. In order to secure that a holographic will is not destroyed or forged, article 1722 allows the testator to deposit it either with a notary public[3] or with a third person. 9.8

Examining the three distinctive elements of a holographic will, the following observations can be made. The requirement that it is handwritten means that any will produced by a mechanical means (eg typewriter, voice recorder) is null and void. If the testator cannot read handwritten documents, article 1723 prevents him from drafting holographic wills. It follows that this prohibition also covers 9.9

1 See Stefanopoulos, '*Die Testameterrictung in Griechenland*' [1961] Oesterreichische Juristenzeitung 376; Stefanopoulos, '*Gueltigkeit Eroeffnung und Vollstreckung des Testaments in Griechenland*' [1962] Oesterreichische Juristenzeitung 372.

2 It is doubtful whether these provisions can be applied by analogy to wills made on airplanes.

3 In Greece the legal status of a notary public is equal to that of an unsalaried civil servant.

testators who, for one reason or another, cannot write without the aid of a third person. It is irrelevant in which language the will is drafted; thus the testator can use a dead language (ancient Greek or Latin) or a cryptographic or stenographic system, provided, of course, that at all times the meaning of the will's text can be ascertained.

9.10 If part of the will was not handwritten, the prevailing legal opinion is that this part is null and void whereas the validity of the remaining text will be decided in accordance with article 181. This provision stipulates that the partial invalidity of a legal transaction will result in the invalidity of the whole transaction, if it can be shown that the latter would not have been concluded without the invalid part.

9.11 Dating the will is of paramount importance, because the date is the crucial element to prove whether the testator had at that particular time the capacity to make wills, whether this was the last of several wills, whether the grounds for disinheritance (see arts 1939 and 1840) invoked by the testator were valid etc. The will must include a full date, ie day, month and year, which, if not explicitly mentioned, may be deduced from a certain and undisputed date or event (eg 'on this day of Christmas 1996'). Problems are encountered when the date is incomplete or non-existent (eg 30 February 1996). However, if the date is untrue or incorrect, article 1721(3) stipulates that this defect alone cannot lead to the invalidity of the will.

9.12 The signature should include the full name of the testator and must be placed at the very end of the will, because text which is not covered by a signature is not recognised as forming part of the will. The aim of this rule is obvious – it prevents third persons from adding provisions to the will in their favour.

9.13 The testator reserves the right to make additions to his will as recognised in article 1721(4); however, such additions should be 'simple' and signed by him, otherwise they are not taken into consideration. What additions are 'simple' is not explained in the Civil Code so it will usually be a question of interpretation for the courts.

Public wills (arts 1724–1738)

9.14 Public wills are defined in article 1724 as oral declarations of last intent (dispositions) made before a notary public and three witnesses and which are later embodied in a document drafted by the notary public in the Greek language. Public wills can also be concluded abroad before a Greek Consular official in accordance with the provisions of the relevant law.[1] Unlike holographic wills, they are considered to be public documents.

9.15 The Civil Code contains detailed provisions as to which notaries public and which witnesses may or may not participate in a public will. More specifically, the spouse and the close relatives of the testator (art 1725) and beneficiaries or executors of the will and their spouses or close relatives (art 1726) are excluded. Furthermore, persons who are blind or deaf, persons who have not completed their eighteenth

1 The so-called consular wills, regulated under art 81 Act 4592/1931, art 27 Act 419/1976, art 1773 and arts 807 and 808 CCP.

year of age, foreigners and those who do not enjoy the legal capacity to enter into contracts can never act as witnesses (art 1728). Both the testator and the witnesses must be known to the notary public. If the testator is unknown to the notary public, the witnesses must testify as to his real identity (art 1728) and they will suffer criminal sanctions should they give false testimony.

Once the testator has made his oral declarations (art 1730) and the witnesses have taken the oath stipulated in article 1731, the notary public will draw up the relevant document, which should include all items and formalities mentioned in articles 1732 and 1734. The document will then be read aloud to and be signed by all participating parties (art 1733). Foreigners have the opportunity to make public wills; this conclusion is based on the wording of article 1737, which provides that, if it appears to the notary public that the testator is ignorant of the Greek language, a public will is validly concluded if an interpreter is employed for the duration of the procedure. Although the interpreter must be chosen by the testator and all provisions relating to witnesses apply to him as well, he never becomes a participating party and his signature is not required. 9.16

Secret wills (arts 1738–1747)

The secret will is an intermediate type between the holographic and the public will and shares characteristics of both. It consists of two separate documents: the testator submits to a notary public a sealed document, written in any language, and declares to him and to the bystanding three witnesses that this is his true last intent (art 1738) and the notary public draws a protocol which records the submission (art 1743). The document handed in by the testator may be written by a third person (art 1740); if it is not signed, the testator must explain to the notary public the reasons which prevented him from signing (art 1744). If the reason invoked is that he is not able to read, the notary public cannot accept it as a secret will (art 1748) but he can suggest the making of a public will. 9.17

A secret will is subject to many formalities, omission of any one of which will lead to its invalidity. However, the observance of these formalities is not necessarily connected to the validity of the testator's dispositions as expressed in the document; thus, article 1747 provides that a secret will which has been declared null and void will have the legal force of a holographic will, if it is valid as such. 9.18

EXTRAORDINARY WILLS

As the name suggests, these wills cater for specific and uncommon circumstances which fall within one of the following three types. First are wills made on a Greek-flagged commercial or war ship for the duration of the voyage (arts 1949–1952, 1955–1956).[1] If the voyage is a relatively short one, the testator must put forward good reasons why he requests the drafting of such will; eg he suffered 9.19

---

1 The prevailing view is that these provisions do not apply by analogy to wills made on airplanes. Which vessels are regarded as ships and which as Greek will be considered in accordance with the Code of Private Shipping Law and Decree 187/1973.

a severe stroke and the next port of call will not be reached for a considerable period of time, thus reducing his chances of surviving the stroke. Second are 'military wills' which can only be drafted by members of the armed forces in war situations (arts 1753–1755). Third are 'blockade wills', which are made by persons residing in areas with restricted access, because of outbreaks of illnesses, war hostilities etc (art 1757).

9.20 The nature of these wills makes it imperative that their temporal effect is restricted to the period corresponding to the extraordinary events. Thus, article 1758 stipulates that an extraordinary will is considered as not having been drafted if three months have elapsed since such events ceased to exist and the testator is still alive, in which case the will loses all its validity.

LEGAL CAPACITY TO MAKE WILLS

9.21 The Civil Code prescribes which persons are capable of making wills *a contrario*; by stipulating those circumstances where a person does not have the necessary capacity to become a testator. Broadly speaking, these can be divided into two categories. The first covers circumstances affecting specific persons, which have been examined above. The second refers to persons who are not regarded by the legislature as being in a position to determine freely their last intent without the danger of having been influenced by others.

9.22 These persons are enumerated in article 1719: minors; judicially interdicted persons; those who have been placed under judicial supervision because of prodigality;[1] those who, at the time the will was made, were either not conscious of their actions or did not enjoy the use of reason because of mental illness.[2] Since a person will be judicially interdicted or placed under judicial supervision only after the relevant court judgment has become *res judicata*,[3] any will made before this procedural stage will remain valid if the testator dies in the meantime (art 1720).

REVOCATION OF WILLS (ARTS 1763–1768)

9.23 The right of the testator to revoke his will is based upon his fundamental right to decide on the future of his property in the way he personally chooses. It follows that the right of revocation is unlimited and it can neither be excluded nor curtailed. Revocation is possible in the following cases, which can be divided into 'general' and 'specific' cases.

9.24 The two general cases are as follows.

---

1 See art 1705(3): 'Anyone who because of prodigality endangers the welfare of himself or his family will be placed under judicial supervision'.

2 See also arts 1686 *et seq*. Distinguish judicial interdiction from legal interdiction, which occurs when a person has been convicted of a felony and lasts for the duration of his punishment (art 1700). Legally interdicted persons are allowed to make wills.

3 See arts 1694 and 1706 respectively.

(1) The making of a subsequent will. Here revocation is either explicit, when the testator declares that he changes, wholly or partly, his previous will, or implicit, when its contents simply contradict, wholly or partly, the contents of the previous will (art 1763). The subsequent will is not required to be of the same type as the previous one; a public will can be revoked by a holographic will.
(2) A declaration by the testator before a notary public and three witnesses that he considers his will to be revoked (art 1764).

Revocation of a revocation is possible only in these two cases and can be effected in either way.

The specific cases apply solely to holographic and secret wills. **9.25**

(1) In the case of holographic wills, the testator can at any time physically destroy a will or make such fundamental changes to its text (eg erasing his signature or crossing out whole parts) that the only conclusion to be reached is that, in this way, he demonstrated his clear decision to revoke the will (art 1765).
(2) In the case of secret wills, when the testator requests the notary public to return to him personally the sealed document and the latter does so, this automatically constitutes revocation. However, the return of a holographic will which was given to a notary public for safekeeping purposes is not considered as a revocation (art 1766).

THE CONTENTS OF WILLS (ARTS 1781–1808)

Contrary to the prevailing opinion before the entry into force of the Civil Code, it is now accepted that the purpose of a will is not necessarily to establish heirs to take over the deceased's assets but it may contain provisions solely dealing with the estate and/or personal and family matters of the testator. The usual dispositions made in a will include: establishment of heirs, legatees or *fideicommissarius*; substitution of heirs etc; conditions imposed on heirs etc; disinheritance of specific relatives; revocation of earlier wills; determination of how the estate is to be distributed; appointment of testamentary executors; appointment of guardians (art 1599); recognition of illegitimate children (art 1476). **9.26**

It is the testator's decision as to whom he would like to become his testamentary heir. However, this decision is not always expressed in clear and unambiguous terms. Should doubts be raised regarding the identity of the designated heirs or the extent of their entitlement to the estate, these will be resolved according to the interpretative rules of articles 1800–1806. Thus, when the will simply stipulates that A, B, and C are entitled to the estate or parts of it, these are considered to be the heirs, even though they are not expressly referred to as 'heirs'. **9.27**

Should the testator have established heirs only to a part of the estate, the remaining part is subject to intestate succession (see arts 1813–1824); correspondingly, if the percentages left to each heir exceed the disposable estate, they will have to be reduced accordingly (art 1803). If the testator specifies more than one **9.28** heir without specifying the heirs' respective shares in the estate, article 1804 provides that they are entitled to equal shares.

9.29 The testator is allowed to include conditions (reservations) or postponing and annulling clauses in the will so as to give effect to his last wishes. Their validity and interpretation will be examined in accordance with the general rules on conditions and clauses stipulated in Book I of the Civil Code (arts 201–209). These rules are supplemented by articles 1794–1799, which cater for specific circumstances. Thus, an incomprehensible condition (ie a condition whose contents cannot be ascertained even by interpreting the whole will) is considered as if it were never written but does not impair the will's validity (art 1794). The same applies to the so-called 'condition of celibacy'; this is the condition which prohibits the heir from entering into marriage (art 1795(a)). However, the courts may allow this condition to stand if the heir is prevented from marrying specific persons (eg people with whom the testator had hostile relationships) or before the heir reaches a certain age.

9.30 The condition of widowhood (ie that the surviving spouse will not marry again) is valid (art 1795 (b)). According to article 1798, this condition operates as an annulling clause, which means that the surviving spouse will continue to be treated as an heir as long as the spouse remains widowed and not remarried. An enticing or alluring condition (*conditio captatoria*, art 1796) as well as any illegal, immoral or impossible condition will render the will partially null and void (art 208). The possibility that the existence of such clauses may lead to the invalidity of the whole will has to be examined in accordance with the general rule of article 181.

9.31 The so-called 'forfeiture clauses' (*clausula cassarotia*) are not regulated in the Civil Code but are treated as annulling clauses. They are defined as conditions in a will which stipulate that the heir will lose, wholly or partly, all his rights if he acts in a way contrary to the testator's wishes. For such dispositions to be valid, they must be clearly set out in the will: usually they are to the effect that the heir should never challenge the validity of the will.

9.32 According to article 1785, any disposition of the testator in favour of the surviving spouse is voidable if their marriage was invalid (art 1372) or was dissolved while the testator was still alive (art 1438), or he had begun a divorce action that was prima facie well-founded (arts 1439 *et seq*). In order to prevent the avoidance of such dispositions, the surviving spouse must prove that the true volition of the testator would not have been different even if at the time the will was made he was aware of the nullity or of the dissolution of the marriage. In other words, the spouse should prove that the fact he was established as heir was not affected by their marital status.[1]

1 See Case 2493/94, Court of Appeal of Athens [1994] Nomikon Vima 1177.

SUBSTITUTION OF HEIRS (ARTS 1809–1812)

Substitution occurs when the testator establishes A as the heir and B (simple substitution) or B and C (parallel substitution) as his substitute heirs for the eventualities that A is disqualified from succession, or dies before the testator, or a disqualifying event stipulated by the testator himself materialises, or A renounces the succession, or is subsequently disinherited. It is possible for the testator to establish a substitute for the designated substitute. Generally speaking, when substitution is effected, the inheritance goes to the substitute heirs, who, however, should be alive when the testator died, in order to be regarded as heirs. Where substitution occurred because the original heir renounced the inheritance (arts 1847–1859) or was declared unworthy (arts 1860–1864), the passing over of the inheritance is considered as having taken place *ex tunc*, from the day the testator died. 9.33

VALIDITY OF WILLS (ARTS 1781–1788)

Validity depends on a number of different considerations. The contents of the will must be precise. Any unclear disposition will be struck out; if it happens to be the most important one, then the whole will becomes null and void under the general rule in article 1781. The only specific provision on imprecise dispositions contained in the Civil Code concerns the identity of the beneficiary (art 1781: 'Disposition in favour of a person, which is so vague that this person cannot be clearly identified is invalid'); it is accepted that this provision can be applied by analogy in all unclear cases. This 'vagueness' does not include persons who were not conceived at the time of the testator's death (art 1924), provided that the will reveals, beyond doubt, the identity of such persons. 9.34

All dispositions must correspond precisely to the real wishes of the testator. This is regulated in article 1783, which provides that a disposition is voidable if the testator erred *vis-à-vis* the identity of the heir (ie he wanted to establish A as heir but in the will he wrote the name of B) or of the property (ie the testator wanted A to inherit his apartment in Athens but he actually left him the apartment in Corfu). Should the disputed disposition be declared null and void, neither A nor B will be established as heirs and, equally, A will not inherit either of the apartments. In practice, such problems are eliminated with a realistic interpretation of the will, which is aided by the rule *falsa demonstratio non nocet*: the false description of persons or items of the estate does not prejudice the validity of the disposition (art 1783). 9.35

The will must reflect only the volition of the testator and not that of third parties. Article 1789 places great importance on the fact that the testator may not make the operation of dispositions subject to the opinion of a third person (eg 'A is to become my heir only if B approves') nor may he allow third persons to decide who is to be established as heir or which items of the estate will be inherited by whom. The result of including such dispositions is that they are automatically null and 9.36

void and, on most occasions, they will constitute sufficient grounds to render the whole will invalid.

9.37 The volition of the testator is vitiated if the events which led him to make specific dispositions were the product of misapprehension, fraud or psychological threat (arts 1784, 1782(1) and 1782(2) respectively). In the case of a disposition inserted by fraud, this is voidable irrespective of the person who defrauded the testator; in other words, even if this person is not the one who will benefit from the fraud the disposition is still voidable.

9.38 Dispositions should not be against the law or prevailing good morals (*bonos mores*).[1] Since the rules of succession law do not contain any specific provisions in this area, the general rules of article 3 ('the volition of an individual may not disapply the rules of public order'), article 174 ('legal transactions which infringe prohibitory rules of law are null and void') and article 178 ('legal transactions that violate good morals are null and void') will be applied by analogy. The illegal or unethical nature of the disposition will usually be concluded from its contents (eg where the testator specifies that the only reason why he established A and B as his heirs is that he was deeply impressed by their illicit activities) and will be judged according to the circumstances existing at the time of drafting the will, and not at the time of the testator's death. The actual determination of what constitutes behaviour against *bonos mores* is made by the courts, and the litigating parties may not contest the findings.[2]

9.39 Whether a disposition infringes *bonos mores* appears usually in wills where the testator has established as heir a person with whom he maintained a sexual relationship. The position of the Greek courts has been that such dispositions are not *per se* against *bonos mores* unless they could be regarded as a clear manifestation of unacceptable scorn or contempt for his closest relatives, including brothers and sisters. When the sole reason that led the testator to establish his sexual partner as heir has been his willingness to maintain such a relationship or to reward the partner for sexual 'services' rendered, the courts have held that the relevant dispositions do infringe *bonos mores*.[3]

1 According to consistent case-law, the establishment as his heir of a person with whom the testator maintained extra-marital sexual relations is not contrary to *bonos mores*; Case 4975/93, Court of Appeal of Athens [1994] GJ 477; Case 781/89, Arios Pagos (Supreme Court) [1992] GJ 136.

2 In Case 1117/90 [1992] GJ 349, the Court of Appeal of Athens held that the illegitimate child of the son of the testator, who was recognised *after* the death of the testator and who was not mentioned in his will, had *locus standi* to challenge the validity of the will but, in the circumstances, the rules of *bonos mores* were not breached.

3 See Case 821/1977, Arios Pagos (Supreme Court) [1978] Nomikon Vima 669; Case 781/89, Arios Pagos [1992] GJ 136; Case 4975/93, Court of Appeal of Athens [1994] GJ 477.

LEGAL CONSEQUENCES OF INVALID OR VOIDABLE WILLS

By applying the general rule enshrined in article 180 ('a null and void legal transaction is considered as if it were never concluded'), it follows that an invalid will is not required to be declared as such by the courts because, legally speaking, it never existed in the first place. However, if a litigant disputes the will's invalidity anyone who can show a sufficient interest in the outcome of the case may petition the courts to declare it null and void and this right is not subject to any statutory time limitations. The will's invalidity is absolute in the sense that not only does it not have any legal effects but also it can never be regarded as valid. The latter is true, even if the person who has a legitimate interest in invoking the invalidity withdraws from so doing or recognises the will's validity. However, if the invalid will is viewed as a legal document drawn up before a notary public, it can have legal effect if it is converted into another valid legal document. To give an example, if a will is invalid because one or more of the formalities were not observed but it contained clauses which established a trust fund or recognised the parentage of a child born outside wedlock, each of these dispositions could very well be considered as separate legal documents, producing, on their own, the legal effect which the testator had originally anticipated. 9.40

However, in the case of voidable testamentary dispositions, it will be the competent court which will decide on the fate of the disputed dispositions. The plaintiff (ie the person who enjoys the right to request the invalidity) may not only be a person who has an inheritance interest but also anyone who benefits directly from having the disposition declared null and void, whereas the defendant will be the person who benefited under the offending disposition, eg the heir, the legatee and their substitutes. The burden of proof lies upon the plaintiff.[1] 9.41

However, for as long as a voidable will is not challenged before the courts, it continues to have legal effect as if it were a valid one. If a voidable disposition is declared by the courts to be invalid, it is considered as null and void *ab initio* (art 184: 'a voidable legal transaction is equated after its annulment with an initially invalid transaction'). 9.42

The plaintiff's right to have the will declared invalid is extinguished in the following circumstances: when the plaintiff chooses not to exercise it (art 156: 'the direct or indirect withdrawal by the beneficiary of his right to request the invalidity of the legal transaction results in its redemption'); when it is not exercised within two years after publication of the will (art 1788); and when the validity of the will was expressly recognised by the plaintiff. 9.43

1 See Case 787/89, Arios Pagos [1990] GJ 1275.

PUBLICATION OF WILLS (ARTS 1769–1780)[1]

9.44 Publication is the procedural act whereby the competent court or consular office of a Greek embassy discloses in an official and public way the contents of a will. It should be noted that lack of publication is not connected with the will's formal validity; this follows from the general rule in article 1779, which stipulates that non-performance of any of the provisions relating to publication does not result in the will's invalidity. The practical importance of publication is that not only the contents but also the existence of the will are made known; therefore, it is of some importance that all wills, including those which were declared null and void or were revoked, are published. Only the original will can be published, never a copy, even if it was officially certified.[2]

9.45 Depending on the type of will, certain persons are under a strict obligation to present the will to the competent court for publication. More particularly, in public, secret and extraordinary wills, the duty lies upon the notary public in whose archive the will is kept (art 1769), whereas in the case of holographic wills it lies upon any person who has possession of the will at the time (art 1774). Delay, refusal or failure to surrender a will is treated as a civil (arts 914 CC and 811 CCP) and criminal offence (art 222 PC) and the latter is punishable with a maximum term of imprisonment of two years and a fine.

9.46 The competent court for publication is the One-Member First Instance court of the region where the notary public has its seat (arts 1769 CC and 807 CCP) and, only in the case of holographic wills, the court in whose region the testator was or the holder of the will is habitually resident (art 1774). The consular sections of Greek embassies will assume competence either when the will has been deposited with them (art 1773), or when the holder of the will resides abroad (arts 1775 CC and 807(2) CCP). The secretariat of all courts and consular offices must keep complete registers with details of all published wills and there is a central register which is located in the First Instance Court of Athens (arts 1778 CC and 809 CCP).[3]

9.47 Finally, it should be mentioned that mere publication of holographic wills does not automatically result in them being considered as true and genuine. Article 1777 introduces the presumption that if, five years after publication, its validity has not been challenged in legal proceedings, a holographic will is authentic. This presumption results in reversal of the burden of proof.

THE TESTAMENTARY EXECUTOR (ARTS 2017–2031)

9.48 The role of the testamentary executor comes into play when the testator, for one reason or another, expresses the wish that a specific person should conduct the affairs of his estate (dealing with assets and liabilities) or implement the various

1 As amended and augmented by Articles 807 to 809 CCP.
2 See Case 1231/87, Court of Appeal of Piraeus [1989] GJ 1036.
3 These registers are regulated under Royal Decree 375/1970.

dispositions themselves. The testator can appoint, only through his will, one or more executors, who can be natural or legal persons (art 2017 (1)); in accordance with article 2018, an heir with full contractual capacity can be appointed as executor. The functions of the executor are of a strictly personal nature and, therefore, they cease as soon as he dies or becomes incapable of carrying out legal transactions (art 2029). A person can never be compelled to act as executor and, in effect, the executor must first accept his office unconditionally by making a relevant declaration before the competent court (art 2019). It follows that the executor has the right to choose to resign at any time (art 2030). Pursuant to article 2028, the office of the executor will be vacated when the heir affords to the court the necessary guarantees that he himself will carry out the will's dispositions for which the executor was appointed. The executor is always remunerated unless the testator has ordered otherwise; the exact amount, if not laid down in the will, will be fixed by the competent court upon his request (art 2027).

The executor's role is to implement the various dispositions and the administration of the estate. The Civil Code bestows upon him wide-ranging authorities and powers (art 2020). However, certain acts, which are exhaustively enumerated in article 2021, are considered to be rather important and, in order to perform them, the executor must seek the prior consent of the courts: eg if selling immovable assets, bonds or shares; concluding out of court settlements;[1] borrowing money; or incurring expenses which do not meet with the heir's approval.[2] Since the carrying out of the executor's duties requires full contractual capacity, article 2018 provides that the appointment will be invalidated if, at the time when the executor accepts the office, he is legally incapable of entering into contractual relationships. **9.49**

The law affords adequate protection to heirs who claim that they have been compromised by the executor's actions. In the first instance, article 2023(1) stipulates that the executor is liable to the heir(s) for any damage caused to the estate as a result of his own actions. His liability will be decided in accordance with the relevant provisions of Book II, Law of Obligations, articles 713–725. In case of repeated maladministration in the affairs of the estate the heir, or any person who can show a legally justifiable interest, may petition the court having jurisdiction over succession to have the executor removed and his office terminated (arts 2031 CC and 815 CCP). **9.50**

3. INTESTATE SUCCESSION (ARTS 1813–1824)

When the deceased did not leave a will or he left a will which was subsequently declared null and void or was cancelled for some other reason, three specific dilemmas arise: what is to happen to the estate; which persons should become **9.51**

1 For out of court settlements, see Magliveras, 'Greece' in Carey Miller (ed), *The Option of Litigating in Europe*, UK National Committee of Comparative Law, 1993, pp 102–104.

2 Note that, under article 2022, the testator can decide to dispense with such restrictions.

beneficiaries; and whether the testator's perceived wishes should be taken into consideration. Since it is practically impossible to decide each case individually, the legislature took the view that intestate succession should only take place in accordance with the provisions of the law. As already mentioned, one of the fundamental principles of succession law is that the family of the deceased must always be protected. Since 'family' is founded on kinship by blood (art 1463) and by marriage (art 1464), the protection afforded to certain relatives must take precedence.

9.52 However, this principle gave rise to two further, complicated problems: first, it is necessary to decide which relatives deserve mandatory protection and, second, it is necessary to distinguish between close and distant relatives and to establish a hierarchy between them. The solution to the former problem is to protect the surviving spouse and the descendants to the exclusion of all other relatives. The second is solved by adopting the system of classes (generations), which operates in a quite simple way: all blood relatives are divided into four generations, each one following the other. The first generation has as its leader the deceased and comprises all descendants without any restrictions. In case there is no person left in the first generation, it is followed by the second, which has as leaders the parents of the deceased and as members their descendants, ie the brothers, nephews etc of the deceased.

9.53 In the same way the third generation ensues with the grandfathers and grandmothers of the deceased as leaders and their descendants as members (ie the uncles and first cousins of the deceased). Finally, the fourth generation includes only the great-grandfathers and great-grandmothers of the deceased, to the exclusion of their descendants; thus the brothers and sisters of the grandfather of the deceased can never inherit from him, even if there are no other relatives alive.

9.54 The various classes can be further divided into roots which comprise one member of the class as leader and all his descendants as members. For example, if the deceased had three children A, B and C, each of them becomes the leader of his own root in the first generation, and their children become members of the respective roots. Equally, the descendants of A, B, and C are the leaders of their own roots and their children (ie the grandchildren of A, B, and C) become members. It should be noted that the system of roots applies only to the first three classes of intestate succession.

9.55 The classes of blood relatives in intestate succession correspond to the generations described above, but are modified in order to take into consideration the succession rights bestowed upon the surviving spouse. The Civil Code recognises that the surviving spouse should be given a general right to inherit, irrespective of which class has priority in the succession line. More specifically, the first four classes are identical to the four generations, the only exception being the addition of the spouse as a compulsory heir. The latter is entitled to pre-determined shares of the estate; if the spouse inherits with the first class (ie the descendants of the deceased), the spouse is entitled to one-quarter of the estate and, if the spouse inherits with any other class, the spouse's share is increased to half the estate (art 1820).

The aim of the Civil Code to promote the position of the spouse *vis-à-vis* the blood relatives of the deceased is obvious and is reinforced by the provision of article 1820(2), which allows the spouse to retain the so-called *preciput*. This consists solely of movable objects which were used by the spouses in their everyday lives, eg furniture, clothing and domestic appliances. The surviving spouse is not entitled to *preciput* even if the spouse inherits together with the descendants of the deceased, whose needs will, however, be taken into consideration. It should be noted that the *preciput* will be received by the surviving spouse only if he becomes heir by intestate succession; thus if he was established as heir by virtue of a will or renounced the inheritance, he is not entitled to it. 9.56

In addition to the above four classes, the Civil Code introduces a fifth and sixth class. The fifth caters for those cases where the deceased had no blood relatives to succeed him and stipulates that the surviving spouse will inherit the whole estate (art 1821). The sixth provides that, if the deceased had no relatives alive in any class, the Greek State is established as sole heir automatically (art 1824). Because the legislature takes the view that no one's assets should be left uninherited, the Greek State is denied the right to renounce the inheritance (art 1848 (2)). 9.57

The actual operation of intestate succession is quite complex, but it can be summarised as follows. 9.58

For one class to succeed another there must be no members of the previous class left who are capable of becoming heirs (art 1819). For example, heirs in the second class will inherit if the deceased had no descendants or he disinherited his only child or his children died before him. It follows that the existence of even one relative in the previous class prevents the members of the next class from inheriting and he will be entitled to the whole estate. The reasons why there were no members left in a class are of no significance. 9.59

Succession *per stirpes* is only possible in the context of the same class. When the leader of the root does not, for one reason or another, become an heir, his share in the estate is taken by his immediate descendants, ie his children and, if they are unable to inherit, by his grandchildren and so on. 9.60

Which persons qualify as descendants is not regulated by the law of succession but determined in accordance with the rules of Book IV, Family Law, articles 1463 *et seq*. In the first class the following persons qualify: the children from all valid marriages of the deceased; the children from invalid or void marriages, even if these were dissolved by court judgment (art 1438); children whose parentage was validly recognised by the deceased (art 1484) and adopted children, provided that the adoption was not dissolved (art 1579; the adopted child inherits from his natural parents as well, art 1588). All descendants are entitled to equal shares between them. 9.61

For the purposes of succession in the second class, the term 'parents' includes: the natural parents of the deceased; the persons who recognised the deceased as their child; and the natural parents of an adopted child. It should be noted that the persons who adopted a child never have the right to inherit from the child (art 9.62

1579).[1] In the second class, the parents and brothers of the deceased also inherit in equal shares.

9.63 For the surviving spouse to inherit there must be a valid marriage at the time of death. Thus, the spouse is deprived of succession rights in the following cases: if the marriage was dissolved by means of divorce (art 1438); if, from a legal point of view, it never existed, because one or more of the mandatory prerequisites were not observed (art 1372); or if the marriage was declared null and void by a court judgment that had reached the procedural stage from which no further right of appeal exists (*res judicata*, art 1376).

4. FORCED HEIRSHIP (ARTS 1825–1845)

9.64 The rules of succession law afford a very high degree of protection to certain persons, in the sense that they not only oblige the deceased to establish them as heirs but also determine what percentage of the estate must be inherited by them. These persons are the very close relatives of the deceased (descendants, parents and surviving spouse) and are collectively known as 'compulsory heirs'. The part of the inheritance to which they are always entitled is referred to as the 'rightful share' (*legitima portio*).

9.65 The rationale behind restricting the power of the deceased to decide that his immediate family should not inherit from him is primarily based on the general principle of the protection of his family and on the moral duty which the deceased has towards all compulsory heirs (*officium pietatis*). Exclusion of compulsory heirs can occur both in testamentary succession (eg the testator establishes as sole heir his lover to the exclusion of his wife and children), and also in intestate succession (eg the deceased, during his life, transferred all property to his lover through donations and gifts so that, at the time of his death, there were no assets left to satisfy the compulsory heirs' rightful share).

9.66 According to article 1825(2), the compulsory heir is a true heir and his rightful share is part of the inheritance (*pars hereditatis*). Compulsory heirs are divided into two classes: following the pattern described above, the first includes the descendants and the second the parents; the surviving spouse is included in both classes. The rules which apply to intestate succession govern, *mutatis mutandis*, the succession of compulsory heirs (art 1826). The percentage of the rightful share is determined at half the intestate succession share (art 1825(1)(b)); in other words, half the hypothetical share to which the compulsory heir would have been entitled, had he become heir by intestate succession.

9.67 This hypothetical share is calculated in accordance with article 1830. First, it should be established which persons would have become heirs by intestate succession; for present purposes, those persons who were disinherited or renounced the inheritance or were declared unworthy are also counted. Then the

1 Adoption is regulated in Book IV, Family Law, articles 1568–1588, supplemented by Decree 610/1970.

estate is distributed between them and the result will be the intestate succession share. For example, if a testator with a surviving spouse (A) and two children (B and C) left the whole estate to his lover, the situation will be as follows: A, B and C as intestate succession heirs in the first class should have received, respectively, two-eighths, three-eighths and three-eighths of the inheritance. As compulsory heirs, A, B and C receive half such hypothetical intestacy share so A is entitled to two-sixteenths and each child to three-sixteenths of the estate.

The final calculation is to ascertain the value of the deceased's estate at the time of his death; this is particularly important in those cases where the estate is not adequate to satisfy all rightful shares. Any debts which the deceased had incurred and not repaid are deducted, whereas all donations made and all assets transferred to compulsory heirs while he was alive (eg after his daughter was divorced, he transferred to her the only house he owned) and to third parties in the ten years preceding his death are notionally added to the estate (arts 1831 and 1833). All such donations and transfers must be taken into consideration by the compulsory heirs when ascertaining the amount to which they are entitled, unless they were made because the deceased thought he had a particularly strong moral duty towards a specific heir (eg he transferred his house to his daughter because she was the only one of his children who looked after him when he became an invalid). **9.68**

In order to safeguard the succession rights of compulsory heirs, article 1829 provides that any dispositions made in a will which infringe or restrict the rightful share are considered as non-existent. Furthermore, if the deceased's actual assets are insufficient to satisfy rightful shares then the compulsory heirs can overturn donations made by the deceased to his relatives while he was alive or to third parties during the last ten years of his life because they offend their rightful shares (arts 1835 *et seq*). The relevant action (known as 'censure of unkind donations', *querella inofficiosae donationis*) must be raised before the competent court within two years of the deceased's death. It is brought against the donee and seeks to reverse the donation to the extent it infringes the rightful share; in other words, the heir can demand that his insufficient rightful share is completed by taking back the donation (or part of it) which the deceased made years ago. If the compulsory heir is successful in his action, the donee can choose between returning the donation which infringes the heir's rightful share or paying an equivalent sum of money, thus preventing its reversal (art 1836). **9.69**

5. DISINHERITANCE (ARTS 1839–1849)

As already mentioned, the deceased is able to leave his estate to whomsoever he likes, provided he observes the requirement to leave the rightful share to the compulsory heirs. The question raised is whether the deceased should enjoy the right to deprive them of the rightful share, in other words, to disinherit them. The Civil Code acknowledges that the protection offered to the compulsory heirs should not be unlimited, and should be taken away in those cases where they committed such grave acts that the deceased can legitimately decide that they **9.70** should not be entitled to any part of the estate. Disinheritance can be made only through a will and the grounds which led to it must be clearly mentioned.

9.71 The circumstances for the disinheritance of descendants, which are enumerated exhaustively in the Civil Code (arts 1839(a) and 1840) are as follows.

(1) They attempted to take the life of the testator, of his spouse or his other descendants. Acts of preparation are considered adequate to trigger this provision.
(2) They wilfully caused bodily harm to the testator or to his spouse (arts 308–310 PC); if the harm was caused simply through negligence (art 314(2) PC), disinheritance is not possible.
(3) They intentionally committed felonies or grave misdemeanours against the testator or his spouse. In these three cases it is not necessary that the disinherited descendant has been convicted by a criminal court.
(4) They neglected maliciously to perform their legal obligation to sustain the testator according to articles 1456 *et seq.*
(5) They led an immoral or amorous life against the wishes of the testator. However, if the will was written a long time before the death of the testator and the descendant has, in the meantime, ceased leading such a life, disinheritance is invalid; in other words, the crucial time element is the death of the testator, not when the will was drafted.

9.72 Disinheriting of parents is possible for any of reasons (1), (3) or (4). The testator is allowed to disinherit his spouse if, at the time of his death, he had the right to file for divorce, on the basis of grounds for which the spouse was *prima facie* responsible (art 1842).

6. UNWORTHINESS (ARTS 1860–1864)

9.73 It is possible that, although the heir, legatee or any other beneficiary had committed grave crimes against the life or the honour of the deceased, the latter was prevented from disinheriting them or otherwise stopping them acquiring parts of the estate. In the following cases, which are exhaustively enumerated in article 1860, the Civil Code stipulates that the heir, legatee or other beneficiaries are regarded as unworthy of inheriting in the public interest, and are deprived *ex tunc* of their succession rights by a court judgment:

- they intentionally murdered (art 299 PC) or attempted to murder the deceased, his descendants, parents or spouse;
- they were convicted by a criminal court for falsely accusing the deceased of a felony (art 229 PC);
- they intentionally and illegally hindered the deceased from making or revoking his will;
- they fraudulently, illegally or against *bonos mores* forced the deceased to make or alter his will;
- they falsified or destroyed the will of the deceased.

If the deceased wishes the heir, legatee or other beneficiary not to be declared unworthy, he must pardon him either in a public document (eg declaration before a notary public) or by mentioning it in his will (art 1861). However, the deceased should be aware that, once he has granted his pardon, he cannot revoke it. The unworthiness can only be proclaimed by a final court judgment, ie a judgment against which there is no further right of appeal. The relevant action is raised, in the words of article 1862, by 'anyone who has a legally justifiable interest in the disqualification of the unworthy heir within two years from the date the succession devolved upon him'. **9.74**

The decision declaring the heir unworthy is valid *vis-à-vis* all interested parties (*erga omnes*), whereas the decision rejecting the action is valid only between the parties involved in the litigation; it follows that, in the latter case, any other person showing the required interest can institute fresh proceedings against the unworthy heir. The result of a successful action for unworthiness is that the heir is considered as not having any inheritance rights and his place is taken by the person who would have inherited had the heir not been alive (art 1863). **9.75**

7. ACCEPTANCE OF SUCCESSION – THE BENEFIT OF INVENTORY (ARTS 1901–1912)

The passing of the estate to the heirs is direct and occurs *ipso jure* the moment the deceased expires (art 1846). Since the Civil Code allows the heir (with the exception of the Greek State when it takes the estate as the heir in the sixth class of intestate succession) to renounce the inheritance (art 1847), he is assumed to have acquired it only temporarily. Acceptance of the succession can be either express or implicit. Although the Civil Code does not prescribe how the former is to be effected, it is generally accepted that it can take the form of a declaration before a notary public or before the court competent to deal with the inheritance in which he is interested. The declaration must concern the whole part of the inheritance to which he is entitled, because partial acceptance is neither allowed nor taken into consideration (art 1851(b)). The determination as to whether the heir has implicitly accepted the inheritance will be decided objectively on the basis of the acts he has undertaken. For example, the request that a certificate of inheritance be issued (see arts 1956–1966) or the bringing of actions to protect the assets of the estate clearly indicates his decision to accept the inheritance.[1] **9.76**

On most occasions the inherited estate will comprise assets and liabilities. If the net amount of the assets is negative (ie liabilities exceed assets), the heir finds himself in an extremely difficult position, because article 1901 provides that he is liable to the extent of his own personal wealth to pay the creditors of the estate. To **9.77**

1 See Case 811/76, Arios Pagos [1977] Nomikon Vima 183. Other similar acts include the lodging with the Inland Revenue an application to have the inheritance tax assessed or the writing off of a claim forming part of the estate.

allow the heir to accept an indebted estate, the concept of 'acceptance with the benefit of inventory' has been developed. This concept, which is *jus congens* and cannot be excluded by the testator, stipulates that the heir (and his own heirs) are only responsible for an amount equal to the estate's assets (art 1904). Should there be more than one heir and one of them accepted his inheritance with the benefit of inventory, then the remaining heirs must follow suit, because the heir's acceptance of his inheritance with the benefit of inventory does not cover all other heirs. It should be noted that heirs with limited or no capacity to conclude contracts must always accept their inheritances with the benefit of inventory.

9.78 The heir[1] must notify the court having jurisdiction over succession that he wishes to take advantage of the benefit of inventory during the time-limit for renouncing the succession (arts 1902 (1) CC and 812 CCP). In the next four months he is required to conclude the inventory of the estate (arts 1903 CC and 838–842 CCP). From the moment of notification the estate is separated from his personal wealth and forms a separate entity (*separatio bonorum*, art 1905), which is administered by him (art 1907). The sole purpose of this entity is to satisfy the estate's creditors, and the personal creditors of the heir may never be satisfied from it. If, after all debts have been fully paid up, there are still assets left in the entity, these become part of the heir's personal wealth and can be used for any purpose.

9.79 The heir will be deprived of the benefit in the cases mentioned in Article 1911: if the inventory was not drawn up on time; if it was intentionally drafted incorrectly to defraud creditors; if the heir administers the entity fraudulently or if he disposes of immovable property, shares or bonds belonging to the estate without the required court permission under article 1908. Although not expressly stipulated in the Civil Code, it is generally accepted that if the heir attempts other acts, such as donations, writing-off debts and compromising claims, he will be similarly deprived of the benefit of inventory. Being deprived of the benefit means that the heir will be liable to the extent of his own wealth for the estate's debts.

8. RENUNCIATION OF SUCCESSION (ARTS 1847–1859)

9.80 The temporary heir is granted four months (one year if he or the deceased had their residence abroad) in order to determine whether or not he would like to accept the inheritance (*spatium deliberandi*, art 1847). If he decides to renounce it, the legal effect is that the devolution of the estate is reversed *ex tunc* and the disclaiming heir is considered as never having become an heir (art 1856(a)). As is the case with acceptance, renunciation must be declared to the court concerned with succession (art 1848(1)).

1 With the exception of the Greek State, which, according to Article 118 of the Introductory Act to the Civil Code, is always considered as heir 'with the benefit of inventory', the State is not required to conclude the inventory.

Upon renunciation, the new heir becomes the person who would have priority in the succession line, if the disclaiming heir were not alive at the time of death (art 1856(b)). Since, as mentioned before, upon renunciation the devolution of the estate is reversed *ex tunc*, the new heir is considered to have assumed his inheritance at the moment the deceased expired (art 1856(c)). If the renouncing heir was made heir by the deceased's will and there was no provision for substitution, the courts will interpret the will in order to determine whether his share should augment the shares of the other heirs or whether his share should lapse and pass according to the rules for intestate succession. In the latter event, article 1852 expressly provides that the disclaiming heir is entitled to accept the share, if entitled to it by virtue of intestate succession. **9.81**

The decision to accept or renounce the succession is irreversible; except that it may be reversed if the heir reached his decision through deception, threat or fraud (art 1857).[1] The right to renounce is not only conferred upon the first entitled heir, but is carried on to every subsequent heir (art 1854). Theoretically speaking, a succession can be renounced by all heirs in the first five classes and this will result in the Greek State being called as heir in the sixth class with no right of renunciation (art 1848(b)). **9.82**

9. CONTRACTUAL RENUNCIATION WHERE FOREIGN SPOUSE INVOLVED

Legislative Decree 472/1974 allows the spouses, provided one of them is not a Greek citizen, to conclude between them a contract, whereby the foreign spouse resigns his rights in the other's estate. This contract may also be concluded before the matrimonial ceremony has actually taken place. Before the contract is validly concluded, the following four prerequisites must be fulfilled: **9.83**

(1) it must be signed in a foreign country;
(2) it must be done in a written form and preferably before a notary public;
(3) both parties, one of whom is a foreign national, must reside abroad at the time of signing;
(4) the parties must either have already been married or plan to get married; however, until they enter into a valid marriage, the contract does not enter into force.

The term of the contract is that the foreign spouse agrees to resign all or part of the succession rights or the rightful share of the Greek spouse. It is of no importance whether the foreign spouse receives any assets in exchange for his willingness to enter into the contract. Decree 472/1974 is applied *ex tunc* and, in effect, all such contracts concluded before 26 June 1974 (date of entering into **9.84**

1 This follows from the general rule enshrined in Book I, General Principles, that all legal transactions concluded under deception, threat or fraud are voidable; see respectively, articles 140, 147 and 150.

force) are recognised as valid, provided that the Greek spouse was alive on this date.

10. THE *FIDEICOMMISSUM* (ARTS 1923–1941)

9.85 This is defined in article 1923(1) as a situation where the testator orders the heir to pass over all or part of his inheritance to another person (the post-heir) when a specific and future event has occurred or a certain period of time has expired. The testator is allowed to set up only one *fideicommissum* but there is no time restriction for the estate to be transferred to the post-heir. The *fideicommissum* caters for those instances where the testator wishes to establish two or more persons as heirs successively. It follows that the *fideicommissum* differs significantly from the substitution of heirs (arts 1809–1812).

9.86 The *fideicommissum* can only be set up in a will. In those cases where the obvious intention of the testator was to create a *fideicommissum* but he did not include any relevant dispositions in the will, the Civil Code allows the existence of the so-called 'presumed *fideicommissum*', *inter alia,* in the following circumstances:

(1) the testator established as heir a natural person who had not been conceived or a legal person which had not been incorporated at the time of his death (art 1924);
(2) the heir was established by virtue of a condition which was not fulfilled before his death (art 1925(1));
(3) the designation of the post-heir depends on an event which should materialise after his death (art 1925). For example, the testator stipulates that the first of his three nephews that is married will be established as heir, but up to the time of his death none of them has married.

9.87 For as long as the inheritance is not passed over to the post-heir, it must be administered diligently by the heir who was established under the will (art 1937(1)). Since the heir is entitled to all proceeds and benefits of the estate and is free to keep them (art 1941(1)(a)), article 1938 orders him to pay the necessary expenses for maintaining the estate. The deceased's creditors will seek satisfaction from the original heir, who is obliged to pay all debts from the estate assets.

9.88 While the inheritance stays with the original heir it becomes part of his personal wealth, but as soon as the future event has occurred or the time-limit has expired, he must transfer the inheritance (or whatever is left of it) promptly to the post-heir (art 1935). The latter enjoys an absolute right to inherit as from the testator himself. Because of the existence of this right, if the original heir refuses to pass over the estate the post-heir is entitled to raise the so-called 'action for the delivery of possession of the estate's assets', which is regulated by articles 1871–1883.

9.89 This is a general action, which can be used as a procedural weapon by any heir in order to sue any persons who unlawfully possess the assets that the heir has inherited. The heir requests the courts to recognise his succession rights and to order immediate delivery of the estate or relevant parts of it. If the person who possesses the estate acted in bad faith, the heir can further demand that he pay compensation for any damage he suffered.

11. LEGACIES (ARTS 1967–2010)

Article 1714 provides that the testator may leave assets to someone without necessarily establishing him as heir, ie make a 'legacy' of assets to a third person known as the 'legatee'. Unlike the person who receives the *fideicommissum*, the legatee is not a true heir and, in effect, he is not liable to pay any debts of the estate which correspond to his legacy. However, under article 2004, he may be asked by the heir to compensate him for any expenses which the heir incurred in order to maintain it or for any liabilities he had to pay (eg the legacy was a mortgaged property and the heir had to pay interest in arrears). 9.90

A legacy can only be made in a will. On most occasions the testator obliges the established heir to give the legatee the assets of the estate he has set aside for him.[1] In this respect, the legacy resembles the *fideicommissum* in the sense that, in both cases, the inheritance is first taken by the heir who is under a strict obligation to transfer it or particular assets within it to other persons. Any natural or legal person, even if he or it was not conceived or incorporated at the time of the testator's death, can be designated as legatee. If the legatee dies (or in the case of a legal person, is dissolved) before the testator, the legacy is invalid (art 1978). This is an application of the principle that the legatee does not enjoy any succession rights *per se* and, therefore, the legacy cannot be inherited. Another application of this principle is the provision of article 1971, which allows the testator to entrust to a third person the choice of the legatee.[2] 9.91

The legacy is also invalid if it refers to assets which did not belong to the testator's estate at the time of his death (art 1984(1)) or if its provisions were illegal or impossible to be executed (art 1980). Like heirs, legatees may accept or renounce their benefits but they are not restricted by any deadlines (art 2001). If they elect to renounce, the legacy will go to their substitutes, if any (art 2008), or to the other legatees (art 1976); otherwise it will be kept by the heir. 9.92

12. THE CERTIFICATE OF INHERITANCE (ARTS 1956–1966)

This is the certificate which is granted by the court usually to the heirs in order to prove their succession rights (arts 1956 CC and 819 CCP). The certificate operates both for the benefit of the heirs, so that they can easily prove their capacity, and 9.93

1 Debts which the testator owed to the legatee may also become the object of a legacy; in this case the heir is compelled to pay to the legatee a sum equal to the amount of the debt (art 1992).
2 As will be recalled, the heir must always be chosen by the testator himself (art 1789).

also for the benefit of third parties (eg creditors of the estate), who are reassured that they are dealing with the true heirs.

9.94 Apart from the heirs, a certificate of inheritance can also be requested by the *fideicommissarius*, the legatee or the testamentary executor. They must all prove to the court's satisfaction that the details mentioned in their application are correct (art 1959). If the court is satisfied, the certificate will be issued forthwith (art 1961(1)); otherwise, the request is dismissed. It is possible that during the proceedings important issues are raised such as the validity of the will, possible disinheritance of the requesting heir etc. The court is not allowed to deal with such issues of its own accord, but reserves the right to postpone its decision on the application until such issues are fully resolved and clarified.

9.95 In accordance with article 1962, read in conjunction with article 821 CCP, the certificate creates the presumption that the heir, legatee etc whose name appears on it enjoys the rights indicated subject to any restrictions which may have been imposed by the court. This presumption can be overturned by anyone who has a legitimate interest in the succession and can prove successfully that the contents of the certificate are untrue. Irrespective of any inaccuracies in the certificate, legal transactions which were entered into by third parties on the basis of the certificate (eg acquisition of immovable assets of the estate) are always valid in favour of the third parties, provided that the inaccuracies were not known to them at the time (art 1963 CC in conjunction with art 822 CCP).

9.96 The problems created by incorrect certificates are obvious and may lead to situations which can be very difficult to reverse at a later stage. The law affords to those people whose position may be compromised a number of procedural weapons. The true heir can request whomsoever possesses the inaccurate certificate to surrender it immediately to the court (art 1964); anyone with a vested interest can apply to the competent court to have the certificate amended or revoked or, should this prove to be impossible, to have it declared ineffective (art 1965 CC in conjunction with art 823 CCP). It should be noted that the court may, on its own initiative, decide to revoke or amend any certificate of inheritance (art 1966).

13. PRIVATE INTERNATIONAL LAW (ART 28)

9.97 The usual question which the rules of conflict of laws have to answer in civil law countries (which do not have the artificial common law concept of domicile) is whether the applicable succession law (*lex hereditatis*) should be based on the last habitual residence or on the last nationality of the deceased; in other words, whether the decisive link between the deceased and the legal system which will regulate his succession should be his habitual residence (*lex domicilii*) or his nationality (*lex patriae*).

The first Greek legislation on the subject was promulgated in 1856 and was in force until the introduction of the Civil Code. This law broke new ground in the sense that it did not follow the prevailing approach in European laws which, at the time, favoured the law of habitual residence. More particularly, the Act of 1856 drew a distinction between testamentary succession and movable objects of intestate succession on the one hand and immovable assets of intestate succession on the other hand. The former were regulated under the *lex patriae*, whereas the latter under the law of the place where the property was located (*lex rei sitae*). 9.98

Nine years later, article 8 of the Preliminary Provisions of the Italian Civil Code of 1865 stipulated that the *lex patriae* applied to all assets of the deceased, thus adopting the unitary system. It is regrettable that when in 1990 Haopei Lei delivered his lectures on conflict of laws in succession to the Hague Academy, he did not mention the revolutionary Greek Act of 1856, but only referred to the Italian Civil Code as the first example of a legal system which made the deceased's nationality law applicable to both intestate and testamentary succession.[1] 9.99

The Italian Code has influenced the current Greek Civil Code in its rules of Private International Law enshrined in Book I, articles 4–33. Of particular importance is the provision of article 28: 9.100

> 'Succession relations are governed by the law of nationality, which the deceased had at the time of his death.'

The primary consideration which led the legislator to opt for *lex patriae* for testate and intestate succession was the large number of Greek citizens who reside abroad; nowadays this number is thought to exceed the actual population of Greece.

The provision of article 28 should be contrasted with the 1988 Hague Convention on the Law Applicable to the Estates of Deceased Persons, where its basic provision, in an attempt to reconcile the civil law and common law traditions, stipulates that: 9.101

> 'Succession is governed by the law of the State in which the deceased at the time of his death was habitually resident, if he was then a national of that State.'[2]

The choice of the law of nationality in the Greek Civil Code did entail a serious problem in the case of testamentary succession, when the testator changed nationality after his will had been made. The problem centred on article 11, which provides that: 9.102

> 'legal transactions are valid as to their form, if they are in accordance . . . with the law of nationality of the persons who concluded them.'

To offer an illustration, if a British subject, after making a will valid under English law, became a Greek citizen, his will had to be valid under Greek law as well;

---

1 Haopei Li, 'Some Recent Developments in the Conflict of Laws of Succession' Collected Courses of the Hague Academy of International Law, 1990V, Vol 224, p 33.

2 Article 3(1). The Convention was adopted at the 16th session of the Hague Conference on Private International Law on 20 October 1988, see Scoles, 'The Hague Convention on Succession' [1994] 42 *American Journal of Comparative Law* 85.

otherwise, there would be no testamentary succession and the Greek intestate succession rules would apply. Happily, this is no longer an issue, because Greece ratified in August 1983, by virtue of Act 1325/1983, the Hague Convention of 5 October 1961 on the Conflicts of Laws relating to the Form of Testamentary Dispositions, which provides in article 1(b) that a will is formally valid, if it was drafted, *inter alia*, in accordance with the law of the testator's nationality either at the time he made the will or at the time of his death.

9.103 Article 28 covers almost all issues relating to succession, except for article 32 which rejects the doctrine of *renvoi* and so simplifies matters where foreigners are concerned, as discussed. However, as the object of separate regulations are the questions of when a person is considered to be dead (art 5), whether the testator was capable of drafting the will (art 7) and which form should be followed by the heir who renounces the succession (art 11). Since the solution to all three questions is that the *lex patriae* is applied, there is no deviation from the general rule of article 28.

14. MINIMISATION OF PROBLEMS WHERE FOREIGN ELEMENTS ARE INVOLVED

9.104 Like The Netherlands, Portugal (arts 16 to 19 Civil Code) and the 1988 Hague Convention on Succession (art 17), Greece rejects the doctrine of *renvoi*. In particular, article 32 stipulates that:

> 'The rules of the private international law of the foreign state are not included in the foreign law which is to be applied.'

Take the example of a British national, who at the time of his death was permanently resident in England and owned immovable property in Greece. According to the Greek conflict of laws rules (art 28), all issues relating to his succession will be dealt with by determining the law of nationality at the time of death; in our case this will be the English *lex successionis*. The latter stipulates that the *lex situs – in casu*, the Greek law – is to govern succession to immovables. Thus, we return to Greek law, which, because it rejects *renvoi* (in other words, it does not accept that the English rules of private international law form part of English law in these circumstances), will not be applied. The result is that the English *lex successionis* will be applied to his immovable property in Greece.

9.105 Dealing with property in Greece will be facilitated if the testator makes a Greek will using Greek concepts and takes care that another non-Greek will does not accidentally revoke the Greek will. If a testator's foreign will deals with Greek property it should be worded as simply as possible to avoid mistranslation of legal terminology (particularly if no Greek counterpart exists). For tax reasons, executors should be close relatives of the deceased.

15. TAXES ON DEATH

THE CONSTITUTIONAL PROVISIONS ON TAXATION

The fundamental principles of taxation law are enshrined in Chapter VI of Book II of the Greek Constitution 1975/1986 (arts 78–80). More particularly, article 78 imposes upon the State specific restraints and limitations which aim at preventing the individual from being exploited by the State. Thus no tax may be introduced or collected if Parliament has not previously promulgated the relevant legislation detailing the purpose of the tax and the income or other property to which it will apply. Furthermore, even if Parliament promulgates such legislation, its application may not be extended retrospectively beyond the previous financial year. Finally, Parliament may not delegate to the government or any other state authority its powers to regulate the object and the rate of taxation as well as exemptions from it. 9.106

THE PANACEA OF THE GREEK TAXATION SYSTEM

Greece has traditionally been plagued with widespread tax evasion, a phenomenon which, from a socio-legal point of view, is not restricted only to this country but rather characterises the whole Mediterranean basin. The widely acknowledged reality of tax evasion together with an ever-increasing black economy (recently calculated to exceed 50% of the official gross national product) and with an erratic tax collection system have two negative results. 9.107

The first is that Greek tax legislation has become very complicated and extremely difficult to enforce with any degree of success; the mutual distrust between tax authorities and citizens has led to a surge of taxation-generated litigation, which is extremely slow and prevents the state from collecting revenue.[1] Second, the State's inability to collect direct taxation of personal income has led the State to rely heavily upon indirect taxation in order to generate the needed revenue; nowadays, indirect taxation amounts to almost 70% of all revenue. When VAT was introduced in Greece in the early 1980s, a wide range of goods were branded as 'luxury items' and an exorbitant tax rate of 36% was imposed upon them. 9.108

Reference has been made to the problem of enforcing tax legislation. This could be attributed to the fact that the Greek tax system operates on the premise of the reporting obligation of the taxpayer, be it a natural or a legal person. Since the tax demand will be based exclusively on the tax return filed, the tax payer will only be required to pay additional tax (and any penalties that may be imposed as a result) if his tax return is audited and found to be incorrect. 9.109

---

1 For an applicant to contest in court the decision of the tax authority, he has only to pay upfront 20% of the assessed tax; considering that a case before first instance tax courts may take between 2 and 3 years before a judgment is delivered, the loss suffered by the State becomes apparent.

9.110 However, since it is logistically impossible for the tax authorities to audit the three million plus tax returns filed annually, only a small percentage is audited at random each year. Even though recent legislation has increased significantly the level of penalties for late, inaccurate or false tax returns (the Finance Ministry has even set up a kind of 'tax evasion police force'), the cumbersome tax system still favours those who choose not to abide by the law.

AN OVERVIEW OF THE GREEK TAX SYSTEM

9.111 Natural persons domiciled in Greece and legal persons registered in Greece are subject to income tax in Greece irrespective of the country where the income was earned or derived (the so-called 'universal principle'). The rules governing domicile are stipulated in articles 51–56 of the Civil Code (Book I: General Principles of Civil Law). For present purposes, domicile should be understood as physical presence in a particular place with the clear intention of making this place the centre of a natural person's social, economic and professional activities.

9.112 Natural persons who are not ordinarily domiciled in Greece are taxed only in respect of the income that has been generated in Greece (eg employment, provision of services, renting out immovable property, or investments like deposit accounts, state bonds, shares etc). An exception to this rule is the so-called 'companies established under Act 89/1967'; this instrument aims at making Greece attractive for the establishment of foreign companies which, if they obtain the approval of the Ministry of National Economy to set up branches, are not subject to income taxation in Greece provided that they import annually at least US$50,000 to cover the branches' expenses. Act 89/1967 has proved very popular with Greek shipowners, whose fleets are registered with 'paper companies' in Panama, Liberia, Malta etc but who retain 'management offices' in Greece which are entrusted with day-to-day activities.

BILATERAL TREATIES FOR THE AVOIDANCE OF DOUBLE TAXATION

9.113 Greece has entered into treaties, the most recent of which usually follow the OECD Model Convention on Double Taxation of April 1977, with the following eighteen countries (in chronological order):

Country	*Place of signature*	*Date*
United States	Athens	20 April 1952
United Kingdom	Athens	25 June 1953*
Sweden	Athens	6 October 1961
France	Athens	21 August 1963
India	New Delhi	11 February 1965
Italy†	Athens	3 September 1987
Germany	Athens	18 April 1966
Cyprus	Athens	30 March 1968
Belgium	Athens	24 May 1968
Austria	Vienna	22 September 1970
Finland	Athens	21 January 1980
The Netherlands	Athens	16 July 1981
Hungary	Budapest	25 May 1983
Switzerland	Bern	16 June 1983
Czechoslovakia	Athens	23 October 1986
Poland	Athens	20 November 1987
Norway	Oslo	27 April 1988
Denmark	Copenhagen	8 May 1989

* Reproduced with commentary in British Tax Agreements, CCH Editions.
† Replacing the previous treaty of 19 March 1965.

TAXATION OF SUCCESSION

All assets of the deceased are taxable. Inheritance tax will be assessed on the estate regardless of whether its assets were situated in Greece (and owned by Greek nationals or foreign nationals domiciled in Greece) or outside Greek territory (and owned by Greek nationals domiciled in Greece or abroad). Tax authorities will calculate the assets' gross market value[1] from which all debts and liabilities of the deceased or of the estate (eg loans secured on mortgages) will be deducted. 9.114

Heirs are granted six months (one year if the deceased or their heirs reside abroad) from the day of death in order to notify the competent tax authority of the assets and liabilities which comprise the deceased's estate; if this time-limit is not observed, the tax authority will impose a penalty equal to 2.5% of the amount of the inheritance tax for each month of delay. The net value of the estate will be taxed according to the degree of kinship: the closer to the deceased, the lower the taxation. Currently, the tax bands are as follows (calculated at £1 = 420 drachmas): 9.115

1 In the case of immovable property located in Greece this is usually undertaken by the so-called 'method of objective assessment', which estimates the value of property on the basis of its geographical location, year of construction, number of rooms etc, and does not take into account its overall condition (eg expensive construction, in need of refurbishment, dilapidated etc).

Net value of estate (million of drs/£)	*Children Spouse*	*Grandchildren Brothers/First Cousins*	*Third persons*
1/2,380	no tax	no tax	245,000
5/11,900	175,000	390,000	1,645,000
20/47,620	2,425,000	3,390,000	9,180,000
50/119,050	9,925,000	13,890,000	28,645,000
100/238,095	22,425,000	31,390,000	61,145,000

Greece has also entered into a limited number of bilateral treaties concerning avoidance of double taxation on death duties and succession to property with the following countries (in chronological order):

Country	*Place of signature*	*Date*
Germany	Athens	18 November 1910
Spain	Madrid	16 March 1919
USA	Athens	20 February 1950†
Italy	Athens	13 February 1964

† With supplementary protocol of 18 July 1953 and modifying protocol of 12 February 1964.

CHAPTER 10

ITALY†

1. INTRODUCTION

The Italian law of succession fully exemplifies the principles of the civil law, and in particular those of universality and unity of succession (art 588 CC). It is based on inheritance, so that the heirs, as successors of the deceased for all purposes, succeed jointly between them to the estate in its entirety or an undivided portion of it, both as to assets and liabilities (art 752 CC). From this follows the clear distinction between heirs and legatees (arts 649 *et seq*) who inherit specific assets only and generally assume no responsibility for debts (art 756 CC though an exception is made for a mortgagee's rights over the assets in question). 10.1

The succession process is considered to have opened at the date of death, from which moment the assets devolve upon the heirs. The Italian system is also characterised by the scheme whereby 'legitimate portions' of the total estate pass by law to various next of kin, irrespective of the wishes of the deceased; they cannot be disinherited. Testamentary freedom is therefore limited. 10.2

FIDUCIARY OBLIGATIONS IN ITALIAN LAW OF SUCCESSION

Although the concepts of the trust and legal and equitable ownership are not part of Italian domestic law, fiduciary obligations under a will do, however, receive very limited recognition, in particular in article 627 of the Civil Code, but this in itself illustrates the gulf between the civil law and common law. This provides that while an action cannot be brought to enforce a fiduciary provision of a will by the claim that a gift apparently to one person was in reality intended for another, because the obligation is basically moral and not legal, nevertheless, where a donee duly transfers the assets in question to the beneficiary indicated by the testator, he cannot later claim them back, as he might otherwise do under the general principle of Italian law that a person making a payment for which he is not liable is entitled to claim it (art 203 CC). In this situation, the law, nevertheless, regards the donee as the heir and the subsequent transfer as a separate transaction; it is thus very far from the equitable principles of the common law. As will be seen below, Italian law does, however, take cognisance of other systems, both in questions of form and those of substance. 10.3

---

† This chapter was written by D B Macfarlane, Solicitor, via Visconti Pi Modrone, 32; 120122, Milan, tel 7600 6425 fax 799564.

2. FORMALITIES FOR A VALID WILL IN ITALIAN DOMESTIC LAW

THE NOTARIAL FUNCTION

10.4 One must preface any description of the formalities for transactions under Italian law, including those of a testamentary nature, with mention of the notarial function and its importance. While many functions of the notary may also be carried out by public officials, such as municipal officers (art 2699 CC; Law 15 of 4 January 1968), the notarial profession plays a pre-eminent and public role, and the notary's seal bears the emblem of the Italian State. His records are public records, and a formal act or deed or instrument received by him is considered a public instrument and carries the title of the Italian Republic (art 2699 CC), requiring no further authentication or proof in any proceedings, (art 2700 CC); the same is true of notarially authenticated copies of such documents (art 2714 CC), even though registration or transcription in particular registers may also be required (arts 2643 *et seq*).

FORMS OF WILL

10.5 In Italian domestic law, a will may be made in one of three principal ways.

(1) In holograph form, which means it must be entirely written, signed and dated in the hand of the testator (art 602 CC). Should this not be done, the will is invalid; if notepaper is used in which the date is already partly printed, the date should still be written by hand. No witnesses are required. This is the most usual form in which wills are made in Italy.
(2) By public, ie notarial, act or deed. The testator appears with two witnesses before a notary who records the will as a formal act, after having read it to the testator and the witnesses (art 603 CC). It then forms part of the notary's official records.
(3) By 'secret will' (art 604 CC) which may be written either by the testator or some other person. This is handed to the notary by the testator in a sealed envelope and in the presence of two witnesses; the notary in receiving the will records the testator's declaration that the envelope contains his last will. The document is signed by the notary, the witnesses and the testator (art 605 CC). It is to be noted that the notary does not have sight of the will itself. The envelope is held by the notary unless the testator requires it to be returned to him, its return being recorded by the notary in the presence of two witnesses (art 608 CC).

10.6 Other special forms of will are provided for exceptional circumstances (arts 609–619 CC).

10.7 Pursuant to the Basle Convention of 16 May 1972, Italy has instituted a General Registry of Wills with the Ministry of Justice for wills made in notarial form or holograph wills deposited with a notary.

REVOCATION

A will may be revoked. Express revocation may only be by another notarial act or another will. Where there is no express revocation in a later will, the earlier will is revoked only to the extent that the two are incompatible (arts 679–682 CC). 10.8

The destruction of a holograph will by the testator (unless a contrary intention is proved) is considered to revoke it (art 684 CC). 10.9

3. THE DOMESTIC LAW OF SUCCESSION

No distinction is made between movable and immovable property in relation to rights of succession in either law – ie intestate succession – or by will. Having regard to the substantial portions of the estate to which next of kin are by law entitled, the view is frequently taken that there is no particular advantage in making a will. 10.10

RESERVED PORTIONS

While there is no mandatory provision to be made, certain 'legitimate' portions of the estate are, as mentioned, reserved to certain persons and are not freely disposable by the testator. 10.11

There is no way of avoiding the operation of these provisions of law. Under article 458 of the Civil Code, any agreement whereby a person attempts to regulate his own succession is void, as is one for the alienation or waiver of future rights of succession. Any attempt to impose conditions or charges on reserved shares is likewise void (art 549 CC). 10.12

The reserved or legitimate portions may be considered rights *in rem.*[1] Where the disposable estate is insufficient to satisfy the provisions of the will, without encroaching on the reserved portions, the legacies or other benefits under the will are reduced (art 554 CC) *pari passu* (unless the deceased has indicated some order of preference in making reductions (art 558 CC)), provided, however, that legacies and donations received from the deceased are brought into account in calculating the reserved portions (art 564 CC). 10.13

The disposable estate is taken as a percentage of the total of all assets after deducting debts, and bringing into account donations, valued at the date of death, or their presumed value where the property donated no longer exists or has diminished in value through use (art 556 CC). 10.14

---

1 Ferri, *Commentario del Codice Civile di Scialoja e Branca.*

10.15 Italian law has similar principles to those of hotchpot in English law, whereby issue and spouses as heirs must bring into account donations received, unless the deceased has relieved them of doing so within the limits of the disposable estate (arts 737–751 CC).

10.16 Those entitled to reserved portions are the spouse, children (both legitimate and illegitimate) and remoter issue, parents and forebears (or ascendants). The provisions in their favour are as follows.

10.17 Where the deceased leaves one child and no spouse, the child is entitled to half the estate, and where more than one and no spouse, the children are entitled to two-thirds in equal shares between them (art 537 CC).

10.18 Where the deceased leaves a spouse and no children the spouse is entitled to half the estate (art 540 CC). Where the deceased leaves a spouse and one child, each succeeds to one-third of the estate; where there are a spouse and more than one child, the children succeed to one half between them in equal shares and the spouse to one-quarter (art 542 CC).

10.19 The spouse's rights apply where the parties are separated under order of the court, provided the order was not made by reason of the fault of the surviving spouse. Where it was, but the surviving spouse was nevertheless in receipt of some form of maintenance from the deceased, such rights may continue, though possibly in a reduced amount having regard to the value of the estate, the number of heirs and who they are (art 548 CC).

10.20 The spouse is also entitled to the use of the family home and its contents whether they were in the name of the deceased or both jointly. These rights are considered a charge on the disposable portion of the estate, or if that is insufficient, on the spouse's reserved share and after these on those of the children (art 540 CC).

10.21 Where a child predeceases the deceased or cannot or does not accept his inheritance but leaves issue, the latter take equally between them *per stirpes* the parent's share (arts 467–469 CC).

10.22 Where there are no children, ascendants succeed to one-third of the estate (art 538 CC), or a quarter where there is a spouse, who in such case receives one half (art 534 CC). Ascendants succeed in order of degrees of kinship, with division within the same degree equally between the maternal and paternal lines of ascent (art 569 CC).

10.23 Where a legacy is given in satisfaction of a reserved share, the legatee may waive the legacy and accept the reserved share; whereas if he accepts the legacy he loses the right to the reserved share unless the will expressly entitles him to claim the difference (art 551 CC).

TESTAMENTARY CAPACITY; GROUNDS OF VITIATION

10.24 Minors, persons of unsound mind and those who for any reason lack the necessary understanding or intention temporarily or permanently, or have been declared legally incapable, do not have testamentary capacity (art 591 CC). A will or a clause in it may also be set aside when shown to have been induced by error, violence or fraud (art 624 CC).

CAPACITY TO SUCCEED AND DISQUALIFICATION

Heirs must have the capacity to succeed and be born or conceived (which in the absence of contrary proof is presumed to have been 300 days earlier) at the date of death, although assets may devolve by will to the unborn child of a person living at the testator's death (art 462 CC). 10.25

Persons disqualified from succeeding include those convicted of homicide or a similar offence against the deceased or his next of kin, or who have destroyed, altered or hidden the will, or made or used a false will (art 463 CC). A minor may succeed under Italian law but may only accept (unless with 'benefit of inventory') or renounce on reaching majority. In the meantime the assets come under the jurisdiction of a particular magistrate, the *giudice tutelare*. 10.26

A witness to a will, a notary receiving it or a person writing a secret will, and illegitimate children beyond certain limits are disqualified from taking under it (arts 592, 597, 598 CC). 10.27

Without government permission, corporations (not being trading companies) may not accept legacies (arts 17, 473 CC). The underlying intention is, like that of the old English statute of mortmain, to prevent assets becoming tied up in perpetuity and not subject to the laws of succession. The prohibition is thus considered also to affect foreign corporate bodies which have been left assets in Italy[1] and to be in the public interest. Inheritance by a corporate body is in any case deemed to be with 'benefit of inventory'. 10.28

A testamentary disposition in favour of an unincorporated body – ie one that has not been granted legal personality – as distinct from its members, is invalid, unless it makes application for incorporation within a year (art 600 CC). Dispositions may be made in favour of the poor, and unless otherwise indicated are treated as being in favour of the local welfare authority (art 630 CC). 10.29

ACCEPTANCE WITH BENEFIT OF INVENTORY AND RENUNCIATION

Acceptance with the benefit of inventory is a procedure enabling the heir to accept within the limits of the available assets and thus avoid responsibility for liabilities (arts 484 *et seq*). The procedures are complicated and onerous and it is not a course to be followed unless there appears to be reason for doing so. An heir may also unconditionally renounce the inheritance (arts 519 *et seq*). 10.30

1 Ferrar, 'Le Persone Giuridiche' – *Tratto di Diritto Civile,* Vassali.

OTHER PROVISIONS: CERTAINTY; DELEGATION; CONDITIONS; PUBLIC ORDER

10.31 A will must be certain in indicating a beneficiary (art 628 CC) and may not leave the choice to a third person, without specifying at least the persons or classes of persons from among whom the choice is to be made (art 631 CC). Nor may the amount of a legacy be left to a third party's discretion (art 632 CC).

10.32 The dispositions in a will may be subject to conditions precedent or subsequent (art 633 CC), provided they are not impossible or contrary to public order or morality. 'Public order' is similar to the idea of public policy in English law. It is a phrase of which no single definition exists although there have been a vast number of judicial decisions on it. It may be considered to reflect the 'imperative objectives' of the legal system. Offending provisions include those considered to apply undue pressure on a person or unduly restrict his liberty, such as a prohibition on marriage.

10.33 As mentioned above, a gift to a corporation may fall into this category. Where, therefore, a condition is illegal or impossible, it is to be disregarded, unless it forms the underlying objective or the sole motivation of the bequest in which case the bequest itself is void. Thus, where a foreign testator bequeathed property to the Italian state on the misguided terms that the whole estate was to be exempt from whatsoever taxes, a condition that was both impossible and contrary to public order, the Court held the whole bequest to be void, both under foreign and Italian law (art 634 CC; Tribunale di Genova, *Brown and Petit v Minister of Finance, Rivista di Diritto Privato Internazionale* (1990) 674).

EXECUTORS

10.34 Executors may be appointed under an Italian will, (arts 700 *et seq*) but their powers and duties are strictly limited. Their duty is to ensure that the provisions of the will are duly observed, and in particular to take possession of and administer the assets. Their term of office is limited to one year from the date of acceptance, unless extended by the court. They are required to act according to one of the common criteria of Italian law, that is, as 'a good father of a family'. They may carry out all necessary administrative acts but require the consent of the court to any disposal of the assets of the estate (art 703 CC). The executors may make a division or distribution of the assets among beneficiaries only when directed by the will and they are not themselves interested as beneficiaries (art 706 CC). On termination of their duties, and in any case within a year from the testator's death, the executors must render an account to the heirs (arts 703, 709 CC).

INTESTATE SUCCESSION

Those entitled on an intestacy are the spouse, issue (legitimate and illegitimate), ascendants, other relatives and finally the State (art 565 CC). The principal provisions are as follows. 10.35

Where the deceased leaves children and no spouse, the former succeed (art 566 CC). Where there is a spouse, the latter succeeds to one half (if there is one child) or a third (if there are more) (art 581 CC). 10.36

Where the deceased leaves brothers, sisters, parents and ascendants they succeed in equal shares *per capita*, provided that the share of the parent or parents may not be less than one half (art 571 CC). Where, however, there is also a spouse, the latter takes two-thirds and the share due to the others is reduced, the ascendants receiving one-quarter (art 582 CC). If only one of these persons or classes of persons survives, they succeed to the whole estate (arts 568, 570, 583 CC). A separated spouse has the same rights unless the separation was held to be due to his or her fault (art 585 CC). 10.37

ADMINISTRATIVE PROCEDURES ON DEATH

The testamentary procedures of probate or granting letters of administration, or indeed the resealing of a grant of administration, have no part in the Italian system. It is necessary, instead, that an heir establish his title to succeed. The usual manner is by means of an 'act of notoriety', a notarial deed or act made at the request of an heir who is a party to it and sworn by two independent persons, who must be Italian citizens or residents of full age (Law 89 of 16 February 1913 as amended), stating who are the heirs, whether under a will or by law. For certain purposes (in particular in dealings with the public administration such as the land registrars) the simpler form of a declaration in substitution sworn by the heir may suffice (Law 15 of 4 January 1968). 10.38

In addition, a holograph will must be presented for 'publication' by the notary, a formal procedure requiring an act or deed executed with two witnesses, which renders it a public document so that it forms part of the official notarial record (art 620 CC). The will itself remains in the records and thereafter copies are issued and authenticated by the notary. 10.39

A will made in notarial form is automatically published. The notary, following publication, must send a copy to the lower court or *pretura* (art 622 CC) and notify heirs and legatees, where their addresses are known (art 623 CC). 10.40

A foreign will of which probate has been obtained abroad clearly cannot be 'published' in Italy, but the grant of administration with the copy of the will annexed, 'legalised' by the Italian consulate, or where the Hague Convention of 1961 applies, the foreign ministry of the country concerned – in the case of Britain, the Foreign and Commonwealth Office – with a sworn translation into Italian may be deposited with an Italian notary. 10.41

10.42 These formalities may not always be required: a bank, for example with whom a deceased of foreign nationality held an account, may be satisfied with the production of the grant of administration, duly legalised and translated.

10.43 Where a declaration in substitution of an 'act of notoriety' is made, this is sworn by the heir alone, either before a notary or a public official (such as the appropriate officer of the local authority or *comune*), and is clearly much simpler. This is accepted as proof by public authorities but not by banks or companies.

Succession taxes

10.44 Succession taxes are payable in the case of Italian residents on their world-wide estate and for non-residents on their property situated in Italy. Naturally, account must be taken of relevant double tax conventions.

10.45 The heirs of residuary beneficiaries are jointly liable for the payment of taxes on the whole estate. For such purposes, real or immovable property is valued according to a particular formula based on the notional income value ascribed to all properties in the local registers. These values are in turn based on particular criteria such as the type of building, number of rooms and location. Generally the resulting value will be found to be notably less than the market value, but in a few cases it may be more. As well as a succession tax, immovable property bears a land registry tax of 2%.

10.46 Shares, bank accounts and assets on any kind of register are valued in the appropriate manner – unquoted shares, for example on the basis of the last accounts. Furniture and personal effects are deemed in the absence of an inventory drawn up by a notary to be 10% of all other assets. The tax authority may contest the values declared within two years of payment of the principal tax. Certain assets are exempt, for example government and certain European securities, (those of the EIB, ECSC and Euratom), the termination payments accruing to employees over the course of their employment, the proceeds of life policies and assets of recognised historic or artistic value. In the case of co-ownership, the owners are presumed to have equal shares.

10.47 As to deductions, funeral expenses may be deducted for up to 2 million lire, medical expenses incurred in the last six months of the deceased's life as well as liabilities relating to the declared assets (such as mortgages), unpaid taxes and certain other liabilities provided they are supported by documentary proof.

10.48 Legacies to recognised charities and public bodies are exempt from succession tax. Legacies to foreign charities are only exempt on the basis of reciprocity – that is to say to the extent that the other State grants similar treatment to Italian charities. Independently of double tax conventions, there is relief in respect of foreign succession taxes on the same assets (100% on estates of up to 100 million lire in value, thereafter one-third).

10.49 Succession tax is graduated, as well as following different scales according to the degree of kinship of the particular beneficiary to the deceased. The tax is divided into two component parts – a global tax on the whole net estate and a tax on each beneficial interest. The former commences at 300 million lire. Spouses, issue and parents of the deceased are exempt from the latter tax, and thus receive the most favourable treatment; the next group comprises brothers, sisters and their children; the third group, other specified relatives; and the fourth group, who receive the least favourable treatment, all others, including persons having no ties of kinship at all.

For the purposes of this calculation, life interests, or usufructs, and reversionary interests are valued on an actuarial basis. There is graduated relief for quick successions, ie when the property is the subject of two successions within five years. 10.50

A tax now being phased out is INVIM – *Imposta sull Incremento del Valore degli Immobili* – or capital gains tax on real property exceeding 250 million lire in value, arising during the period of the deceased's ownership until 31 December 1992, when the tax ceased to accrue, that is to say on the difference between the initial value, as increased by proven capital expenditure, and the value at the latter date. The tax is structured to make allowance for inflationary increases. There is a 50% reduction for spouses and issue and a similar exemption as above in favour of charitable bodies. The INVIM is deducted from the succession tax so that, in effect, one pays the higher of the two taxes. 10.51

A declaration of succession must be completed by the beneficiaries or executors and filed with the authorities in the place where the deceased resided, or, in the case of a non-resident, Rome, within six months of the date of death; no declaration, however, is required where the value of the estate does not exceed 50 million lire and devolves to the spouse, issue or parents, and does not include real property. 10.52

A receipted copy of the declaration must be presented to banks and other third parties holding assets of the deceased before such assets can be released. Safe deposit boxes must be opened in the presence of a notary who records the contents, with notice to the revenue authority who may also attend. 10.53

Apart from the land registry tax (para **10.45**) and certain others, amounting to 4% in all, which are payable on presenting the declaration, taxes are payable on receipt of the demand from the revenue authority, and in the case of immovable property become a charge on it, including in the hands of third party purchasers, until paid. One may apply for payment by instalments, over five years with interest, giving suitable security. One may also appeal against the assessment. There are penalties both for late or incomplete presentation or non-presentation of a declaration of succession (two to four times the tax where the delay is more than 30 days). Under-declarations of value are also penalised. Late payment of the tax attracts interest and a surtax of 20%. 10.54

4. INTERNATIONAL ASPECTS

CONNECTING FACTORS; *RENVOI*

The rules of Italian private international law are now to be found in Law 218 of 31 May 1995, which reformed this branch of the law. This contains the important 10.55

innovation that references to foreign law are to include the *renvoi* provisions of the law in question – previously they were excluded. Article 13(1) provides that references to foreign law shall take account of the reference operated by that law to that of another State, where the latter accepts the reference to it, or to Italian law. This provision does not apply, however, to the form of documents (art 13(2)(b)). Under article 15, moreover, foreign law is to be applied according to its own rules of interpretation. This means that 'domicile' in the common law sense, which is not a concept of Italian law, may nevertheless be relevant.

FORM

Governing law

10.56 Under article 48 of Law 218, the form of a will is governed either by the law of the place where it is made, by the law governing its substance, by the national law of the deceased or by that of his country of residence or of his *domicilio* or centre of his affairs at the time of death.

Proof of compliance with foreign law

10.57 Where, therefore, the national law of the deceased requires the will to be made in a particular form, it will be necessary to demonstrate that it complies with that form.

10.58 The usual way is by the production of probate or a similar document: the onus is on whoever is setting up a foreign will to prove its formal validity.

10.59 The question was examined by the Supreme Court of Cassation in a case involving a grant of probate of the will of an Italian citizen living in New York (*Gatta v Gatta* Sez II, 30 April 1955, no 1217). It was stated that the onus is on whoever seeks to establish foreign law, unless the instrument or act of a foreign public authority is produced, in which case there is a presumption of compliance with the foreign law in question. While the court made reference to a textbook of American law, it was clear that the grant of probate, authenticated or 'legalised' by the Italian consul, was to be regarded as conclusive, and is to be treated in Italy as a foreign judgment: this is certainly so where probate is granted in solemn form, but also where it is granted in common form.

10.60 The court, nevertheless, recognised that a grant of probate was not essential provided the onus of proving the foreign law was discharged. It may be that probate cannot be obtained in the country concerned because there is no basis on which its courts are able to claim jurisdiction: the deceased may not, as for example, in the case of the UK, have possessed assets in that country at the date of death or they may have been excluded from the ambit of the will (such as where the deceased has made two wills, one for UK assets, the other for non-UK assets). In these circumstances it will be necessary to prove the formal validity of the will to the Italian authorities.

In practice, a certificate from that country's consular authorities in Italy will suffice. For many consular authorities, however, such as those of the UK, it is not the practice to give certificates as to what they consider legal matters; in these circumstances the affidavit of a practising lawyer of the particular jurisdiction that the formal requirements have been satisfied will probably be accepted. In any proceedings, the judge is required to ascertain the foreign law by having resort *inter alia* to international conventions, information acquired through the Ministry of Justice, experts and specialised institutions, failing all of which, Italian law may be applied. 10.61

Washington Convention on the International Will

In 1990, Italy ratified and enacted the provisions of the Washington Convention of 1973 on the Uniform Law on the Form of the International Will (Law 387 of 29 November 1990), which recognises a will as formally valid until the contrary is proved when signed and acknowledged in the presence of two witnesses and authenticated by a third person, qualified in the country concerned under the legislation which signatory states are required to enact, who makes an attestation, in the prescribed form, to the effect that the document is the will of the testator, signed in the required manner, and that the latter understood its contents (art 4). In the case of Italy, the person so qualified is a notary, although Italian consular officials abroad may fulfil this function where so permitted by local law (art 3, Law 307). 10.62

The procedure will be useful in obviating the need for a grant of administration, or otherwise proving the will if made in one of the signatory States.[1] 10.63

SUBSTANCE

Governing law

Under article 46 of Law 218, succession on death is governed by the national law of the deceased. Where the will of the deceased so provides, succession may be governed by the law of the State in which the deceased then resided and continued to reside at the date of death. In the case of an Italian citizen, this may not prejudice the reserved rights of next of kin under Italian law (art 46(2)). Where the beneficiaries so agree, distribution of the estate may be according to the law of the place of death or of where any of the assets were situated. 10.64

Where there is an intestacy, and the deceased was of Italian and some other nationality, Italian law will be followed. 10.65

Relation to *lex situs*

Article 51 of Law 218 provides that rights in movable and immovable property are to be governed by the *lex situs* except in cases of succession. Nevertheless, a foreign 10.66

1 Currently, Canada, Cyprus, Ecuador, Libya, Niger, Portugal and Yugoslavia.

will cannot attempt to impose rights of ownership unknown to the Italian legal system, such as a joint tenancy with rights of survivorship.

Proof of foreign law

10.67 Once more, the onus is on whoever is relying on foreign law to prove it. For many administrative and similar purposes, an act or declaration of notoriety will suffice, stating who are the successors to the deceased in respect of the assets in question (Law 15 of 4 January 1968). Where for example there is a sale of real – or, more correctly, immovable – property this is likely to be a useful step.

Proof of foreign will

10.68 The foreign will and probate, 'legalised' by the Italian consulate or the foreign ministry of the country concerned, where the Hague Convention of 1961 applies, will, as mentioned, be treated as a foreign judgment. It may be deposited with an Italian notary to form part of his official records, and authenticated copies thereafter may be issued by the notary for production to authorities and third parties generally. It may also be lodged at the Land Registry and the accompanying notarial deed may incorporate a declaration as to the devolution of the assets according to the terms of the will in order to remove any doubts.

The absence of a system of trusts

10.69 A series of problems has always been found to arise because of the absence of any system or notion of trusts in the civil law, of any distinction between legal and equitable ownership, or of any of the various incidents of the law of trusts existing in common law countries. Such problems might be fiscal: who, for example, for the purposes of the tax legislation are the true successors to the deceased? They may relate to the powers of the executors in ascertaining whether they can exercise wider powers than those permitted to Italian executors, or they may relate to those of infant or unborn children.

Infant beneficiaries

10.70 Where there are infant beneficiaries, the *giudice tutelare* would, in an Italian situation, assume control over the assets passing to the infants. While questions of guardianship are a matter for the national law of the minor (art 36 of Law 218, whereby relations between parent and infant child are a matter of the latter's national law, and art 42 of Law 218 which adopts the provisions of the Hague Convention of 5 October 1961 on the Protection of Minors), the jurisdiction of the *giudice tutelare* depends on where the property is administered (art 24 Code of Civil Procedure). The Hague Convention of 1961 recognises the jurisdiction of the country where the minor is habitually resident to take measures for the protection of his person and property. The authorities of the minor's country of residence or nationality may, in particular, authorise those of the country where assets are situated to adopt any particular measures for their protection (art 6). There are also provisions for cases of urgency (art 9).

While the assets may be vested in the names of the infant beneficiaries of a will, a problem arises as to disposal of the assets: under English law, for example parents have no power to dispose of assets belonging to their children. Commonsense would seem to require the executors to do so, but in Italy the question then arises as to their power to dispose of assets that are not in their name. Difficulties of this nature were examined in a case where real property situated in Italy was left in trust under a foreign will for the benefit of infant children (*Tribunale di Casale Monferrato*, 1984 N 85 RG 84). The judge held the foreign executors were empowered to sell the property, even though Italian executors might not, by what amounted to an effective recognition that the executors' position under the foreign law did not conflict with Italian law. It might be hoped that the case (which was cited in the report to Parliament when it ratified the Hague Convention of 1 July 1985 on the Recognition of Trusts) would now be resolved by reference to the Convention. 10.71

The Hague Convention on the Recognition of Trusts

The Hague Convention of 1 July 1985 (ratified by Law 364 of 16 October 1989), however, which represents a compromise between numerous points of view, between common law and civil law countries, may well be found to raise as many problems for the Italian legal system as it solves. 10.72

It commences with a description of a trust: the assets of the trust are separate from those of the trustee in whose name they are held, who is both empowered and obliged to administer and deal with them according to the terms of the trust and is accountable accordingly (art 2). 10.73

The governing law is selected by the settlor, whether expressly or by implication having regard to the terms of the trust, provided it is one that provides for the creation of trusts (art 6): this rules out the selection of Italian law. 10.74

Where there is no such selection, the trust is governed by the law of the place with which it is most closely connected, having regard in particular to where it is to be administered, where the assets are situated, the residence of the trustee or the centre of his affairs and where its objects are to be carried out (art 7). This enables, and indeed requires, a very broad view to be taken in determining the governing law. 10.75

However, a court has a discretion not to recognise a trust if, according to the above criteria excluding those of choice of law, place of administration and residence of the trustee, it is most closely connected with a place whose law does not provide for trusts (art 13). 10.76

This may well prevent a trust from being set up, say in Italy, by an Italian settlor with Italian beneficiaries, but under a foreign law with a foreign trustee and administration, with the ostensible object of its being treated as a foreign trust and circumventing the ordinary provisions of Italian law (such as those relating to 'legitimate portions') but article 15(1)(c) could, instead, be relied upon. 10.77

10.78 This would appear both clear and reasonable, but the intermediate situations give rise to difficulties: where, for example, a non-Italian, possibly British, settlor creates a trust over Italian assets for beneficiaries or objects partly in Italy and partly elsewhere. In these circumstances, the Italian court would have to decide with which country the trust was most closely connected, and if it decided this was Italy then it would have a discretion to refuse recognition of the trust.

10.79 It may also be argued that the Convention actually reduces the efficacy of foreign trusts under Italian law. Before its ratification by Italy, the generally held view was that under the rules of private international law in Italy, a trust validly created under foreign law, by a foreign settlor, would be recognised as creating rights and duties *in personam*, but not *in rem*, as far as Italian assets were concerned; if, however, under the Convention, the court exercises its discretion to refuse to recognise the trust for the reasons mentioned, then it can be argued that the trustee is under no obligation at all in the eyes of Italian law. However, the court could still give effect to the objects of the trust by *in personam* means: cp article 15(2) of the Hague Convention.

10.80 A further limitation, and one to be expected, is that the trust does not conflict with the notions of public order described above. It has been argued that the creation of a trust over Italian realty conflicts with public order, a view rejected by the court in the case mentioned in para **10.71** above in which an executor's right to sell Italian property for the benefit of infant beneficiaries was upheld (see art 18).

10.81 The power of foreign trustees to designate beneficiaries, even though impossible in Italian law, has also been upheld (see *Gatta v Gatta* cited at para **10.59** above). Notwithstanding these decisions, in which the Italian courts have clearly not wished to disallow the provisions of a foreign will, considerations of public order are among those that anyone setting up a foreign will must be prepared to satisfy.

Tax considerations

10.82 An important exception to the principles of the Hague Convention is article 19 which states that the Convention shall not prejudice the powers of signatory States in fiscal matters.

10.83 This, in fact, is the area in which the non-recognition of the trust can have the most onerous consequences. In Italy, a succession tax (*Imposta Sulle Successioni e Donazioni*) (see para **10.44** above) is payable at differing rates depending on the degree of kinship of the successor to the deceased: at one end of the scale, property passing to spouses and issue receives the most beneficial treatment; at the other, property passing to persons having no ties of kinship bears the heaviest rates. If, therefore, the executors are to be treated as the successors of the deceased to whom legal ownership passes, as must indeed be the strict interpretation, the result may be very onerous, except in cases where the executors are next of kin.

10.84 Other taxes, in particular income taxes arising or deemed to arise on property, will be chargeable on assets in the hands of the executors as owners.

Notarial considerations

Doubts have been raised about the usefulness of the 1985 Hague Convention by a writer in the notarial review, the *Rivista del Notariato* Vol XLIV p 91. The writer points out that an Italian notary called upon to record or receive an act or deed is required under the notarial laws (Law 89 of 16 February 1913, Royal Decree Law 166 of 14 July 1936) to satisfy himself of its validity and legality; and if a foreign trust is involved he will have to address himself to problems of the kind mentioned above. He faces a difficult task with a foreign trust deed, a private, unregistered (and therefore unproven) document, subject to a system of law of which he knows nothing. 10.85

One of the preliminary questions will be what is the governing law, if it has not been specified; and if it has been specified, has it been validly specified, having regard to the provisions of articles 6 and 7? What is the law with which it is most closely connected? Is it valid in terms of article 13? He must also satisfy himself that the provisions of the trust do not contemplate an infringement of the requirements of Italian public order. He may in short be faced with a series of problems made no easier if he is relying on a translation of a foreign trust deed, possibly one of considerable complexity with technicalities of terminology that only a practitioner in that system can properly explain. Indeed, it would not be unreasonable to require an opinion from such a lawyer. 10.86

The reluctance of the Italian notarial profession to accept and act on a foreign trust deed is therefore to be expected; if it becomes widespread, the convention will remain largely ineffective in Italy. 10.87

Following from such problems is the question of registration of fiduciary interests in real, or immovable, property. Registration constitutes constructive notice (art 2644 CC), and one may see the logic of providing for registration in the absence of a body of equitable rules. Naturally, Italian law does not in fact contain any provisions for registering separate beneficial and equitable interests, but nor is there any provision of Italian law forbidding registration. It is arguable, therefore, that such interests are now to be considered as registrable, with the consequence that they are to be recognised and protected by the Italian legal system. 10.88

Apart from the broader problems mentioned, the writer of the article sees technical and formal problems both for the notary and the land registrars (which may, indeed, be insurmountable in the distinctive tabular system of land registration of Austrian origin obtaining in the north-eastern part of the country). 10.89

A further problem, and one not canvassed in the article, is that it may not be sufficient to refer to the existence of the trust but necessary to spell out its precise terms, and this may require the deed either to be set out, *verbatim*, in translation, and incorporated, as an appendix or otherwise, or possibly in *précis* form. 10.90

The conclusion of the writer of the article is that the attempt to import foreign trusts into Italy is to be avoided, and that it would be better to attempt to reach the same result through one of the existing institutions of Italian law, such as the creation of a foundation, or the grant of a mandate, although he does not suggest 10.91

a solution for a testamentary trust. However, Professor M Lupoi takes a more favourable view in Chapter 7 of his book, *Trusts* (1977, Milan, Dott A Guiffrè).

JURISDICTION

10.92 The Italian courts claim jurisdiction over foreign nationals *inter alia* where at the moment of bringing proceedings such a person had either his residence or centre of his affairs (or *domicilio*) in Italy, where the question concerns property in Italy, the succession to the estate of an Italian citizen or a succession opened in Italy or obligations to be performed in Italy. They also claim jurisdiction if the claim is connected with another claim properly pending in Italy, is one for provisional relief to be enforced in Italy, or concerns matters already within their jurisdiction.

10.93 There is also jurisdiction where the courts of the State to which the foreign national belongs would in the same situation claim jurisdiction over an Italian national (art 4 Code of Civil Procedure).

10.94 In matters of succession, article 50 of Law 218 provides for Italian jurisdiction:

(1) where the deceased was an Italian citizen at the moment of his death;
(2) if, in effect, the centre of the deceased's interests at his death was in Italy;
(3) if the greater part of the assets in terms of value is situated in Italy;
(4) if the defendant in the proceedings was resident or has the centre of his interests in Italy, or has accepted Italian jurisdiction, except where the proceedings relate to immovable property situated abroad;
(5) if the proceedings concern assets situated in Italy.

10.95 In the case, therefore, of the estate of a foreigner whose affairs and interests are centred abroad, but who owned property in Italy, the Italian courts will claim jurisdiction in relation to that property, and the particular court will be the territorially competent court for the place where the greater part of the property is situated.

10.96 The fact, therefore, that a foreigner died in Italy, or was resident in Italy at his death, would not in itself seem to give the Italian courts jurisdiction over his estate: some other element is necessary, such as that the proceedings concerned assets in Italy, or the defendant was resident in Italy.

10.97 The principle of *forum conveniens*, it may be noted, has no part in Italian private international law.

5. THE MINIMISATION OF PROBLEMS WHERE FOREIGN ELEMENTS ARE INVOLVED

10.98 As will be seen from the above, Italy's accession to the Hague Convention on the Recognition of Trusts has by no means removed the problems affecting this area of the law.

The draftsman of a will made under some law other than Italian law but disposing of Italian property, especially immovables or registered property, will be well advised to follow certain principles. The will should be as simply worded as possible, to avoid mistranslations of legal terminology, which may in any case have no counterpart in the Italian system; the creation of complicated trusts that may give rise to problems in their application to the Italian context should be avoided; where possible, executors should be next of kin, for basically fiscal reasons; and finally, unusual provisions, certainly in the Italian context, should be avoided so as not to risk unintentional infringement of some aspects of public policy or order. **10.99**

CHAPTER 11

THE NETHERLANDS†

1. DOMESTIC LAW[1]

FORMALITIES FOR A VALID WILL

Wills must be made by a notarial deed (art 4:985).[2] There are some, not very important, exceptions, eg the so-called 'codicil' (art 4:982), which is a hand-written instrument dated and signed by the testator. Only a few dispositions may validly be made in a codicil, such as the appointment of an executor and the legacy of special jewellery and furniture. Other assets like money, securities and real property, may not be validly bequeathed by a codicil. 11.1

The *notaris* plays an important part in drawing up wills. A *notaris* is a fully qualified lawyer appointed by the Crown to serve as a public official. 11.2

Dutch wills, codicils excepted, have to be registered in the Central Registry of Wills. Only the name of the testator and the date of the will are recorded on the register and the name and place of office of the *notaris* before whom the will was executed; the contents of the will are not recorded. 11.3

Any person of 16 years and over and of sound mind may make a will. Mutual wills are not allowed (art 4:977). 11.4

THE LAW OF SUCCESSION

Who may or may not benefit

One has to be alive at the time of a person's death if one is to inherit from that person or to receive a legacy out of the deceased's estate (arts 4:883 and 4:946). However, any unborn child expected at such time is considered as having been born (art 1:2). 11.5

---

† This chapter was written by FAA Duynstee and KMFJ Houben of De Brauw Blackstone Westbroek of The Hague, tel (70) 328 5328, fax (70) 328 5325 and of Rotterdam, tel (10) 240 6500, fax (10) 411 3548.

1 For further reference see (1) C Asser, *Handleiding tot de beoefening van het Nederlands Burgerlijk Recht,* Volume Erfrecht, edited by E M Meijers, 12th edn updated by S Perrick, W E J Tjeenk Willink, Zwolle, 1996 (2) *Huwelijksgoederen – en erfrecht,* Tweede gedeelte: Erfrecht, Klaasen – Eggens, 10th ed edited by E A A Luijten, W E J Tjeenk Willink, Zwolle, 1989 (3) *Het Nederlands Burgerlijk Wetboek,* Deel 5, Het Erfrecht, A Pitlo, 9th edn, edited by G van der Burght, Gouda Quint, Arnhem, 1997.

2 References are to the Dutch Civil Code, unless indicated otherwise.

11.6 A person who has been convicted of killing the deceased or a person who has destroyed or forged a deceased's will, or prevented the deceased from making, revoking or amending his will, cannot benefit from the estate of the deceased (arts 4:885 and 4:959).

Unity of the estate

11.7 The estate of a deceased passes as a whole. That means that irrespective of movable or immovable property located abroad belonging to the estate, only one legal system can apply to the devolution of such estate. Even if the deceased left immovables abroad which, according to the *lex situs* devolve according to that law, Dutch law will in ascertaining the size of heirs' portions or of heirs' intestacy rights take those immovables into account (see also para **11.52**).

Succession rules on intestacy (arts 4:899 *et seq*)

11.8 If a married person dies intestate without leaving issue, the spouse will be the only heir. If the deceased in addition to the spouse also leaves children, the spouse and children will each inherit an equal portion of the estate. If the deceased is single and leaves children, the latter will inherit the estate in equal portions. If children have died prior to the death of their parents, their descendants will take their place as heirs *per stirpes*.

11.9 If the deceased is single and leaves no descendants, the parents and the brothers and sisters, if any, will inherit the estate. If the deceased leaves both parents and a brother (or sister), each one of them will inherit one-third of the estate. If the deceased leaves both parents and two or more brothers or sisters, the parents will each receive one-quarter of the estate and the brothers and sisters will equally share the remaining half of the estate.

11.10 If one of the parents died prior to the deceased, the surviving parent will, in the event of the deceased leaving only one brother or sister, inherit one half of the estate and the brother or sister the other half. If the deceased left two brothers or sisters, the surviving parent and the other two heirs will inherit equal portions.

11.11 If the deceased leaves one parent and more than two brothers or sisters, the parent will receive in any event one-quarter of the estate and the brothers and sisters will equally share the remaining three-quarters of the estate.

11.12 If the brothers and sisters include half brothers and sisters, the inheritance will be divided in equal portions between the lines of the father and of the mother. The full brothers and sisters will each get their portion from both the line of the father and of the mother. The half brothers and sisters get their portion only from the line from which they descend. Other members of the family are not entitled to the estate as long as there are parents and/or (half) brothers or sisters.

11.13 If the deceased leaves no issue or parents or brothers or sisters, the estate will be split in two. One half will pass to the next of kin on the father's side and the other half to the next of kin on the mother's side.

In each half of the estate the closest related ascendants will inherit equally. If there are no ascendants, the other blood relations in the side line will inherit, but not beyond the sixth degree of kinship. 11.14

If there are no ascendants or blood relations within the required degree on the side of either the father or the mother then the entire estate will descend to the heirs in the other line. 11.15

An illegitimate child (and its descendants) takes the same position as a legitimate child of its mother and, upon recognition by its father, as a legitimate child of its father (arts 1:222 and 4:879). On 17 January 1997 the Supreme Court decided that even if 'a family life' has existed between the biological father and a child, in the meaning of Article 8 of the European Convention for the protection of human rights and fundamental freedoms, such child, if not recognised by the biological father, may not claim the same position in the estate of his biological father as a legitimate child. The heirs of a father who has an unrecognised child may, however, be forced by such child to pay for the child's care and education a lump sum not exceeding the value of the 'statutory portion' (see paras **11.21** *et seq*) to which such child would have been entitled had it been recognised. Such liability can, however, not be qualified as a liability under the law of succession but must rather be qualified as alimony (art 1:406). 11.16

Testamentary powers of disposition

A person is free to dispose of his estate by will (arts 4:921 *et seq*). However, should the dispositions in his will infringe upon the rights of a descendant or a parent to receive a statutory portion, the aggrieved party may as far as such infringement is concerned oppose the will. He will then receive his statutory portion as an heir (see paras **11.21** *et seq*). 11.17

Restrictions on powers of disposition

Testamentary dispositions which are immoral or contrary to the law and dispositions based on motives which are immoral or contrary to the law are null and void (arts 3:40 and 4:938). 11.18

The law is in general hostile to successive interests in property. It explicitly prohibits *fideicommissa* (art 4:926), albeit with certain exceptions. *Fideicommissa* are dispositions by means of which the testator leaves the estate or part of it, or a specific property to A, under the proviso that upon A's death it will pass to B. The allowed exceptions are: 11.19

(1) if A is a child of the testator or a child of a predeceased child or its brother or sister or a predeceased child of a brother or sister, and B is a child of A (arts 4:1020 *et seq*);
(2) in all cases where A is free to spend the capital and is not restricted to the use of the income only, the so-called *fideicommissa de residuo* (art 4:1036 *et seq*).

Furthermore, the law specifies certain categories of persons who may not inherit by virtue of dispositions made by a deceased (arts 4:951 *et seq*). For instance, the doctor or nurse who treated the deceased during the illness causing death, and 11.20

ministers or priests who assisted during the last stages of illness. Also persons who run, or are in charge of, or are working in an institution designed for elderly and mentally disabled persons, may not derive any advantage from a will which may have been made by such person during his stay in such institution. It is self-evident that the *notaris* before whom the will was executed cannot enjoy anything on the basis of such will.

Statutory portions

11.21 Children have the right to receive a so-called 'statutory portion' (also called *legitime* or 'forced heirship portions') of the estate of their parents (arts 4:960 *et seq*). Such statutory portion does not just confer the right to a portion of the value of the estate, but also the right to receive this portion in kind in the form of assets belonging to the estate free from any encumbrances. The statutory portion is, if the parent left one child, half of the portion which such child would have inherited on intestacy. If two children survive, the statutory portion will be two-thirds of the intestacy portion, and if the deceased leaves three or more children, the statutory portion will be three-quarters of the intestacy portion.

11.22 Descendants of predeceased children are entitled to receive the statutory portion of the predeceased child, if, failing a will, they would have been the heirs of the deceased by virtue of intestacy law. Spouses, ascendants, brothers and sisters are not entitled to any statutory portion.

11.23 In order to satisfy statutory portions, the dispositions made by will (those benefiting heirs and legatees alike) will be reduced on a *pro rata* basis unless the testator has indicated another method of reduction in his will (art 4:973).

11.24 If gifts have been made by the deceased during his life, the values of those gifts are added to the value of the estate for the purpose of the calculation of the statutory portions (art 4:968); if it appears that the gifts infringe upon the statutory portion and the estate is not sufficient to meet the statutory portions as a result of such gifts, the gifts may even be quashed (art 4:971).

Avoiding statutory portions

11.25 The Supreme Court of the Netherlands has decided that, if a deceased made dispositions to satisfy his non-enforceable obligations to provide for his spouse financially upon his death, such testamentary dispositions cannot be challenged on the basis of the statutory portion.

11.26 It will be evident that, because the Supreme Court has only formulated a general rule, the operation of such rule will depend on the circumstances of the case.

11.27 The said obligation established in case-law may constitute the basis for an entire or partial escape from the legal provisions in respect of the statutory portion. Spouses with children in particular may avail themselves of a will, in which they leave the surviving spouse a larger portion than the portion of the estate which is freely at their disposal on the basis of the law, in order to satisfy the obligation of financial maintenance. The children's statutory rights are wholly or partially subordinated to the maintenance obligation of the surviving spouse which is recognised in case law.

A typical kind of testamentary disposition often used where there are parents and children is the so-called 'parental division', whereby the testator uses the legal opportunity to divide his estate in his will between his children and his spouse (arts 4:1167 *et seq*). In such division, one gives the entire estate to the surviving spouse; then the children are given a claim in the amount of their portion against the surviving spouse, which claim is in principle only payable at the date of death of the surviving spouse. The result is that the surviving spouse retains the disposal of the entire estate. 11.28

Unmarried co-habitants may use a co-habitation agreement to escape the statutory portions of their children; they may agree that, on the death of one of them, any jointly owned assets will by virtue of the agreement accrue to the surviving co-habitant. Only if the chances of survival are very unequal will those entitled to a statutory portion have the opportunity to attack such an agreement. 11.29

Succession and matrimonial property regime

The estate of the deceased will pass on his death. If the deceased was married at the time of his death, the matrimonial property law regime existing at the time of his death is important in order to determine what belongs to the deceased's estate. If the deceased and his spouse did not make any marriage contract, then complete legal community of property exists between the spouses if Dutch matrimonial property law is applicable. Any and all assets acquired by the spouses before and during the marriage form part of such community and all the spouses' debts may be recovered from the community property (art 1:94). Each spouse is entitled to one half of the community property. Only assets acquired under the law of succession or by way of a gift do not form part of the community property, but only if expressly so provided by the will or by the donor. 11.30

The spouses may deviate from the statutory regime by marriage contract (art 1:121). This may be done both before and during the marriage, but during the marriage only with the consent of the *rechtbank* (District Court). A marriage contract must be executed by a notarial deed. A marriage contract is recorded on the Matrimonial Property Register held by the District Court; this register is open for public inspection. 11.31

Bewind (quasi-trust)

A testator may provide by will that assets left to an heir or a legatee shall, during the latter's life or for a certain period, be placed under administration called *bewind* (arts 4:1066 *et seq*). Those assets are then not controlled by the heir or legatee acquiring title to the assets but by the administrator designated for such purpose. Within the scope of his powers, the administrator is the representative of the heir or legatee. It is true that the assets placed under administration belong to the heir, yet his debts cannot be recovered from the administered estate during the administration where such debts did not arise in relation to the assets under administration. 11.32

Transactions *inter vivos* relating to inheritances

11.33 One cannot waive the right to be someone's heir or legatee before the inheritance has crystallised upon the death of the *de cujus*. Legal acts performed *inter vivos* in respect of the expectation of an inheritance, either one's own or someone else's, are null and void to the extent that such acts would amount to the irrevocable disposition of the whole or a proportion of an estate at death or would have the effect of impeding the *de cujus* in the disposition of his estate (art 4:921).

11.34 Spouses, however, can give the whole or a proportion of their future estate or assets to be comprised in their future estate to each other by marriage contract (art 1:146).

ADMINISTRATION AND DIVISION

Saisine;[1] transmission of title

11.35 An heir (*erfgenaam*) is the person who succeeds to the whole or a proportionate part of an estate either on intestacy or by virtue of a will. Under Dutch law, the heirs acquire the deceased's rights immediately upon the death of the deceased (arts 4:880 and 4:1002) and from that moment they are also personally liable for his debts, subject to their unconditional acceptance of the estate (art 4:1146).

11.36 A legatee should be distinguished in this respect from an heir. The legatee acquires under a will only the right to receive one or more specific assets of the estate. The testator's death does not automatically entitle the legatee to the assets bequeathed to him. The legatee has only the right to demand delivery of such assets from the heirs.

Unconditional acceptance

11.37 The unconditional acceptance of an estate need not be made formally; it may also be evident from the actual conduct of the heirs. If one conducts oneself as heir one is deemed to have accepted the estate. Heirs have the opportunity to consider whether or not to accept an estate. For that purpose they may file a statement with the competent court (art 4:1070).

Benefit of inventory

11.38 The heirs have the right to accept the estate under the *beneficium inventarii* (arts 4:1075 *et seq*); minors and other incapacitated persons can only accept under the *beneficium inventarii* (arts 1:253 and 1:353). Such acceptance is also made by filing a statement with the competent court. If an heir accepts an estate under the *beneficium inventarii*, the heir will not be liable for the deceased's debts beyond the value of the deceased's assets inherited by him. The law provides special rules for the liquidation of estates accepted under the *beneficium inventarii*.

1 Civil law doctrine by which the heirs by operation of the law enter into possession of the assets of the deceased with effect from the day of his death.

Certificate of inheritance

An heir who has accepted an estate can identify himself as such against third parties by the production of a certificate of inheritance. Such a certificate is issued by a *notaris*. If there are several heirs, the heirs will usually grant powers of attorney authorising one or more persons to represent them in winding up the estate. The certificate of inheritance generally specifies such power of attorney. 11.39

Renunciation

An heir, whether by virtue of a will or intestacy, may renounce his rights by filing a statement to that effect with the competent court, provided he has not earlier, expressly or tacitly, accepted the inheritance (art 4:1103). Upon renunciation, the heir is considered retroactively never to have been an heir (art 4:1104). 11.40

Executor

A testator may appoint an executor (arts 4:1052 *et seq*). Usually, the testator will give the executor the right to take and hold possession of the estate until the final liquidation of the same. Such powers are considered to infringe upon the rights of those entitled to a statutory portion to receive such portion free of any encumbrance; that is why, if there are persons entitled to a statutory portion, an executor will not be able to exercise his powers if such persons do not waive their right to oppose such appointment. Within the scope of an executor's powers the executor is the representative of the heirs. In general, executors are not authorised to alienate assets belonging to the estate; the heirs will therefore often supplement the powers of the executors by giving them additional powers of attorney to liquidate the estate. 11.41

Probate and liquidation

There are no probate procedures nor specific administrative procedures applying to the liquidation of an estate which is accepted unconditionally by all the heirs. The law provides special rules for the acceptance of the estate in the event that minors or other incapacitated persons are entitled to the estate; in such cases the estate has to be accepted under the *beneficium inventarii* (see para **11.38**). 11.42

Although not normally required by law, notaries are often involved in the winding up of estates. 11.43

Division of the estate

The division of the estate between the heirs, completely or partially as the case may be, is in principle not subject to special formalities, provided they unanimously agree about their shares and provided there are no minors or other incapacitated persons amongst the heirs. Division requires the co-operation of all the heirs or their (legal) representatives (arts 3:182 *et seq*). 11.44

If the heirs disagree about their shares in the estate or when minors or other incapacitated persons are entitled to the estate, the division must be effected by notarial deed and requires court approval. 11.45

11.46 A division of real estate situated in the Netherlands or of registered shares in Dutch companies must also be effected by notarial deed.

11.47 If the heirs cannot reach an agreement between them as to the division of the estate the most interested party may request the court to make the division itself.

2. PRIVATE INTERNATIONAL LAW[1]

INTRODUCTION AND SOURCES

11.48 For the purpose of this outline of Dutch private international law and other features of Dutch law relevant to international succession matters, it is useful to distinguish between:

(1) the law applicable to succession to estates;
(2) the law applicable to the administration and the liquidation of estates;
(3) the law relating to the form of testamentary dispositions;
(4) the jurisdiction of Dutch courts in international succession matters; and
(5) the recognition and enforceability of foreign court orders.

11.49 The Netherlands are a party to the Hague Convention of 5 October 1961 on the Conflicts of Laws Relating to the Form of Testamentary Dispositions. The Netherlands have also ratified the Hague Convention of 1 August 1989 on the Law Applicable to Succession to the Estates of Deceased Persons ('the Succession Convention'); none of the reservations permitted by article 24 of the Succession Convention have been made. Although the Succession Convention has not entered into force since the required number of three ratifications has not yet been obtained, the Dutch legislature has nevertheless introduced the rules of the Succession Convention by reference as part of Dutch private international law as of 1 October 1996. Also on 1 October 1996 the Act on the Conflicts of Laws in Matters of Succession ('the Succession Conflicts Act') came into force, dealing with matters not covered by either of the above conventions such as the administration of estates. Finally, a few bilateral conventions for recognition and enforcement of foreign court orders (see para **11.68** below) are effective in the field of succession law.

THE LAW RELATING TO THE FORM OF TESTAMENTARY DISPOSITIONS

11.50 The rules of the 1961 Hague Convention on the Conflicts of Laws relating to the Form of Testamentary Dispositions apply. The Netherlands have, however, made the reservation under article 10 of this Convention to the effect that oral

1 For further references see *Inleiding tot het Nederlands Internationaal Privaatrecht* by L Strikwerda, (4th edn) Wolters-Noordhoff, Groningen, 1995; *Twee Haagse Verdragen* by K D de Lange and W Westbroek, Kluwer, Deventer, 1990 and *Internationaal en Interregionaal Erfrecht in het Koninkrijk der Nederlanden* by M H ten Wolde, Kluwer, Deventer, 1996.

dispositions are not recognised. Mutual wills are not allowed under Dutch domestic law, but mutual wills validly made under the *lex loci* are recognised.

THE LAW APPLICABLE TO SUCCESSION TO ESTATES

Succession Convention: scope

The Dutch conflict rules in respect of succession are found in the Succession Convention, which is universal in its application, ie the succession law designated under the Convention is applicable, even if it is the law of a non-contracting State. *Renvoi* is not permitted (art 17 of the Succession Convention).[1] 11.51

Unity of the estate versus scission

Article 7(1) of the Succession Convention upholds the principle of the unity of the estate, so that one set of mandatory family protection rules will apply to the whole estate. To this principle, only one exception is permitted. Article 4 of the Convention accepts the *renvoi* with respect to the whole *or part* of the succession by a non-contracting State, whose domestic succession law would be applicable under the Succession Convention, to the law of another non-contracting State which would apply its own domestic law. The principle of the unity of the estate does not prevent the incorporation by substantive reference of the law of another state but only for the extent permitted under the law applicable under the Succession Convention (art 6 and arts 8 *et seq*).[2] 11.52

Of course, the unity rule cannot be imposed in respect of property situated in jurisdictions applying the scission rule: if a Dutchman residing in the Netherlands dies owning English immovables then English law as the law of the *lex situs* will govern the devolution of such immovables. Under article 2 of the Succession Conflicts Act the acquisition by the beneficiaries under the law of England is recognised. However, if the beneficiaries under the law of England are also amongst the beneficiaries under the Dutch succession law which is applicable under the Succession Convention, other beneficiaries under the Dutch succession law whose interests may be prejudiced by the application of the *lex situs* in respect of the English immovables may seek compensation out of other assets of the estate. 11.53

Objective connecting factor

Under article 3 of the Succession Convention, in the absence of a valid express choice of the *lex successionis*, succession to an estate is governed by the law of the State of which at the time of his death the deceased was a national if he was then habitually residing in that State (para 1). If the deceased at the time of his death was habitually resident in a State other than that of his nationality, the succession 11.54

---

1 Generally see W M Waters, Official Report on the Convention. The text of the Convention is set out in the Appendices at paragraphs A1.12 to A1.25.

2 Also, under article 12 of the Succession Convention the validity of an agreement as to succession may not be contested on the ground that it would be invalid under the law applicable under the Succession Convention. However, the rights of persons who may have an indefeasible interest in the estate under the law applicable under the Succession Convention and who are not a party to such agreement, shall not be affected by such agreement.

law of the State of his habitual residence will apply if he was a resident[1] in that State for five years or more immediately preceding his death (para 2);[2] if, however, the deceased had at the time of his death not completed the five years residence term, or if he had no habitual residence at all, his estate will be governed by the succession law of the State of which he was a national at the time of his death (para 3).[3]

Subjective connecting factor

11.55 Article 5 of the Succession Convention allows a person to deviate from the objective connecting factor and to designate the law of a particular State to govern succession to his estate. In accordance with the unity principle, the designation of the applicable law will only be valid if it is made for the whole of the estate. Scission of the estate by designation of separate applicable laws to distinct parts of the estate is not available under the Succession Convention.[4] Under the Succession Convention, a choice of the following laws is available:

(1) the law of the State in which the deceased had his habitual residence at the time of the designation;
(2) the law of a State of which the deceased was a national[5] at the time of the designation;
(3) the law of the State in which the deceased had his habitual residence at the time of his death;
(4) the law of a State of which the deceased was a national[6] at the time of his death.

Scope of the succession law

11.56 The scope of the succession law under the Succession Convention (see art 7) includes:

(1) (in)capacity of persons to inherit or to be beneficiary under a will, including *commorientes* and *nasciturи*;
(2) devolution upon intestacy, including determination of the respective portions of the heirs;
(3) legacies;
(4) contribution to the estate of gifts received by the heirs[7] from the deceased *inter vivos*;

---

1 Not necessarily a habitual resident for the whole of the period.

2 Unless, in exceptional circumstances, the deceased was at the time of his death manifestly more closely connected with the State of his nationality, in which case the succession law of that State will be applicable.

3 Unless the deceased was more closely connected with another State, in which case the law of that State will be applicable.

4 Apart from the substantive law reference of article 6 of the Succession Convention.

5 If the deceased had the nationality of more than one State, the law of each such State will qualify.

6 See note 5.

7 In Dutch law the equivalent word for heir (*erfgenaam*) is also used for those who take as residuary beneficiaries under a will; in this chapter the term heir includes residuary beneficiaries.

(5) statutory portions and the reduction of gifts made by the deceased *inter vivos* for the benefit of those entitled to statutory portions (unless excluded from the scope of the Convention by article 1(2)(d) as discussed above in paras **1.52** to **1.53**);
(6) *fideicommissa* and the continued administration of inheritance portions or legacies beyond the liquidation of the estate (*bewind*);
(7) (in)validity of agreements *inter vivos* in respect of one's future estate.

The Dutch domestic provisions in respect of the (in)capacity of persons to inherit or to be beneficiaries under a will, statutory portions and reduction of gifts, *fideicommissa* etc and agreements *inter vivos* in respect of a future estate contain elements of mandatory law which cannot be affected by testamentary dispositions whether specifically or by making use of a substantive law reference to a foreign law under article 4 of the Succession Convention. 11.57

Concurrence with matrimonial property law[1]

In most States, domestic matrimonial property law and succession law are tuned into each other. In consequence, inconsistencies may occur if succession to a deceased's estate is governed by the law of one State and his matrimonial property regime is governed by the law of another State. For example, if the German *Zugewinngemeinschaft* is dissolved by the death of one of the spouses whose succession is governed by Dutch law, the problem arises that the German domestic law does not account for the partition of the *Zugewinn* in the sphere of its matrimonial property law but in the sphere of its succession law by granting to the surviving spouse by way of allowance one-quarter of the estate of the deceased spouse in addition to his or her intestate portion. A legalistic solution would leave the surviving spouse with nothing: neither the applicable German matrimonial property law nor the applicable Dutch succession law would lead to adequate surviving provisions for the surviving spouse. In applying Dutch law to the succession, the courts would, however, in such cases take into account the consequences of the German succession law in winding up the *Zugewinngemeinschaft*. 11.58

Agreements as to succession

Although Dutch domestic succession law does not allow *pactes successoraux*[2] the Netherlands have not made the reservation permitted under article 24 para 1(a) of the Succession Convention; in consequence *pactes successoraux* validly made under the Succession Convention and the applicable domestic law will be recognised. 11.59

1 The Netherlands are a party to the 1978 Hague Convention on the Law applicable to Matrimonial Property Regimes.
2 There is one exception: *pactes successoraux* may be made under Dutch domestic law between spouses in their marriage contract.

THE LAW APPLICABLE TO THE ADMINISTRATION AND THE LIQUIDATION OF ESTATES

Objective connecting factor

11.60 Article 4 of the Succession Conflicts Act provides for a unilateral Dutch conflict rule designating Dutch domestic law as the law applicable to the liquidation of an estate if the deceased at the time of his death was habitually resident in the Netherlands. In consequence, the estate of an Englishman habitually residing in the Netherlands at the time of his death will be liquidated with the application of Dutch domestic law, even if the succession to his estate would be governed by English law, both from the English perspective because he was still domiciled in England and from the Dutch perspective because he was not resident in the Netherlands for a period of five or more years immediately preceding his death.

11.61 In the Explanatory Memorandum to the draft of the Succession Conflicts Act, it was stated by the Government that a conflict rule which would also apply if the deceased was at the time of his death habitually residing abroad could be ineffective because local authorities, bound to their own conflict rules, would normally be involved in the liquidation of such estates. Whatever the merit of this explanation, there is nothing in the Explanatory Memorandum which leads one to believe that it was the intention to change the then prevailing unwritten multilateral Dutch conflict rule designating the law of the last habitual residence[1] of the deceased as the law governing the liquidation of his estate.

11.62 The conclusion may be that in respect of assets in the Netherlands belonging to the estate of a deceased who was at the time of his death habitually residing abroad, the domestic law pertaining to the administration and liquidation of estates in the State of his habitual residence will be honoured, and administrators or executors duly appointed under such law will be recognised in the Netherlands. If no personal representatives have been appointed in the jurisdiction of the last habitual residence of the deceased or would or could not exercise their function outside their own jurisdiction, personal representatives duly appointed under the applicable succession law could also be recognised. In the last resort, Dutch domestic law as the law of the *situs* of the assets may be applied.

11.63 As an example, if a Dutchman was to die intestate as a non-domiciled but habitual resident of England, having resided in England for fewer than five years, the succession to his estate would be governed by Dutch law: from a Dutch perspective by the application of the Succession Convention and from an English perspective because he was, we will assume, domiciled in the Netherlands. The administration and liquidation of his estate would, however, from a Dutch point of view be governed by English law as the law of the State of his habitual residence; only if a grant of representation could not be obtained in England, or if the English administrator were to refrain from exercising his functions in the Netherlands,

1 Some legal writers hold that in this respect residence in the meaning of arts 1:10 of the Civil Code *et seq* is the connecting factor rather than the habitual residence which is a concept under private international law.

would Dutch domestic law be applied in the Dutch jurisdiction for the administration and liquidation of the estate.

Scope of the law applicable to the administration and liquidation of estates

The following matters fall under the scope of the law applicable to administration and liquidation: **11.64**

(1) the direction transmission of assets (*saisine*) to the heirs,[1] or judicial or testamentary administration as the case may be;[2]
(2) the liability of the heirs *vis-à-vis* the creditors of the deceased; *beneficium inventarii*, ie acceptance by the heirs of the estate on the condition that their liability for obligations of the deceased will not exceed the value of the assets belonging to the estate;
(3) the scope and the authority of judicial or testamentary administrators and executors;
(4) the partition of the estate between the heirs;[3]
(5) the administration of unattended estates, ie estates not claimed by personal representatives or heirs.

Executors

In line with article 4 of the Succession Conflicts Act (see paras **11.60** and **11.61**), article 5 of this Act provides that the duties and authorities of a liquidator (*executor*) designated by the deceased[4] are governed by Dutch law if the deceased, at the time of his death, was habitually resident in the Netherlands. No corresponding rule is provided in respect of the duties and authorities of executors and administrators of estates under foreign law if the deceased was not habitually resident in the Netherlands; according to the Explanatory Memorandum this deliberate omission was not meant to create doubt about the validity of their appointment abroad, but to provide a certain discretion for such executors or administrators if the applicable succession law under the Succession Convention would not be the applicable succession law in their own jurisdiction. However, each person having an interest to do so may ask the court for an order for measures, including an order to grant security, safeguarding the proper application of the rules of the succession law applicable under the Succession Convention in respect of assets of the estate situated in the Netherlands. **11.65**

1 See footnote 3 to para **11.54**.

2 According to prevailing opinion in legal doctrine; however, some legal writers are of the opinion that direct transmission falls under the scope of the succession law.

3 Under article 4, para 2 of the Succession Conflicts Act the heirs of the estate of a deceased who had his last habitual residence in the Netherlands may jointly designate the law of another State to govern the partition of the estate, without prejudice to the requirements of the *lex situs* of the assets.

4 Under Dutch domestic law, administrators are unknown; the heirs have direct access to the assets belonging to the estate.

INTERNATIONAL JURISDICTION OF DUTCH COURTS IN MATTERS OF SUCCESSION

11.66 Most proceedings in succession matters must be initiated by a summons; in those cases a Dutch court will assume international jurisdiction if:

(1) the deceased was resident in its jurisdiction at the time of his death;
(2) at least one of the defendants is resident or has a permanent address in its jurisdiction;
(3) at least one of the plaintiffs is resident in its jurisdiction, provided that there is no defendant resident or with a permanent address in the Netherlands;
(4) the litigation is about real property situate in its jurisdiction;
(5) the litigation is about attached assets situate in its jurisdiction; or
(6) all parties concerned have agreed to submit the case to it, provided they have a reasonable interest to involve a Dutch court.

Neither Dutch nationality of any of the parties nor the applicability of Dutch law to the succession of an estate is sufficient ground for Dutch courts to assume international jurisdiction.

RECOGNITION AND ENFORCEABILITY OF FOREIGN COURT ORDERS

Recognition

11.67 Dutch courts have full discretion to recognise foreign court orders. In practice, they will take into account and respect a foreign court order satisfying the following conditions:

- it must have been given by a court competent to decide on the matter;
- it must be final;
- it must not conflict with Dutch public order;
- adequate legal procedures must have been observed.

If those conditions are met the case decided by the foreign court will not be materially tested again by the Dutch court.

11.68 The Belgian–Dutch Execution Convention of 1925, the Italian–Dutch Execution Convention of 1959 and the German–Dutch Execution Convention of 1962 contain provisions for mandatory recognition in succession matters. Furthermore, the Charter for the Kingdom of the Netherlands provides for recognition of court orders made in any of the other autonomous parts of the Kingdom of the Netherlands.[1] The Brussels Execution Convention and the Lugano Parallel Convention do not apply to succession matters.

1 The Kingdom of the Netherlands in the political sense of the word consists of the Netherlands, the Netherlands Antilles, and Aruba, each being an autonomous entity within the Kingdom, and each having its own domestic legislation and private international law. The Supreme Court of the Netherlands serves also as the Supreme Court for the Netherlands Antilles and for Aruba. This chapter deals with the Netherlands only and not with the Netherlands Antilles and Aruba.

Enforceability

Foreign court orders in succession matters cannot be enforced in the Netherlands, with the exception of Belgian, Italian, and German court orders which may be enforced in the Netherlands upon the *exequatur* by a Dutch court having been obtained under the respective Execution Conventions; Netherlands Antilles and Aruban court orders may also be enforced in the Netherlands under the Charter. **11.69**

If a foreign court order has been obtained a new procedure may be started before a Dutch court in order to procure a court order enforceable in the Netherlands; in such procedure the court may at its discretion attach value to foreign court orders obtained earlier. **11.70**

3. WAYS TO MINIMISE PROBLEMS WHERE ELEMENTS OF FOREIGN LAW ARE INVOLVED

CHOICE OF LAW CLAUSES (*PROFESSIO JURIS*)

In case of a conflict between the law of the nationality and the law of the habitual residence, a choice between either of those laws may solve the conflict; such choice is permitted under the Succession Convention (see para **11.55**). **11.71**

SUBSTANTIVE LAW REFERENCE

Within the framework of the succession law, applicable either by virtue of the objective connecting factor or by virtue of a valid choice of law clause, it is possible to make a reference to another law to govern the succession to certain assets belonging to the estate (eg assets situated in a jurisdiction other than that of the applicable succession law). It should be emphasised that a substantive law reference does not set aside the mandatory rules of the applicable succession law, such as statutory portions (see para **11.57**). **11.72**

TRUSTS

Although the concept of the Anglo–American trust is not known in Dutch domestic law, this does not mean that such foreign trusts cannot have any effect when they touch the Dutch legal domain. In fact, the Netherlands have from 1 February 1996 implemented the 1985 Hague Convention on the Law Applicable to Trusts and their Recognition, and trusts qualifying under this Convention will be recognised and given effect in accordance with this Convention. Article 4 of the 1995 Trusts Conflicts Act, indeed, is designed to ensure that the trust fund is a separate autonomous patrimony, not part of the trustee's private patrimony. **11.73**

REPLACEMENT OF ASSETS

11.74 Sometimes it may be helpful to convert the nature of real property into personal property, eg if real property situated in a scission jurisdiction is vested in a company, the shares in the capital of such company might be considered as personal property and therefore not governed by the *lex situs* of the real property but by the succession law governing the personal assets of the estate. Similarly, it may be possible to replace shares in a company governed by a certain jurisdiction by shares in a company governed by another more favourable jurisdiction by transferring the shares of the former company into the latter.

TONTINE ARRANGEMENTS

11.75 Legal devices like *tontine* arrangements used in purely domestic cases to avoid statutory portions (see para **11.29**) may also be helpful to procure solutions outside the scope of the succession law in cases where international elements are involved.

4. TAXES ON DEATH

BASIC PRINCIPLES OF TAXATION

11.76 Dutch taxes on death (succession taxes) are a levy upon the beneficiaries of the estate of a deceased resident[1] in the Netherlands at the time of his death,[2] and their calculation is based on the value acquired by each particular beneficiary of the world-wide net assets of the estate.

DEEMED ACQUISITIONS

11.77 Certain benefits which technically are not derived by succession from the estate of the deceased, such as life insurance payments, gifts by the deceased within 180 days of his death and the value of assets in respect of which the deceased had reserved a life interest during his lifetime are for the purposes of the succession taxes fictitiously deemed acquired out of the deceased's estate upon his death.

1 Residence for the purpose of the succession taxes is the place where the deceased had – taking account of all circumstances – the enduring centre of his life; the term seems to be somewhat more broadly defined than the term habitual residence under the Succession Convention; in consequence, in the absence of a last habitual residence of a deceased in the Netherlands he may still have been resident there for the purposes of the succession taxes.

2 For the purposes of the succession taxes a Dutch citizen is deemed to be a resident in the Netherlands for 10 years after leaving the country.

TAXATION ON DEATH OF NON-RESIDENTS IN RESPECT OF DUTCH *SITUS* ASSETS

If the deceased was not a resident of, but owned *situs* assets in the Netherlands, the acquisition of *situs* assets by the beneficiaries is also subject to succession taxes. *Situs* assets are non-incorporated enterprises conducted in the Netherlands, including permanent establishments of foreign enterprises owned by the deceased, and real property situated in the Netherlands. 11.78

VALUATION

Valuation of the assets acquired by beneficiaries is made at their full economic value, except for the value of the family home[1] which is valued at 60% of its full economic value. Life interests are calculated at 6% interest *per annum* and capitalised according to the age of the beneficiary with the following factors: 11.79

– age under 20:	16
– age between 20 and 30:	15
– age between 30 and 40:	14
– age between 40 and 50:	13
– age between 50 and 55:	12
– age between 55 and 60:	11
– age between 60 and 65:	10
– age between 65 and 70:	8
– age between 70 and 75:	7
– age between 75 and 80:	5
– age between 80 and 85:	4
– age between 85 and 90:	3
– age over 90:	2

Residual interests are taken at the balance of the full value of the underlying assets and the value of the life interest. Annuities are also capitalised according to the age of the beneficiary with the above factors.

1 A home is deemed a family home if at the time of his death the deceased lived there together with his spouse, partner and/or one or more blood relatives, and one or more of them inherited it.

EXEMPTIONS

11.80 Acquisitions by a beneficiary may be wholly or partially exempt from succession taxes. The most important exemptions are the following:[1]

– surviving spouse or partner[2]	:	NLG 565,868[3]	
– children under 23	:	NLG 7,933	for each year under 23 but not less than NLG 16,167
– children over 23	:	NLG 16,167	provided total acquisition does not exceed NLG 48,502
– parents	:	NLG 80,837	
– other ascendants and descendants	:	NLG 16,167	provided total acquisition by beneficiary does not exceed this amount
– charities[4] etc	:	NLG 16,167	provided total acquisition by beneficiary does not exceed this amount
– others	:	NLG 1,616	provided total acquisition by beneficiary does not exceed this amount

There are no exemptions available if the deceased was a non-resident and taxes are only due in respect of Dutch *situs* assets (see para **11.78**)

RATES

11.81 The rates vary according to the relationship between the deceased and the beneficiary (with one exception; see below).

There are five classes:

(1) surviving spouse, partner[5] and children;
(2) grandchildren;
(3) parents, brothers and sisters and ascendants;
(4) charities;[6]
(5) others.

1 The amounts given are those for the fiscal year 1998; the amounts are adjusted annually.

2 For the purpose of this exemption a partner will only enjoy the full exemption if he or she lived together with the deceased for at least five years preceding the death of the latter.

3 This amount is decreased by the capitalised value of pension rights and certain other benefits which are in themselves not taxable or are exempt; the exemption will, however, not fall below NLG 161,676.

4 Only charitable legal entities established in the Netherlands qualify; charities include churches, political parties and institutions for general welfare. Charities in some other countries (like France) may also qualify on the basis of reciprocity.

5 A partner will only qualify for this category if he lived together with the deceased for at least 5 years preceding the death of the latter.

6 See note 2 to para **11.76**.

The rates are as follows:[1] 11.82

value of part of the acquisition between NLG	class (1)	class (3)	class (5)
0– 40,428	5%	26%	41%
40,429– 80,848	8%	30%	45%
80,849– 161,686	12%	35%	50%
161,687– 323,363	15%	39%	54%
323,364– 646,715	19%	44%	59%
646,716–1,616,771	23%	48%	63%
over 1,616,771	27%	53%	68%

The rates in class (2) are those of class (1) plus 60%.
In class (4) a flat rate of 11% applies.

DOUBLE TAXATION

The Netherlands have concluded bilateral conventions for the avoidance of double taxation on death with Switzerland, Sweden, Finland, the UK, Israel and the USA. Further, the Tax Act for the Kingdom of the Netherlands contains provisions in respect of double taxation in relation to the Netherlands, Antilles and Aruba. Finally, if double taxation occurs in relation to States or territories other than those above, relief may be found, wholly or partially, in the unilateral Ordinance for the avoidance of double taxation. 11.83

TAX DECLARATION

A succession tax return must be filed with the tax authorities by the heirs or the executor within eight months after the day of death. 11.84

ASSESSMENTS AND PAYMENT

The tax authorities must impose the final assessment within three years after the death of the deceased came to their knowledge. Pending the final assessment a provisional assessment may be imposed. Assessments are payable within two months from their date. 11.85

1 See **11.80**, note 1.

CHAPTER 12

PORTUGAL†

1. INTRODUCTION

HISTORICAL BACKGROUND

Mortis causa succession is regulated under Portuguese law in accordance with Book V of the Civil Code (arts 2024–2334) which was approved under the terms of Decree Law no 47,344 of 25 November 1996 and which came into effect on 1 June 1967. 12.1

After the 1974 Revolution, several important alterations were made to the Civil Code, which is based on the Germanic classification of civil law and in which both German and Italian law have had a marked influence. These alterations were introduced to the Civil Code by Decree Law no 496/77 of 25 November 1977 and adapted the Civil Code to the new principles introduced by the new constitution of the Portuguese Republic of 1976. 12.2

The modifications made to the Civil Code under the 1977 reform have mainly affected the Books dealing with Family Law (Book IV) and the Law of Succession (Book V). It can be said that several of the most important alterations made to the law of succession are merely a reflection of parallel modifications of family law. 12.3

The following were the most significant alterations made to Book V under the 1977 reform. 12.4

(1) The elimination of the distinctions between the eligibility in terms of succession of children born or conceived within a marital status existing between their parents (commonly known as legitimate children) and children who were born or conceived outside a marital status between their parents (commonly known as illegitimate children). This alteration was made on the basis of the constitutional imposition of the elimination of the distinctions between legitimate and illegitimate children.

(2) The improvement of the position of the surviving spouse. In the initial version of the Code, the surviving spouse was not a mandatory or 'legitimary heir' (*herdeiro legitimário*) and, in intestate succession, was classified fourth in line of succession after descendants, ascendants and relatives in the second degree of the collateral line and their descendants. The spouse became a 'legitimary heir' after the 1977 reform and then became part, together with

---

† This chapter was written by Grupo Legal Português (F Castelo Branco, Nobre Guedes & P Rebelo de Sousa in association with Simmons & Simmons, Pinheiro Neto & Co and J & A Garrigues) Lisbon, tel (351) 1 352 1318, fax (351) 1 352 1418.

descendants, of the first category of intestate successors, or, in the event of there not being any descendants of the deceased, the second category of intestate successors in competition with ascendants. However, preference was granted to the surviving spouse in relation to the right of abode in the family home and use of its contents.

(3) The exclusion of the more distant relationships from eligibility to inherit. In the original version of the Code, relatives up to the sixth degree of the collateral line could be called upon as successors. This is now only the case with regard to relatives up to the fourth degree of the collateral line.

GENERAL LAYOUT AND BASIC CHARACTERISTICS OF SUCCESSION LAW

The scope of succession

12.5 Succession consists of the 'summoning of one or more persons to the entitlement to the legal assets of a deceased person and the consequent devolution of the assets belonging to him' (art 2024 of the Civil Code).

12.6 In accordance with this definition, it may appear that only rights having a patrimonial or proprietary nature ie those rights which are meant to satisfy the economic needs of their title holder and which, for this reason are quantifiable in monetary terms, may be transmitted upon the death of their title holder. This is not, however, the position where there are personal rights which are transmissible by death, such as authors' moral rights (which consist of the right to lay claim to the ownership of intellectual works and to safeguard their integrity by taking action against plagiarism or adulterations) or in the case of certain aspects of the rights of personality such as the right to a name (arts 71, 72 and 73 of the Civil Code).

12.7 It is important to stress that not all of the patrimonial or proprietary rights to which the deceased held title are transmitted on his death. This is because there are patrimonial rights which are not transmissible on death. One example of this is the right of *usufruct*, which consists of the right fully but temporarily to enjoy something belonging to another person without altering its form or substance and which, by law, is not transmissible *mortis causa*, being in the nature of a life interest.

12.8 It is, therefore, more accurate to state that succession involves the transmission of all the rights and obligations of the deceased, with the exception of those which are necessarily extinguished by his death, as is the case with most rights of a personal nature and with some patrimonial rights.

Types of *mortis causa* succession recognised by Portuguese law

12.9 The Civil Code establishes that succession can be regulated 'by law, testament or contract' (art 2026 of the Civil Code). There are two basic source types of succession: legal and voluntary.

(a) Legal Succession

Legal succession is a direct result of the law and consists of two categories, the applicability of which depends on whether the legal rules may or may not be subject to the will of the title holder of the assets (the deceased or *de cujus*): 'legitimate succession' (*sucessão legítima*) and 'legitimary or compulsory succession' (*sucessão legitimária*), which may, respectively, be regarded as intestate succession and forced heirship. 12.10

The rules governing 'legitimate succession' are supplementary in nature and are applied whenever the deceased has not expressed wishes on the use to be given to his assets or whenever the will of the deceased is not valid or does not cover all his assets. In this latter case the laws of 'legitimate succession' will obviously only be applied to the transmission, on death, of the assets in relation to which the deceased has failed to make his wishes known. Based on the assumption that there are no arrangements for the last wishes of the deceased, the laws of 'legitimate succession' are also known as *ab intestato* succession. 12.11

Unlike the case of 'legitimate succession', the rules of 'legitimary succession' are mandatory and are not subject to the will of the deceased. It is for this reason that this type of succession is known as mandatory or forced succession. To protect interests which are considered to be untouchable, the law reserves a mandatory part of the estate known as the 'reserved part' (*legítima*) for a specific category of persons (the legitimary heirs) over which the deceased has no control. It is, however, only in this sense that the succession can be claimed to be mandatory or forced. It is, therefore, mandatory or forced upon the deceased who is not able to impose his will upon the law, but not upon the eligible heirs, because 'legitimary heirs' enjoy the ability to accept or reject the inheritance. In addition, the deceased's right, in certain cases, to disinherit his 'legitimary heirs' must be taken into account (art 2166 of the Civil Code). 12.12

(b) Voluntary Succession

Voluntary succession is the result of the unilateral desire of the deceased (succession by testament) or an agreement of wishes between the deceased and another person (succession by contract). 12.13

As stated, voluntary and intestate succession referring to the same assets are mutually exclusive, with the former taking precedence. 'Legitimary succession' always takes precedence over voluntary succession. It is, however, possible for there to be four different types of competing succession applicable to the same case. 12.14

It should, finally, be added that succession pursuant to contract is of little practical relevance in Portuguese law because donations made on death are only accepted in a very limited number of cases. 12.15

In dealing with the assets which are actually transmitted by death, Portuguese law makes a distinction between universal succession in the form of an inheritance and individual succession in the form of a legacy. The Civil Code, on the basis of this premise, refers to successors as being heirs or legatees (art 2030 of the Civil Code). 12.16

12.17 An heir is a person who inherits 'the total amount or a part share of the patrimony of the deceased' whereas a legatee is a person who inherits 'specific assets or amounts'. The distinction is important because the legal status of the two categories of potential successors is different, with different legal consequences regarding the qualification of an eligible person as an heir or legatee. For example, heirs are responsible for the debts incurred by the estate (up to the value of the assets) while legatees, who do not receive the whole of the estate, are not liable for the estate's debts.

12.18 Although it is possible for there to be heirs and legatees in both of the types of succession referred to above, 'legal' legatees are not common in Portugal. The situation closest to this idea is the preference given to the surviving spouse in respect of the right of abode in the family home and use of its contents.

2. DOMESTIC LAW OF SUCCESSION

SUCCESSION BY TESTAMENT

General aspects

12.19 Subject to restrictions imposed under the rules governing 'legitimary or mandatory succession', Portuguese law provides for the effecting of testamentary arrangements in respect of assets after death.

12.20 In accordance with the legal definition, a testament is 'a unilateral, revocable act by means of which a person makes arrangements for after death, for all or part of his assets' (art 2179, no 1 of the Civil Code). It is, however, possible for dispositions of a non-patrimonial nature to be part of a testament.

12.21 A testament, in accordance with the Civil Code, has four basic features: it is a unilateral, personal, revocable and formal act.

12.22 The importance attributed to the free expression of the will of the testator is a basic guiding principle covering succession by testament in Portugal. It is on the basis of this principle that joint testaments (an act by means of which two or more persons simultaneously make arrangements for their wishes after death either reciprocally or on behalf of a third party) are prohibited.

12.23 In addition, emphasis is explicitly placed on the personal nature of the act of making a testament which cannot be performed through a representative. Minors or persons suffering from psychiatric problems are not therefore allowed to make a testament since it is deemed that they do not have the capacity to do so and their legal representative may not make a testament on their behalf (art 2189 of the Civil Code).

12.24 As mentioned, a testament is also an act which is freely revocable at any time. It is described as being a solemn or formal act, because it is only valid if it is performed in accordance with one of the legally established forms.

Capacity to make a will

All persons not declared by law to be incapable are allowed to make a testament (art 2188 of the Civil Code). Unemancipated minors and persons with psychiatric problems are considered to be incapable of making a testament. 12.25

In accordance with Portuguese law, a person is considered to be an adult when he reaches the age of 18 (art 130 of the Civil Code). The law, at the present time, only establishes one case in which minors are considered to be emancipated and this is as a direct result of marriage (art 132 of the Civil Code). Minors who have come of age through marriage are able to make a testament. This latter possibility will only occur in the case of 16 or 17 year old minors, because matrimonial capacity in Portugal is only acquired at the age of 16. 12.26

In order for a person to be declared psychiatrically unfit, legal proceedings must be brought and a judgment must be delivered by a judge. A testament made by a person whom the law declares unfit to make a statement is null and void (art 2190 of the Civil Code). The capacity of the testator is established by reference to the date upon which the testament is made. 12.27

Forms of testament

As mentioned above, a testament is always a formal or solemn act and should be performed in accordance with one of the legally established forms. Portuguese law establishes common and special forms of testament. 12.28

Special forms

The special forms established by law are military testaments, a testament made on board a vessel, a testament made on board an aircraft and a testament made in the event of a public disaster. 12.29

All these forms of testament are considered to be exceptional and allow persons, in light of the situation in which they find themselves (military personnel or civilian personnel on military campaigns, persons making a sea or air journey or persons who are in a place in which an epidemic has broken out) and who are unable to have recourse to the normal forms of making a testament, to express their wishes for the distribution of their assets after their death. The law establishes that these testaments cease to be valid two months after the cessation of the event preventing the testator from using one of the common forms (art 2222 of the Civil Code). In each case the legally required formalities are very simple and are adjusted to the circumstances in which the testator finds himself. 12.30

Common forms

Normal or common forms of testament are public and sealed testaments. A public testament is a testament which is drawn up by a notary and registered in a specific book and kept at the notary's office. The fact that a testament is called a public testament could lead to the assumption that these testaments are accessible to the public in general. In reality, the situation is that during the lifetime of the testator only the testator himself or his proxy may apply for copies of a public testament (art 164, no 2 of the New Notaries Code). 12.31

12.32 A sealed testament is drawn up and signed by the testator himself or by another person at his request, or drawn up by another person at the request of the testator and signed by the testator. In order to be valid, a sealed testament must be subject to the approval of a notary. This takes the form of a declaration drawn up by the notary which bears witness to the verification of compliance with various requirements. A sealed testament may be kept by the testator or by a third party or be filed at a notary's office.

Contents of a testament

12.33 Although a testament will normally make arrangements of a patrimonial nature, Portuguese law accepts the inclusion in a testament of arrangements of a non-patrimonial nature or even a testament which only contains arrangements of a non-patrimonial nature (art 2179, no 2 of the Civil Code).

12.34 Heirs (persons who inherit all or part of the estate of the deceased) or legatees (persons who inherit specific assets or amounts) may be nominated by a testament. The nomination of an heir or legatee by means of a testament may be subject to a proviso or conditioning factor or, in addition, may contain duties to be performed by the heir or legatee. In either of these cases, the law specifies several restrictions on the validity of accessory clauses.

12.35 Conditions which are physically or legally impossible, in addition to conditions which contravene the law, are considered not to have been written and will not, in principle, prejudice the heir or legatee (art 2230 of the Civil Code). Any disposition, however, made on the condition that the heir or legatee should, in his testament, make a disposition in favour of the testator or another person will be null and void (art 2231 of the Civil Code).

12.36 The testator can also make arrangements for a situation in which another person may substitute the heir or legatee nominated by him in the event that they do not wish to or cannot accept the inheritance or the legacy. This is known as direct substitution (arts 2281 *et seq* of the Civil Code).

12.37 There are, however, other methods of substitution accepted under Portuguese legislation. The most important is '*fideicommissary*' substitution which consists of 'arrangements under which the testator forces the nominated heir to accept the condition of preserving the inheritance in order for it to revert, upon his death, to another person' (art 2286 of the Civil Code). An heir having this responsibility (which the law terms fiduciary) has the right to manage and enjoy the assets of the inheritance, but may not sell these assets except with permission of the court in the case of obvious need or use of the assets (arts 2290 and 2291). A third party to whom the inheritance will revert upon the death of the fiduciary is known as the '*fideicommissary*'. This form of substitution is restricted by law to one degree ie it is not possible to stipulate that the inheritance, upon the death of the *fideicommissary*, should revert to a third party.

Restrictions on the content of testaments

As already stated, Portuguese law establishes a general restriction upon the freedom to make a testament. The testator cannot dispose of that part of the estate which the law reserves for 'legitimary heirs'. This part of the estate is, as mentioned above, called the 'reserved part' (*legítima*). This means that if there are any 'legitimary heirs', the deceased may only dispose of a part of the inheritance. This is called the 'available part'. If there are no 'legitimary heirs', the testator is free to dispose of the whole of the patrimony. 12.38

Portuguese law has established various measures for the protection of the 'reserved part'. The most important of these consists of the right given to 'legitimary heirs' and their successors to apply for a reduction in the unofficial donations ie gifts made between people while alive or on death which affect the 'reserved part' of the inheritance. The law is very precise in regulating the terms under which this reduction should be applied (arts 2171 *et seq* of the Civil Code). The period of time for applying for the reduction of the gifts is two years from the date of the acceptance of the inheritance by a 'legitimary heir'. 12.39

In addition to this general restriction, there are several restrictions on the freedom to make arrangements for after death. These are situations in which, because of the special relations existing between the testator and other persons, the testator is forbidden from making a testament in favour of these other persons in order to protect him. For example, the Civil Code considers that dispositions made in favour of a doctor or nurse who looks after the testator are null and void if made during the illness of the testator from which the testator dies (art 2194 of the Civil Code). 12.40

Revocation and lapse of the will

Revocation of testaments

As mentioned, one of the fundamental characteristics of testaments is their capacity to be revoked. Portuguese law, in its concern that the testament should reflect the last wishes of the testator, ensures by several methods that testaments which have been made can be revoked. 12.41

In addition to testaments being revocable at any time, the testator is not forced to specify the reasons for revoking a previous testament either wholly or in part (revocation *ad nutum* or *ad libitum*). The law, additionally and explicitly, states that the ability to revoke testaments cannot be renounced and that any clause contravening the ability to revoke a testament is considered as being non-existent (art 2311 of the Civil Code). 12.42

Revocation may be explicit or tacit. The latter occurs in the event of the appearance of two contradictory testaments. If the two testaments have different dates and the more recent of the testaments does not explicitly revoke the former, it will, in principle, be considered to revoke only those parts of the former testament which are incompatible with it. In the event of there being two testaments of the same date and it is not possible to determine which is the more recent, and if there are any contradictions between the respective arrangements, 12.43

then the contradictory arrangements in both of them are considered not to have been written (art 2313 of the Civil Code).

12.44 A testament which has explicitly or tacitly revoked a former testament and which is, in turn, revoked, will not affect the revocation of the former testament unless the testator declares that it is 'his will that the dispositions of the former be re-established' (art 2314 of the Civil Code).

Lapse of testaments

12.45 Article 2317 of the Civil Code specifies that testaments will lapse in the following cases:

(1) if the successor, being an heir or legatee, dies before the testator, unless the heir or legatee has left descendants who represent him and the right of representation is not excluded;
(2) if the testamentary dispositions are subject to a condition and the successor dies before the condition stipulated is satisfied;
(3) if the eligible heir becomes incapable of accepting the inheritance or legacy;
(4) if the person nominated for accepting the inheritance was the spouse of the testator at the time of the making of the will, but at the date of death they were divorced or separated with a legal division of assets or the marriage had been declared null and void or if, after the date in question, the marriage had been dissolved, annulled or declared void or a legal separation is decreed between the spouses;
(5) if the person nominated for accepting the succession rejects the inheritance or legacy, except when his descendants have the right of representation.

SUCCESSION BY CONTRACT

12.46 Succession by contract is the result of an agreement which can only be altered by a new agreement which contradicts the original agreement. The Portuguese legislature, although having recognised the concept of succession contracts in article 2028 of the Civil Code, has established that 'contracts of succession are only admissible in legally specified cases, all others being void'. With this prohibition as a principle, the objective of the Portuguese legislature was to protect the complete freedom of choice of the testator since a contract is not subject to modification by the unilateral desire of one of its parties.

12.47 All of the cases in which succession agreements are allowed relate to marriage and they are only permitted as part of pre-nuptial agreements. The law establishes three types of these agreements (art 1700 of the Civil Code):

(1) the naming of an heir or the appointing of a legatee made on behalf of one of the spouses by the other;
(2) the naming of an heir or the appointing of a legatee on behalf of one of the spouses made by a third party;
(3) the naming of an heir or the appointing of a legatee on behalf of a third party made by one of the spouses.

The naming of an heir and the appointing of a legatee by contract, as part of a pre-nuptial agreement, by one of the spouses on behalf of the other may only be revoked (by mutual agreement) up to the date of the wedding. From then on they become irrevocable because they are subject to the principle of the immutability of pre-nuptial agreements. If the naming or appointing is effected by a third party on behalf of one of the spouses, it may only be revoked by the mutual agreement of the parties to the contract. Revocation in respect of the third type of succession agreements is possible by mutual agreement and also by unilateral revocation, provided that the third beneficiary has taken part as an acceptor in the pre-nuptial agreement and the institutor has declared that this power could be used. 12.48

It should be noted that Portuguese law permits donations to be made between people while they are alive, whether or not limited by way of *usufruct*, covering all or part of their assets to one or several of the presumed 'legitimary heirs' (with the consent of the others). The donees pay (or accept responsibility for the payment) to the other 'legitimary heirs' the value of the parts of the donated assets to which they would be proportionally entitled (art 2029 no 1 of the Civil Code). This contract (which the law explicitly states is not a contract of succession but rather a donation) is called a distribution of assets during life (*partilha em vida*). 12.49

COMPULSORY SUCCESSION SHARES

'Legitimary succession' occurs whenever there are 'legitimary heirs' (*herdeiros legitimários*) and restricts the deceased's ability freely to dispose of his assets. Spouses, descendants and ascendants are 'legitimary heirs', in accordance with the order and the rules governing intestate succession (*sucessão legítima*). The part of the estate or share over which the deceased has no control (the reserved part) varies in accordance with the number and the category of 'legitimary heirs' in question. 12.50

If the spouse is the only applicant for the estate the 'reserved part' is half of the inheritance. If the spouse is competing with the children of the deceased, the total amount of the 'reserved part' will be two-thirds of the estate. If there is no surviving spouse the 'reserved part' for the children is either a half or two-thirds of the estate in accordance with whether there are only one or two or more children. 12.51

It should be noted that if a child of the deceased is already dead at the deceased's death, descendants of the second and following degrees enjoy the right to the 'reserved part' to which their ascendant would be entitled, with the part attributable to each of them being established by the terms prescribed for intestate succession. 12.52

If the spouse and ascendants of the deceased are applying for the estate (which will only occur, in principle, if there are no children), the total combined amount of the 'reserved part' will be two-thirds of the estate. If the testator does not leave descendants or a surviving spouse the 'reserved part' for the ascendants is half or one-third of the estate, depending upon whether there are parents or ascendants of the second and following degrees. 12.53

12.54 'Legitimary heirs' may only be deprived of their share of the estate when the deceased disinherits them by testament in the event of the existence of one of the situations which the law considers to be a basis for disinheriting (art 2166 of the Civil Code).

12.55 The following should be taken into account for the calculation of the value of the 'reserved part':

(1) the value of the existing assets which are part of the patrimony of the deceased upon the date of death;
(2) the value of donated assets;
(3) the amount of the expenditure incurred by the deceased on behalf of his descendants (with several exceptions, such as those incurred on the weddings of the descendants);
(4) the debts of the estate.

INTESTATE SUCCESSION

12.56 Intestate heirs are, by law, split into categories of eligible heirs, with the estate being divided up by categories and with preference being given within each of the categories to heirs with a closer degree of kinship with the deceased, without prejudice to the right of representation (see below).

12.57 There are the following categories of eligible heirs:

(1) spouse and descendants of the deceased;
(2) spouse and ascendants of the deceased;
(3) brothers and their descendants;
(4) other collateral relations up to the fourth degree in the collateral line;
(5) the State.

12.58 The point at which a change is made to a subsequent category of eligible heirs occurs when all of the eligible heirs of the preceding category, who have been simultaneously called upon to accept the inheritance, have not been able or have not wanted to accept it. If, within any category, one or more of the eligible heirs cannot or will not accept the inheritance, the part to which they are entitled will be added to the part of those belonging to the same category.

12.59 It is, however, necessary to make a proviso in respect of the first category of eligible heirs and the position of the surviving spouse. If there are no descendants, instead of the surviving spouse being called upon as the only representative of the first category, the eligible heirs of the second category are immediately summoned and share with the surviving spouse. The rule governing the way in which the estate is distributed in each of the categories is that relations of the same degree should have an equal part of the estate (art 2136 of the Civil Code). Attention should also be paid to the specific rules governing each of the categories of eligible heirs which are as follows:

Category 1 – spouse and descendants

12.60 If there is no surviving spouse, the estate is split up among the children in equal parts, with no distinction being made between the legitimate and illegitimate children of the deceased (art 2139 no 2 of the Civil Code). If, in the case of their being one or more of the children who cannot or do not wish to accept the estate, their descendants are called upon to accept the estate through right of representation and they will inherit to the extent that their ascendants would have inherited (art 2140 of the Civil Code).

12.61 If the surviving spouse competes with the descendants the estate will, in principle, be split into equal parts. As the law establishes that the surviving spouse can never receive less than a quarter of the inheritance, the rule of the division into equal parts is only effective if, together with the spouse, a maximum number of three descendants compete for the inheritance. If there are more descendants, the spouse will receive a quarter of the inheritance with the remainder being divided up into equal parts among the descendants.

Category 2 – spouse and ascendants

12.62 When the deceased does not have any surviving descendants (children, grandchildren, great grandchildren etc), and the testator leaves a spouse and ascendants, the spouse has the right to two-thirds of the inheritance and the ascendants one-third. If there is no spouse, the total amount of the inheritance will belong to the ascendants.

12.63 In accordance with the rules of preference set out above, ascendants who are first summoned for inheritance purposes are the parents of the testator with the one-third share of the ascendants being equally divided among them (if there is a surviving spouse) or the whole of the inheritance (if there is no surviving spouse).

12.64 If there are no parents and because there is, in this case no right of representation, ascendants of the second degree (grandparents) are summoned and so forth. The division among ascendants will always be in equal parts.

12.65 If one or more ascendants cannot or do not wish to accept the inheritance, their part will be added to that of the other ascendants and only if there are no ascendants will their part be added to that of the surviving spouse (art 2143 of the Civil Code).

Category 3 – brothers and sisters and their descendants

12.66 In the absence of a spouse, descendants and ascendants, the brothers and sisters of the deceased are summoned to take up the inheritance. If one of the brothers or sisters cannot or does not wish to accept the inheritance, then his descendants are called upon to assume his position through the right of representation.

12.67 In respect of the division of the inheritance between brothers, the Civil Code makes a distinction between brothers-german (those who are sons of the same father and mother) and unilateral brothers (those who are the sons of the same father (blood brothers) or sons of the same mother (uterine brothers)). Article

2146 of the Civil Code specifies that, if brothers-german and blood or uterine brothers are competing for the same inheritance, the portion available to each of the brothers-german or the descendants representing them should be double the amount of the portion of the blood or uterine brothers.

Category 4 – other collateral relations up to the fourth degree

12.68 In the absence of heirs in the categories referred to above, the remaining collateral relations are called upon up to the fourth degree, with preference always being given to the closest relations (art 2147 of the Civil Code). The estate will always be divided in equal parts, even if one of the successors is 'doubly related' to the deceased (art 2148 of the Civil Code).

Category 5 – the State

12.69 In the absence of a spouse and all eligible relations, the State is called upon to accept the estate and has the same rights and obligations as in the case of any other heir (arts 2152 and 2153 of the Civil Code). The State is not required to accept the inheritance, since it acquires the inheritance automatically, but it cannot reject the inheritance.

3. ASPECTS COMMON TO THE DIFFERENT TYPES OF SUCCESSION

OPENING OF THE SUCCESSION AND SUMMONING OF ELIGIBLE PERSONS

12.70 The procedure of succession normally commences with the death of the person in question. However, it is possible for the succession to be opened without the death of a person having been effectively verified. The law, under certain circumstances, will allow a submission to account for the presumption of death of a person who is absent or whose whereabouts are unknown. If the court issues this declaration, the succession will be opened on the basis of the presumed death of the person. This is because the law equates the presumption of death with the actual death. The heirs and legatees are summoned at the opening of the succession and the first matters to be dealt with will be to check if there are 'legitimary heirs' and if the deceased has left a testament.

12.71 The eligible persons must have capacity to inherit. In addition to the State, all persons born or conceived at the time of the opening of the succession, provided that there is no cause for disqualification (established in art 2033 no 1 of the Civil Code) have capacity to inherit. Cases (described in art 2034 of the Civil Code) in which an eligible heir commits a serious crime or tort (such as murder for example) against the testator or his close family provide a basis for disqualification.

In the case of succession by testament or contract, persons who as yet have not been conceived, but who potentially are children of a specific living person on the date of the succession, and collective persons (art 2033 no 2 of the Civil Code) are also eligible as heirs. 12.72

RIGHT OF REPRESENTATION

Representation for the purposes of succession consists of the legal summoning of the descendants of an heir or legatee to assume the position of an eligible person who could not or who did not wish to accept an inheritance or legacy. 12.73

Representation is allowed both in intestate and testate succession (art 2040 of the Civil Code), although there are several restrictions. We have already seen that, in the case of intestate succession, representation is made on behalf of the descendants of the children of the testator and on behalf of the descendants of the brother or sister of the deceased (art 2042 of the Civil Code). In the case of succession by testament, the descendants of a person who dies before the testator or of a person who rejects the inheritance have in principle the right of representation (art 2041 of the Civil Code). 12.74

It is considered, in the case of intestate succession, that the eligible person could not or would not accept the inheritance or legacy whenever: 12.75

(1) he has already died;
(2) he rejects the inheritance or legacy;
(3) his whereabouts are not known;
(4) he has been declared unfit or has been disinherited.

ACCEPTANCE AND REJECTION OF INHERITANCE

After the opening of the succession and after establishing that there are heirs, the heirs may either accept or reject the inheritance or the legacy, ie they may state whether or not they want to accept the inheritance or legacy of the deceased. Both acceptance and rejection are unilateral, indivisible, unconditional and irrevocable acts. Indivisibility means that a person cannot accept one part and reject another. However, if a person is called upon to accept in different capacities eg as an heir and as a legatee, he may in principle, accept the inheritance and reject the legacy. 12.76

Acceptance and rejection are unconditional acts because the eligible person cannot subject acceptance or rejection to any condition. He either accepts or rejects. The only possible variation is that acceptance can be acceptance *per se* or by inventory. Acceptance by inventory is made on the basis of an inventory already submitted or by means of an application to be submitted for a legal inventory. The difference between acceptance *per se* and acceptance by inventory relates to the burden of proof in respect of the assets and debts of which the succession is comprised. 12.77

12.78 In several cases the acceptance of an inheritance by inventory is mandatory: these include inheritances left to a minor, a disabled person or a collective person. Acceptance may, in addition, be either explicit or tacit, although some acts of administering the inheritance may not imply its acceptance even on a tacit basis. The maximum period of time in which an inheritance can be accepted is ten years, commencing from the date upon which the eligible person was summoned to take up the inheritance.

12.79 With regard to rejection, it should be noted that rejection is always a formal act and should be in the form of a written document or, in certain cases, a notarial deed.

ADMINISTRATION OF INHERITANCE

12.80 The inheritance must be administered from the moment of the opening of the succession up to its liquidation and distribution. Portuguese law gives the name of *cabeça-de-casal* to the party responsible for managing the inheritance. The law specifies, in decreasing order of preference, four categories of persons for assuming the role of *cabeça-de-casal* (art 2080 of the Civil Code). In accordance with this order, it is the responsibility of the surviving spouse to assume this position, provided that he is an heir or has the right, based on the matrimonial property regime, to half of the assets of the household.

12.81 The *cabeça-de-casal* administers the estate but does not enjoy extensive legal powers because the established principle is that the rights pertaining to the inheritance can only be exercised jointly by or against all of the heirs (art 2091 of the Civil Code). If the duties are not properly carried out, the incumbent *cabeça-de-casal* may be replaced.

DISTRIBUTION OF THE ESTATE

12.82 Heirs have the right to submit an application for the distribution of the inheritance at any time. No heir may be forced to accept that the inheritance remains undistributed, although it may be agreed that the inheritance should not be distributed for a period of five years. This period is renewable. The division may be made on a judicial or private basis. After the division has been made, each of the heirs is considered, from the time of the opening of the inheritance, as the sole successor to all of the assets attributed to him' (art 2119 of the Civil Code).

4. ASPECTS OF PRIVATE INTERNATIONAL LAW

CONFLICTS OF LAWS

General rule

Portuguese law adopts the principle of the unity of succession even in the area of private international law. In fact, under Portuguese legislation different conflicts of law rules for the succession to movable and immovable assets do not exist. The general rule in matters concerning succession is that the personal law (ie law of nationality) held by an individual at the date of his death is applicable (art 62 and 31 no 1 of the Civil Code). 12.83

The statute of succession is responsible for regulating all matters pertaining to the opening, devolution, transmission and distribution of an estate. The scope of competence of the law of succession also includes (under art 62 of the Civil Code) the definition of the powers of the administrator of the estate and the executor of the testament. 12.84

With regard to the opening of the succession it should be pointed out that presumptions of death and survival are regulated by the national law of the individual in question. There is, however, a special regulation covering the possibility of the existence of presumptions of survival which are incompatible in light of the national laws of the subjects involved. In accordance with article 26, no 2 of the Civil Code, the rule set out in internal Portuguese law is applicable and this rule states that in the event of the existence of any doubt it is assumed that both of the parties died at the same time (art 68 no 2 of the Civil Code). 12.85

It should be added that Portugal is a signatory to the Hague Convention concerning the International Administration of the Estates of Deceased Persons (2 October 1973). A distinction must be made between succession by testament and succession by contract in the case of voluntary succession. 12.86

Succession by testament

Both the statute of succession and the law regulating the dispositions and declarations set out in the testament govern the deceased's estate. There are also specific rules in respect of the form in which the expressions of the final will should be set out. 12.87

By article 63 of the Civil Code, it is the national law of the deceased at the time he makes his testament which regulates the deceased's capacity to make, change or revoke a testamentary disposition. However, if the testator, after having made his testament, should acquire a new national law and if this law does not grant him the capacity to make a testament, he will retain the capacity necessary for revoking the arrangements already made in accordance with the terms of the previously applicable law. 12.88

12.89 By article 64 of the Civil Code, the same law (ie the law of nationality held by the testator at the time of his testament) is also responsible for regulating:

(1) the interpretation of the clauses and dispositions of the testament, unless a specific or implied reference is made in the testament to another law;
(2) questions relating to the absence of and defects in the will of the testator;
(3) the admissibility of joint testaments.

12.90 The application of the law of the nationality held by the testator at the time at which he made his testamentary dispositions is justified by the need to protect the wishes and the expectations of the testator, because the testator will have relied upon the law in existence at the time the testament was made. Outside of these questions, the law which is applicable in the case of succession by testament is the law referred to in article 62 of the Civil Code. In accordance with these terms it is the law of the nationality of the deceased at the time of his death which is responsible for deciding, *inter alia*, on his freedom to make a testament and the restrictions to which he is subject, on the admissibility of certain clauses or arrangements for after his death, on the capacity to receive under a testament and the admissibility and the regime of direct or *fideicommissary* substitution.

Form of testament

12.91 Another aspect, which is not subject to the general conflicts of laws rule on succession, is the form of testaments. Portuguese legislation is very generous in this area and is inspired by the principle of *favor testamenti*. Article 65, no 1 of the Civil Code establishes a conflicts of laws rule (with alternative connecting factors) in accordance with which the form of arrangements for death, in addition to the form of their revocation or modification, will be considered valid if they satisfy the requirements set out by one of the following laws:

(1) the law of the place at which the act was signed (*lex loci celebrationis*);
(2) the national law of the deceased at the time of making the testament;
(3) the national law of the deceased at the time of his death;
(4) the law which is applicable in accordance with the conflict of laws rules of the *lex loci celebrationis* (admission of *renvoi* based on *favor negotii*).

12.92 However, article 65, no 2 of the Civil Code establishes an important restriction upon the principle of *favor testamenti*. If the national law of the deceased when he made the testament requires, under penalty of nullity, compliance with a specific form (even if the act is performed in a foreign country), then this requirement should be respected. Rules of this type exist, for example, in Dutch law (art 4:992 of the Civil Code) and in Portuguese law. Article 2223 of the Civil Code states that a testament made by a Portuguese citizen in a foreign country in compliance with the applicable foreign law will only be valid in Portugal if its preparation and approval is in a 'solemn form'. 'Solemn form' for these purposes means in written form.

12.93 It should also be noted that any special form requirements of the testament based on the age of the testator, made by the national law of the deceased at the time of the statement, should be complied with (art 63 of the Civil Code).

Portugal is a signatory to the Convention providing Uniform Law on the Form of an International Will, which was signed in Washington on 26 October 1973. Accordingly, Portuguese law recognises a testament which has been drawn up in accordance with the form specified in the Uniform Law annexed to the Convention. 12.94

Succession by contract

By article 64, para (c) of the Portuguese Civil Code it is the national law of the deceased at the time he makes his testament which is responsible for deciding the admissibility of succession contracts. If there are several persons making arrangements for their last wishes in the same contract the respective national law is applied to each of them. 12.95

The conditions set out in article 53 of the Civil Code constitute a proviso to para (c) of article 64, and, accordingly, if the contract is part of a pre-nuptial arrangement its admissibility is not dependent on the national law or laws of its institutors but the law which article 53 of the Civil Code requires to be applied to the pre-nuptial arrangements. This law is, in principle, the national law which is common to the parties at the time of the wedding ceremony. If they do not share the same nationality the law of the shared, common residence on the date of the wedding will be applied. If they do not share a common residence, the law of the place of the first residence of the married couple is applicable. 12.96

In the case of contracts of succession and in respect of the capacity to dispose on the basis of a contract and the absence of or defects in the expression of the will of the disposer, the regulation covering testaments is applicable. This means the applicability of the national law of the deceased at the time of the testament (arts 63 and 64, para (b) of the Civil Code). The same is true on matters of form since article 65 of the Civil Code also applies to the arrangements for after death. 12.97

Corrective mechanisms for the operation of the conflict of laws rules

The operation of the conflicts of laws rules may be affected by several corrective mechanisms which are well known to all private international law specialists. These are the cases of *renvoi*, public order or fraudulent manipulation of the law. 12.98

The position of Portuguese law on *renvoi* is complex and is set out in articles 16–19 of the Civil Code. On the basis of the principle that any reference made by a Portuguese conflicts of laws rule to a foreign law encompasses only the material internal rules of the law in question and not also its conflict of laws rules (art 16 of the Civil Code which adopts a position which is, in principle, opposed to *renvoi*), *renvoi* is not accepted as a general principle but only when it results in situations considered to be valid in terms of private international law. 12.99

The first of the objectives which may justify the adoption of the *renvoi* doctrine is the harmonisation of judgments. The admission of *renvoi* is provided by articles 17, no 1 (transmission) and 18, no 1 (remission) of the Civil Code. In accordance with the first of these rules, if the conflicts of laws rule of the law referred to by 12.100

Portuguese law refers to another system of law and this system considers itself to be competent for regulating the case, it will be the internal (material) law of the latter system which should be applied.

12.101 This rule is subject to an important restriction on matters relating to 'personal status' in article 17 no 2 of the Civil Code which states that there will be no *renvoi* if the law referred to by the Portuguese law is the national law of a person and this person usually resides in Portuguese territory or in a country in which the conflicts of law rules consider that the internal (material) law of the State of his nationality is competent.

12.102 This restriction is based on the concept that, within the scope of the 'personal status' (which also includes succession on death by art 25 of the Civil Code) it is only desirable to apply a law with which the individuals concerned are closely associated, this being the case with the laws of nationality and habitual residence. Therefore, in order for a law which is different from these two to be applied, it is in principle, necessary for both of these laws to be in agreement with the application of the third law.

12.103 The restriction in question is, however, subject to a limitation which is of special relevance in the field of succession. Article 17, no 3 of the Civil Code establishes that *renvoi* to a third system of law becomes acceptable in the case described in article 17, no 2 of the Civil Code when the matter to be resolved falls inside one of the areas referred to in article 17, no 3 of the Civil Code (which specifically includes succession) and provided that the national law specified by the Portuguese conflicts of laws rule transfers competence to the law of the place of the immovable assets and provided that this law considers itself to be competent. Thus, if an English citizen died habitually resident in Portugal owning immovables in France, the French *les situs* would govern succession to the French immovables.

12.104 Article 18, no 1 of the Civil Code establishes that *renvoi* to Portuguese law is only acceptable if the private international law of the law assigned by the Portuguese conflict of laws rules devolves responsibility to Portuguese internal (material) law. It is once again the idea of international legal harmony which justifies *renvoi* in this case.

12.105 Article 18, no 2 of the Civil Code, in turn, reverts to the idea which underlies article 17, no 2 of the Civil Code by stating that in the case of matters which are subject to 'personal law', Portuguese law is only applicable if the interested party has his habitual place of residence in Portuguese territory or, if he does not reside in Portugal, if the law of the country of his habitual residence considers Portuguese internal (material) law to be equally competent. Thus, if an English citizen died habitually resident in Portugal or in England owning immovables in Portugal, Portuguese law would govern succession to the Portuguese immovables.

12.106 To complete this overview of the Portuguese system of *renvoi*, reference should be made to three other rules.

The first is article 19, no 1 of the Civil Code which imposes a general restriction on the admissibility of *renvoi*. This is based on the premise of *favor negotii*. The article states that *renvoi* will not be accepted whenever its acceptance causes a legal act to become invalid or to be rejected which would otherwise be valid and acceptable in accordance with the law which the Portuguese conflicts of laws rule orders to be applied, or the illegitimacy of a *status familiae* which would otherwise be legitimate. 12.107

The second is set out in article 65, no 1 of the Civil Code, which was referred to above, and which, based on the same premise of *favor negotii*, leads to the acceptance of *renvoi* in the case of the form of testaments. 12.108

Finally, article 31, no 2 of the Civil Code states that the legal acts made in accordance with the laws of the habitual place of residence of the *de cujus* are recognised in Portugal. This is important because on the subject of personal status Portuguese law opts for the law of nationality and not for the law of habitual residence or the law of domicile. What the rule set out in article 31, no 2 of the Civil Code is saying is that, in spite of the fact that the law considered to be competent by Portuguese law is the law of the nationality of the individual, the legal acts made in accordance with the law of the place of his habitual residence will be recognised as being valid in Portugal. This is an example of the principle of the recognition of acquired rights. 12.109

Public order

Another possible exception to the application of the normally applicable law is the effect of the general clause concerning public order. In all laws, it is accepted that the law which is ordered to be applied for the settling of conflicts may not be *de facto* applied if its application contradicts any principle or fundamental tenet of the *lex fori*. This exception is specifically established in article 22 of the Civil Code which specifies that, if the precepts of a foreign law which is normally applied is contrary to the Portuguese public order, then the more appropriate rules of foreign legislation should be applied or, on a subsidiary basis, national Portuguese regulations. It can therefore be seen that (unlike other legal jurisdictions) under Portuguese law the public order clause does not immediately have the effect of making the local law applicable. 12.110

Fraus legis

The theory of *fraus legis* is explicitly established in Portuguese law. This is referred to in article 21 of the Civil Code, which establishes that: 12.111

> 'in the application of the conflict of laws rules, the *de facto* or legal situations created with the fraudulent intention of avoiding the applicability of a law which, in other circumstances (ie if it were not for the fraudulent activities of the party(ies) involved) would be competent, are irrelevant.'

If an English citizen chooses to own a Portuguese immovable indirectly by owning shares in a company, which directly owns the immovable, so that he owns movables (succession to which is governed by English law) rather than an immovable (subject to Portuguese forced heirship rules), it is considered unlikely that *fraus legis* will apply where the above steps were taken to enable an equitable 12.112

distribution of the deceased's property under one law rather than in a blatant attempt to disinherit forced heirs.

CONFLICTS OF JURISDICTIONS

12.113 It is a general principle of Portuguese law that Portuguese courts enjoy international jurisdiction whenever, in accordance with the national rules concerning the attributing of competence based on territory, Portuguese courts are competent to deal with a dispute (principle of the coincidence between international and territorial competence (art 65, no 1, para (b) of the Code of Civil Procedures).

12.114 In accordance with these terms, the rules which establish the territorial competence of local courts in the field of succession *mortis causa* (art 77 of the Code of Civil Procedures) are also applied for determining international jurisdiction of the Portuguese courts in the same area.

12.115 In accordance with the first of these rules, Portuguese courts have international jurisdiction for carrying out the inventory procedure or on matters concerning the qualification of a person as an heir of others when the deceased had his last place of residence in Portugal. Even in the case in which the deceased had his last place of residence in a foreign country, Portuguese courts may have jurisdiction for the procedures for carrying out the inventory and qualification, provided that the deceased has assets in Portugal. In this case, the competent court will be the court of the place at which the property or greater part of the property is located or, if there is no property, the court of the place at which most of the movable assets of the deceased are located.

12.116 Lastly, even if the deceased does not have any assets in Portugal, but the eligible person has a place of residence in Portugal, then the Portuguese court of the place of residence has international competence in matters concerning qualification as an heir.

12.117 One point which has been much discussed is, in the event that the deceased has assets both in Portugal and abroad, whether Portuguese courts have international competence only for the distribution of the assets placed in Portugal or also for the distribution of the assets in a foreign country. Although several Portuguese jurists have defended the point of view that Portuguese courts have competence for the distribution of assets in a foreign country, the Portuguese courts have not always accepted this opinion.

CHAPTER 13

SPAIN†

1. INTRODUCTION

PLURALISM OF SPANISH SUCCESSION LAW

Historically, Spain has been a State comprising several territorial units, each of which has its own system of rules on succession. Before the Constitution of 1978, this situation was recognised by article 13 of the Civil Code (below CC) of 24 July 1889 and provisions on this matter were included in the Compilations on Civil Law enacted later on: for Vizcaya and for Ayala (Law of 30 July 1959, arts 6–40, 62 and 63), for Catalonia (Law of 21 July 1960, arts 61–276), for the Balearic Islands (Law of 19 April 1961, arts 6–53 and 69–84), for Galicia (Law of 2 December 1961, arts 84–87), for Aragon (Law of 8 April 1987, arts 59–142) and for Navarra (Law of 1 March 1973, arts (laws) 148–375). 13.1

The Constitution of 1978 enshrined this legal pluralism of civil law (art 149.1.8) and the Autonomous Communities, into which Spain is divided, assumed the power to enact legislation on the civil law of their own territories. As a consequence, the Compilations of Civil Law have been partly revised or amended by the Acts of the Legislative Assemblies of these political bodies, namely those of Catalonia (Law of 20 March 1984), of Aragon (Laws of 21 May 1985 and of 29 March 1995), of Navarra (Law of 1 April 1987), of the Balearic Islands (Law of 28 June 1990) and the Basque country (Law of 1 July 1992). Moreover, the amendments to the compilation of Civil Law of Catalonia 1984, 1987 (Law on Intestacy) and 1990 have been replaced by the new Code on Succession to the estates of deceased persons (Law of December 1991). Finally, a new law substitutes in Galicia the compilation (Law 24 May 1995, arts 117–170). Some amendments to notarial wills have also been made in the Civil Code (1991). It is worth noting that some rules of Autonomous Communities have been declared unconstitutional (as, for example, art 2 of the Law of the Balearic Islands, in the Constitutional Court Judgment 156/1993 of 6 May, so that article was modified as a consequence by the Law of 20 October 1993). 13.2

† This chapter was written by Professor Julio D González Campos of the Autonomous University of Madrid and Judge at the Spanish Constitutional Court and Professor Alegría Borrás of the Univerity of Barcelona.

SUCCESSION IN SPANISH LAW – GENERAL CHARACTERISTICS

13.3 All civil law systems in force in Spain distinguish between the two kinds of succession: the testamentary one (disposal upon death by will, *sucesión testamentaria*) and intestacy (*sucesión legítima*). However, two points should be stressed: first, agreements as to succession, including mutual or reciprocal wills, are in principle excluded by the Civil Code with some exceptions; but largely allowed in other systems, as those of Aragon, the Balearic Islands, Catalonia, Galicia and Navarra. Mutual or reciprocal wills are also admitted in Aragon and Navarra. Second, the compatibility between testate succession and intestacy is established by the Civil Code (arts 658, 764 and 912), as well as by other systems of law in this matter. However, the principle of Roman law *nemo pro parte testatus, pro parte intestatus decedere potest* is enshrined by the Civil Law of Catalonia (Code on Succession, arts 3, 41 and 322) and the Balearic Islands (Comp, art 7).

13.4 Broadly speaking, succession law in Spain, as in other civil law countries, is characterised by the continuity of a person, the heir, succeeding to the estate and the legal relationships of the deceased. The subject matter of succession law is the *hereditas (herencia)*, comprising all assets, rights and debts of the *de cujus* which are not extinguished at his death (art 659 CC). Nobility titles, for example, not having patrimonial contents, are not integrated in the estate of the *de cujus* (arts 657, 659 and 661 CC). Therefore, they are not governed by the legal regime established for succession in the CC – or, if it is the case, in the 'foral' laws –, but by an exceptional system of succession, with an entailed character, established by historical laws still in force (Code of the *Siete Partidas, Partida* 2.15.2 and *Leyes de Toro* of 1505). The deceased's estate is, therefore, construed as a kind of *universitas iuris* for the purposes of succession.

13.5 Accordingly, the heir (*heredero*) is defined as the person entitled to the whole estate of the *de cujus*: the legatee being only entitled to a specific asset of the deceased's estate or to a right to be transmitted to him according to the testamentary disposition (art 660 CC). In the Civil Code, it is possible, however, for the heir also to be made a legatee and for the deceased's estate to be distributed by way of legacies under some circumstances.

13.6 The unity and universality of the *hereditas*, as just indicated, does not exclude the presence of special rules of succession law with regard to certain immovables or some special categories of assets, which institute particular inheritance regimes in respect of such assets. In general, this is the case for succession with regard to family farms (*explotaciones familiares agrarias*) in accordance with the Law of 24 December 1981. Moreover, this is also the case with immovables, which appertain to a stirpital family line (*bienes troncales*) in the civil law of Vizcaya, Aragon and Navarra.

13.7 Finally, Spanish rules of succession law are founded on the devolution of the deceased's estate to the persons who are his close relatives. Thus, the freedom of disposing of the estate by will – like the liberty of making gifts – is restricted in the interests of the next of kin and the surviving spouse, to whom an indefeasible share (*legítima*) is attributed by law. Moreover, some particular assets of the estate must also be reserved under particular cicumstances to specific relatives determined by law (*reserva*).

The law on succession is closely related to legal rules on gifts and matrimonial property, two areas of law also largely differing amongst the various systems in force in Spain. It suffices to indicate here: first, that gifts might have to be restored to the estate if they surpass the testator's freely disposable share; second, that questions concerning matrimonial property are to be dealt with prior to determining rights under the *lex successionis* in order to ascertain the extent of the disposable estate of the *de cujus*. In some civil law systems, like that of Catalonia, they may be determined in agreements on matrimonial property (*heredamientos*) or that of Galicia (*usufructo voluntario de viudedad*). 13.8

2. DOMESTIC LAW ON SUCCESSION

WILLS

General aspects

The will (*testamento*) is defined as the act or declaration by which a person disposes *post mortem* of all his estate or a part of it (art 667 CC). However, as will be indicated below, a will may also contain other declarations not relating to the disposal of the estate upon death, like the recognition of a child or the appointment of a guardian for a minor (arts 120 and 223 CC). Generally, in Catalonia and the Balearic Islands, however, naming of the heir is a necessary element of the will in accordance with Roman law principles of succession. 13.9

Declarations with *post mortem* effects may also be made in Catalonia and Navarra in a postscript to a will (*codicilo, memoria testamentaria*); if these declarations are incompatible with those made previously in the will the formal requirements of the will have to be fulfilled. A new naming of heir(s) in these documents is excluded. 13.10

The will has some distinctive elements: 13.11

(1) it is a unilateral declaration of the testator; although the strict unilaterality required by art 669 CC is excluded by other civil law systems in force in Spain, like those of Aragon, Vizcaya, Galicia and Navarra, which admit joint and mutual or reciprocal wills;

(2) it is a personal act under the Civil Code, prohibiting any delegation to a third person in order to dispose of the deceased's property upon his death; the identity of the testator must be clearly established when making the will. In other civil law systems, however, the will made by a commissioned person – either the spouse or a third person – is admitted (Vizcaya, Aragon);

13.12 (3) moreover, the will is a formal or solemn act in all civil law systems in force in Spain. The testator is therefore obliged to declare his intention upon death in accordance with one of the testamentary forms provided for by the law; each system offering a diversity of them, before a notary, before a witness or by a private document, as will be indicated below. Otherwise, the consequence is the nullity of the declaration (art 687 CC).

(4) a will is, by its essence, revocable and the revocation of the will is possible at any moment, even if the testator had previously agreed otherwise (art 736 CC). Codicils and other postscripts to a will may also have a revocatory effect, as indicated above. But revocation must satisfy the formal requirements provided by law in each of the civil law systems.

13.13 Wills may be made in any of the official languages of Spain or in a foreign language, by Spanish nationals or by foreigners. In respect of the 'open' notarial will, the presence of an interpreter is required when the testator makes his will so as to translate into Spanish (or another official language in Spain) the declaration made by the testator (art 684 CC, art 109 Catalonian Code on Succession). But this provision does not affect 'closed' notarial wills or holograph wills, although a translation will be required in order to include them in the records of a notary after the death of the testator.

13.14 As a declaration having legal effects upon death, a will may be vitiated by *duress* – physical or moral – and also by *fraud* of a third person. A particular aspect of fraud is undue influence exercised upon the testator so that he makes a testamentary disposition in favour of the influencer or of a third person. A will made under duress or fraud is void (art 673 CC; but *mistake* does not in principle involve the nullity of the will: so, *error personae* in respect of the heir may be corrected (art 733 CC); and the testator's mistaken motives in determining the choice of the heir or legatee will not be taken into account unless such a motive was essential for the choice made (art 767 CC).

Capacity to make a will

13.15 All persons not expressly excluded by law have testamentary capacity (art 662 CC). Disability is an exception, limited to some specific circumstances:

(1) minors under 14 years; although full age is required for some kinds of wills (art 688 CC);
(2) mental illness, whether permanent or temporary (art 633 CC).

In the civil law of Navarra, however, prodigality which has been judicially declared is also considered a disability (Comp, art 184, 3).

The testator's capacity is to be determined at the time of making the will (art 660 CC). If the will is made by a person who has testamentary capacity and afterwards this same person becomes mentally impaired, the validity of the will is accepted (art 664 CC).

In respect of wills made in the presence of a notary, the testator's capacity is attested by the personal judgement of the notary. The judgment by witnesses of the testator's capacity is only required for special situations (art 697 CC; art 106 Code of Succession of Catalonia; art 30 Vasc Law). No previous medical examination is required, except in the case of a person suffering from mental illness who intends to make a will at a period of remission of madness (art 665 CC). 13.16

Reference in a notarial will to the personal judgement of the notary on the testator's capacity is considered a necessary element of the act; its absence invalidates the will. But such a judgement does, in fact, only constitute a presumption *iuris tantum*; other evidence may attest the disability of the testator. 13.17

Formal validity. Types of wills

In accordance with articles 676 and 677 CC, wills are either 'common' (holograph, 'open' and 'closed' wills) or 'special' (military, maritime and wills made by Spanish nationals in a foreign country). Other civil law systems in force in Spain provide other testamentary forms as will be indicated below. 13.18

Private wills (holograph) are generally allowed. The same happens with wills made only before witnesses if special circumstances occur at the time of making it. But notarial wills, either 'open' or 'closed', constitute the habitual testamentary forms, given that the intervention of the notary – a public officer – assures the observance of legal provisions, the notary being liable under articles 705 and 715 CC when formal requirements of 'open' and 'closed' wills have not been observed. 13.19

Holograph wills

Private or *holograph wills* need to be entirely handwritten and signed by a testator having full age, and reference to the year, month and day when made must be added by him; this requirement is essential to the validity of the declaration as a will (arts 678 and 688 CC).[1] However, as a private document, its legal effects *post mortem* are dependent upon two subsequent formalities: the verification of its authenticity (*adveración*) and, if attested, the inclusion of the document as a will in the records of a notary (*protocolización*). For the first, a strict term of five years from the testator's death is provided: on expiry of this term the private will ceases to be capable of having any effect (art 689 CC.) The verification is made in the course of a judicial procedure by three witnesses who know the handwriting and signature of the testator or, failing such witnesses, by expert evidence. The surviving spouse and the relatives of the *de cujus* are present in this procedure and may dispute the authenticity of the document (arts 691 and 692 CC). 13.20

Open notarial wills

The *open notarial will* is made by the testator declaring his *post mortem* intent in the presence of a notary and the witnesses, if required. The notary drafts the will in accordance with the testator's declaration and it is read aloud by him in the 13.21

1 On the requirements of holograph wills, see Supreme Court decisions of 24 April 1895, 13 May 1942, 11 April 1945, 30 November 1956, 24 February 1961; also, T Torres, *El testamento ológrafo*, 1976. Article 688 admits that foreigners may make holograph wills in their own language; this faculty has been extended to any other foreign language.

presence of the testator and the witnesses, if required, in order to verify that it gives effect to the testator's wishes. If the testator agrees then the instrument will be signed by the testator, the notary and, if needed, by the witnesses (arts 694, 695, 696, 697 and 698 CC). It is possible, however, for the testator, instead of making an oral declaration to the notary, to give the latter a minute or draft of the will, on the basis of which the open will will be drafted; but it is necessary, as in the first case, that the will is read in the presence of the testator and then signed (arts 695 and 696 CC). Some special provisions are applicable to wills made by deaf or blind persons (art 697 CC) to assure the right expression of their intent.

13.22 In any case, the testator's knowledge of the contents of the will and the signatures of him and the notary constitute essential elements.[1] Moreover, article 699 CC requires that all formalities indicated above must be accomplished in a single continuous act. It is acceptable, however, for the notary to prepare the formal will upon receiving the declaration of the testator and then to convene the testator for a later meeting at which it will be read and signed.[2]

Open wills before witnesses

13.23 The civil code also admits *open wills before witnesses* under two particular circumstances: first, when the testator is close to dying, to be made before five witnesses; second, in case of an epidemic, in the presence of three witnesses (arts 700 and 701 CC). The oral declaration will be, if possible, written down. These wills become ineffective after two months if the testator survives or the epidemic comes to an end; if the testator dies during this term, the will only has legal effect if included in the records of a public notary within three months of the testator's death (arts 703 and 704 CC).

Closed notarial wills

13.24 The *closed notarial will* is made when the testator, without manifesting its content, declares before a notary and five witnesses that his *post mortem* dispositions are contained in a closed and sealed written document, or in a written document to be closed and sealed in the presence of the notary. The notary receives the written document and writes certain details on its cover, which will thereafter be signed by the testator, the notary and, if required, the witnesses (arts 680, 706 and 707 CC). To prevent fraud, illiterate or blind persons are excluded from this testamentary form (art 708 CC).

13.25 The will may be written by the testator himself, signing at the end of the document. In this case, although it may be invalid as a closed notarial will, it is valid as a holograph one (art 715 CC). The will may also be written by mechanical means or by another person at the request of the testator; although the latter will have to sign all the pages and at the end of the document, this circumstance must be indicated to the notary, and be expressed in the document. In all cases, after the formalities already indicated, the will can be kept by the testator or handed to

---

1 Supreme Court decisions of 14 July 1899, 18 November 1915 and 8 April 1965. The notary will attest at the end of the will that the testamentary forms required by law have been observed. See Cano Martinez de Velasco, 'Solemnidades y formalidades de los testamentos según doctrina del Tribunal Supremo', *Revista de Derecho notarial* (1978) 139.

2 Supreme Court decisions of 28 June 1909 and 10 April 1987.

the notary or to a third person (arts 710 and 711 CC). The person holding the will is obliged to present it to the judge a short while after the testator's death, to be openly read and then included in the records of a notary (art 714 CC and art 1956 LEC).

Territorial variations

The testamentary forms of the Civil Code just indicated are also applicable in those territories where a particular system of civil law is in force, according to the provisions of the respective Compilations of civil law or new laws including rules on succession. These, however, modify to some extent the rules laid down in the former. Only two witnesses are required for notarial wills in Aragon; the same number is required in Navarra for open notarial wills, while seven are needed for a closed one. In Catalonia and Galicia, no witnesses are required, except in special situations (art 107 Code on Successions of Catalonia and art 136 Law of Galicia). 13.26

The Compilations provide for particular testamentary forms especially as concerns wills made when the testator is close to dying. In those cases the intervention of the parson and two witnesses is admitted in Aragon, Catalonia and Navarra, the latter also admitting a priest of the place. Similarly, wills made before three witnesses are provided for in Navarra and Vizcaya. However, all these cases require a procedure for attesting the testator's will. 13.27

Registry of wills

Notarial wills are registered in a Central Registry at the Ministry of Justice and in particular registries in each notarial district, as well as by each notary authorising them.[1] These registries of wills have, however, only an informative purpose and do not prejudge the validity or legal effect of the wills. Holograph wills may, of course, revoke a notarial will already registered. Information on registered wills may be obtained by any person who produces a death certificate of the person who supposedly has made a will. 13.28

For this reason, when anyone dies, it is necessary: first, to obtain the death certificate; second, to ask after 15 days from the date of death for the certification of the Central Registry of wills; third, to obtain, in the case of notarial wills, a copy of it and, if this is not the case, to initiate the procedure of the heirship declaration. 13.29

Spain is a party to the European Convention of 16 May 1972 instituting a uniform system of registration of wills, together with Belgium, Cyprus, France, Italy, Luxembourg, the Netherlands, Portugal and Turkey. Under this Convention, the registering of a will is not subject to a condition relating to the nationality of the testator; it may be communicated to other countries and information on wills is 13.30

1 The Central Registry is in the charge of the *Dirección General de los Registros y del Notariado,* dependent upon the Ministry of Justice. Address, c San Bernardo 62, E-28015-Madrid. The notarial Registry of wills is regulated by Annex II to the Notarial Rules of 2 June 1944. About how to act in international situations, see A Calvo in J D González Campos and al. *Derecho internacional privado. Parte especial,* vol II. Madrid (1991) 553.

facilitated through co-operation amongst the Central Registries of the States parties to the Convention.

The contents of the will

13.31 In accordance with article 764 CC, a will is valid although it names no heir or if the disposal upon death only concerns a part of the *hereditas* or the person named as heir does not accept it. However, the naming of the heir is usually the main element of the will; it is a necessary one for its validity in the civil law of the Balearic Islands and Catalonia. In general, the heir is qualified as such when a person succeeds to the *de cujus* in the universality of the *hereditas*, as distinct from being a legatee; and the consequence of this is the heir's liability in respect of debts relating to the *hereditas*.

The heir

13.32 It is required that the heir be certain, this being assured when his name and, if necessary, other personal qualities, are indicated (arts 750 and 772 CC). But the heir may also be identified by reference to a later event, like the children not yet born of a person, if the birth occurs; and when two or more persons are instituted as heirs, some rules are provided to determine the testator's choice (arts 765, 769, 770 and 772 CC), as well as when 'relatives', in general, are indicated as heirs in the will (art 751 CC). On the other hand, the testator may name the heir under a suspensive or resolutive condition, subject to a term and *sub modo* (arts 790, 791, 797 and 805 CC). In these cases, the legal position of the heir in respect of the *hereditas* is modified in accordance with the condition, term or charge imposed upon him by the testator.

13.33 A subordinated creation of an heir can be made by *substitution*. The person first named as heir occupies the place of the first heir. Substitution is also allowed in respect of a legatee (art 789 CC). In the so-called 'direct' substitution, the condition is either that the first heir does not survive the testator or, although surviving him, that the *hereditas* is not accepted or may not be accepted (art 774 CC); a substitution made by parents or ancestors can be due to the fact that the first heir is a minor under 14 years (art 775 CC) or, that although aged more than 14 years, his disability owing to mental illness has been judicially declared (art 775 CC).

13.34 In the *fideicommissary substitution*,[1] however, the estate or part of it passes to the first heir, but he has the obligation to transmit the *hereditas* to a third person. The first is then a fiduciary heir. But this kind of substitution is limited under art 781 CC: only two successive persons are admitted as *fideicommissary* heirs. Forced shares (*legítimas*) are excluded from substitution. The historical tradition of *fideicommissary* substitution in Catalonia is reflected in a detailed regulation in the new Code on Successions (arts 180–248).

1 On the elements of fideicommissary substitution, see Supreme Court decisions of 6 April 1954, 25 October 1954 and 3 July 1963; see also, L Puig Ferriol, *El heredero fiduciario*, Barcelona, 1965 and M Albadalejo and S Diaz Alabart in *Comentarios al Código civil y Compilaciones forales*, t 10, vol 2, Madrid, 1984.

The legatee

A person (including the heir) may also be made a *legatee* by will. In the Civil Code, as in other civil law systems in force in Spain, different kinds of legacy are specifically regulated (arts 858–891 CC) but their content is generally either a specific part of the estate or a new right created for the benefit of the legatee by the testator's disposition. In fact, the legatee acquires the asset or a creditor's rights against the heir or, otherwise, the executor of the will. The testator may charge a legatee with making another legacy (*sublegado*). 13.35

The legatee (*legatorio*), as distinct from the heir, is not liable for the debts of the estate, except in some particular cases (arts 858 and 1029 CC). The payment of the legacy may be secured by an entry in favour of the legatee in the Land Registry (*Registro de la Propriedad*) when the estate includes immovables; the creation of a mortgage is also possible in the same case if the legacy is a pension or a periodical payment (arts 47, 88 and 90 LH). However, legacies may be restored to the estate in some cases, for the benefit of the heirs to whom an indefeasible share (*legítima*) is allocated (arts 820 and 822 CC). 13.36

Spiritual or altruistic purposes

Finally, the will may contain disposals of the whole estate or a part of it for the benefit of the testator's soul or for other pious purpose (art 747 CC), and also for the benefit of poor persons (art 749 CC). Other provisions not having a dispositary character, (recognition of a child, appointment of a guardian) may also be included. 13.37

Legal restrictions upon the disposal of the estate by will

One characteristic of Spanish succession law is the limited freedom of the testator to dispose of his estate by will, due to two significant concepts. First, the concept of the indefeasible share (*legítima*) in favour of some relatives and, in some measure, the surviving spouse. Second, the concept of the legal reserve (*reserva*) relating to some assets, also for the benefit of a determined class of relatives. Both aspects are common to the Civil Code and to other civil law systems in force in Spain, but the latter differs in many points from the former on these restrictions, as well as differing amongst themselves. 13.38

The indefeasible share (*legítima*) has to be calculated on the basis of the deceased's estate (*relictum*), deducting debts of the *hereditas* and adding all gifts made by the testator (*donatum*); the inclusion of gifts (*colación de donaciones*) is founded on the idea that a person may only dispose by gift of what he can dispose of by will (art 636 CC). The persons entitled to the *legítima* (called *herederos legitimarios*) and the indefeasible share allocated by law to them are as follows. 13.39

(1) The children and other progeny, in respect of succession to the estates of their parents and ancestors, are entitled to two-thirds of the total, calculated as indicated above; the remaining third is left to the free disposal of the testator (art 808 CC). In Aragon, the same share is provided, but the testator possesses more freedom in order to attribute it amongst the heirs; and in other civil law systems, this share goes from the four-fifths of Vizcaya to a very 13.40

limited (one-quarter in Catalonia) or symbolic share (as in Navarra and Ayala).

(2) If the *de cujus* has no children or progeny, the parents and ancestors are entitled to receive the indefeasible share in respect of his estate with the amounts established by the civil law of the *de cujus.*

(3) The surviving spouse who has not separated from the *de cujus* is only entitled to a usufruct in the estate, the extent of which differs depending upon whether the spouse inherits with children or progeny of the *de cujus* (one-third), with ancestors or children of the latter (one-half), or with other heirs (two-thirds), under articles 834, 837 and 839. However, this is not the case in other civil laws in force in Spain.

13.41 It is worth noting, however, that, in the Civil Code, the testator has the power to dispose by will of a third of the *legítima,* in order to improve the situation of one of his children or progeny on his death in respect of succession to his estate (*mejora*);[1] the forced heirs (*herederos legitimarios*) are then entitled to a strict *legítima* of one-third. The *mejora* may also be made as a gift, if it is so expressly declared (art 825 CC), as well as by agreements on matrimonial property (arts 826 and 827 CC). In these cases, the *mejora* is not revocable; and it is possible to accept the latter and renounce the *hereditas* (art 833 CC) if the *mejora* was made as a legacy, being subject to the same principle of article 890 CC. The *majora* does not exist in other civil systems in Spain, but in some systems it has special forms, eg in Galicia.

13.42 As an indefeasible share, the *legítima* is protected in different ways. First, as indicated above, gifts are restored to the estate and all gifts surpassing the part left for free disposal by the testator are ineffective. Second, no charge, condition or substitution of any kind, except (if it be the case) for the usufruct of the surviving spouse, is allowed in respect of the *legítima*; nor are agreements allowed between the testator and the persons entitled to this *legítima* (art 816 CC). Finally, if the latter are intentionally excluded by the testator in his will (*preterición*), the *legítima* may be claimed against the other heirs (art 814 CC); exclusion of persons from the *legítima* is only possible if they were disinherited by the testator for any of the causes fixed by the law (arts 852–855 CC), although the *legítima* will then pass to the children of the person who was disinherited (art 857 CC).

13.43 The *reserve* concerning particular assets may also restrict the disposal of the estate by will. The first reserve is imposed upon the widow if she enters into a subsequent marriage and is for the benefit of the children and progeny of the first marriage. It affects the ownership of all assets received by the *de cujus,* by will or otherwise, as well as property acquired by the widow from the children of the first marriage or from relatives of the *de cujus* (arts 968, 969 and 980 CC). This kind of reserve is also established in Catalonia and Navarra. The second reserve is for the benefit of persons belonging to a family line (*reserva lineal*) in respect of assets which are acquired by an ancestor from a direct descendant or a brother and which have been the appurtenance of the family. It is imposed upon the person who acquires

1 Fuenmayor, *La mejora en el sistema sucesorio español,* Coimbra, 1946; Elfenger, 'la mejora en el vigente derecho español', *Revista de Derecho Notarial* (1969) 7.

such assets (art 811 CC).[1] Other reserves on the basis of assets belonging to a family line also exist in Aragon, Navarra, Galicia and Vizcaya (*reserva troncal*).

Testamentary executors

13.44 The testator may entrust a person – or two or more persons, to act in common – with the task of carrying out, wholly or in part, the provisions of his will (art 892 CC). This executorship is called *albaceazgo*, and *albacea* (testamentary executor) the person entrusted with this task;[2] it is only required that the person so appointed has capacity to bind himself (art 893 CC). The testamentary executor is akin to an agent, but his task is one of confidence and is not remunerated unless the will provides for remuneration (art 908 CC). The person appointed as *albacea* may accept the task or, having a legal cause, renounce it. When no testamentary executor is appointed by will, or the person appointed renounces, the heir is entrusted with the task (art 911 CC); and if not fulfilled by the heir, or under the circumstances prescribed in article 966 CC, the judge will appoint another person as *albacea*.

13.45 The testamentary executor possesses the powers expressly entrusted to him by the will or, otherwise, those provided in article 901 CC; he is accountable to the heir as well as liable in the fulfilment of his task under the general rules on obligations (art 907 CC). The *albaceazgo* may not be delegated to a third person because it is founded on confidence. Finally, the testamentary executor must finish the task within one year, unless otherwise provided in the will (arts 909 and 904 CC).

13.46 Different from *albaceazgo* is the case where the testator entrusts to someone the sole power of distribution among the heirs. This person receives the name of *comisario* or *contador-partidor* (art 1057 CC).

13.47 In Navarra, testamentary executors (*albaceas*) may also be appointed but the powers of testamentary executors are enlarged in this civil law system, as in others, when a person is entrusted not only with the performance of the will, but also with the distribution of the estate. This is the case of fiduciary succession (Aragon, Navarra) or when an 'heir of confidence' (*heredero de confianza*) was appointed by will (Catalonia, Navarra).

AGREEMENTS AS TO SUCCESSION

Contracts of succession

13.48 Agreements on succeeding to someone's estate when he dies (either succeeding or not succeeding) are forbidden by the Civil Code in accordance with the Roman law tradition (arts 658 and 1271). However, as in other civil law systems in Europe,

1 Supreme Court decisions of 19 November 1910, 7 November 1928, 2 March 1929, 1 February 1957. See Doral Barcia, 'La reserva hereditaria común', *Anuario de Derecho civil* (1977) 497; J B Vallet de Goytisolo, 'La jurisprudencia del Tribunal Supremo y el art 811 del Código civil', *Anuario de Derecho civil* (1957–1960).

2 On the powers of testamentary executors, see Supreme Court decisions of 14 May 1891, 6 May 1903, 24 December 1909, 25 March 1914, 24 May 1954, 27 November 1972 and 23 November 1974. Also M Albadalejo, *El albaceazgo en el derecho español*, Madrid, 1969.

the inclusion of some dispositions *mortis causa* in marriage contracts is allowed (arts 826 and 831 CC), as well as gifts in favour of the other spouse of some goods subject to the restrictions upon disposing by will above indicated (art 1341 CC).

13.49 However, agreements as to succession between two or more persons creating, modifying or terminating the rights of one or more of these persons to inherit in the future are known in other civil law systems in force in Spain (Aragon, the Balearic Islands, Catalonia, Galicia and Navarra). They are also allowed, in general, with regard to family farms, by the Law of 24 December 1981.[1]

13.50 These inheritance agreements are generally made in favour of the spouses in marriage contracts by their parents or grandparents or by the spouses themselves. There is the case of the *heredamientos* (inheritance agreements) in Catalonia, where a marriage contract instituting an heir is required. In Aragon and Navarra, disposal of the estate in favour of one or both of the spouses, or of a third party (usually the spouses' children or progeny or a relative), may be agreed either in a marriage contract or other public document. But Aragon also allows a reciprocal agreement for the surviving spouse to inherit (*pacto al más viviente*) and Navarra allows a contract of inheritance between the adopting and the adopted persons. Finally, agreements as to succession extend to the whole estate as in the Balearic Islands and Catalonia. Agreements as to succession, with specific express exceptions, are not revocable, but they may revoke a previous will; and they may involve, too, an anticipated transmission of the estate to the beneficiaries.

Mutual wills

13.51 The Civil Code forbids joint wills made by two or more persons in one document (see Supreme Court decision of 13 February 1984) as well as mutual or reciprocal wills (art 669 CC), the will being, by its essence, a unilateral act of disposal *post mortem*. This prohibition extends to Spanish nationals subject to the Civil Code when making such a will in a foreign country (art 733 CC).

13.52 In Aragon and Galicia, however, the spouses subject to this civil law system may dispose by a joint will (*testamento mancomunado*); in Aragon, also, mutual or reciprocal disposal is possible, unless otherwise provided in the will, which has the legal effect of an inheritance agreement in favour of the surviving spouse (*pacto al más viviente*). In Navarra too, a joint will (the so-called *testamento de hermandad*) may contain a reciprocal disposal. For Aragon, any testamentary form is admitted; but the holograph form is excluded in Navarra for joint wills. In both civil law systems, revocability is admitted in some cases. It is worth noting, finally, that a kind of inheritance agreement as to succession, the mutual one (*heredamiento mutual*), has in Catalonia a similar function to the above-mentioned mutual wills, although it is made by marriage contract.

1 See Martinez Vazquez de Castro, 'El pacto sucesorio en el nuevo estatuto de la explotación familiar agraria', *La Ley* (1982) 1074. In general, Castán Vazquez, 'Notas sobre la sucesión contractual en el Derecho español', *Anuario de Derecho civil* (1964) 367.

INTESTACY

General aspects

Intestacy arises in the absence of a will or an agreement as to succession, or in the case of an ineffective naming of an heir. However, as mentioned at the outset, while in the Civil Code (art 658) the compatible interrelationship between wills and intestacy is accepted, it is not accepted in other systems. 13.53

As common characteristics of the different civil law systems in force in Spain, it is worth stressing the following. Intestacy is based on a familial relationship, being the relation by kin (as a consequence of marriage or without marriage) or by adoption, as a consequence of the principle of non-discrimination among the different kinds of children.[1] The bases of the Spanish system are in Roman law, *successio gradum et ordinum*. In this way, there are *kinds* of possible heirs, having in each group the same degree of relation (progeny, ancestors, collaterals, spouse, the State or other public institutions). Inside every kind, *lines* are distinguished, which are the divisions inside every kind, with different *degrees* in every line and excluding the next of kin of the most remote relatives. 13.54

The general rule is equality among relatives in the same degree and the right of accretion or survivorship (*derecho de acrecer*) among them. However, the right of representation (*derecho de representación*) (art 921 CC) is an exception to this rule and is attributed to certain relatives when there is no person of intermediate degree (eg to the grandchildren if the children predecease). The exception exists without limit in the descending direct line and with limits in the collateral line, since it is only recognised for the children of brothers or sisters, without being allowed for the ancestors. 13.55

Besides the rules of the Civil Code, other civil law systems in force in Spain also include rules about intestacy. They are mostly limited to a reference to the Civil Code, including some peculiarities. In some cases, regulation is more complete and peculiar, as happens in Catalonia, with the above-mentioned Code on Succession of 1991. Although inheritance on the basis of the family line of provenance of certain assets (*sucesión troncal*) is an historical remnant in the Civil Code, its importance is maintained, especially in intestacy, in Vizcaya and, in a most limited way, in Aragon (for the so called *bienes troncales de abolorio*), Navarra and Catalonia (in the succession of the *de cujus* who has not reached puberty). 13.56

1 Taking into account changes in filiation by the law of 1981 and, mainly on adoption, by law of 11 November 1987. See M D Nuñez Boluda, 'El orden de suceder abintestato y personas con derecho a legítima después de la reforma del Código civil de 1981', *Revista de Derecho privado* (1986) 715; P Salvador Coderch, 'Adopción y sucesión intestada', *Revista Jurídica de Catalunya* (1986) 655 and in *Comentarios al Codigo civil y compilaciones forales*, t XXIX, vol 3, 1.

The priority order

13.57 Generally speaking, the order of priority is as follows.

(1) The first in the order of priority is the *direct descending line,* without limitation in degree. In this way, children and their descendants succeed the parents and other ancestors without distinction due to sex, age or filiation (art 931 CC). When all the progeny is in the same degree, the estate is divided in equal parts; when the progeny is in different degrees the most remote inherits by right of representation.

13.58 (2) Then comes the *direct ascending line* also without limitation in degree, excluding the next of kin of the most remote ancestor. Parents inherit in equal parts if both are alive or inherit the whole of the *hereditas* if only one of them is alive. For other ancestors, there is no right of representation. If they pertain to the same line, the estate is divided apiece and when this is not the case it is divided into halves which are attributed to each line and afterwards divided apiece (arts 935–941 CC).

13.59 (3) One of the consequences of the evolution of the family is the modification of the situation of the *surviving spouse.* In order for a spouse to be considered a surviving spouse it is necessary that the marriage actually existed, that is to say, the marriage should not have been declared void, nor should there have been a divorce nor should the judge have declared a separation nor should there be any evidence that there was a factual separation. As seen above, the surviving spouse has a usufruct in the estate, which also exists in intestacy when the spouse is not the heir. The rules for the surviving spouse differ from one legal system to the other, because while in the places where the Civil Code is in force (in Navarra, in the Balearic Islands and in Aragon) the spouse inherits only in the absence of ancestors and progeny, in a more progressive approach, the spouse can be ranked immediately after the children and other progeny as happens in Catalonia.[1]

13.60 (4) In respect of *collaterals,* in all the civil systems in force in Spain preference is given to brothers and sisters and their children. Special rules for more complex cases have also been established (such as the difference between brothers and half-brothers, etc). The right of accretion and the right of representation are limited to brothers and sisters, nephews and nieces, and do not exist for other relatives. The claim for collateral relatives is not without limit, being generally limited to the fourth degree (Civil Code, Catalonia, Balearic Islands, Aragon, Vizcaya) with the exception of Navarra where the limit extended to the sixth degree.

---

1 For the rights of the surviving spouse in Catalonia, see J M Garcia, 'El usufructo vidual abintestado en Cataluña', *Revista Juridica de Catalunya* (1980) 865 and articles 11 and 147 *et seq* of the law on intestacy of Catalonia. Also see M Carcaba, 'Derechos del cónyuge viudo en la sucesión intestada tras la reforma del Código civil', *La Ley* (1986) 1177; J M Chico Ortiz, 'Usufructo vidual', commentary to the decision of the *Dirección General de los Registros y del Notariado* of 27 September 1974, *Anuario de Derecho civil,* (1977) 145.

(5) In the case of the estate of a deceased dying without an intestate heir, Spanish law adopts the *ultimus heres* approach, clearly expressed in the Civil Code (arts 956 *et seq*) in respect of the Spanish State. The same approach has the result that this rule is not in force either in Navarra or in Catalonia; instead, Navarra, Catalonia, Aragon or Galicia takes the property as *ultimus heres*. There also exist several exceptional cases eg for family farms under articles 14 and 27 of the Law of 24 December 1981. 13.61

MATTERS COMMON TO THE DIFFERENT KINDS OF SUCCESSION

The formal opening of the succession process

The only ground for opening the succession process is the *de cujus's* death (art 657 CC); the declaration of decease (*declaración de fallecimiento*) has, however, the same effect as far as succession is concerned (art 196 CC). 13.62

Where two or more people are entitled to inherit property from each other and the order in which their deaths occurred is uncertain, the person who maintains that one of them died first will have to prove it; in the absence of such a proof, there is a presumption that they all died simultaneously (*presunción de conmoriencia* or *commorientes* clause) (art 33 CC). 13.63

A person's entitlement as heir is proved through a *determination (vocación)*, that can follow from a will, from the law and in certain cases from a contract. The specification of the determination is done through a reporting process (*delación*), which begins when the *de cujus* dies: there should be a deed of declaration of inheritance or in the case of intestacy a deed of declaration of heirs. 13.64

The determination as an heir and the *ius delationis* can be transmitted if the heir dies without either accepting or rejecting the estate; this right is called the 'right of transmission' or *ius transmissionis* (art 1006 CC). 13.65

From the moment of death until the heir accepts the estate, there is a *vacatio* in the estate, which is called a 'lying estate' (*herencia yacente*). The person entitled to inherit is generally considered a provisional heir during this period for the purpose only of administering and preserving the estate. For certain particular cases,[1] there are special provisions. 13.66

Capacity to inherit

As a general rule, everyone whose incapacity has not been declared has capacity to inherit (art 744 CC), individuals as well as juridical persons (arts 38 and 746 CC). It is possible to distinguish between an *absolute* incapacity which refers to all possible inheritances and a *relative* incapacity referring to a particular estate. 13.67

---

1 As is the case with the inheritance under suspensive condition and with the rules of articles 965 *et seq* CC in the case of designation of a *nasciturus*. In general, about administration in Spanish law, see Gitrama, *La administración de la herencia en el derecho español*, Madrid 1950.

13.68 The so-called '*absolute* incapacities' affect (art 745 CC) 'abortive creatures', which are the ones not fulfilling the requirements of article 30 of the Civil Code and associations not allowed by the law.

13.69 Birth determines personality (art 29) and in order to have the capacity to be an heir or a legatee the decisive point in time will be the moment of death of the testator or intestate (art 758 CC). Nevertheless, there is no doubt about the rights of succession of a then existing embryo in the womb if he is actually born in the conditions required by article 30.

13.70 The *relative* incapacities refer only to a particular estate. Although there are peculiarities in some Spanish territories,[1] generally it can be said that these relative incapacities refer to three situations. First, the case of dispositions made by the testator during his last illness in favour of the assisting priest, his relatives up to the fourth degree or his church, community or institute (art 752 CC). Second, any disposition made by a pupil in favour of his guardian before the approval of the final account between them (art 753 CC), although this prohibition will not be applicable if the guardian is the pupil's ascendant, descendant, brother or sister or spouse. Third, the testator cannot dispose of his property in favour of the notary or relatives up to the fourth degree (art 754 CC).

13.71 There are cases where the law deprives an heir or legatee of his inheritance on grounds of *unworthiness*. The grounds established are very specific and refer to serious offences, such as parents who abandoned their children or forced their daughters into prostitution; those who attempted to take the life of the testator or some relative; those who accused the testator of having committed a severe crime, if this accusation is declared a calumny; the heir who being of full age has not denounced the violent death of the testator; those who, using menace, fraud or violence, forced the testator into making or revoking a will or those who, by the same means, hindered him from making a new will or substituted, altered or hid a subsequent one; also, any person who knowingly did not present the 'closed' will in his possession in the period of time established by the law.

Acceptance and rejection of the estate

13.72 Acceptance and rejection are unilateral declarations of a person concerning whether or not he wants to be an heir. These declarations cannot be made until there is certainty about the *de cujus*'s death (art 991 CC); they cannot be revoked (art 997 CC) and are indivisible and unconditional (art 990 CC), but they have no personal character: they can be made by a representative expressly empowered to do so (art 1713 CC). There are special provisions (in the Civil Code, in Aragon, Catalonia and Navarra) dealing with the case of minors, incapable and deaf-mute people as well as concerning the case of estates left to the poor or in favour of the soul.

---

1 In Navarra, Catalonia and the Balearic Islands there are incapacities aimed at the protection of the children born of the first wedlock; there are legal limitations as to what the second spouse and the children born in the second wedlock can receive.

Although Catalonia and Navarra follow more closely the system of Roman law, the Civil Code (arts 1004 and 1005) establishes that a claim against the heir that he accepts or rejects the estate can only be introduced nine days after the *de cujus*'s death. The judge will then give the heir a period not exceeding 30 days in which to accept or reject the inheritance, after which period he will be treated as accepting the estate. 13.73

The heir, however, has the so-called *right to deliberate*, that is, he can ask for an inventory before accepting or rejecting the estate. 13.74

The heir may either purely and simply accept the estate or accept it with benefit of an inventory. Pure acceptance can eigher be express or tacit (arts 998–1002). 13.75

In the case of *pure acceptance* it is express if it is done in writing, whether in a public or a private document. Acceptance is tacit in those cases where there are certain acts which are positive and unequivocal and entail acceptance. Acceptance can also derive from the law (art 1002) in the cases where the heirs have either taken out or hidden assets belonging to the estate. 13.76

The judge can also authorise the acceptance by creditors if the heir rejects the estate to their detriment. 13.77

The general principle is that of immediate fusion of the patrimonies of the *de cujus* and the heir and its consequence is the unlimited responsibility of the heir taking all benefits and burdens. In order to maintain the dissociation of patrimonies, the heir can ask for the *benefit of inventory* (arts 1010 CC *et seq*) even in the case of prohibition by the testator. 13.78

The acceptance of the estate with the benefit of inventory can take place before the notary or the judge who has jurisdiction in respect of the will (*juicio de testamentaria*) or intestacy, according to the criteria laid down in article 64, 5 LEC. If the heir is abroad (art 1012) he can undertake this action before a Spanish diplomatic or consular agent in that country. Acceptance with the benefit of inventory or the right to deliberate can only be made before expiry of the limitation period for the action to claim the estate. There are specific provisions (arts 1014 and 1015) for the cases in which the heir already possesses some of the assets which have been left or when a time-limit for acceptance has been fixed. 13.79

The inventory has to be started in the 39 days following a convocation of the heirs and legatees and it has to be finished in another 60 days, unless there is an extension because of special circumstances. In no case can it exceed the period of a year (art 1017 CC). There are special provisions concerning this matter in Catalonia. 13.80

The advantages of acceptance with the benefit of inventory will be lost if by guilty or negligent behaviour the inventory is not finished on time or if the formalities required by the law are lacking; it will also be lost if some assets, rights or actions belonging to the estate are knowingly not included (arts 1018 and 1024 CC). 13.81

The main effect of acceptance is that of acquisition of the status of heir; the effects of acceptance (and rejection) are retroactive; beginning at the moment of the *de cujus*'s death (art 989). The responsibility of the heir will then depend on whether 13.82

the estate's acceptance is pure and simple or with the benefit of inventory. Responsibility towards the legatees for their legacies will also depend on the kind of acceptance. Finally, it is important to note provisions about preferences among the creditors and among the legatees (arts 1027, 1029, 1034 and 1082 CC).

13.83 As will be seen below, several people can be jointly entitled to the estate which they have to share in equal parts: this is the situation of 'estate community' (*comunidad hereditaria*), which is a provisional situation where the heirs are granted the utmost individual independence possible under such circumstances. The Roman system survives in Catalonia and Aragon[1] in the so-called consortium or '*fideicomiso foral*' which does not appear in any provision of the Civil Code.

The distribution of the estate

13.84 The provisional 'estate community' culminates in distribution of the estate. Article 1052 CC provides the general rule according to which any joint heir can ask for distribution of the estate at any moment. If he does not have the power of administering and disposing of his goods, this will be done through his legal representatives. This means that nobody is forced to remain in the 'estate community'. The testator can moreover distribute his goods both partially or totally (*institutio in re certa*), even in the case where the heirs are also entitled to forced shares (*legitimarios*) (arts 815 and 1056).

13.85 Powers of and opportunities for testamentary executors have already been mentioned in paras **13.44–13.47** above, as well as the obligation of bringing into hotchpot (*colación*): see paras **13.40** and **13.42**. If there are no testamentary executors, the heirs proceed on their own to distribution (art 1058). But if they do not reach an agreement amongst themselves, any joint heir may start a distribution process *ab intestato* or by will (*juicio divisorio de abintestato* or *testamentaria*, arts 1002, 1037 and 1038 CC), which means that distribution will be judicial. Arbitration is also possible (following the rules laid down in art 1057) but judicial approbation will be necessary, except in the case where all the heirs and legatees give their express confirmation.

13.86 The general effect of distribution is to attribute to the heir exclusive ownership of the assets which have been adjudicated to him (art 1068). The heirs will be under the reciprocal obligation of 'reparation and eviction' (*saneamiento y evicción*) in respect of the assets which have been attributed to each of them (arts 1069–1072).

One also needs to consider the opportunities to rescind a distribution on the same grounds as those provided in the law of obligations (art 1081), eg for mistake or to rescind on the grounds of damage in those cases where the heir has suffered severe harm. Article 1074 specifies the latter by providing that damage has to exceed one-quarter of the total value at the time when the assets were adjudicated.

1 See on Aragon, Merino Hernandez, *El cousorcio foral*, Zaragaza, (1976); for Catalonia, L Puig Ferriol and E Roca Trìas, *Fundamentos del derecho civil de Cataluña*, t III vol 2, Barcelona (1980) 545.

3. PRIVATE INTERNATIONAL LAW ON SUCCESSION

GENERAL ASPECTS

Due to the diversity of civil law systems in Spain, as indicated above, private international law rules on this matter have a twofold scope. First, they decide in respect of international or external situations, when the circumstances of the case point to one or more foreign legal systems. Second, they decide the position, too, with regard to internal situations, when the *de cujus* is a Spanish national and different civil law systems in force in Spain are connected by the circumstances of the case. The same principle of personality shapes the conflict of law rules on succession in both situations, but different connecting factors are provided for in articles 9, 8 and 16 respectively, and there are other differences with regard to the application of these rules. Therefore, international and internal aspects of succession deserves a distinct treatment. 13.87

In spite of the existing diversity of substantive law on succession, private international law rules in this matter are enacted by the State Parliament (art 149.1.8 of the Constitution). Therefore, they are general in character and are applied by all courts and authorities in Spain as a single private international law system. The following should be noted. 13.88

(1) The jurisdiction of courts in international cases concerning succession is determined in accordance with the Organic Law on Judiciary of 1 July 1985.[1] The last domicile (see (3) below) of the *de cujus* in Spain, or the fact that the *situs* of immovables belonging to the estate is in Spanish territory, are the specific circumstances attributing jurisdiction to the Spanish courts on this matter. But the domicile in Spain of the defendant, or the express or tacit choice by the parties of Spanish courts when the case is connected in some respect to Spain also constitute a general basis of jurisdiction. With regard to internal situations, the territorial jurisdiction of the courts is determined in accordance with the last domicile of the *de cujus*, although particular rules are provided for specific procedures relating to succession (art 63, rules 5, 6, 7 and 22 of *Ley de Enjuiciamiento civil*, 'LEC', the Code of Civil Procedure). 13.89

(2) Choice of law rules, as indicated above, are also general in character. Nevertheless, some of the Compilations of civil law in force in Spain include substantive rules for foreign facts as well as 'unilateral' choice of law rules.[2] But there are also special rules for questions relating to those civil law systems: this is the case, in particular, of Aragon and Navarra, whose laws establish the 13.90

1 M A Amores Caonradi, "La nueva estructura del sistema español de competencia judicial internacional en el orden civil: art 22 LOPJ", *Revista Española de Derecho internacional* (1989) 113.
2 O Casanovas i La Rosa, 'El derecho interregional e interlocal', in *Llibre del II Congrès Jurídic Català*, Barcelona (1972) and his commentary on article 16 CC in *Comentarios a las reformas del Código civil*, Madrid (1977) 735; E Pecourt, 'El nuevo sistema español de derecho interregional', *Ponencia General de las Primeras Jornadas del Instituto español de Derecho foral*, (1975); H Rau, 'Zur Reform des Spanischen und Interregionalen Privatrechts', *IPrax* (1986) 4, 254.

validity of joint wills made outside the respective territory. Joint wills, as indicated above, are not admitted by the Civil Code; but their validity is affirmed in those systems characterising the matter as one belonging to the personal law of the testator applicable to the succession.

13.91 (3) Domicile in Spanish law does not correspond to domicile in English law: it normally coincides with habitual residence but need not (see art 40 CC and arts 62–69 LEC).

CONFLICTS OF LAWS IN INTERNATIONAL SITUATIONS

Nationality of the *de cujus* as the connecting factor

13.92 Article 9, 8 of the Civil Code provides 'Succession to the estate of deceased persons is governed by the national law of the deceased', this rule having been already established by decisions of the Supreme Court prior to the Civil Code of 1889. The guiding principle is unity and universality of the estate, which is reinforced in the provisions stating that the national law is applicable 'whatever may be the nature of the assets in the estate and whatever may be the country in which they are located'.

13.93 Nationality as a connecting factor is determined at the time of the *de cujus*'s death. However, article 9, 8 deals with conflicts resulting from a change of nationality as discussed below in paras **13.98** and **13.115**.

13.94 In case of dual nationalities – largely allowed by Spanish law – the personal law applicable to succession is to be determined in conformity with the provisions of article 9, 9 of the Civil Code, where different situations are considered.[1] The personal law of stateless persons and of those whose nationality is undetermined is the law of the place of their habitual residence.[2]

Wills

13.95 In respect of the *capacity to make a will*, the testator's national law is applicable in accordance with the general provision on capacity of article 9, 1 of the Civil Code; although this is also the law governing succession under article 9, 8 of the Civil Code as indicated above. Incapacity to inherit as well as special prohibitions concerning some persons and estates are governed by the law governing succession.[3]

---

1 M Virgós Soriano, 'Nationality and Double Nationality. Principles in the Spanish Private International Law system', *Nation und Stadt in Internationalen Privatrecht*, Heidelberg (1990) 137. The reform of rules on Nationality (arts 17–26 CC) by the law of 17 November 1990 adds new aspects to the problem, derived from the new article 24.

2 J C Fernandez Rozas, 'Sucesión en el tiempo de la norma de conflicto y ley rectora del estatuto personal del apátrida', *Boletín Informativo del Departamento de Derecho político de la UNED* (1979) 49, commenting on the case *Swinkels* v *Swinkels* (Appeal Court of Granada, decision of 12 February 1975) and his contribution to González Campos *et al*, *op cit*, 15.

3 See E Perez Vera, *Derecho internacional privado. Parte especial*, Madrid (1980) 263; A L Calvo Caravaca in González Campos *et al*, *op cit* 309.

The Civil Code contains a general rule on *testamentary forms* (art 11 CC), as well as other special rules on this matter (arts 732–736). However, from 10 June 1988 Spain is a party to the Hague Convention of 5 October 1961 relating to the form of testamentary dispositions and, since its rules have a universal scope as provided by article 6, they will generally apply to questions concerning the formal validity of wills. Therefore, the *favor testamenti* is the ruling principle in this matter, the 1961 Hague Convention having enlarged the laws under which the formal validity of a will is upheld (*lex loci celebrationis, lex patriae, lex domicilii,* the law of the place of the habitual residence, either at the time of the disposal or at the time of the testator's death and, in respect of immovables, the *lex situs*). However, due to the content of article 4 of the Hague Convention, a problem arises on the applicability of the unilateral conflict of laws rule set out in article 733 of the Civil Code, a provision forbidding joint wills made abroad by a Spanish national whose personal law, on the basis of articles 14 and 16, is the civil law system of the Civil Code.[1] 13.96

The disposal of the estate upon death as the ordinary content of the will is governed by the deceased's national law. Therefore, the freedom of disposition or otherwise the restrictions imposed by law for the benefit of some person (indefeasible shares, reserves in respect of some assets) as well as the duty of restoring to the estate gifts made exceeding the freely disposable portion are subjected to the *lex successionis.*[2] Moreover, the appointment of testamentary executors and the powers given to them are subjected to the same law; although two decisions of the Supreme Court have considered applicable the law of the place where the will was executed.[3] 13.97

Agreements as to succession

Article 9, 8 refers to 'succession to the estates of deceased persons', without distinguishing the origin of the succession rights and, in respect of the change of the deceased's national law, this article expressly deals with contracts on succession (*pactos sucesorios*). Therefore, it is generally accepted that the validity and legal effect of an agreement as to succession are governed by the *lex successionis,* the national law of the *de cujus.*[4] 13.98

---

1 On this problem, see J A Carrillo Salcedo, 'La forma de las disposiciones testamentarias', *Revista Española de Derecho internacional,* 1961, p 169; Calvo Caravaca in González Campos *et al, op cit,* p 533. Spain has not made the reservation allowed by article 11 of the 1961 Hague Convention. For the use of special testamentary forms by foreigners, see A Borrás, 'Los extranjeros y los testamentos especiales', *Materials de les III Jornades de Dret Català a Tossa* (1984) III.

2 The Supreme Court in a confusing, and much criticised, decision of 23 October 1992 has included indefeasible shares in *ordre public.* See J C Fernàndez Rozas and S Sánchez, *Derecho internacional privado* 2nd ed, Madrid (1993) 508.

3 Supreme Court decisions of 27 May 1913 and 11 February 1952, the latter in respect of a will made in Spain by a French national. To the contrary, the application of the law governing the succession is affirmed by the decisions of 1 February 1910, 10 October 1960 and 10 December 1966. In favour of this conclusion, see M Albadalejo, *El albaceazgo en el Derecho español,* Madrid (1969) 691, although he considers that the capacity to be testamentary executor is governed by the personal law of the person appointed to perform this task. The application of the law governing the succession to this question is, however, preferable.

4 This conclusion, now set out by article 9, 8 CC after the reform of 1974, was affirmed in 1971 by J D González Campos in M Aguilar Navarro (ed), *Derecho internacional privado. Derecho civil internacional,* University of Madrid (1971) 240.

13.99 Two questions, however, have to be determined. First, in respect of the moment at which the national law is to be crystallised, it is accepted that it will be the time when the agreement as to succession was made.[1] Second, if the deceased changes his nationality, the content of the agreement has to be adjusted to the national law at the moment of death with regard to the indefeasible shares (*legítimas*) when the latter provides such restriction upon the freedom of disposal of the *de cujus*, as indicated above.[2]

Intestacy

13.100 Since the Spanish system is a system which governs succession by a sole law, determined by nationality of the deceased at the moment of his death this law will, in general, govern intestate succession though, in practice, a foreign *lex situs* may apply to immovables, eg in England, because Spanish law cannot impose its unity rule in respect of immovables situated in a jurisdiction applying the scission rule and so applying the *lex situs* to immovables. The scope of the applicable law is very large.[3] This law determines when intestacy takes effect (and, especially, the question of compatibility with testate succession), the order and limits of inheritance (especially, the situation of the surviving spouse and the limitation upon inheritance for collaterals), the existence of a right of representation and of a right of accretion, etc.

13.101 In the case of existence of a particular inheritance regime in respect of special categories of assets, it must be noted that such provisions have territorial applicability,[4] subject to the need for compensation for the other beneficiaries of indefeasible shares (*legitimarios*) in order to respect the law governing succession generally.

13.102 Where there is no intestate heir, Spain adopts the *ultimus heres* approach. There is no specific provision for international situations. The problem is, therefore, a question of classification that, according to article 12, 1 of the Civil Code must be answered by Spanish law.[5] The classification of the Spanish State as heir has been accepted by the English courts in a case of intestacy of a Spanish national, domiciled in Spain, without relatives who owned movables situated in the UK.[6] Consequently, the assets passed to the Spanish State. When Spanish substantive

---

1 J D González Campos, *op cit* in the previous footnote, p 241, indicating the similarity with the rule on the capacity to dispose by will. Also, A L Calvo Caravaca in J D González Campos *et al, op cit*, 307; A Marin López, *Derecho internacional privado español*, vol II, Granada (1990) 277.

2 On the restrictions that such an adjustment may involve for the agreement as to succession, see also V L Simó Santonja in M Verwilghen (ed), *Régimes matrimoniaux, successions et liberalités*, vol I, Neuchatel (1979) 732.

3 The Supreme Court decision of 10 December 1966 says that 'applying the national law is not just limited, as the appellant demands, to the determination of the heir, but also embraces all the legal limitations established by this law as a part of the succession law and, for this reason, the law excluding the goods of the heir from paying the debts of the deceased'.

4 Decision of the *Dirección General de los Registros y del Notariado* of 1 April 1980, commentary of P Dominguez Lozano in *Revista Española de Derecho Internacional* (1982) 571. Also, in general about this kind of disposition, V L Simó Santonja, *Derecho sucesorio comparado. Conflictos de leyes en materia de sucesiones*, Madrid (1968) 43.

5 E Pérez Vera, *op cit*, 259; A L Calvo Caravaca in González Campos, *op cit*, 557.

6 *In the Estate of Maldonado* (1954).

law has to be applied, the pluralism of Spanish succession law has to be noted and, subsequently, the assets have to be given the destination provided in the substantive law of the applicable law (see para **13.119** below, for the case of being referred to the law of a state with territorial units).

Matters common to the different kinds of succession

Although the personal law determined by nationality has in Spain a large scope in questions related to succession, some matters need to be emphasised. 13.103

Spanish private international law on succession does not contain a rule related to *commorientes*, as in the Benelux Convention or in the Hague Convention of 1 August 1989 (art 13). Therefore, the main solution is to apply the personal laws of the deceased persons; if they are incompatible or say nothing about the question, only the *lex fori* can be applied.[1] 13.104

The *lex successionis* must be applied to the commencement of the succession process and to the declaration of estate, including determining the heirs and legatees and, in any case, the essential validity of the will. It is possible, however, to invoke public policy.[2] 13.105

Since the acceptance of the estate is an essential element of succession, it must be governed by the *lex successionis*, including acceptance with the benefit of inventory. However, other laws may interfere: the personal law of the heir or legatee determines his capacity and the complementary need to accept or to reject the estate, but relative capacity and unworthiness must be governed by the *lex successionis* because they are connected with a particular estate; also, for other questions, the law of acceptance or the *lex rei sitae* may apply. 13.106

The distribution of the estate is governed, in principle, by the *lex successionis*, which also determines who is allowed to ask for the distribution. There is no agreement on whether article 1052, seen in para **13.84** above, has the characteristic of public policy or not. But the *lex successionis* should, in any case, be applied to the bringing of property into hotchpot, the reduction of gifts, the order of legacies, the definitive attribution of the assets, etc. Other laws may, however, have some bearing on the question, such as the law of the co-heirs, the *lex fori* or the *lex rei sitae*. 13.107

When all the requirements for distribution are accomplished and every heir has his 'title of acquisition' (*título de adquisición*), compliance with the requirements of the Spanish *Registro de la Propriedad* (according to art 14 of the *Ley Hipotecaria* and arts 36–37 of the *Reglamento hipotecaria* that almost reproduce arts 600–601 LEC) is then necessary if there are assets requiring inscription. Moreover, it should be remembered that Spain is a party to the Hague Convention abolishing the requirement of legalisation for foreign public documents from 1978. 13.108

---

1 A L Calvo Caravaca in J D González Campos, *op cit*, 561.

2 As in *Ferriol Rodriguez v Ferriol Varela*, Supreme Court decision of 10 October 1960, commentary of E Pecourt Garcia, in *Revista Española de Derecho internacional* (1963) 144–148.

13.109 Property rights, interests or assets created or transferred otherwise than by way of succession, such as property in joint ownership with rights of survival (eg a foreign joint tenancy), pension plans, insurance contracts, or arrangements of a similar nature, are not included as matters of succession. Therefore, they are not governed by the *lex successionis* but by the applicable law for the specific question.

13.110 The rules on foreign investments or on foreign exchange control cause problems of succession, especially as to the ability of foreigners under the law of the *situs* to own certain properties.

13.111 Besides the traditional problems of private international law, fiscal problems related to succession must be taken into account. Until recently, Spain had not paid sufficient attention to tax problems related to succession. Although Spain is a party to a great number of conventions to avoid double taxation on income and patrimony, only two conventions try to avoid double taxation on estates and inheritances (with France and Sweden).[1] There were no internal rules on double taxation on inheritances until the Law of 18 December 1987. The general connection for the obligation to pay taxes is the habitual residence of the deceased person in Spain (art 6) and if he has no habitual residence in Spain, a real obligation would exist as regards the assets situated in Spain (art 7). In order to avoid double taxation, article 23 establishes the tax credit system, but the tax sparing clause is not accepted.[2]

General topics in private international law of succession

13.112 As regards classification or characterisation the rule is classification or characterisation by the *lex fori*.

Special attention must be paid to *renvoi*, because the application of the deceased's national law to govern succession to the whole of his estate movable and immovable may be modified by it. Article 12, 2 of the Civil Code accepts only *renvoi* to the first degree. But the problem arises when the national law is a system providing distinct connecting factors for movable and immovable assets and only the deceased's residence or the *situs* of the immovable assets is in Spain, other assets or the domicile being in a foreign country. This is the case in English law where movables are governed by English law as the law of the deceased's last domicile while immovables are governed by the *lex situs*. The problem becomes acute where Spanish and English law differ eg as to those entitled upon the

1 See González Poveda, *Tratados y convenios internacionales en materia de doble imposición*, Madrid (1988). About the general problems of double taxation in Spain and of the convention to avoid it, see A Borrás, *La doble imposición: problemas jurídico-internacionales*, Madrid (1974), 109, and 'Los convenios internacionales para evitar la doble imposición desde el punto de vista de la teoría general de los tratados internacionales', in *Estudios de doble imposición*, Madrid (1980); J M de la Villa, 'La doble imposición en al ámbito sucesorio: su filosofia y evolución histórica. La realidad española', a study accompanying the Spanish translation of the model convention to avoid double taxation for estates and inheritances, Madrid (1985).

2 On the new situation see A Borrás, 'La nueva regulación del impuesto sobre sucesiones y donaciones. Problemas internacionales de su aplicación', in J Ferreiro (ed), *Comentarios a la nueva ley del impuesto sobre sucesiones y donaciones*, Madrid (1988) 103.

deceased's intestacy and as to whether or not there are any forced indefeasible shares in the estate.

In this situation, *renvoi* to the first degree, as provided by Spanish law, may lead to the scission of the succession with Spanish law governing Spanish immovables, a result contrary to the principle of unity embodied in article 9, 8 of the Civil Code. To exclude such a result, it has been proposed that *renvoi* should not be admitted in this case and although the courts in general apply *renvoi* in the first degree, some recent decisions include the idea of respecting the unity of succession. This interpretation was given some years ago by an English court[1] in a way differing from the Spanish doctrine on *renvoi* as included in article 12, 2 of the Civil Code and as then applied by Spanish courts. The doctrine has been sensitive to the problem,[2] but Spanish courts only recently started to point it out in a decision of the *Tribunal Supremo*[3] and in another case in which *renvoi* is accepted but Spanish law was applicable to the whole estate.[4] It is worth observing, however, that if unity of succession is the paramount criterion under article 9 to admit or to exclude *renvoi*, domicile of a British national either in the UK or in Spain should be the controlling issue: when domicile is in the UK, *renovi* would be excluded and the unity of succession so secured; on the contrary, when domicile is in Spain, the unity of succession is attained by applying Spanish law accepting *renvoi*. 13.113

---

1 The unreported decision of Browne-Wilkinson V-C on 31 July 1985, High Court of Justice, Chancery Division, in which a British national, domiciled in England disposed by will of a Spanish immovable in favour of the surviving spouse and excluded his son, yet the court rejected the son's claim that Spanish, and not English, law applied; see J L Iriarte, 'Doble reenvío y unidad de tratamiento de las sucesiones', *Revista General de Derecho* (1989) 3561.

2 In favour of the construction of preferring article 9 to article 12 and of excluding *renvoi* in the cases in which the result is scission see A L Calvo Caravaca in J D González Campos, *op cit*, 544. Similarly, an article has focused on the situation of English people living in Spain and the Canary Islands: see Perez Voituriez, A 'El reenvío en el Derecho internacional privado español: una interpretación actualizada', *Revista Jurídica del Notariado*, 13, January–March 1995, pp 257–337.

3 In the decision of the *Tribunal Supremo* of 15 November 1996 (published in *La Ley* 13 January 1997, pp 7–10) the unity and universality of Spanish law on succession serves as a basis to refuse *renvoi* and to reverse the decision of the *Audiencia* of Granada of 22 December 1988, in which the succession of a citizen of the State of Maryland (USA) in respect of immovables situated in Spain was governed by Spanish domestic law, as a consequence of the rules of Maryland, which establish that succession to immovables is governed by the *lex situs*. See note on the decision of the *Audiencia* by M Moya in *Revista Española de Derecho internacional*, 1990, 2,634. In the same sense as the decision of Granada, see decision of the *Audiencia* of Barcelona of 9 November 1994, *Revista Jurídica de Cataluña*, 1995, 2, p 345.

4 Decision of the *Audiencia de Málaga* of 18 December 1996 (not yet published) in the case of the succession of a British national domiciled in Spain and with immovables situated in Spain: *renvoi* to the first degree is accepted according to article 12, 2, but attention is paid to the fact that immovables situated in Spain are the only ones he had and, consequently, the unity of succession is maintained, applying Spanish law to the totality of the estate. Problems of relationship between unity of succession and *renvoi* are also pointed out in the decision of the *Audiencia Provincial de Badajoz* of 11 July 1995, although the Court did not have the opportunity to decide on the substance after accepting the existence of the procedural exception that had been presented; see comments to this decision by J Carrascosa, in *Revista Española de Derecho internacional*, 1996, 2 (pp 312–321).

13.114 The applicable law must be excluded if *public policy* or *fraude à loi* intervenes. The ambit of public policy is difficult because of the great differences existing among the different civil law systems of succession in force in Spain and differing between them in essential questions (such as the forced shares, as seen above). In the application of foreign law, the party invoking it must prove its tenor and that it is in force but the judge is allowed to use all his inquisitional powers in obtaining the relevant proof. When the applicable law is that of a State with units where different succession laws apply, the governing law must be determined by the law of that State. There is no rule to cover the void which results when the law of that State does not provide such a rule.[1]

Although strongly related to succession, there is no special provision on the *incidental question* (marriage, filiation). The generally accepted opinion is to apply to the incidental question the *lex formalis fori*.[2]

13.115 The incidence of the time factor must be taken into account especially in relation to two questions:

(1) In relation to the so-called *conflit mobile*, article 9, 8 deals with conflicts resulting from a change of nationality, by providing that testamentary dispositions, as well as agreements as to succession, which were entered into in conformity with the personal law of the testator or of the person making a disposition at the time when the will or other disposition was made, will retain their validity even though the law which governs the succession is different; but the indefeasible shares (*legítimas*), if any, will be governed by the national law at the time of the deceased's death. Adjustment between both personal laws is required for the benefit of those persons entitled to the *legítima* in accordance with the latter.

(2) In relation to the problems deriving from the interrelationship of matrimonial property regimes with succession law and the problem of the succession rights of the surviving spouse, the recent amendment of the Civil Code[3] has established that the rights of the surviving spouse will be governed

1 Article 12 being not exclusive to succession matters, see general commentaries in *Comentarios a las reformas del Código civil, op cit* and in *Comentarios al Código civil y Compilaciones forales, op cit.* About the specific problem of article 12, 5 and the problem of the governing law when the applicable law is that of a State with units where different succession laws apply, M P Andrés, 'El article 12. 5 del Código civil y el problema de la remisión a un ordenamiento purilegislativo', *Revista General de Legislación y Jurisprudenca* (1978) 1; E Jayme, 'Spanisches interregionales und deutsches internationales Privatrecht', *Iprax* (1989), 5, 287. For a case concerned with *renvoi* and with the applicable law in a reference *ad intra*, there is a traditional example in the decision of the judge of the District of the Hospital of Barcelona, of 3 August 1900, about succession of a Scot domiciled in Barcelona, *Revista Jurídica de Cataluña* (1901) 173.

2 J C Fernandez Rozas – S Sanchez Lorenzo, *Curso de Derecho internacional privado*, 2nd edn, Madrid, 1991 p 503.

3 Law of 15 October 1990, modifying the Civil Code in application of the principles of non-discrimination due to sex. About the rights of the surviving spouse, E Zabalo, *La situación juridica del cónyuge viudo. Estudio en el Derecho internacional privado y derecho interregional*, Pamplona, 1993. It is also possible to consider the problems derived from the interrelationship of trust with succession; see M A Asin, 'La ley aplicable al trust en el sistema de derecho internacional privado español', *Revista General de Derecho* (1990) 2089. C González Beilfuss, El trust. *La institución angloamericana y el Derecho internacional privado español*, Barcelona, 1997.

by the same law as that governing matrimonial property, without detriment to the indefeasible shares (*legítimas*) of progeny.

CONFLICTS OF LAW IN INTERNAL SITUATIONS

General aspects

The problem of determination of the applicable law when the law designated by the international conflict of laws rule is that of a State with units where different succession laws apply, is a common problem for all the States, because it is always possible that the conflict of law rule designates a non-unified legal order. But Spain, being a State with different substantive laws on succession, as seen above, has also the internal problem of determining the applicable law when succession to a person's estate is connected with different territorial units. This is dealt with in the so-called *derecho interregional* or private international law for internal situations. 13.116

Article 16 CC is the main rule to determine the applicable law in these cases. It provides that the conflict of law rules for international situations will also be applied for internal situations, but establishes some peculiarities, referring to the connecting factor and to the general topics of private international law.[1] 13.117

The *vecindad civil* of the *de cujus* as connecting factor

For internal situations, the connecting factor is *vecindad civil*. The reason is that in internal situations nationality does not determine one of the Spanish laws on succession, because there are no different nationalities. *Vecindad civil* is a difficult juridical concept,[2] used only to determine the application of one of the civil laws in force in Spain. *Vecindad civil* is not always coincidental with administrative dependence, from which emanates the political quality that determines the appurtenance to one or another Autonomous Community. 13.118

In order to determine the *vecindad civil*, the rules of articles 14 and 15 must be applied. It is worth stressing the following. 13.119

(1) All people with Spanish nationality have a *vecindad civil*, and only Spanish nationals have *vecindad civil*. For this reason, in the cases where Spanish law is applicable to non-Spanish nationals, one of the laws in force in Spain will not be applied as the law of the *vecindad civil*, but only as the law of the domicile, the law of the habitual residence or the *lex situs*.

---

1 See, A Arce, *Comunidades Autónomas y conflicto de leyes, op cit*, A Borrás, *Calificación, reenvío y orden público en derecho interregional español*, Barcelona (1984) and A Borrás, 'Les ordres plurilégislatif dans le droit international privé actuel', *Recueil des cours de l'Académie de Droit international*, vol 249 (1994–V) pp 145–368.

2 See M Coca, 'Vecindad administrativa y vecindad civil: génesis de un concepto legal', *Revista Jurídica de Catalunya* (1981) 133; P Dominguez, *Las circumstancias personales determinantes de la vinculación con el derecho local*, Madrid (1988); I Ribas, *La vecindad civil: problemática en torno a su régimen juridico y a su prueba*, Barcelona (1984).

(2) Many of the questions of *derecho interregional* are focused on the problem of *vecindad civil*, which is the connecting factor upon which the governing law depends; because the substantive laws in force in Spain are so different (and in main questions, such as the amount of the indefeasible shares (*legítimas*) or the rights of the surviving spouse), the fixation of the applicable law is a primary question.

13.120 The incidence of other applicable laws is also possible, especially in the so-called *sucesión troncal*, concerned with inheritance of special family assets. This has already been discussed in para **13.6** but it has a clear territorial element. Other reserves do not have this character.

13.121 The law determined through the connecting factor has, as in the international situations, a large scope, on the one hand as regards wills and agreements as to succession and, on the other hand, concerning the rules for the protection of the family, especially in respect of the indefeasible shares (*legítimas*).

13.122 Besides the general rules, the different civil laws on succession in force in Spain provide for some traditional wills, for which there is no conflict of laws rule but substantive rules as well as 'unilateral' choice of law rules, as seen above, to determine who, and under what conditions, can make such a will. However, in some cases they must be considered as historical vestiges, difficult to understand in a modern world and in a temporal State.

13.123 The applicable law has a very large scope on intestacy, for internal situations as well as for international ones. The problem arises as regards succession to the estate of the deceased when there is no intestate heir. If the same classification allowed for international situations is allowed for internal situations (*ultimum heres* approach), it is clear that the personal law has to determine the destination of the assets and the heir need not be the State because it can be an Autonomous Community as in Catalonia or the territorial unit corresponding to the *vecindad civil* of the *de cujus* as in the Basque country.

General topics in derecho interregional

13.124 The main rule in article 16, 2 of the Civil Code provides that rules 1, 2 and 3 of article 12 do not apply to internal situations. That means that the rules on classification, *renvoi* and public policy are excluded. However, the situation is not so easy; it is clearly impossible to find problems related to *renvoi* and public policy in the present situation in Spain, because there is a single private international law system for internal situations. But this is not the case with the problem of classification: it is a very common question in internal situations and classification is needed. The rule of article 12, 1 establishing a *lex fori* classification is useless, since all the laws are internal ones, so it may be that classification should be determined by the *lex civilis litis* (the law in which the institution is regulated). The other general topics like fraud are possible as well in internal situations; the most common ones are the *conflit mobile* and the problem of the interrelationship between matrimonial regimes and succession law, because they are much more frequent in internal situations than in international ones.

4. TAXES ON DEATH

The law presently in force for inheritance tax is to be found in the Law 29/1987 of 18 December (*BOE* of 19 December 1987).[1] Article 2 provides that the tax will be in force in 'the whole of the national territory' with two exceptions, one relating to the taxation regimes of Covenant and Financial Conventions in force exclusively in the Basque Country and Navarra, the other to 'the provisions of Treaties and International Conventions'. However, it must be said that Spain has only concluded two Conventions in the field of inheritance: one with France, concluded on 8 January 1963 (*BOE* of 7 and 30 January 1964); the other with Sweden, concluded on 25 April 1963 (*BOE* of 16 January 1964). A third Convention, concluded with Greece on 6 March 1919, is not purely a double taxation Convention, but it does establish the rules to be applied to the succession of Spaniards and Greeks in each country (*Gaceta* of 3 December 1920).[2] The absence of any other Conventions leads to the application of Spanish law in most cases. 13.125

Concerning the scope of application of the law, the following must be said: 13.126

(1) Article 1 establishes that the taxes on inheritances and gifts are to be considered as 'direct and subjective' and as taxes on 'increases in the estate of natural persons based on a lucrative title'.
(2) The territorial scope is defined as being the whole of the Spanish territory, with the exceptions contained in article 2, above. Furthermore, according to the first autonomous disposition, 'the cession of the revenue of the tax to the Autonomous Communities shall be governed by the appropriate laws of succession'.
(3) According to article 5, in the following situations certain classes of individuals are obliged to pay tax:

    (a) in *mortis causa* acquisitions, the heirs or beneficiaries;
    (b) with regard to gifts and similar lucrative transfers, the donee or beneficiary;
    (c) with regard to life assurance payments, the beneficiaries.

The law uses personal and real (or territorial) connecting factors to establish liability. 13.127

(1) *Personal liability* derives from the fact that the taxpayer who is the heir or recipient of a gift is habitually resident in Spain, irrespective 'of where the goods or rights which make up the taxable increase of the estate are located' (art 6, para 1). To establish the existence of habitual residence, the law refers

---

1 For an overview of the essential features of this law, see Agulló, A, Borrás, A, Ferreiro, J J, Pérez Royo, F and Ramallo, J (1988) *Comentarios a la nueva Ley de Impuesto sobre Sucesiones y Donaciones*, Madrid.

2 For a detailed review of these Conventions, see Borrás, A, (1980) 'Los convenios internacionales para evitar la doble imposición desde el punto de vista de la teoría general de los tratados internacionales', in *Estudios de doble imposición*, Madrid, pp 23,74, and Sánchez, M A, (1991) *La doble imposición internacional en materia de sucesiones y donaciones*, Granada.

to the provisions of the Law regulating the income tax of natural persons, which establishes that 'a stay for more than 183 days during the natural year in Spanish territory shall be deemed to constitute habitual residence', and goes on to add that 'to estimate the period of habitual residence, absences shall not be taken into account if, due to the circumstances under which these take place, it can be inferred that they do not have a duration of more than 3 years'. Consequently, when the deceased resides in Spain but the beneficiary resides, and the goods are located, outside Spain, there is no liability to pay inheritance tax in Spain.

(2) *Real liability* exists for those taxpayers who do not habitually reside in Spain and for whom the obligation to pay arises out of:

> 'the acquisition of goods or rights, whatever their nature, situated, liable to be exercised or which have to be discharged in Spanish territory, as well as the receipt of sums deriving from Spanish insurance companies or in Spain with foreign companies operating in its territory.'

13.128 In determining the liability to pay tax, two types of deduction exist:

(1) deductions respecting a 'tax-exempt minimum' which take account of the relationship between the deceased and the beneficiary as well as the age of the beneficiary; and
(2) deductions relating to the same goods or their exchange product which have been subject to two or more *mortis causa* transfers in favour of descendants during the previous ten years. In this case, aside from the deductions due to tax-exempt minimum, the amounts of tax previously paid will be deducted from the tax due.

13.129 The rate of the tax has a unified character, independent of the relationship between the beneficiary and the deceased. The minimum is set at 7.65% and the maximum at 34%. The difference in treatment due to blood relationships is achieved by the application of multiplying rates which vary according to the degree of consanguinity. These multiplying rates also take into account the pre-existing estate of the beneficiary.

13.130 To avoid international double taxation, article 23 establishes:

> 'when liability to the tax arises from personal liability, the taxpayer has a right to deduct the smallest of the following amounts:
>
> (a) the actual amount paid in another country for a similar tax affecting the increase of the estate which is subject to tax in Spain;
> (b) the result of applying the actual average rate of this tax to the increase in the estate deriving from goods situated or rights which can be exercised outside Spain when they have been subject to a similar tax abroad.'

The Spanish system thus incorporates the tax credit method; it is not a clause of attribution of unpaid taxes, or a tax exemption clause. Therefore only sums effectively paid are attributed.

13.131 Finally, it is necessary to consider Royal Decree Law 7/1996 of 7 June on urgent fiscal measures and promotion and liberalisation of economic activity (*BOE* of 8 June 1996). This introduced a new paragraph to article 25 of the Law regulating the Inheritance and Gifts Tax. This amendment establishes the mechanism for assessment of the chargeable amount when the benefit on which tax is to be assessed includes the value of a private company or shares in companies to which the exemption established in the Law regulating estate tax applies.

In the event of a *mortis causa* acquisition by the spouse, the descendants or the adopted children of the deceased, notwithstanding other reductions contemplated in the same article which may be applicable, in assessing the chargeable amount a reduction of 95% must be applied. This new paragraph requires that the acquisition be retained for ten years after the death of the deceased, except if the beneficiary dies within that period. *Mortis causa* acquisitions of the deceased's home also benefit from this percentage reduction, subject to a limit of 20 million pesetas per taxable person, when the beneficiaries are the spouse, ancestors or descendants, or collateral relations over 65 years of age who had lived with the deceased during the two years immediately preceding his death. This may be of special interest to foreign spouses who acquire a home in Spain where they usually reside. 13.132

5. WAYS FOR FOREIGNERS TO MINIMISE PROBLEMS

There are two kinds of questions to be considered:

(1) *Succession questions.* It is always easier if the *de cujus* has a will and there is no intestacy. There are, however, the 'three famous falsehoods',[1] which must be excluded. These are: 13.133

   (1) that, if a house has been acquired in Spain, it is necessary to make a Spanish will;
   (2) that, by making a Spanish will, Spanish problems as to succession will be solved; and
   (3) that, in the absence of a Spanish will, all the assets will be seized on death by the Spanish State.

It must be emphasised that it is perfectly sufficient to have a valid will made outside Spain, even if it includes assets located in Spain. However, it may be advisable to have a will made in Spanish and sworn before a Spanish notary to simplify matters. In all cases concerning assets located in Spain, consideration must be given to the indefeasible shares established by the Spanish civil law system in case of *renvoi* to Spanish law. If this has not been done, the will will not be abrogated, but the persons entitled to the indefeasible shares (*legítimas*) will retain their rights. It is worth noting the changing position of Spanish courts as explained in para **13.113**

1 See further Thomas de Maurice B, 'El heredero inglés. El proceso sucesorío inglés y los problemas de conflícto de la ley inglesa' *Boletín del Ilustre Colegio Notarial de Granada*, November 1993. This article also concerned the situation of English people in Spain, in this case the Costa del Sol; and Sain-Lopez Negrete, M 'El derecho de sucesiones inglés. Conflicto entre la ley espagñola y la ley inglesa' *Revista Jurídica del Notariado*, October–December 1994, pp 119–147.

on *renvoi* so that the Spanish immovables of a British national domiciled in England should not be subject to Spanish forced heirship claims.

13.134 (2) *Fiscal questions.* Adequate fiscal planning, not only concerning inheritance tax purposes, but especially in the case of beneficiaries inheriting assets from a non-UK domiciled deceased can result in significant tax benefits. For example, it may help to set up a patrimonial company or a company merely concerned with the owning of assets, particularly if these are immovables; as in this case the succession concerns shares and not immovables, this being particularly useful when the heirs are already shareholders in the company. Other formulae can be used, such as the constitution of an annuity or a donation in usufruct, which enable property to be transmitted and benefits to be reserved.

CHAPTER 14

SWITZERLAND[†]

1. PRIVATE INTERNATIONAL LAW

INTRODUCTION

Switzerland's Federal Code on Private International Law (CPIL) came into force on 1 January 1989 and has replaced the former Statute on the Private Law Conditions of Domiciliaries and Sojourners (*NAG*).[1] Chapter 6 (arts 86–96 CPIL) deals with the law of inheritance. It is subdivided into jurisdiction, applicable law and recognition. 14.1

The connecting factor *Wohnsitz* is translated throughout this chapter as 'habitual residence'. For the purpose of the CPIL, an individual has his habitual residence in the country in which he is living with the intention of residing there permanently (art 20(1)(a) CPIL). The Federal Tribunal has held that an objective test applies to decide whether residence is habitual. Thus, to fulfil this test, it must be recognisable to third parties that the person has made or intends to make his residence the centre of his living. As the establishment of habitual residence does not require a certain duration of sojourn, a person can be habitually resident from the first day of his sojourn. 14.2

According to article 20(2) CPIL, no individual can be habitually resident in more than one place at the same time. If a person has no habitual residence, then his ordinary residence (*gewöhnlicher Aufenthalt*) serves to replace habitual residence. Ordinary residence is circumscribed as being in the country in which the person is living for a certain time, even if this time is limited from the outset (art 20(1)(b) CPIL). 14.3

JURISDICTION

General rule (*habitual residence*)

According to article 86(1) CPIL, the Swiss judicial or administrative authorities at the last habitual residence of the deceased have jurisdiction for probate proceedings and inheritance disputes. This provision confers jurisdiction upon 14.4

---

† This chapter was written by Duri Berther, Attorney-at-Law, Gürtelstrasse 37, 7000 Chur, Switzerland.

1 *Bundesgesetz vom 25 Juni 1891 betreffend die zivierechteichen Verhältnisse der Niedergelassenen und Aufenthalter.*

the Swiss authorities over the deceased's entire estate, wherever his property is situated (universal jurisdiction).

14.5 This Swiss jurisdiction at the deceased's last habitual residence is neither exclusive nor mandatory. Where a foreign country claims exclusive jurisdiction over immovables situated in its territory, article 86(2) CPIL restricts the Swiss authorities' world-wide jurisdiction with regard to that property for reasons of efficacy. By way of such voluntary limitation the Swiss jurisdiction is prevented from competing with the foreign *situs*-State. Furthermore, the parties can by choice of jurisdiction (art 5 CPIL), unconditional appearance (*vorbehaltlose Einlassung*; art 6 CPIL) or arbitration agreement (arts 7 and 177 CPIL) choose another jurisdiction.

Jurisdiction at place of citizenship

14.6 Where the deceased was a Swiss citizen habitually resident abroad, Swiss authorities normally do not have jurisdiction. However, in two cases, article 87 CPIL grants a subsidiary Swiss jurisdiction.

14.7 The first case concerns a situation where foreign authorities do not deal with the deceased's estate, irrespective of whether they remain passive for factual or legal reasons. In this case, para 1 confers jurisdiction upon the Swiss judicial or administrative authorities at the place of the deceased's Swiss citizenship to the extent that foreign authorities do not deal with the estate.

It is noteworthy that where a Swiss national also has the citizenship of another country, then for the determination of the jurisdiction at the place of citizenship his Swiss citizenship alone is relevant (art 23(1) CPIL). This applies whether or not the person has the citizenship of a country with which he has a close connection.

14.8 Second, the Swiss authorities always have jurisdiction where a Swiss citizen dying habitually resident abroad, has, by will or testamentary pact, subjected his assets in Switzerland, or his entire estate, to Swiss jurisdiction or to Swiss law (art 87(2) CPIL). According to this provision, article 86(2) CPIL also applies where Swiss jurisdiction over immovable property situated abroad is based upon *professio fori* or *professio juris*.

Jurisdiction at place of assets

14.9 Article 88(1) CPIL provides for a further subsidiary Swiss jurisdiction. Where a foreigner habitually resident abroad at death leaves movable or immovable property located in Switzerland, the Swiss judicial or administrative authorities at the place of the property have jurisdiction to the extent to which the foreign authorities (for factual or legal reasons) remain passive. If there is property at more than one place in Switzerland, the Swiss authorities first called upon have jurisdiction (art 88(2) CPIL).

Protective measures

Where the deceased (Swiss or foreigner) dies habitually resident abroad and leaves property in Switzerland, the Swiss authorities at the place of the property have to take provisional measures necessary to protect the property (art 89 CPIL). 14.10

APPLICABLE LAW

One characteristic of the CPIL is that the law applicable to the estate (*lex successionis*) always hinges upon the Swiss authorities having jurisdiction, ie it determines the applicable law only to the extent to which Swiss authorities have jurisdiction. 14.11

Objectively applicable law

Person dies last habitually resident in Switzerland

Where a person dies habitually resident in Switzerland, his estate is governed by Swiss law (art 90(1) CPIL). Swiss law applies to all his assets wherever situated (principle of unity), unless a foreign *situs*-State claims exclusive jurisdiction over its immovables. It is noteworthy that although Swiss authorities have to decline jurisdiction over the foreign immovable property in such an exceptional case and the Swiss winding up is subsequently regarded as separate from that of the *situs*-State, commentators generally seem to take the view that principles of justice and equity can demand that the foreign position with regard to the foreign immovables be considered in Switzerland. This approach aims to prevent unjust results with regard to issues like forced heirship and heirship quotas or estate-debts. 14.12

Person dies last habitually resident abroad

Where a person dies habitually resident abroad, his estate is governed by the law determined by the conflicts of law rules of the country of such habitual residence (art 91(1) CPIL). This is one of the few provisions in the CPIL which expressly provides for a *renvoi*. The meaning of this *renvoi*, however, is argued amongst writers and has not yet been settled by case-law. Whilst several commentators construe the *renvoi* as requiring a Swiss judge to accept a referral back (remission) or a referral on to the law of a third jurisdiction (transmission), others construe the *renvoi* as being one in the sense of the foreign court theory, ie requiring the Swiss judge to apply exactly the same law that the foreign judge would apply if he were hearing the case. 14.13

From the Swiss viewpoint this *renvoi*-issue is normally unproblematical because this provision only applies in the exceptional case where Swiss authorities have jurisdiction under article 88 CPIL. However, it becomes more important where questions relating to succession have to be answered by Swiss authorities incidentally. In this case, article 91(1) CPIL also applies to Swiss nationals last habitually resident abroad, unless the Swiss authorities have jurisdiction on the basis of article 87 CPIL and apply the law determined under article 91(2) CPIL. From the point of view of the foreign country of the deceased's habitual residence, 14.14

article 91(1) CPIL becomes relevant if the conflicts of law rules of that country refer to Swiss law including Swiss private international law.

14.15 Article 91(2) CPIL provides a special rule for Swiss citizens dying habitually resident abroad where the Swiss authorities have jurisdiction under article 87 CPIL. In these cases the estate is governed by Swiss law, unless, as will be seen below, the deceased had expressly reserved the law of his last habitual residence by will or testamentary pact.

Professio iuris

In general

14.16 The CPIL contains several options for a *professio*. The exercise of such *professio* is always a substantive law reference. The CPIL requires that the *professio* is made by will or testamentary pact. The question whether such *professio* has to be made expressly is, however, unclear. With the exception of article 91(2), the CPIL does not state such requirement. Prior to the CPIL coming into force, the Federal Tribunal held that a *professio* did not have to be made expressly and that it was sufficient if a choice of law was intended by the testator. Referring to this position of the Federal Tribunal under the old regime, commentators generally take the view that the *professio* has not to be made expressly. However, it is left to the courts to develop the criteria for a *professio* where no express choice has been made.

Foreigner last habitually resident in Switzerland

14.17 According to article 90(2) CPIL, a foreigner dying habitually resident in Switzerland may subject his whole[1] estate, by will or testamentary pact, to the law of one of his countries of citizenship. Such *professio iuris* is, however, subject to the requirement that the testator at the time of his death still has the citizenship of that country, otherwise his choice of law lapses (art 90(2) CPIL). It is noteworthy that Swiss citizens with dual nationality are for reasons of equality deemed to be solely Swiss nationals and, consequently, they are not entitled to the choice of law option.

Swiss nationals habitually resident abroad

14.18 Article 87(2) in combination with article 91(2) CPIL provides for several *professio* options which a Swiss citizen dying habitually resident abroad may choose from, namely:

(1) he may subject his estate located in Switzerland or his entire estate to the Swiss forum whereby such *professio* automatically has the effect that Swiss law applies; or
(2) he may subject his Swiss assets or his entire estate to Swiss law; or
(3) he may choose the Swiss forum and Swiss law; or
(4) he may choose the Swiss forum and expressly reserve the law of his last foreign habitual residence.

---

1 The admissibility of a partial *professio iuris* is generally rejected by commentators.

Scope of the *lex successionis*

In general

14.19 The CPIL distinguishes between the *lex successionis* and the law applicable to the winding-up procedure (*Eröffnungsstatut*). This distinction is an area of great difficulty and has led to much controversy for many years, in particular prior to 1989. The CPIL now contains a qualification guideline in article 92 which helps to mark off the substantial difference between the subject matter falling under the *lex successionis* and the subject matter covered by the law applicable to the winding-up procedure.

14.20 From the Swiss viewpoint the problem of differentiation arises when the winding up of the estate takes place in Switzerland and a foreign *lex successionis* applies. Such is the case:

(1) where a foreigner last habitually resident in Switzerland subjects his estate to the law of the country of his citizenship; or
(2) where a Swiss national last habitually resident abroad makes a *professio fori* in favour of the Swiss jurisdiction and expressly reserves the law of his country of habitual residence; or
(3) where the Swiss authorities have jurisdiction under article 88 CPIL and the *renvoi* contained in article 91(1) CPIL leads to a foreign *lex successionis.*

14.21 Generally speaking, it can be said that the tendency of the CPIL is to give a broad field of application to the *lex successionis.* Thus, in a case of doubt, it is likely that the courts will define a question as a substantive succession matter rather than being of a formal nature. However, since the exact dividing line is not defined by article 92 CPIL, the Federal Tribunal will ultimately have to decide a disputed question.

14.22 The *lex successionis* governs, in particular, questions such as the size of the estate, the beneficial entitlement to the estate and the quota of the shares, the vesting of the estate, the liability for the deceased's debts, the content and effect of the certificate of inheritance and other documents, which remedies and measures are available to an heir or legatee and under what conditions.

14.23 In contrast thereto, the winding-up procedural law is primarily concerned with the way in which measures shall be carried out. It is essentially applicable to the formal aspects of the winding-up procedure and governs questions like, for example, the proceedings with respect to actions for avoidance of a will, for reduction, for partition, the opening of wills, the granting of certificates of inheritance and other documents, and forms of disclaimer of the inheritance.

14.24 The views with respect to the executorship appear to be less clear, although it would seem that the rights and obligations of the executor with regard to the estate and the heirs are governed by the *lex successionis,* while his position, insofar as the formal winding-up procedure is concerned, is governed by the procedural winding-up law.

Form of testamentary dispositions

14.25 For the form of wills, the Hague Convention of 5 October 1961 on the law applicable to the form of wills applies. According to article 1 of this Convention, a will is formally valid either if it corresponds to the law at the place of making the will, or to the law of citizenship, habitual residence or residence of the deceased at the time of making the will or at the time of his death, or in respect of immovables to the law of the place where they are situated.

14.26 As to the form of other dispositions taking effect on death (testamentary pacts and mutual wills) this Convention applies by analogy.

Testamentary pacts and mutual wills

14.27 According to article 95(1) CPIL, a testamentary pact is governed by the law of the deceased's habitual residence at the time of concluding the pact if only one party has obliged himself as testator. In contrast to this, article 95(2) CPIL allows a manner of restricted choice of law. If, in a testamentary pact, the deceased subjects his entire estate to the law of his country of citizenship (*professio iuris*), that law applies instead of the law of the country of his habitual residence. As to mutual testamentary pacts and other mutual dispositions taking effect on death (eg mutual wills) the law requires that they comply with the law of the habitual residence of each of the disposers or with the law of the country of common citizenship chosen by them (art 95(3) CPIL).

Testamentary capacity

14.28 A person may make a testamentary disposition if, at the time of disposal, he had the capacity to dispose under the law of the country of his habitual residence or ordinary residence, or of one of his citizenships (art 94 CPIL).

RECOGNITION OF FOREIGN DECISIONS AND OTHER LEGAL ACTS

14.29 The CPIL generally takes a favourable attitude to recognition matters (*favor recognitionis*). By virtue of article 96(1) CPIL foreign decisions, measures, and certificates concerning the estate as well as rights arising from probate proceedings abroad are recognised in Switzerland:

- if they were rendered, issued, or established in the country of the deceased's last habitual residence, or in the country whose law he has chosen, or if they are recognised in one of these countries; or
- if they concern immovable property, and were rendered, issued, or established in the country in which the immovable property is situated, or if they are recognised there.

14.30 However, this *favor recognitionis* is restricted in two ways. First, where a country claims exclusive jurisdiction over the deceased's immovable property situated in its territory, only that country's decisions, measures and documents are recognised (art 96(2) CPIL). Secondly, protective measures are only recognised if they are taken in the country in which the assets of the deceased are located (art 96(3) CPIL).

The further requirements for recognition (especially grounds for refusal, procedure for recognition and required documents) are dealt with in articles 25–29 CPIL. 14.31

2. SUBSTANTIVE LAW

INTRODUCTION

The Swiss Civil Code (CC) deals with the law of inheritance in its articles 457–640. It is located between family law and the law of property and obligations. The law of inheritance is divided into the two sections: *Heirs* and *Devolution of the Estate.* Particular regulations with respect to the law of inheritance relating to farming are contained in the BGBB (*Bundesgesetz über das bäuerliche Bodenrecht*) which has been in force since 1 January 1994. 14.32

PRINCIPLES

The inheritance is vested as a whole in the heir or heirs by operation of law at the death of the deceased (art 560 (1) CC/ *Universalsukzession* or *Gesamtnachfolge*). An immediate transfer only of parts of the estate by operation of law is not recognised by the Civil Code. At the moment of death, all property of the deceased (ownership, rights of possession and other legal rights including debts due to the deceased) pass automatically (*ipso jure*) to one or more persons as his heirs. Inheritance takes effect even without the knowledge and agreement of the heir. As a consequence of this, the forms of transfer *inter vivos* (eg registration in the land register, delivery, assignment, assumption of debts) need not be complied with. 14.33

According to the principle of universal succession, the estate of the deceased and the assets and debts of the heir melt into one another. Subsequently, the heir is personally liable without limit for the debts of the deceased. 14.34

Where there are several heirs, the inheritance is vested in them jointly. By operation of law they constitute a community of heirs. It is the community of heirs which obtains the inheritance, not the single heir. To enable each heir to obtain possession of his part, partition is necessary. 14.35

Universal succession is mandatory, and cannot be excluded by the deceased, but it is possible for the heir to disclaim the inheritance accrued to him so that the universal succession is repealed retroactively. 14.36

HEIRS ON INTESTACY

14.37 The Civil Code distinguishes between statutory heirs and instituted heirs. Where the right to be heir is given to a person by law, he is called a 'statutory heir', where given by testamentary disposition he is called an 'instituted heir'.

Parentela-system for relatives

14.38 The entitlement of inheritance between relatives is based on the *Parentela*-system.

Parentela-system

14.39 A *Parentela* includes all persons who descend from a common ancestor. To the first *Parentela* belong the descendants of the deceased (art 457 (1) and (3) CC), to the second *Parentela* his or her parents (father and mother) with their descendants, eg brothers, sisters, nephews and nieces of the deceased (art 458 (1) and (3) CC), to the third *Parentela* his or her grandparents (grandfather and grandmother) with their descendants, eg uncles, aunts and cousins of the deceased (art 459 (1) and (3) CC).

Characteristics of the Swiss Parentela-system

14.40 Each relative is entitled to be heir only as a member of one *Parentela*. Where there are relatives who belong to different *Parentelae*, the members of the more distant *Parentela* are excluded from succession as long as members of a nearer *Parentela* exist.

14.41 A *Parentela* itself can be subdivided into *stirpes*. This is the case where a member of a *Parentela* himself becomes the parent of descendants (eg if in the first *Parentela* one of the children of the deceased gets married and himself has children). *Parentela* and *stirpes* are not identical terms.

14.42 The spouses, not being related by blood, are not members of a *Parentela*. The spouse of the deceased inherits as an additional entitled person.

14.43 The principals in each *Parentela* and *stirpes*, unless they are deceased, precede their own descendants. On the other hand, the descendants take the place of predeceased ascendants (arts 457(3), 458(3) and 459(3) CC).

14.44 Where the deceased leaves no descendants, the inheritance is divided into two parts; one of them passes to the father's side, the other to the mother's side (art 458 (1) and (2) CC). Such division takes place where the *Parentelae* of both the parents have members entitled to inherit. If there are no descendants on one side, the whole inheritance passes to the heirs on the other side (art 458(4) CC). This half of the inheritance does not pass to a *Parentela* which is more distant. A competition between *Parentelae* of different proximity cannot exist. The nearer *Parentela* in any case excludes the members of a more distant *Parentela* from the succession.

14.45 Where the deceased leaves neither descendants nor heirs of the *Parentelae* of his parents (parents or their descendants), the right of inheritance passes to the *Parentelae* of his grandparents (art 459(1) CC). Where the deceased leaves members on both the paternal and the maternal side, one half share passes to each side (art 459(2) CC). If on one side one of the *Parentela* is missing, its part passes to the heirs of the existing *Parentela* of the same side. Only if there are no heirs on the paternal or the maternal side, does the whole inheritance pass to the heirs on the other side (art 459 (4) and (5) CC). A competition between *Parentelae* of different proximity cannot exist in this case either.

Where a person is solely related to the father's or to the mother's side, such person is entitled to inherit only on the *Parentela* of an ascendant in common with whom he has the deceased relative. Where a person is several times related, he inherits on all *Parentelae* to whom he belongs, unless the *Parentelae* are of different proximity. 14.46

An adopted child acquires the legal rights and duties of a legitimate child of the adopting parents (art 267(1) CC); the former child relationship is dissolved (art 267(2) CC). The new law of adoption makes no distinction with respect to the inheritance entitlement as between relatives because of an adoption. An exception is made where such adoption was made before 1 April 1973. Such adoptions are governed by the law which came into force on 1 January 1912, provided that the adoption was not made subject to the new law on the request of the adopting parents (arts 12a and 12b of the provisions for the application of the old and new law). Article 465 CC, which has been annulled, is still valid for adoptions governed by the old law.[1] 14.47

According to article 460 CC, the right of inheritance based on relationship ceases with the *Parentelae* of the grandparents. Since 1 January 1988 members of the *Parentelae* of the great-grandparents no longer have any usufruct. 14.48

Right of inheritance of illegitimate children

Where a child–parent relationship according to article 252 CC exists, the child (respectively his relatives) and his parent (respectively his relatives) have a full and mutual right of inheritance. 14.49

Right of inheritance of the surviving spouse

The surviving spouse takes (art 462 CC): 14.50

- one-half of the property where the spouse has to share the estate with descendants: the other half falls to the descendants who (according to art 457 CC) are entitled to inherit;
- three-quarters of the property where the spouse has to share the estate with the heirs of the *Parentelae* of the parents: the remaining one-quarter falls to these heirs and their shares are calculated according to article 458 CC;
- the whole estate where there are no heirs of the *Parentelae* of the parents.

Where there is a surviving spouse, the grandparents of the deceased have no right of inheritance. 14.51

---

1 Article 465 CC in the wording of 1 January 1912:
1. In relation to the adopter the adopted child and his issue have the same right of inheritance as the issue from marriage.
2. In relation to the adopted, the adopter and his blood relations have no right of inheritance.

14.52 One must remember that the surviving spouse is first entitled to matrimonial property (see arts 181–251 CC). Only after the distribution of the matrimonial property can the extent of the property available for inheritance be ascertained.

Right of inheritance of the Canton and Commune

14.53 Where the deceased leaves no heirs of the first three *Parentelae* nor a surviving spouse, the estate devolves upon the *Canton* of the deceased's last habitual residence (see arts 23 *et seq* CC) or to the local *Commune* entitled under the law of the *Canton*.

WILLS AND TESTAMENTARY PACTS (TESTAMENTARY DISPOSITIONS)

14.54 The Civil Code distinguishes between two kinds of testamentary dispositions: wills and testamentary pacts. Sometimes it may be difficult to tell in a specific case whether a legal transaction *inter vivos* or a testamentary disposition has been effected. The distinction is especially important because of the different requirements regarding form and content.

14.55 According to case-law, all the circumstances of each individual case must be taken into consideration, and the differentiation cannot be made schematically according to abstract criteria. In case of doubt, the court will accept a valid legal transaction *inter vivos* rather than an invalid testamentary disposition.

14.56 Testamentary dispositions are considered to be strictly personal acts of the deceased. Thus they can only be effected by the deceased personally: any form of representation is excluded. The deceased has to specify the content of a testamentary disposition, for example the identity of the beneficiaries (heirs or legatees), the exact content of the legacy or the amount of an inheritance. According to case-law, the deceased may not leave such decisions to an heir, an executor, or other third party.

Testamentary capacity

Mental capacity

14.57 The testator must have comprehension (or understanding) before he can make a testamentary disposition.

Age

14.58 He must, furthermore, have completed his eighteenth year (age of majority) to be able to make a will or to conclude a testamentary pact (arts 467 and 468 CC).

14.59 Where in a testamentary pact both parties mutually dispose (in the event of their death) in favour of each other, both testators must have attained their age of majority and act personally. Where in a testamentary pact one party disposes as testator, these requirements must be fulfilled by him. As to the other party, the general rules on contractual capacity apply (see arts 12 *et seq* CC).

14.60 The following points are noteworthy.

- A person who has mental capacity and who has been placed under a guardian after attaining majority has capacity to dispose by will. He needs neither parental consent nor the consent of the guardian. In contrast to this, minors cannot dispose by testamentary pact even if the parents or the guardian have consented.
- Even an insane person who is placed under guardianship can make a will in a lucid period (*lucida intervalla*).

Void dispositions (art 469 CC)

All testamentary dispositions may be made null and void where the testator has made them under the influence of mistake, fraud, threats or violence. It must be noted that they become operative where the testator fails to revoke them within one year of discovering the mistake or fraud, or after ceasing to be under influence of threats or violence. Where the disposition contains an evident misdescription of a person or thing and the true intentions of the testator can be established with certainty, the mistake must be rectified accordingly. 14.61

Consequences of missing testamentary capacity

A testamentary disposition made by a testator having no testamentary capacity or made under the influence of mistake, fraud, threats or violence is not from the first null and void. But the judge declares such a will or testamentary pact null and void if an heir or beneficiary who is an interested party brings a court action to avoid the will or testamentary pact (art 519 CC). According to article 521(1) CC, the action must be brought within one year from the date when the plaintiff had cognisance of the testamentary disposition and of the ground for nullity and, in any case, not later than ten years from the date of the opening of the will. If the action is not brought within these time-limits, then the testamentary disposition is effective. 14.62

The fact that the will or testamentary pact is voidable on one of the above-mentioned grounds can always be pleaded as a defence to an action to enforce it (art 521(3) CC). 14.63

A deficient testamentary disposition may also be declared partially void by the court. 14.64

Freedom of disposition

In general, where the deceased does not dispose otherwise, the whole inheritance passes to the statutory heirs. Where the testator, by will or testamentary pact, prescribes who shall obtain how much of the estate, this takes precedence over the rules of intestate succession; but the extent to which effect can be given to a will or pact is restricted by the rules relating to the compulsory portion. 14.65

Compulsory portion and devisable portion

Certain statutory heirs are by law entitled to a quota of the inheritance (compulsory portion). The testator cannot dispose by will or testamentary pact so as to oust the compulsory portion. However, he can freely dispose of the devisable portion. The devisable portion is equal to the statutory share of the inheritance less the compulsory portion. The total of the compulsory portions is equal to the whole estate less the total of the devisable portions. 14.66

Heirs entitled to a compulsory portion and size of the compulsory portion

14.67 According to article 471 CC, the compulsory portion is as follows:

- for a descendant three-quarters of his statutory share of inheritance;
- for each of the parents one half of his statutory share of inheritance;
- for the surviving spouse one half of his statutory share of inheritance.

Statutory heirs are entitled to receive their compulsory portion in its full amount and therefore without any financial burden. Burdens which are only of ideal nature are allowed.

Gifts to surviving spouse (art 473 CC)

14.68 A testator can by testamentary disposition favour the surviving spouse. He can leave to his surviving spouse the usufruct in the whole of the share of the inheritance devolving on their common descendants or the non-common descendants begotten during the time of their marriage and their descendants. Such usufruct is taken to be in satisfaction of the right of inheritance conferred by law on the surviving spouse where these descendants are co-heirs with the spouse.

Reduction of testamentary dispositions

14.69 Where a testator has exceeded his rights of disposition, those heirs who have not received the full value of their compulsory portion can demand the reduction of the bequests to their proper limits (art 522(1) CC). The right to demand reduction is inheritable. Only in exceptional cases do non-heirs also have the right to demand reduction (the administrator in a testator's bankruptcy or the testator's creditors; see art 524 CC). The executors have neither the power to sue nor the power to be sued.

14.70 The action for reduction must be brought within one year from the time when the heirs had cognisance of the infringement of their rights, and, in any case, not later than ten years from the opening of the will in respect of testamentary dispositions and from the death of the donor in respect of other gifts (art 533(1) CC). The claim for a reduction can always be pleaded as a defence to an action (art 533(3) CC).

14.71 Where a beneficiary has suffered a reduction of his benefit and he is at the same time charged with a legacy in favour of a third person, the beneficiary (even if he is not a heir) can claim that the amount of this charge be proportionately reduced (art 525(2) CC).

Order of reduction

14.72 Reductions are made in the first place in testamentary dispositions and in the second place in gifts *inter vivos*, beginning with the latest in time and continuing in that order until the compulsory portions are fully restored (art 532 CC). Where there are several testamentary dispositions or gifts *inter vivos* at the same time, in principle a proportionate reduction takes place, unless the deceased intended to favour one of the beneficiaries. As to the calculation of the proportion, the following two situations must be distinguished:

14.73 – The reduction is effected in the same proportion for all instituted heirs, all statutory heirs who are not entitled to a compulsory portion and all other beneficiaries (art 525(1) CC). *Example*: The testator has fully violated the compulsory portion of his only son A; he has bequeathed to B, 36,000 of his estate (which is in total 60,000) and to C, 24,000. The compulsory portion of A is 45,000. In consequence the shares of B and C are reduced in the proportion 36:24 or 3:2. The reduction is 27,000 for B and 18,000 for C, so making up A's 45,000.

- The reduction is effected proportionate to the amounts which exceed the compulsory portion for the statutory heirs who are entitled to a compulsory portion. *Example*: The testator leaves three children A, B and C; his estate is 60,000. The testator bequeathed to A, 36,000 and to B, 24,000. The compulsory portion of C is 15,000 (= three-quarters of his statutory share of inheritance = 3/4 x 1/3 = 3/12 = 1/4 = 15,000). The proportion for the reduction of the shares of A and B is 21,000: 9,000 or 7:3. A has to give 10,500 to C, B has to give 4,500 to C. **14.74**

Disinheritance

The testator has the right to deprive a statutory heir of his compulsory portion by will or testamentary pact only in exceptional circumstances though he may defer descendants' rights by granting a usufruct to his surviving spouse: see para **14.68**. **14.75**

- *Punitive disinheritance*
  Where the heir has committed a serious offence against the testator or one of his near kinsmen or where he has seriously failed in the duties laid upon him by law towards the testator or the latter's family, the testator can deprive the heir of his compulsory portion (art 477 CC).

A disinheritance is valid only where the testator has clearly stated the ground for it in his will or testamentary pact (art 479(1) CC). Where the ground for the disinheritance is not at all stated or stated insufficiently, the disinherited person has the right to contest the testamentary disposition. In such a case the disposition normally will be held valid to the extent to which it does not deprive the disinherited person of his compulsory portion. But where it can be shown that the testator made the disposition under an evident mistake as to the ground for the disinheritance, the disinherited person will not get merely his compulsory portion but his whole statutory share (art 479(3) CC). **14.76**

A disinherited person is fully excluded from the inheritance. He can neither claim a share in the inheritance nor bring the action for reduction (art 478(1) CC). His share passes, where the testator has not directed otherwise, to the latter's statutory heirs, as if the disinherited person had not survived the testator (art 478(2) CC). Nevertheless the descendants of the disinherited person have the same right to their compulsory portion, as if he had predeceased them (art 478(3) CC). **14.77**

- *Disinheritance of insolvent person*
  The testator can deprive an insolvent descendant of the moiety of his compulsory portion, provided he leaves that moiety to the descendant's children (art 480(1) CC).

Formalities required for testamentary dispositions

Significance of the form of testamentary dispositions

14.78 Where a will or testamentary pact is not made in the proper form it is voidable (art 520(1) CC). The action to avoid the will or testamentary pact can be brought by any heir or beneficiary who is an interested party (arts 520(3) and 519(2) CC). It must be brought within one year from the date when the plaintiff had cognisance of the testamentary disposition and of the ground for nullity, and in any case not later than ten years from the date of the opening of the will (art 521(1) CC). If the action is not brought within the time-limit, a testamentary disposition which is not made in a proper form becomes effective. The fact that the will or testamentary pact is voidable because of its improper form can always be pleaded as a defence to an action to enforce it (art 521(3) CC).

Three forms of wills

Holograph will (art 505 CC)

14.79 The holograph will is the common form of private will, and is characterised by its simplicity of establishment and the secrecy of content of the will, as well as the fact of its establishment.

14.80 Where the will is to be a holograph will, the testator must write and sign it himself by hand from the beginning to the end including the mention of the place, year, month and day it was made. Typewriting is void. Later additions must also be dated and signed by hand.

14.81 As to the signature, it is sufficient if the testator signs the document with either his family name or his first name as long as there is no doubt about the identity of the testator (even a pseudonym may be sufficient). With regard to later additions he can sign with his initials if at the end the document is signed with the full name.

14.82 The testator can preserve the document himself, or give it to a person in trust or to some office appointed by *Cantonal* law for that purpose.

Public will (arts 499–504 CC)

14.83 This is made in the presence of two witnesses by an official (notary or other official qualified for that purpose by *Cantonal* law). The public will must point out the importance of the act and secure that the content of the will corresponds to the well-considered intention of the testator. The official charged with making public wills himself preserves the original or a copy of the document, or else deposits it for safe custody at some office created for that purpose.

14.84 – *Principal form (arts 500 et seq CC)*
First of all the testator communicates his wishes, orally or in writing, to the official. Thereupon the official draws up the document and hands it to the testator to read it through in the presence of the official. Subsequently, the document is signed by the testator and then dated and signed by the official. Immediately after that the two witnesses are called and the testator must make a declaration to them in the presence of the official to the effect that he has read the document and that it represents his last will. The witnesses must both sign an attestation clause appended to the document to the effect that

the testator has made this declaration in their presence and that they are of opinion that he had testamentary capacity at the time.

- *Secondary form (art 502 CC)* 14.85
  The testator neither reads nor signs the document. The official must read it out to him in the presence of the two witnesses. Thereupon the testator must make the declaration that the document represents his last will. This form is especially used where the testator cannot read or write, or where he is not capable because of illness or weakness.

Oral will (arts 506–508 CC)

Where a testator by reason of exceptional circumstances (eg imminent danger of death, epidemic, war) is prevented from making his will in any other form, he is entitled to make it orally. He must declare his last wishes in the presence of two witnesses who after that inform judicial authorities. 14.86

Testamentary pact

According to article 512(1) CC, a testamentary pact is valid only where the formalities required by a public will have been observed (of course with some divergences because of its nature as a bilateral transaction). The contracting parties must simultaneously declare their intention to the official and sign the document in his presence and in the presence of two witnesses. For the testamentary pact the law does not provide an official place to deposit the document. 14.87

Revocation of wills

The testator can at any time totally or partially revoke his will by an express declaration, provided he makes use of one of the forms prescribed for the making of the will (art 509 CC). Further, he can revoke his will by destroying the document (art 510(1) CC), eg tearing, burning, crossing out or erasing. Finally, he can revoke his will by making a later will or by disposing of the item bequeathed in some manner inconsistent with the legacy (art 511 CC), eg selling or giving the item away. A declaration of the testator in his will that it shall be final and irrevocable has no effect. 14.88

A later will does not necessarily mean the revocation of an earlier one. The testator can leave an earlier and a later will where he wants both to be valid, provided that the two wills are not mutually exclusive because of their contents. But where a testator makes a will without expressly revoking an earlier one, article 511(1) CC presumes the revocation of the earlier one, unless it clearly purports to be only a supplementary disposition. A person who claims that both wills are valid must prove his or her statement. Such proof must be conclusive and leave no doubt. Thus a testator who wants both his earlier and later will to be valid should be advised to state such intention expressly in the later will. Where a revocation of a will is revoked, in case of doubt the intestacy rules prevail and the old will does not become valid again. 14.89

Rescission of testamentary pacts

14.90 A testamentary pact can at any time be rescinded by the parties by an agreement in writing (art 513(1) CC). Only in exceptional cases does the testamentary pact lapse by operation of law: eg where the document has been destroyed without a possibility to reconstitute it and where the heir or legatee dies before the testator (art 515(1) CC). In the following cases the testamentary pact can be rescinded unilaterally by the testator:

(1) The testator can revoke the institution of his heir or the gift of a legacy under a pact where after its conclusion the heir or legatee commits an act in relation to the testator which would have constituted a good ground for his disinheritance (art 513(2) CC). Such revocation must be made in one of the forms required for the making of a will (art 513(3) CC).
(2) Where a testamentary pact is combined with obligations *inter vivos* and these obligations are not fulfilled, the person entitled can rescind the contract according to the principles of the Code of Obligations (arts 107 *et seq* CO).

Kinds of dispositions in wills and testamentary pacts

14.91 There is a limited number of the kinds of dispositions which can be made in a will or in a testamentary pact. In both of them one can provide for the institution of one's heir, make a legacy, impose conditions or burdens, provide for substitutions, appoint a reversionary heir, or make directions on the mode of partition. The following dispositions can only be made in a will: constitution of a foundation (art 81(1) CC), acknowledgement of a child (art 260(3) CC) and appointment of an executor (art 517(1) CC).

14.92 As the form of testamentary pacts satisfies the formal requirements for wills, testamentary pacts may contain wills, but without binding the testator.

14.93 Where an immoral, illegal or impossible charge or condition is attached the disposition is voidable (arts 482(2), 519 and 521 CC). Where a charge or condition is senseless or merely vexatious to other persons, it is held to be non-existent (art 482(3) CC).

Interpretation of testamentary dispositions

Testamentary pacts

14.94 According to the ruling doctrine in principle the rules for the interpretation of contracts are applicable.

Will

14.95 Where a will needs to be interpreted, the real intention of the testator must be ascertained. Therefore, his usual parlance or the usual parlance of his environment and also his standard of knowledge are to be taken into consideration. External facts and circumstances (eg other written documents, oral remarks, degree of relationship and friendly relations) may be helpful where different interpretations are possible. Where an intention of the testator is not at all indicated in the document, it is irrelevant. Furthermore, for the interpretation of wills, the principle *in favorem testamenti* is applicable.

Dispositions of a general nature

These are the dispositions which can be made by will and by testamentary pact as well as only by will: 14.96

Institution of heir (art 483 CC)

A testator can institute one heir or several co-heirs for the whole or for only a part of the inheritance. Such an institution constitutes a universal succession with the concomitant liability for debts. Further, it gives to the heir a right to demand delivery of the assets (action to recover inheritance; see arts 598 *et seq* CC). Every disposition which purports to give the whole or part of an inheritance to a beneficiary is held to be an institution of an heir. 14.97

Legacy (arts 484–486 CC)

A testator can leave a beneficiary a legacy of some of his property without instituting him heir (art 484(1) CC). He can leave him a specific item forming part of the estate or the usufruct either in the whole or in part of the estate, or charge his heirs or other beneficiaries to give the legatee some benefit out of the estate or release him from some liability (art 484(2) CC). The legatee has the right to demand delivery of the property bequeathed to him. 14.98

Where the legacies exceed either the total value of the inheritance or the benefit conferred upon the person charged with them or the devisable part of the estate, their proportionate reduction can be demanded (art 486(1) CC). Legacies remain operative even where the persons charged with them do not survive the testator, or are unworthy to succeed, or disclaim the inheritance. Then the heirs of those persons are charged with implementing the legacies (art 486(2) CC). 14.99

Special kinds of legacies

(1) *Untervermächtnis*: where a legatee and not an heir is subject to a charge; 14.100
(2) *Vorvermächtnis*: where a testator has made a legacy to a statutory or instituted heir, the latter can claim it even where he disclaims the inheritance (art 486(3) CC);
(3) *Forderungsvermächtnis*: where a claim of the testator is bequeathed to a legatee or where the testator releases the debts of a legatee;
(4) *Verschaffungsvermächtnis*: where an item, which at the time of death is not comprised in the estate, is required to be obtained by a person for delivery to the legatee.

Burdens (art 482 CC)

These are related to legacies. Statutory and institutional heirs, and legatees, can be charged with burdens. In the typical case a burden does not serve a purpose of a financial nature. Each interested person can demand the enforcement of a burden as soon as the disposition itself takes place. The right of enforcement (*Vollziehungsanspruch*) is of a strict personal nature (neither inheritable nor attachable). 14.101

Substitution

A testator can in his will or testamentary pact appoint one or more persons to take the inheritance or legacy if the heir or legatee predeceases the testator or 14.102

disclaims the inheritance or legacy (art 487 CC, *Ersatzerbeneinsetzung* and *Ersatzvermächtnis*).

14.103 A testator can in his will or testamentary pact charge the instituted heir or legatee to pass on the inheritance or legacy to another as reversionary heir or reversionary legatee (arts 488 *et seq* CC, *Nacherbeneinsetzung* and *Nachvermächtnis*).

Foundation (art 493 CC)

14.104 The testator can in his will devote the whole or any part of the devisable portion of the estate for some special purpose by way of a foundation.

Executors (arts 517, 518 CC)

14.105 The testator can in his will appoint one or more persons who have legal capacity to execute his last wishes. The executor (*Willensvollstrecker*) must see that the wishes of the testator are carried out, and in particular he must administer the estate, pay the debts of the testator, give effect to the legacies and carry out the partition of the inheritance according to the directions of the testator or the provisions of the law. Where several executors are appointed, they are, in the absence of a contrary direction, considered to hold their office jointly. The executors are entitled to a fair remuneration for their services.

Specific content of the testamentary pact

Positive testamentary pact (art 494 CC, Erbzuwendungsvertrag)

14.106 This is the case where the testator, by making a testamentary pact with another person, binds himself to leave the inheritance or a legacy to him or to a third person and this pact is combined with a counter-promise. The two parties institute one another heir or make a bequest to one another, or the instituted heir or legatee binds himself to an donation *inter vivos* in favour of the testator.

14.107 A testator who makes a positive testamentary pact retains the right to deal with the property and to dispose of it. Testamentary dispositions and donations, however, which conflict with the testator's obligations, can be avoided by the other party.

Negative testamentary pact (Erbverzichtsvertrag)

14.108 A testator can conclude a testamentary pact with one of his heirs by which the heir voluntarily renounces or sells his rights of inheritance. The renouncing party in consequence loses his rights of inheritance. Where the parties do not expressly provide otherwise the testamentary pact is also binding on the descendants of the renouncing party. To the rule that a renouncing party loses his rights of inheritance the following reservations are to be made:

(1) the renunciation is without effect where in the testamentary pact certain heirs are instituted in place of the renouncing party and for some reason they do not acquire the inheritance (art 496(1) CC);
(2) where the renouncing party received property from the testator by virtue of the pact during the last five years preceding the death of the testator and in consequence the rights of the creditors of the testator are violated (art 497 CC);
(3) where alienations in consideration of a renunciation violate the compulsory portions of statutory heirs (art 527 (figure 2) CC).

A partial renunciation is also possible.

ADMINISTRATION AND DEVOLUTION OF THE ESTATE

In order for the heir to become sole possessor of the part of the inheritance conferred by law or by the testator, three requirements must be fulfilled: 14.109

(1) a succession must have been opened;
(2) the inheritance must definitely have been vested in the heir; and
(3) partition of the inheritance must have been effected where several co-heirs exist.

Opening of the succession

Death of the deceased

The succession opens with the death of the deceased (art 537(1) CC). According to article 538 CC, the succession to the whole estate opens at the last habitual residence of the deceased; and actions for the avoidance or reduction of testamentary dispositions as well as for the delivery of possession or the distribution of the estate must be brought before the court of the place of his last habitual residence. It is the competent probate authority of the deceased's last habitual residence who is required to take all necessary measures to secure the devolution of the inheritance (art 551(1) CC). Furthermore, important declarations and demands (eg declarations of disclaimer or acceptance of the inheritance, demands for public inventory or official liquidation of the inheritance) must be made to the competent probate authority of the deceased's last habitual residence. 14.110

The place of the deceased's death has a subordinated importance. The probate authority of the place of his death must notify the probate authority of his last habitual residence of the fact of death and take all necessary measures to preserve the property left there by the deceased (art 551 (3) CC). 14.111

The person who claims to be entitled to succeed or otherwise to rights under the law of inheritance has to prove the death of the deceased, generally by an extract from the death register. Such proof is not required if a person has been officially declared absent (arts 546 *et seq* CC). 14.112

The time of death is important to determine who is heir, whether a testamentary disposition is valid and what the extent and value of an inheritance is. 14.113

Surviving the deceased

The heir, likewise the legatee, must be alive at the moment of death of the deceased (arts 542 (1), 543 (1) CC). The rights of an heir or legatee who died after the opening pass to their heirs. Where a legatee or instituted heir dies before the testator, in the absence of evidence of a contrary intention on the part of the testator, the institution of an heir respecting the legacy falls away. 14.114

14.115 Where a child has been conceived by the time of death of a testator, the child is capable of inheriting subject to the condition that it is born alive (art 544 CC). It is even possible to leave the whole estate or an item forming part of it to a person who is not born at the date of the opening of the succession; this is the case where it is left to him as a reversionary heir or legatee (art 545 CC).

Capacity to take

14.116 According to article 539(1) CC, every person (natural person and corporate body) can take as heir or otherwise benefit under a will or testamentary pact.

14.117 Where a legacy is left for a definite object to a number of persons together and they do not form a corporate body, the legatees are obliged individually under a charge to apply it for the prescribed object, or, if impossible, the legacy is held to be a foundation (art 539 (2) CC).

Unworthiness (arts 540 et seq CC)

14.118 The law declares the following persons unworthy to take as heir or otherwise to benefit under a testamentary disposition:

- a person who has intentionally and unlawfully caused or attempted the death of the deceased;
- a person who has intentionally and unlawfully made the deceased permanently incapable of making a will or testamentary pact;
- a person who by fraud, force or threats has induced the deceased to make or revoke a testamentary disposition or prevented him from doing so;
- a person who has intentionally and unlawfully suppressed or destroyed a will or testamentary pact under circumstances which prevented the testator from remaking it.

The act causing unworthiness to inherit requires mental capacity and intention. It affects the offender alone. His descendants inherit as if he had died before the deceased. The testator can remove the unworthiness by pardoning the offender.

Administrative processes

Provisional measures

14.119 The purpose of provisional or interim measures is to let the inheritance devolve intact to the heirs and to find out who are the heirs. Some of these measures are dealt with in articles 551–559 CC, others are reserved to the *Cantonal* law (*Einführungsgesetz zum Zivilgesetzbuch*). Some of the provisional measures in the Civil Code are available for each kind of succession (by law, testamentary pact or will), others exclusively apply to protect wills.

General provisional measures

Official administration

14.120 According to article 554(1) CC, this measure will be ordered:

- where an heir is permanently absent and has not appointed an agent to act for him, if such administration is necessary to safeguard his interests;
- where none of the claimants to the inheritance can supply sufficient proof in support of their claims, or where it is uncertain whether there is an heir;

- where all the heirs of the deceased are not known;
- in other special cases specified by law (see arts 490(3), 548, 556(3), and 595 CC).

Where the official administration takes place the heirs cannot dispose of the estate. The official administrator takes it in his care, makes an inventory and carries out the necessary administrative acts. Where the testator has appointed an executor the administration usually is placed in his hands (art 554(2) CC); and where a person dies who is under guardianship, in the absence of a different provision, it is usually placed in the hands of the guardian (art 554(3) CC). 14.121

Affixing of seal

Seals are affixed to property in the cases provided by *Cantonal* law (art 552 CC). 14.122

Inventory

According to article 553(1) CC, the making of an inventory will be ordered: 14.123

- where an heir requires the appointment of a guardian or is under guardianship;
- where an heir is permanently absent and has not appointed an agent to act for him;
- where one of the heirs demands it.

The *Cantons* can make use of the inventory in further cases.

Where heirs are unknown (art 555 CC)

Where the probate authority is not certain whether the deceased has left any heirs at all or whether it knows who all the heirs are, claimants are invited by a public citation to notify the authority of their claims within one year. Where no claims are notified within this period and the authority does not know of any heirs, the inheritance passes, subject to any action claiming the inheritance, to the *Canton* or *Commune* entitled to it. 14.124

Provisional measures in respect of wills (arts 556–559 CC)

Obligation to deliver up

Where a will or several wills are found at the death of the deceased they must be delivered up without delay to the probate authority, even if they appear to be invalid (arts 556(1) and 557(3) CC). Where this obligation is disregarded the law imposes a personal liability upon the person in charge of the will or the person who has found the will among the testator's effects (art 556(2) CC), but the disregard of the obligation does not affect the validity of the will. 14.125

Administrative measures

After the will has been delivered up, the probate authority either gives provisional possession of the estate to the statutory heirs or orders official administration of it (art 556(3) CC). The will (or wills) must be opened by the competent probate authority within a month from delivery to the authority. All the heirs that are known to it are summoned to the opening ceremony (art 557 (1) and (2) CC). The legatees receive only a copy of the portion of the will that concerns them (art 558(1) CC). According to article 559(1) CC, at the expiration of one month after notice to the interested parties, the instituted heirs, whose claims have not been openly contested by the statutory heirs or by beneficiaries under an earlier will, 14.126

can obtain from the probate authority a certificate to the effect that they are recognised as heirs subject to an action to void the will (arts 519 *et seq* CC) or to claim the inheritance (arts 598 *et seq* CC). With this certificate the instituted heirs put themselves in possession of the estate.

14.127 This document does not amount to a final decision on the rights of succession. Even if the statutory heirs or the beneficiaries under an earlier will neglect to contest the rights of the instituted heirs they can still claim for their own rights. But their position in the litigation has become disadvantageous. Where the instituted heirs now possess the estate, the statutory heirs are the plaintiffs and must bring an action to void the will or an action for reduction or an action to recover the inheritance. This is in contrast to the situation prior to such possession when the instituted heirs had to sue. The statutory heirs can ask for a certificate too.

Vesting and disclaimer of the inheritance

14.128 According to article 560 CC, the inheritance is vested as a whole in the (statutory and/or instituted) heirs by operation of law, *ipso iure*, at the death of the deceased. Nevertheless the heirs can make a declaration to accept the inheritance. Such a declaration is none other than a renunciation of a disclaimer. Where a statutory or instituted heir wants to be liberated from the rights and liabilities of the inheritance, he must disclaim the inheritance by a written or oral declaration to the competent probate authority (arts 566(1) and 570(1) CC). It must be made unconditionally and without any reservation (art 570(2) CC). The disclaimer normally has to be made within a time-limit of three months from the day when the statutory heir had cognisance of the death of the deceased or from the day on which the instituted heir was officially notified of the disposition in his favour (arts 567–569 CC). An extension or renewal of the time-limit is possible on material grounds (art 576 CC). Where an heir does not make the required declaration of disclaimer within the time-limit, the inheritance passes to him unconditionally (art 571(1) CC). An heir further loses his right of disclaimer where he has within the time-limit intermeddled with the inheritance or done acts which were not required for the mere management of the estate and the carrying on of the affairs of the deceased, or appropriated or concealed anything forming part of the estate (art 571(2) CC).

14.129 The Civil Code in principle distinguishes three cases of disclaimer.

(1) Where the deceased has died *intestate* and one of several statutory co-heirs disclaims, his share devolves as if he had not survived the deceased (art 572(1) CC). If the disclaiming statutory co-heir has descendants, they are substituted for him, otherwise his share passes to his co-heirs.
(2) Where the deceased has died *testate*, and one of the instituted heirs disclaims, his share passes, in the absence of a contrary intention shown by the testator, to the latter's nearest statutory heir (art 572(2) CC).
(3) Where all the nearest statutory heirs of the deceased disclaim the estate available for inheritance, it will be wound up by the official in bankruptcy (art 573(1) CC; exception: arts 574 and 575 CC). Surplus assets left after payment of all the debts pass to the persons entitled as if no disclaimers had been made (art 573(2) CC).

Securing heir's creditors (art 578 CC)

Where an insolvent heir has disclaimed for the purpose of depriving his creditors of the estate, they themselves or the official in bankruptcy can within six months oppose the disclaimer, unless their claims are duly secured. Where the disclaimer is declared void in consequence, the inheritance will be wound up officially. Surplus assets are assigned in the first place for the satisfaction of the claims of the creditors who have opposed the disclaimer and in the second place for the payment of the other creditors; the balance, if any, falls to the heirs in whose favour the disclaimer was made. Where the deceased by testamentary disposition has disposed of the devisable portion of a statutory heir, then the creditors are entitled only to his compulsory portion. 14.130

Securing creditors of the inheritance (art 579 CC)

Where heirs disclaim an insolvent inheritance they are held liable to the creditors of the estate to the extent of the property which they have received from the deceased within the five years preceding his death. Heirs who have acted *bona fide* are liable only to the extent to which they were enriched at the time. Customary gifts received by the heirs by way of dowry on marriage and money laid out on their education and training do not fall under this liability. 14.131

Vesting and disclaimer of legacies

Voting of legacies

Legatees have a personal action against the person charged with the legacy, or if no such person has been specifically appointed, against the statutory or instituted heirs (art 562(1) CC). Where no other intention appears from the will the right of action accrues as soon as the person charged has acquired the inheritance (art 562(2) CC). 14.132

Where a movable or immovable is bequeathed or devised, the legatee can claim transfer of possession and the devisee can require co-operation of the charged person in order to be entered on the land register. Where the persons charged fail in their obligation towards the legatee or devisee, they can be sued for the transfer or for damages (art 562(3) CC). Where the movable or immovable is encumbered, it must be delivered in the state and condition in which it was at the date of the opening of the succession (art 485(1) CC). 14.133

Disclaimer

In the absence of evidence in the will of a contrary intention, the disclaimer by a legatee of his legacy operates in favour of the person charged with effecting it (art 577 CC). 14.134

Legatees and creditors of the deceased

According to article 564(1) CC, the rights of the creditors of the deceased take precedence over those of legatees. 14.135

Legatees and creditors of the heir

The deceased cannot reduce the compulsory portion of his statutory heirs by making legacies. If he does so, these heirs can claim for reduction of the legacies. The right to demand the reduction passes to the creditors of the heir if the heir does not demand the reduction himself (art 524 CC). 14.136

14.137 As for heirs without a compulsory portion the situation is totally different. Where the estate of the deceased and the assets of the heir are kept separated the legatee precedes the creditors of the heir. But if the estate of the deceased consolidates with the assets of the heir, then according to case-law the creditors of the heir precede the legatee.

Reduction

14.138 Where the legacies exceed either the total value of the inheritance or the benefit conferred upon the person charged with them or the devisable part of the estate, their proportionate reduction can be demanded (art 486(1) CC).

Public inventory

Purpose

14.139 Where an heir does not have a clear idea of the assets and debts of the inheritance of the deceased, he risks either failure to participate in a surplus of the estate if he disclaims the inheritance or being liable for a surplus of debts if he does not make a disclaimer.

14.140 The public inventory serves to enlighten the heir on the financial situation of the inheritance and to limit his liability.

Procedure

14.141 Every heir who is entitled to disclaim the inheritance can orally, or by writing, demand within a month from the opening of the succession, a public inventory from the competent probate authority. This authority is appointed by the *Cantonal* law. The procedure in its leading features is dealt with by the Civil Code. Even if only one heir demands the making of a public inventory it always includes the whole estate available for inheritance.

14.142 The procedure is characterised as follows:

- Statement of the assets and debts of the estate, combined with a valuation of every item of property in it (art 581(1) CC).
- Public citations to the creditors and debtors of the deceased to state their claims and their debts respectively within a certain fixed time. The attention of the creditors is at the same time called to the consequences of their failure to comply with the notice (art 582 CC). Pending the making of the inventory, only necessary acts of administration are allowed (art 585 CC). Except in urgent cases, legal proceedings which have already been instituted are suspended and no new proceedings can be instituted; furthermore, the period for the limitation of actions does not run and no execution in respect of the debts of the deceased is allowed (art 586 CC).
- After the closing of the inventory each heir is called upon to declare within one month what his intention is with regard to accepting the inheritance (art 587(1) CC).

Various possibilities for decision

14.143 The heir has within the period fixed the right to disclaim the inheritance, to demand its official liquidation, or to accept it either subject to an inventory or unconditionally. Silence on his part is held to be an acceptance, subject to an inventory (art 588 CC).

Limitation of the liability for debts

Where an heir accepts the inheritance subject to an inventory, the debts of the deceased as specified in the inventory pass to him together with the assets (art 589(1) CC). For these debts the heir is personally and fully liable (art 589(3) CC). 14.144

An heir is not liable, either personally or to the extent of the assets, to those creditors of the deceased whose claims are not specified in the inventory because they neglected by their fault to state them within the time fixed (art 590(1) CC). Where, however, the creditors omitted to state their claims through no fault of their own, the heir is liable to the extent to which he is enriched by the inheritance (art 590(2) CC). Special rules are provided by the law where an inheritance devolves upon the *Canton* or the *Commune* (art 592 CC) and in respect of the liability on guarantees (art 591 CC).

Official liquidation

Purpose

The official liquidation has as its purpose the separation of the estate from the assets and debts of the heir and to limit his liability. 14.145

Procedure

Every heir, instead of disclaiming the inheritance or accepting it subject to an inventory, can demand its official liquidation (art 593(1) CC). Furthermore, the creditors of the deceased, where they have reasonable grounds for anxiety lest they might not be paid and their claims have not been satisfied on demand nor has security been given, can demand an official liquidation (art 594(1) CC). The time-limit for the demand is three months. It will only be acceded to where none of the co-heirs accepts the inheritance unconditionally (art 593(2) CC). But where a creditor of the deceased demands an official liquidation it takes place even against the will of all heirs. The liquidation is carried out by the competent probate authority appointed by the *Cantonal* law or at its request by one or more administrators and begins with an inventory and the public citations connected with it (art 595 (1) and (2) CC). 14.146

According to article 596(1) CC, in liquidating an estate the administrator must settle the current affairs of the deceased, perform his obligations, recover the debts due to him, as far as possible discharge the legacies, obtain where necessary a judicial pronouncement on his rights and obligations, and realise the deceased's property. Where the estate is insolvent, the liquidation is carried out by the official in bankruptcy according to the law of bankruptcy (art 597 CC). Where the liquidation is carried out by an administrator the heirs can appeal to the probate authority against any measures he intends to take or has already taken (art 595(3) CC). 14.147

Effects

In the case of an official liquidation the heirs are not liable for the debts of the estate (art 593(3) CC). Where, despite the public citation after the closing of the procedure, further claims come up, according to case-law the heirs are liable to the extent to which they are enriched by the estate. 14.148

Action to recover an inheritance

Term and field of application

14.149 Where a person considers that he has as statutory or instituted heir a better right to an inheritance or to property forming part of it than the person who has been put in possession of it, he can enforce his rights by an action for the recovery of an inheritance (art 598(1) CC).

14.150 The action for the recovery of an inheritance must be brought against a *bona fide* possessor within one year of the date on which the plaintiff first had cognisance of the defendant's possession and of his own superior title, but in any case, not longer than ten years from the date of death of the deceased or of the opening of the will (art 600(1) CC). As against a *mala fide* possessor, the period of limitation is in all cases 30 years (art 600(2) CC).

Effect

14.151 Where the action succeeds, the party in possession must restore the inheritance or the property forming part of it to the plaintiff in accordance with the law relating to possession (arts 599(1), 939–940 CC). According to article 599(2) CC, the defendant cannot in this action plead that he has acquired a title to the property by prescription.

Partition of the inheritance

Community among heirs

14.152 Where there are several heirs, all the rights and obligations comprised in the inheritance constitute an undivided community among the heirs until partition (art 602(1) CC). The heirs are joint owners of the property and joint creditors of the claims forming part of the inheritance (art 602(2) CC). An individual heir has no independent right of ownership to a certain share of the property; his share is latent as long as the community among the heirs exists.

14.153 According to article 602(2) CC, the heirs deal jointly with the property forming part of the estate, subject to the rights of representation and administration conferred by agreement or by law. In this way, a co-heir is prevented from dealing with assets of the inheritance selfishly and from damaging the co-heirs. On the other hand, the requirement to deal jointly often renders it difficult to make decisions. Thus, case law has made exceptions to the requirement to deal jointly. Where an heir has renounced a claim, his co-operation with the other heirs is not necessary. Furthermore, where all heirs make a claim regarding the inheritance against a co-heir, his consent is not necessary. An heir can also act alone as representative of the community of heirs and bring an action to court in the name of the community of heirs where it is important to observe a time-limit, or where it is important to act very quickly in order to preserve the community of heirs from damage.

14.154 By unanimous vote the heirs can authorise a co-heir or a third person to represent the community. Furthermore, each co-heir is entitled to demand that the competent probate authority appoint an agent to represent the community until partition (art 602(3) CC). To the extent of his authorisation to make decisions the agent has to act independently and on his own responsibility. Each heir has the right to appeal against his decisions or acts.

Liability for debts

According to article 603(1) CC, the heirs are liable jointly and severally for the debts of the deceased. This liability lasts until a certain time after partition. The heirs are jointly and severally liable for legacies too, unless only certain heirs are charged with implementing them. 14.155

Termination of the community among heirs

The community among heirs is a provisional stage until the partition. Each co-heir has at all times the right to demand the partition of the estate, unless he is expressly bound by agreement or by law to continue the community (art 604(1) CC). 14.156

Carrying out the partition

Principle of free agreement

Partition is a matter for the heirs. In principle, the heirs can freely agree among themselves as to the mode of partition to be adopted (art 607(2) CC). An agreement of the heirs prevails over directions of the testator as to partition. 14.157

Directions of the testator

The testator can by will or testamentary pact give directions to his heirs on the mode of partition and implementing their shares (art 608(1) CC). Each heir who is interested in complying with these directions can refer to them. Article 608(3) CC states the important principle that, in the absence of evidence of a contrary intention in the testamentary disposition, the allotment by the testator of a specific item to an heir is not held to be intended as a specific legacy but as a direction for the purpose of partition. 14.158

Appointment of an executor

Where the testator appoints an executor, he has the right and duty to carry out the partition according to the directions of the testator or the provisions of the law (art 518(2) CC). Where such directions are missing and the executor has to carry out the partition according to the provisions of law, he has to respect the unanimous wills of the heirs. 14.159

It is uncertain whether heirs may carry out the partition according to their unanimous wills where the testator has given directions for partition to the executor. 14.160

Collaboration of the probate authority

Where the heirs cannot agree on the division of the estate into shares or lots, any one of them can require the competent probate authority to settle the lots (art 611(2) CC). The probate authority has to divide the estate into as many shares or lots as there are heirs entitled or *per stirpes* (art 611(1) CC). According to article 611(2) CC, the competent probate authority settling the lots has to take into account local custom, the circumstances of the heirs and the wishes of the majority of them. As to differences in values a compensation in money takes place. The lots are distributed in the first place by agreement among the heirs and in the second place by drawing for them (art 611(3) CC). 14.161

Action for partition

14.162 Where the heirs do not agree on the partition, each of the co-heirs has in principle at all times the right to demand the partition of the estate (art 604(1) CC). Depending on the request, the court sentences the defensive co-heir to co-operate or it decides upon substantial questions of partition, eg reductions, hotchpot, approving or correcting an official proposal for partition, extent of the shares. Where a corresponding request is made the court carries out the partition itself.

Principles for partition

14.163 The following principles apply where the heirs have not agreed unanimously on the partition and unless there are no other directions for partition given by the testator.

Assets

14.164 In principle, all heirs have in a partition equal rights to the distribution of the property forming part of the inheritance (art 610(1) CC). As to the value of the items forming part of the inheritance, the date of the partition is decisive. Where the house or the apartment in which the spouses lived or household effects are part of the inheritance, the surviving spouse can demand that they become the spouse's property with corresponding compensation (art 612a(1) CC).

14.165 For certain special cases the *Cantonal* law (*Einführungsgesetz zum Zivilgesetzbuch*) and the Civil Code render it possible to deviate from the principles of equal rights and distribution *in natura*, eg where the deceased has claims against one of the heirs (art 614 CC); where an article would materially lose in value by being divided (art 612 CC); where there are items which by their nature belong together and where family papers and articles valued for their family associations form part of the assets (art 613 CC).

Debts

14.166 According to article 610(3) CC, each co-heir can require that the debts of the deceased shall all be paid or secured before partition. In this way the heir can eliminate the risk of being liable after the liquidation of the community among heirs. Where the request is not made the debts are distributed to the heirs proportionately to the extent of their shares. As to property charged with debts a reservation is to be made. Where at partition an heir receives property forming part of the inheritance which the deceased had charged for his debts, the heir takes over with the property the liability for these debts (art 615 CC).

Law of inheritance relating to farming

14.167 Especially to protect against danger flowing from land being charged with debt or divided up into small shares, special regulations regarding the law of inheritance relating to farming are contained in the BGBB (*Bundesgesetz über das bäuerliche Bodenrecht*), in force since 1 January 1994. Articles 613a and 619 CC are the only two rules regarding the law of inheritance in the Civil Code.

Hotchpot

14.168 Where the deceased has made gifts during his lifetime, two questions arise: whether the heir has to bring such gifts into hotchpot and, if so, how this shall be done.

The starting point is the will of the deceased; but this will cannot prejudice the compulsory portion of the heirs. Where the will does not deal with the heirs' liability to bring gifts into hotchpot, the law states several rules. 14.169

(1) Customary presents need not be brought into hotchpot (art 632 CC).
(2) In the absence of a contrary intention expressed in the will, gifts made by the deceased to his descendants by way of dowry or by way of surrender of property, or as the remission of a debt, and other similar gifts must be brought into hotchpot (art 626(2) CC: presumption of equal rights of the descendants).
(3) Where the gifts are in excess of the statutory share of inheritance, the excess is, subject always to the action for reduction, not liable to hotchpot, if it can be shown that the deceased intended it as an extra benefit to the donee (art 629(1) CC). This intention is presumed in the case of gifts made to descendants in the customary amounts to set them up on their marriage (art 629(2) CC).
(4) Costs of education, in the absence of evidence of a contrary intention on the part of the deceased, are liable to hotchpot only to the extent to which they exceed the customary limit (art 631(1) CC). Children who at the death of the deceased had not yet completed their education or training or are subject to some infirmity must be allowed at partition to receive a fair amount paid in advance (art 631(2) CC).
(5) A special liability to bring into hotchpot gifts in favour of certain children and grandchildren is stated in articles 334, 334 bis and 603(2) CC.
(6) Where there are statutory heirs other than descendants, these heirs are mutually obliged to bring into hotchpot all that the deceased has given to them in his lifetime by way of advancement on their share in the inheritance (art 626(1) CC). In case of doubt, preference is presumed.

The rules regarding the liability to bring gifts into hotchpot are designed for statutory heirs. But the deceased can also refer to articles 626 *et seq* CC for instituted heirs. 14.170

Where an heir loses his right of inheritance either before or after the opening of the succession, the persons who inherit in his stead take over at the same time his liability to hotchpot (art 627(1) CC). According to article 627(2) CC, the descendants of an heir who has received a portion by way of advancement are bound to bring it into hotchpot even where it has not passed into their possession. 14.171

An heir can elect whether he will bring the property he has received into hotchpot and then participate in the partition like the other heirs, or keep the property and forfeit his share or part of it according to the value of the property received (art 628(1) CC). The computation for hotchpot is made by taking the value of the gifts at the date of the opening of the succession or, where the donee has already sold what he received before that date, the amount of the proceeds of sale (art 630(1) CC). 14.172

Completion and effect of partition

The partition becomes binding on the heirs upon its completion. Apart from the judgment of partition the heirs are bound as soon as either the lots have been 14.173

'formed and distributed' or the partition agreement has been concluded (art 634(1) CC).

14.174 'Forming and distribution' of the lots, according to article 634(1) CC, means the transfer of the property forming their shares into the ownership of the heirs.

14.175 The heirs can bind themselves by a partition agreement even before the partition is carried out. Such a partition agreement is valid only if it is in writing (art 634(2) CC). Where the heirs have made a partition agreement they are obliged to carry out the acts required for the execution of the agreement.

Contracts relating to rights of inheritance

14.176 According to article 635 CC, the co-heirs are entitled to make a contract between them for the assignment of their rights of inheritance. Such contracts must be made in writing.

Contracts before the opening of the succession (art 636 CC)

14.177 Contracts made between two or more heirs, or between an heir and a third person with regard to a succession which has not yet been opened, are valid only if they were made with the consent and concurrence of the testator leaving the inheritance. Such contracts bind only the two contracting parties, not the testator leaving the inheritance. The contract has to be made in writing.

The time after partition

14.178 After partition, the heirs remain for a certain time and in certain respects legally related to one another and to the creditors of the deceased.

14.179 After partition, the heirs are mutually liable *inter se* for the property forming part of the inheritance, as if they were vendors or purchasers (art 637(1) CC). Further, they mutually guarantee the existence of the debts and other *choses in action* allotted to each heir at partition (art 637(2) CC).

14.180 The heirs are entitled to rescind the partition agreement under the same conditions as any other contract (art 638 CC).

14.181 Where an heir has paid a debt of the deceased for which he was not made liable at partition, or a greater part of a debt than the amount which he had undertaken, he is entitled to be indemnified by his co-heirs (art 640(1) CC).

14.182 For debts relating to the estate, heirs even after partition are liable jointly and severally to the extent of the whole of their own property, provided the creditors have not expressly or tacitly assented to the division of the liability among the heirs or to its delegation to one or more of them (art 639(1) CC). This liability ceases at the expiration of five years from the partition or from the time when the claims can be enforced, whichever is later (art 639(2) CC).

3. THE WAY FOR FOREIGNERS TO MINIMISE PROBLEMS

There is a simple way for a foreigner who is habitually resident in Switzerland to deal with property in Switzerland so as to avoid the application of any Swiss law on forced indefeasible shares of his heirs. By virtue of article 90(2) CPIL he can, by will or testamentary pact, choose the law of his nationality to govern succession to his estate. It is advisable expressly to choose the foreign law to avoid any uncertainties as to the validity of his *professio*. It is, furthermore, vital to appreciate that this choice of law will, as has been mentioned above, be ineffective if at his death the testator no longer has this nationality or has become Swiss. Furthermore, article 96 CPIL ensures that foreign decisions and certificates are recognised in Switzerland. Thus, where an Englishman, whether dying habitually resident in Switzerland and domiciled in England or habitually resident and domiciled in Switzerland, has expressly chosen English law to govern succession to his estate, it would seem that an English judge putting himself in the shoes of a Swiss judge, would be likely to accept such *professio iuris* and apply English law as *lex successionis* (see the Maine Supreme Court decision in Estate of Wright (1994) 637 A 2d 106 which provides support for this approach). 14.183

If, on the other hand, an Englishman dies habitually resident and domiciled in England or habitually resident in England and domiciled in Switzerland, *renvoi* complexities arise. However, in the first case where English conflicts of law rules refer to the Swiss jurisdiction only with regard to the Swiss immovables, the *renvoi* uncertainties can be avoided if the Englishman owned the immovables not directly but through a company because shares are movables governed by the English *lex domicilii*. Since the English grant will be recognised under article 96 CPIL, the English personal representative can apply for recognition of his English grant under the procedure provided for in article 29 CPIL. This enables him to prove his title to the satisfaction of third parties and Swiss authorities and thus to recover the deceased's Swiss property. 14.184

One should note that if A and B purchase property by way of a *tontine* arrangement whereby the survivor shall obtain his deceased co-owner's share, then such arrangement must be made in the form required for a will or a testamentary pact or it will be void (see arts 519 CC *et seq*). Furthermore, those heirs whose compulsory portion is violated by such an arrangement can demand a reduction of the donated share (arts 522 CC *et seq*). 14.185

As far as Swiss immovable property is concerned, persons who are not entitled to take up residence in Switzerland need an authorisation from the relevant *Cantonal* authority in order to acquire and retain such property, unless ranking as a statutory heir entitled under Swiss law if the deceased died intestate: article 7 Federal Law on Acquisition of Real Property by Non-residents of 16 December 1983. In the absence of proving a special reason for authorisation the immovable will have to be sold within two years (art 8). The acquisition of shares in companies owning immovables is also subject to restrictions (see articles 4 and 6). 14.186

4. TAXES ON DEATH

GENERAL

14.187 Taxes upon inheritances are levied on the transfer of a deceased person's assets. These taxes are purely within the jurisdiction of the *Cantonal* authorities. Thus the Confederation levies no taxes upon inheritances. With the exception of one *Canton*,[1] all other 25 *Cantons* levy taxes upon inheritances. In a few *Cantons* the communities take a share of the *Cantonal* taxes. In others the communities levy supplementary taxes.

14.188 Under *intercantonal* rules, a *Canton* is entitled to levy tax if the deceased had his last place of residence there. In the case of real estate, the property is taxed in the *Canton* in which it is located, debts being apportioned according to the location of the assets.

14.189 In most *Cantons*, taxes upon inheritances take the form of an inheritance tax (*Erbanfallsteuer*). This means the heirs and legatees are taxed on their share of the estate.[2] Only three *Cantons*[3] levy a tax on the estate itself (an estate tax or *Nachlasssteuer*) in addition to or instead of the inheritance tax.

LIABILITY TO TAX

14.190 Unlimited tax liability applies when the deceased had his last place of habitual residence in Switzerland. In such cases the estate or the inherited share of the estate is fully taxable at the deceased's last place of habitual residence. Only transfers of real estate situated abroad or outside the *Canton* are exempt from taxation. Limited tax liability applies if real property[4] located in the *Canton* belongs to the estate of a person whose last place of habitual residence was outside the *Canton*. Liability to taxation does not, therefore, depend on the deceased's nationality.

14.191 In general, moreover, an heir resident in Switzerland is not liable to tax if the estate was inherited from a deceased habitually resident abroad unless Swiss real estate is inherited. Liability to taxation rests with the heirs in the case of inheritance tax and with the estate in the case of estate tax. The residence of the heirs is of no relevance.

14.192 In many cases, contributions to public and charitable institutions are tax-free. This is always the case if the institution is situated in the *Canton* levying the tax. Institutions domiciled outside the *Canton* are often only exempted from tax if a reciprocal arrangement exists. This is also the case with institutions abroad,

---

1 Schwyz.

2 Subsequent references to heirs also apply to legatees.

3 Solothurn, Graubünden, Neuchâtel.

4 Limited rights in real property (servitudes and pledges) are as a rule treated in the same way as real property.

providing that an exemption is at all possible. Two *Cantons*[1] levy only half the inheritance tax in the case of foreigners who never worked in Switzerland.

BASIS FOR TAXATION

In various situations, the Swiss Civil Code provides for the drawing-up of an inventory on the death of a person (see arts 553 and 580 *et seq* CC). *Cantonal* law may provide for such an inventory to be drawn up in additional situations. The Confederation, moreover, imposes a general requirement to draw up an inventory to determine whether there is any indication of earlier tax evasion. 14.193

In certain cases, gifts come under death duty provisions, as for example in the case of gifts and transfers made by the donor a few years before his death. The assets being transferred are valued at the market value prevailing at the date of death or of making the gift. The valuation arrived at for the individual assets for net wealth tax is generally used. The valuation of a usufruct or other periodic payment is often determined by calculating its capital worth. Minor contributions as well as household effects are usually not valued. Proven debts can be deducted. 14.194

TAX CHARGE

Certain tax-free amounts are allowed in respect of the net assets subject to death duties. The inheritance tax is generally levied on a progressive basis with the following aspects being taken into account: 14.195

(1) degree of kinship; and
(2) size of the share of the inheritance.

The inheritance of the surviving spouse remains tax-free in most *Cantons* and that of the offspring in about one-third of the *Cantons*. For more distant relatives and non-relatives (including institutions which are not tax-exempt), the rate can rise to approximately 55%.

Estate tax is levied at a gradually progressive rate irrespective of the share of the estate accruing to the individual heirs. 14.196

DOUBLE TAXATION CONVENTIONS

The principle that real estate is taxed in the *Canton* in which it is located also applies in international relations. Beyond that, however, Swiss tax law does not contain any provisions for the avoidance of double taxation in the area of inheritance taxes. In particular, there is no provision for crediting foreign taxes against Swiss taxes. 14.197

1 Vaud, Geneva.

14.198 Switzerland has concluded double taxation conventions with several countries[1] to prevent inheritance taxes from being levied twice. The majority of these conventions follow the OECD's model convention of 1966 for the avoidance of double taxation of estates and inheritances. In most conventions, the right to levy death duties is accorded to the country in which the deceased was last resident. However, immovable property and the assets of a permanent establishment are taxed in the country where they are situated. The conventions with the UK, the USA and Germany contain special regulations.

1 Austria, Denmark, Finland, France, Germany, Netherlands, Norway, Sweden, the UK and the USA.

APPENDICES

APPENDIX A

CONVENTION ON THE LAW APPLICABLE TO TRUSTS AND ON THEIR RECOGNITION

The States signatory to the present Convention, AI.1

Considering that the trust, as developed in courts of equity in common law jurisdictions and adopted with some modifications in other jurisdictions, is a unique legal institution,

Desiring to establish common provisions on the law applicable to trusts and to deal with the most important issues concerning the recognition of trusts,

Have resolved to conclude a Convention to this effect, and have agreed upon the following provisions –

Chapter I

Scope

Article 1

This Convention specifies the law applicable to trusts and governs their recognition. AI.2

Article 2

For the purposes of this Convention, the term 'trust' refers to the legal relationships created – *inter vivos* or on death – by a person, the settlor, when assets have been placed under the control of a trustee for the benefit of a beneficiary or for a specified purpose.

A trust has the following characteristics –

(a) the assets constitute a separate fund and are not a part of the trustee's own estate;
(b) title to the trust assets stands in the name of the trustee or in the name of another person on behalf of the trustee;
(c) the trustee has the power and the duty, in respect of which he is accountable, to manage, employ or dispose of the assets in accordance with the terms of the trust and the special duties imposed upon him by law.

The reservation by the settlor of certain rights and powers, and the fact that the trustee may himself have rights as a beneficiary, are not necessarily inconsistent with the existence of a trust.

Article 3

The Convention applies only to trusts created voluntarily and evidenced in writing.

Article 4

The Convention does not apply to preliminary issues relating to the validity of wills or of other acts by virtue of which assets are transferred to the trustee.

Article 5

The Convention does not apply to the extent that the law specified by Chapter II does not provide for trusts or the category of trusts involved.

Chapter II

Applicable law

Article 6

AI.3 A trust shall be governed by the law chosen by the settlor. The choice must be express or be implied in the terms of the instrument creating or the writing evidencing the trust, interpreted, if necessary, in the light of the circumstances of the case.

Where the law chosen under the previous paragraph does not provide for trusts or the category of trust involved the choice shall not be effective and the law specified in Article 7 shall apply.

Article 7

AI.4 Where no applicable law has been chosen, a trust shall be governed by the law with which it is most closely connected.

In ascertaining the law with which a trust is most closely connected reference shall be made in particular to –

(a) the place of administration of the trust designated by the settlor;
(b) the situs of the assets of the trust;
(c) the place of residence or business of the trustee;
(d) the objects of the trust and the places where they are to be fulfilled.

Article 8

AI.5 The law specified by Article 6 or 7 shall govern the validity of the trust, its construction, its effects, and the administration of the trust.

In particular that law shall govern –

(a) the appointment, resignation and removal of trustees, the capacity to act as a trustee, and the devolution of the office of trustee;
(b) the rights and duties of trustees among themselves;
(c) the right of trustees to delegate in whole or in part the discharge of their duties or the exercise of their powers;
(d) the power of trustees to administer or to dispose of trust assets, to create security interests in the trust assets, or to acquire new assets;
(e) the powers of investment of trustees;
(f) restrictions upon the duration of the trust, and upon the power to accumulate the income of the trust;
(g) the relationships between the trustees and the beneficiaries including the personal liability of the trustees to the beneficiaries;

(h) the variation or termination of the trust;
(i) the distribution of the trust assets;
(j) the duty of trustees to account for their administration.

Article 9

In applying this Chapter a severable aspect of the trust, particularly matters of administration, may be governed by a different law. A1.6

Article 10

The law applicable to the validity of the trust shall determine whether that law or the law governing a severable aspect of the trust may be replaced by another law.

Chapter III

Recognition

Article 11

A trust created in accordance with the law specified by the preceding Chapter shall be recognised as a trust. A1.7

Such recognition shall imply, as a minimum, that the trust property constitutes a separate fund, that the trustee may sue and be sued in his capacity as trustee, and that he may appear or act in this capacity before a notary or any person acting in an official capacity.

In so far as the law applicable to the trust requires or provides, such recognition shall imply, in particular –

(a) that personal creditors of the trustee shall have no recourse against the trust assets;
(b) that the trust assets shall not form part of the trustee's estate upon his insolvency or bankruptcy;
(c) that the trust assets shall not form part of the matrimonial property of the trustee or his spouse nor part of the trustee's estate upon his death;
(d) that the trust assets may be recovered when the trustee, in breach of trust, has mingled trust assets with his own property or has alienated trust assets. However, the rights and obligations of any third party holder of the assets shall remain subject to the law determined by the choice of law rules of the forum.

Article 12

Where the trustee desires to register assets, movable or immovable, or documents of title to them, he shall be entitled, in so far as this is not prohibited by or inconsistent with the law of the State where registration is sought, to do so in his capacity as trustee or in such other way that the existence of the trust is disclosed.

Article 13

No State shall be bound to recognise a trust the significant elements of which, except for the choice of the applicable law, the place of administration and the habitual residence of the trustee, are more closely connected with States which do not have the institution of the trust or the category of trust involved.

Article 14

The Convention shall not prevent the application of rules of law more favourable to the recognition of trusts.

Chapter IV

General Clauses

Article 15

A1.8 The Convention does not prevent the application of provisions of the law designated by the conflicts rules of the forum, in so far as those provisions cannot be derogated from by voluntary act, relating in particular to the following matters –

(a) the protection of minors and incapable parties;
(b) the personal and proprietary effects of marriage;
(c) succession rights, testate and intestate, especially the indefeasible shares of spouses and relatives;
(d) the transfer of title to property and security interests in property;
(e) the protection of creditors in matters of insolvency;
(f) the protection, in other respects, of third parties acting in good faith.

If recognition of a trust is prevented by application of the preceding paragraph, the court shall try to give effect to the objects of the trust by other means.

Article 16

A1.9 The Convention does not prevent the application of those provisions of the law of the forum which must be applied even to international situations, irrespective of rules of conflict of laws.

If another State has a sufficiently close connection with a case then, in exceptional circumstances, effect may also be given to rules of that State which have the same character as mentioned in the preceding paragraph.

Any Contracting State may, by way of reservation, declare that it will not apply the second paragraph of this article. [The UK has made this reservation and excluded para 2 of Art 16 from the Recognition of Trusts Act 1987.]

Article 17

A1.10 In the Convention the word 'law' means the rules of law in force in a State other than its rules of conflict of laws.

Article 18

The provisions of the Convention may be disregarded when their application would be manifestly incompatible with public policy (*ordre public*).

Article 19

Nothing in the Convention shall prejudice the powers of States in fiscal matters.

Article 20

Any Contracting State may, at any time, declare that the provisions of the Convention will be extended to trusts declared by judicial decisions.

This declaration shall be notified to the Ministry of Foreign Affairs of the Kingdom of the Netherlands and will come into effect on the day when this notification is received.

Article 31 is applicable to the withdrawal of this declaration in the same way as it applies to a denunciation of the Convention.

Article 21

Any Contracting State may reserve the right to apply the provisions of Chapter III only to trusts the validity of which is governed by the law of a Contracting State. AI.11

Article 22

The Convention applies to trusts regardless of the date on which they were created.

However, a Contracting State may reserve the right not to apply the Convention to trusts created before the date on which, in relation to that State, the Convention enters into force.

Article 23

For the purpose of identifying the law applicable under the Convention, where a State comprises several territorial units each of which has its own rules of law in respect of trusts, any reference to the law of that State is to be construed as referring to the law in force in the territorial unit in question.

Article 24

A State within which different territorial units have their own rules of law in respect of trusts is not bound to apply the Convention to conflicts solely between the laws of such units.

[Arts 25–32 are omitted as of little substantive significance.]

APPENDIX B

CONVENTION ON THE LAW APPLICABLE TO SUCCESSION TO THE ESTATES OF DECEASED PERSONS

The States signatory to this Convention, AI.12

Desiring to establish common provisions concerning the law applicable to succession to the estates of deceased persons,

Have resolved to conclude a Convention for this purpose and have agreed upon the following provisions –

Chapter I

Scope of the Convention

Article 1

1 This Convention determines the law applicable to succession to the estates of deceased persons. AI.13

2 The Convention does not apply to –

(a) the form of dispositions of property upon death;
(b) capacity to dispose of property upon death;
(c) issues pertaining to matrimonial property;
(d) property rights, interests or assets created or transferred otherwise than by succession, such as in joint ownership with right of survival, pension plans, insurance contracts, or arrangements of a similar nature.

Article 2

The Convention applies even if the applicable law is that of a non-Contracting State.

Chapter II

Applicable Law

Article 3

1 Succession is governed by the law of the State in which the deceased at the time of his death was habitually resident, if he was then a national of that State. AI.14

2 Succession is also governed by the law of the State in which the deceased at the time of his death was habitually resident if he had been resident there for a period of no less than five years immediately preceding his death. However, in exceptional circum-

stances, if at the time of his death he was manifestly more closely connected with the State of which he was then a national, the law of that State applies.

3 In other cases succession is governed by the law of the State of which at the time of his death the deceased was a national, unless at that time the deceased was more closely connected with another State, in which case the law of the latter State applies.

Article 4

A1.15 If the law applicable according to Article 3 is that of a non-Contracting State, and if the choice of law rules of that State designate, with respect to the whole or part of the succession, the law of another non-Contracting State which would apply its own law, the law of the latter State applies.

Article 5

1 A person may designate the law of a particular State to govern the succession to the whole of his estate. The designation will be effective only if at the time of the designation or of his death such person was a national of that State or had his habitual residence there.

2 This designation shall be expressed in a statement made in accordance with the formal requirements for dispositions of property upon death. The existence and material validity of the act of designation are governed by the law designated. If under that law the designation is invalid, the law governing the succession is determined under Article 3.

3 The revocation of such a designation by its maker shall comply with the rules as to form applicable to the revocation of dispositions of property upon death.

4 For the purposes of this article, a designation of the applicable law, in the absence of an express contrary provision by the deceased, is to be construed as governing succession to the whole of the estate of the deceased whether he died intestate or wholly or partially testate.

Article 6

A1.16 1 A person may designate the law of one or more States to govern the succession to particular assets in his estate. However, any such designation is without prejudice to the application of the mandatory rules of the law applicable according to Article 3 or Article 5, paragraph 1.

Article 7

1 Subject to Article 6, the applicable law under Articles 3 and 5, paragraph 1, governs the whole of the estate of the deceased wherever the assets are located.

2 This law governs –

(a) the determination of the heirs, devisees and legatees, the respective shares of those persons and the obligations imposed upon them by the deceased, as well as other succession rights arising by reason of death including provision by a court or other authority out of the estate of the deceased in favour of persons close to the deceased;
(b) disinheritance and disqualification by conduct;
(c) Any obligation to restore or account for gifts, advancements or legacies when determining the shares of heirs, devisees or legatees;

(d) the disposable part of the estate, indefeasible interests and other restrictions on dispositions of property upon death;
(e) the material validity of testamentary dispositions.

3 Paragraph 2 does not preclude the application in a Contracting State of the law applicable under this Convention to other matters which are considered by that State to be governed by the law of succession.

Chapter III

Agreements as to succession

Article 8

For the purposes of this Chapter an agreement as to succession is an agreement created in writing or resulting from mutual wills which, with or without consideration, creates, varies or terminates rights in the future estate or estates of one or more persons parties to such agreement. **A1.17**

Article 9

1 Where the agreement involves the estate of one person only, its material validity, the effects of the agreement, and the circumstances resulting in the extinction of the effects, are determined by the law which under Article 3 or 5, paragraph 1, would have been applicable to the succession to the estate of that person if that person had died on the date of the agreement.

2 If under that law the agreement is invalid, it is nevertheless valid if it is valid under the law which at the time of death is the law applicable to the succession to the estate of that person according to Article 3 or 5, paragraph 1. The same law then governs the effects of the agreement and the circumstances resulting in the extinction of the effects.

Article 10

1 Where the agreement involves the estates of more than one person, the agreement is materially valid only if it is so valid under all the laws which, according to Article 3 or 5, paragraph 1, would have governed the succession to the estates of all those persons if each such person had died on the date of the agreement. **A1.18**

2 The effects of the agreement and the circumstances resulting in the extinction of the effects are those recognised by all of those laws.

Article 11

The parties may agree by express designation to subject the agreement, so far as its material validity, the effects of the agreement, and the circumstances resulting in the extinction of the effects are concerned, to the law of a State in which the person or any one of the persons whose future estate is involved has his habitual residence or of which he is a national at the time of the conclusion of the agreement.

Article 12

1 The material validity of an agreement valid under the law applicable according to Article 9, 10 or 11 may not be contested on the ground that the agreement would be invalid under the law applicable according to Article 3 or 5, paragraph 1. **A1.19**

2 However, the application of the law applicable according to Article 9, 10 or 11 shall not affect the rights of anyone not party to the agreement who under the law applicable to the succession by virtue of Article 3 or 5, paragraph 1, has an indefeasible interest in the estate or another right of which he cannot be deprived by the person whose estate is in question.

Chapter IV

General Provisions

Article 13

A1.20 Where two or more persons whose successions are governed by different laws die in circumstances in which it is uncertain in what order their deaths occurred, and where those laws provide differently for this situation or make no provision at all, none of the deceased persons shall have any succession rights to the other or others.

Article 14

1 Where a trust is created in a disposition of property upon death, the application to the succession of the law determined by the Convention does not preclude the application of another law to the trust. Conversely, the application to a trust of its governing law does not preclude the application to the succession of the law governing succession by virtue of the Convention.

2 The same rules apply by analogy to foundations and corresponding institutions created by dispositions of property upon death.

Article 15

A1.21 The law applicable under the Convention does not affect the application of any rules of the law of the State where certain immovables, enterprises or other special categories of assets are situated, which rules institute a particular inheritance regime in respect of such assets because of economic, family or social considerations.

Article 16

Where under the law applicable by virtue of the Convention there is no heir, devisee or legatee under a disposition of property upon death, and no physical person is an heir by operation of law, the application of the law so determined does not preclude a State or an entity appointed thereto by that State from appropriating the assets of the estate that are situated in its territory.

Article 17

In this Convention, and subject to Article 4, law means the law in force in a State other than its choice of law rules.

Article 18

The application of any of the laws determined by the Convention may be refused only where such application would be manifestly incompatible with public policy (*ordre public*).

Article 19

A1.22 1 For the purposes of identifying the law applicable under this Convention, where a State comprises two or more territorial units, each of which has its own system of law or its own rules of law in respect of succession, the provisions of this article apply.

2 If there are rules in force in such a State identifying which law among the laws of the two or more units is to apply in any circumstance for which this article provides, the law of that unit applies. In the absence of such rules the following paragraphs of this article apply.

3 For the purposes of any reference in this Convention, or any designation by the deceased pursuant to this Convention,

(a) the law of the State of the habitual residence of the deceased at the time of designation or of his death means the law of that unit of the State in which at the relevant time the decreased had his habitual residence;
(b) the law of the State of the nationality of the deceased at the time of designation or of his death means the law of that unit of the State in which at the relevant time the deceased had his habitual residence, and in the absence of such an habitual residence, the law of the unit with which he had his closest connection.

4 For the purposes of any reference in this Convention, the law of the State of closest connection means the law of that unit of the State with which the deceased was most closely connected.

5 Subject to Article 6, for the purposes of any designation pursuant to this Convention whereby the deceased designates the law of a unit of the State of which at the time of designation or of his death,

(a) he was a national, that designation is valid only if at some time he had had an habitual residence in, or in the absence of such an habitual residence, a close connection with, that unit;
(b) he was not a national, the designation is valid only if he then had his habitual residence in that unit or, if he was not then habitually resident in that unit but was so resident in that State, he had had an habitual residence in that unit at some time.

6 For the purposes of any designation under Article 6 with regard to particular assets whereby the deceased designates the law of a State, it is presumed that, subject to evidence of contrary intent, the designation means the law of each unit in which the assets are situated.

7 For the purposes of Article 3, paragraph 2, the required period of residence is attained when the deceased for the five years immediately preceding his death had his residence in that State, notwithstanding that during that period he resided in more than one of the units of that State. When the period has been attained, and the deceased had an habitual residence in that State at that time, but no habitual residence in any particular unit of that State, the applicable law is the law of that unit in which the deceased last resided, unless at that time he had a closer connection with another unit of the State, in which case the law of the latter unit applies.

Article 20

For purposes of identifying the law applicable under this Convention, where a State has two or more legal systems applicable to the succession of deceased persons for different categories of persons, any reference to the law of such State shall be construed as referring to the legal system determined by the rules in force in that State. In the absence of such rules, the reference shall be construed as referring to the legal system with which the deceased had the closest connection. A1.23

Article 21

A Contracting State in which different systems of law or sets of rules of law apply to succession shall not be bound to apply the rules of the Convention to conflicts solely between the laws of such different systems or sets of rules of law.

Article 22

A1.24 1 The Convention applies in a Contracting State to the succession of any person whose death occurs after the Convention has entered into force for that State.

2 Where at a time prior to the entry into force of the Convention in that State the deceased has designated the law applicable to his succession, that designation is to be considered valid there if it complies with Article 5.

3 Where at a time prior to the entry into force of the Convention in that State the parties to an agreement as to succession have designated the law applicable to that agreement, that designation is to be considered valid there if it complies with Article 11.

Article 23

1 The Convention does not affect any other international instrument to which Contracting States are to become Parties and which contains provisions on matters governed by this Convention, unless a contrary declaration is made by the States Parties to such instrument.

2 Paragraph 1 of this Article also applies to uniform laws based on special ties of a regional or other nature between the States concerned.

Article 24

A1.25 1 Any State may, at the time of signature, ratification, acceptance, approval or accession, make any of the following reservations –

(a) that it will not apply the Convention to agreements as to succession as defined in Article 8, and therefore that it will not recognise a designation made under Article 5 if the designation is not expressed in a statement made in accordance with the requirements for a testamentary disposition;

(b) that it will not apply Article 4;

(c) that it will not recognise a designation made under Article 5 by a person who, at the time of his death, was not or was no longer either a national of, or habitually resident in, the State whose law he had designated, but at that time was a national of and habitually resident in the reserving State;

(d) that it will not recognise a designation made under Article 5, if all of the following conditions are met

- the law of the State making the reservation would have been the applicable law under Article 3 if there had been no valid designation made under Article 5,
- the application of the law designated under Article 5 would totally or very substantially deprive the spouse or a child of the deceased of an inheritance or family provision to which the spouse or child would have been entitled under the mandatory rules of the law of the State making this reservation,
- that spouse or child is habitually resident in or a national of that State.

2 No other reservation shall be permitted.

3 Any Contracting State may at any time withdraw a reservation which it has made; the reservation shall cease to have effect on the first day of the month following the expiration of three months after notification of the withdrawal.

[The final clauses in Arts 25–31 are omitted.]

GUIDE TO LAWS OF DIFFERENT STATES

A1.26

The following table shows whether States are unitarian (one law for movables and immovables) or schismatic (separate laws for movables and immovables), which States have succession laws based on habitual residence, nationality or domicile, which States reject the application of *renvoi* and which States have forced heirship rules.

State	*Unitarian*	*Schismatic*	*Habitual Residence*	*Nationality*	*Domicile*	*Renvoi Rejected*	*Forced Heirship*
Austria	✓			✓			✓
Belgium		✓	✓				✓
Denmark	✓		✓			✓	✓
England		✓			✓		
Finland	✓		1	✓		✓	✓
France		✓	✓				✓
Germany	✓			✓			✓
Greece	✓			✓		✓	✓
Ireland		✓			✓		
Isle of Man		✓			✓		
Italy	✓			✓			✓
Jersey		✓			✓		✓
Netherlands	✓			✓		✓	✓
Portugal	✓			✓			✓
Scotland		✓			✓		✓
Spain	✓			✓		✓	✓
Switzerland	✓		✓	2			✓

1 If deceased was habitually resident in a Nordic country.
2 If resident foreigner expressly chooses his nationality law.

INDEX

R